MW01200310

"For over fifty years, the Institute for Spirituality and Health has explored the relationship between spirituality and health in its strategic location in the heart of the Texas Medical Center. This book offers not only an important history but perhaps a springboard to the future."

L. James Bankston, D.Min., *Senior Minister, St. Paul's United Methodist Church.*

"Texas Medical Center started with a dream to create a medical center where people from all walks of life could have access to the best health care anywhere—whether they were rich, poor, famous, alone, young or old. Our founder, Dr. Fred Elliott, also envisioned an unprecedented way to bridge religion and medical practice. Today, the Institute for Spirituality and Health is one of some fifty member institutes that make up Texas Medical Center, and it continues to fulfill that first vision of serving as a cornerstone for our world-renowned complex, bringing together faith, medicine and healthcare. As I look toward my retirement at the end of 2012, I am proud to have been a witness to this organization's growth over the years."

Richard Wainerdi, P.E., Ph.D., *Former President and CEO, Texas Medical Center.*

"In a world where healthcare is increasingly secularized, this book is a refreshing reminder of the need to include spirituality in our approaches to health and healing. Cathey Nickell tells the story of a few committed individuals, who with a few small seed grants, realized their dream of an institute blending spirituality and health for the then-burgeoning Texas Medical Center. The book—and the creation of the Institute for Spirituality and Health—is an inspiration for those who believe in the power of commitment to holistic healthcare."

Patricia Gail Bray, Ph.D., *Executive Director, St. Luke's Episcopal Health Charities.*

"St. Luke's Episcopal Hospital is a church owned and operated hospital in the Texas Medical Center. It delivers a unique brand of *Faithful, Loving, Care.* At its founding in 1954, Bishop John Hines said, "We won't just build another hospital. That would be a betrayal of our commission as a church of God. We shall build a church hospital in which all the mountain-moving powers of faith and prayer and human skill can be brought to bear upon individuals in need. It will be a hospital in which the chapel will stand close to its very heart. It will be a witness to the gallant and decisive fact of human experience, namely, that 'We are children of God.'" To this day, the Institute for Spirituality and Health shepherds the contributions of faith in the healthcare setting. We all have much to learn from its staff and history."

David J. Fine, FACHE, *President and CEO, St. Luke's Episcopal Health System.*

UNITING FAITH, MEDICINE AND HEALTHCARE

A 60-Year History of
The Institute for Spirituality and Health
at the Texas Medical Center

CATHEY GRAHAM NICKELL

UNITING FAITH, MEDICINE AND HEALTHCARE:

A 60-Year History of The Institute for Spirituality and Health at the Texas Medical Center

Softcover ISBN: 978-0-692-42612-8

Hardcover ISBN: 978-0-692-42613-5

First Edition published in 2012.

Lightning Source, La Vergne, TN, USA

Cover design and book layout by Barbara Lindenberg, Bluebird Designs.

"The Institute of Religion and the far outreach of its
work may be described by this word: 'Imagineering.'
To all of you who in your imagination have seen the
dream and are constructively working that it be
engineered into reality — Welcome!"

Excerpt from a speech written by Dr. Dawson Bryan, 1959

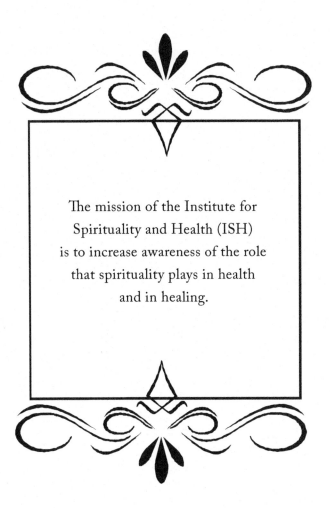

The mission of the Institute for
Spirituality and Health (ISH)
is to increase awareness of the role
that spirituality plays in health
and in healing.

ᏑᎯ—ACKNOWLEDGEMENTS—᠍᠍ᏳᎯ

I want to thank several individuals who were instrumental in bringing the historical chronology of the Institute for Spirituality and Health to life. I first must thank Jim Walzel who, during his tenure as Chairman of the Board of Trustees, made it his personal quest to see that the complete history be written for posterity. I don't think either of us knew how much time it would take to accomplish this task. Jim hired me to write the book in 2011, it was completed and printed in 2012, and I am pleased to release this updated version for a second printing in 2015. Secondly, I would like to thank my father, John K. Graham, M.D., D.Min., who serves as President/CEO of the Institute; it was he who knew of my journalism and writing background, and of my training in oral history, which led him to submit my name as a potential freelance writer to Jim Walzel. For that, and for the ensuing journey on which this project took me and continues to take me, I want to thank them both. Their support, suggestions, interviews and ideas were invaluable.

Next, I must acknowledge the many people who welcomed me into their personal homes or places of business so that I could conduct the face-to-face interviews and record their oral histories. They are: Jim Bankston, D.Min.; Baruch Brody, Ph.D.; Rev. Julian Byrd; Carolyn Clarke; Jerri Doctor; Nancy Gordon; John K. Graham, M.D., D.Min.; Karen Hahn, Ph.D.; Susan Josey; Rabbi Sam Karff, D.H.L.; James W. Lomax, II, M.D.; Rabbi David Lyon, M.H.L.; Ken Pargament, Ph.D.; Ted Smith, D.Min.; Betsy Garlington Striegler; Ron Sunderland, Ed.D.; the late Allen Verhey, Ph.D. (1945-2014); and Jim Walzel. Without their memories and willingness to take the time to reveal their recollections, I could not have written this book. Bonnie Weekley, Stuart Nelson and other staff and board members were helpful as I revised the original book in recognition of the Institute's 60th anniversary in 2015.

Thanks must be given to Sister Agnes Mary Joy, M.M., who, several years ago, spent countless hours outlining the board minutes; her document gave me an early starting point. Thanks to Jerri Doctor, ISH Manager of Operations, who provided me with archives and contacts and who answered many questions. I also want to thank my good friend and proofreader, Elizabeth Fortner Hall. Thanks to Barbara Lindenberg for her graphic design work on the original book and on the updated anniversary edition. Thanks to Helen Taylor, Ph.D., of Louisiana State University-Shreveport, who guided me through the editing process of turning this book into a thesis for my Master of Arts degree in 2013. My deepest appreciation goes to my mother, Pat Graham, for always being able to see the big picture. Finally, thanks and love to my family and especially to my incredible husband, Kevin Nickell, M.D.

Cathey Graham Nickell
Houston, Texas

ꙮ CONTENTS ꙮ

Foreword 11

Chapter One: A Vision Fulfilled 15

Chapter Two: Breaking New Ground 23

Chapter Three: Change is in the Air 31

Chapter Four: Medical Ethics and Identity Issues 39

Chapter Five: From the Nineties to the Millenium....61

Chapter Six: The Institute Today................................69

Appendix...81

Chronology of the Board of Trustees 87

Chronology of the President/CEO 99

ISH Adjunct Faculty Members 101

References 105

Index..113

FOREWORD

In 1955, the Institute of Religion was formed at the Texas Medical Center in Houston to bring the spiritual dimension back into medicine. Historically, these two traditions worked together, but mankind's fascination with science and the hope it offered led to a clear separation over time. With the conviction that healthcare and religion should reunite, a unique group of individuals in Houston set out to try to make that happen.

The same year that the Institute of Religion was formed, I enrolled in college, majored in pre-medicine, and four years later entered Tulane Medical School in New Orleans. During my senior year I had a rotation in psychiatry. One day I was with a group of students who were watching a fellow student interview a patient who was on a surgical ward. We were told she had chronic drainage from her left lung that had been unresponsive to treatment. The interview was to teach us to appreciate the psychological aspects of a patient who had come in for a medical problem, not a psychiatric one.

We were seated behind a one-way mirror and sat quietly until our fellow student asked his patient, "I was wondering, did you ever feel God was punishing you with your illness?" We groaned audibly and felt embarrassed for our fellow student. Someone said, "Why did he ask that?" Dr. Frank Heath, head of the Department of Psychiatry, was sitting with us and said, "That's a great question!" And, to our amazement, the patient began sobbing, wiping tears from her eyes, and said, "Yes, that is exactly why I am sick. I have committed adultery, and God is punishing me. That's why I can't get well."

In a debriefing that followed, a student said, "Give the lady the right antibiotic, and she will get well." Dr. Heath said, "Yes, and she will return in six months with another illness. You must learn to listen to your patient. She is telling you why she is sick. What she needs is not just another antibiotic. What she needs is to see her priest so he can pronounce absolution for her sins. And your role as a physician is to see that that happens." Other

11

than that one isolated incident in medical school, I did not hear any other professor discuss a blending of religion and medical care.

Today, things are very different. Over 100 medical schools offer a course in spirituality related to medical care, providing instructions on how to take a religious history. In some schools, students are invited to look at their own spirituality in order to better understand themselves and their patients. They are taught meditation, yoga and other stress-relieving techniques that can help prevent burnout.

It is a new day, and the Institute of Religion has had a major role in bringing about this transition. Students no longer need be embarrassed when asking a patient about his or her spiritual concerns. In fact, not to ask those kinds of questions could be seen as insensitive by some. Spirituality is a part of what it means to be human, and studies reveal that it should not be ignored in modern healthcare.

During the sixty-year period from 1955 to present, researchers began to collect data and submit their findings to medical journals. Among the early scholars in this field were: Harold Koenig, M.D., at Duke University; Kenneth I. Pargament, Ph.D., at Bowling Green State University; and Jeff Levin, Ph.D., M.P.H., at Baylor University. It took great courage and fortitude on the part of these pioneers, who were often fighting an uphill battle. At first their papers were rejected by major medical journals as being "unscientific." But, article after article was eventually published, and today over 3,000 articles have appeared in literature, with the majority showing a positive correlation between religion and health.

Research reveals that regular, weekly attendance at religious services results in measurable benefits to health. For example, studies show that a high commitment to one's faith results in a higher sense of well-being, less frequent and shorter hospital stays, less time in the Intensive Care Unit, lower rates of depression and suicide, and even increased longevity. These studies are now recognized as valid papers on spirituality and health issues and are regularly accepted in major medical journals such as the *Journal of the American Medical Association* (JAMA). These studies also have been compiled into a great work entitled *Handbook of Religion and Health*, by Harold Koenig, Michael McCullough and David Larson. The Second Edition was published in March 2012, and it is considered "the Bible" for those interested in knowing more about spirituality and health.

The book you are about to read is a history of one of the most important institutions that contributed to the restoration of the union of medicine and spirituality in American medicine. Other institutions played a role, but the story of the Institute of Religion is particularly noteworthy because it took place in the Texas Medical Center, which today has become the largest medical complex in the world. During this same sixty-year period, the TMC, as it is often called, would produce five great hospitals and two medical schools that have trained thousands of physicians from all over the world. These hospitals, with over 80,000 dedicated professionals, daily serve tens of thousands of patients. Men and women in every field of medicine have been brought to Houston to serve at the forty-nine institutions that make up the TMC. These include: Baylor College of Medicine, Houston Methodist Hospital, St. Luke's Episcopal Hospital, M.D. Anderson Cancer Center, Memorial Hermann Health Care System, Ben Taub General Hospital, and more. Many innovations in medicine happened here in Houston. Heart surgeons Michael DeBakey and Denton Cooley brought their field forward and made the front cover of *Time* magazine in the process.

In this book you will encounter the names of many prominent men and women of Houston who gave their hearts and money to ensure the success of the Institute for Spirituality and Health, as we are now called. Among the family names you will find in this manuscript are: Scurlock, Fondren, Hankamer, Tellepsen, Barrow, West, Fairchild, Barrow, Moody, Farnsworth, Birdwell, Elkins, as well as Houston Endowment, Inc. You will also encounter beloved leaders in our medical community like Dr. "Red" Duke, and religious leaders like Rev. Charlie Shedd, Rev. John E. Fellers, and Rabbi Hyman Judah Schachtel. From its beginning, the Institute has been ecumenical, and it continues to be a meeting place for people of all faiths.

We changed our name several times over the decades to better express our role in the community. But our mission always has been the same: to increase knowledge of and sensitivity to the role that spirituality plays in health and in healing.

Prepare your heart now to be enriched by a remarkable story. It is a story of the creation of a unique organization at the Texas Medical Center that seeks to increase knowledge about treating the whole person. Medicine and religion came together. Really? Science and spirituality, together? Absolutely! When hearts are open to hear the spirit within, this can truly happen.

John K. Graham, M.D., D.Min.
President/CEO of the Institute for Spirituality and Health
2010 – Present

CHAPTER ONE

A VISION FULFILLED

"A small body of determined spirits fired by an
unquenchable faith in their mission can alter
the course of history." – Mohandas Gandhi

The charge was clear: develop a new program that combines religious ministry, teaching, research, and holistic care of the patients in Houston's emerging Texas Medical Center. The year was 1955, and in the mid-1950s, the United States was living in the height of the Cold War, McCarthyism was in full force, the first McDonalds fast food chain opened, families were delighted by the new Disneyland California, and the Civil Rights Movement was just beginning to stir. Partly in reaction to some of these factors, religion and patriotism were sometimes comingled in an attempt to promote positive slogans for the good of the nation. America was inserting religion into ordinary life, where it had been separated before, and references to God seemed to multiply. In June of 1954, for example, the phrase "Under God" was added to the otherwise secular U.S. Pledge of Allegiance by a joint resolution of Congress that amended the original 1942 Flag Code. Additionally, the 84th Congress, under President Dwight D. Eisenhower, passed a law that adopted the phrase "In God We Trust" as the official motto of the United States in 1956. That same motto has been printed on American paper currency since 1957 (History 2). In the midst of all these national social changes, the founders of Houston's up-and-coming Texas Medical Center, just ten years old at this time, dreamed of combining religion and medicine to better serve the health needs of their growing patient constituency.

Frederick C. Elliott, D.D.S., Executive Director of the Texas Medical Center, had a unique vision. His plan was to embark upon a pioneering adventure to build a religious program that would serve to better the Texas Medical Center (Bryan, *An Evaluation* 2). Dr. Elliott's grandfather was a Methodist lay minister, his uncle was a homeopathic doctor, and his father was a pharmacist who owned his own drugstore. In his early years, his mother died while he was just in kindergarten; he also survived a bout with polio, and, then tragically lost his first wife and infant son to influenza. Over time, Dr. Elliott became a successful dentist and dental educator who also loved to cook, travel, write poetry, and attend church. Dr. Mavis P. Kelsey, Sr., founder of Houston's Kelsey-Seybold Clinic, knew Dr. Elliott very well and once said, "I guess you could call Fred Elliott a kind of Renaissance man. Although he was a dentist, he thought in terms of the entire health care profession. Dr. Elliott had a broader vision for Houston's health care" (Elliott, *Birth* 19). Dr. Elliott's familial roots and personal life challenges certainly influenced his desire to address patients and their families in a holistic manner, and this became his life's work. In 1952, he took the helm of the state's largest medical facility, referred to at that time as the "$110-million Texas Medical Center" (Wilburn). Two years into this new position, he approached the Council of Churches of Greater Houston to begin studying his innovative idea of creating a religious presence throughout the campus. On December 9, 1954, a group called the Committee on Religious Activities Development, initially referred to as RAD for short, met for the very first time. Twelve Houston leaders, including Dr. Elliott himself, were present: Milton A. Backlund, Julia A. Bertner, Dawson Bryan, D.D., Ella F. Fondren, Earl C. Hankamer, Charles L. King, M.D., Rev. Virgil Lowder, Otis Massey, Latimer Murfee, Howard T. Tellepsen, and Wesley W. West (Council 1).

Dr. Bryan was elected Director of RAD and was asked by Dr. Elliott to resign officially from his co-pastor position at Houston's First Methodist Church and begin full-time work on January 1, 1955 (Fondren, *Minutes of Dec. 9, 1954* 3). The proposed start date was just one month away from that first organized December meeting. Plans were rolling along quickly. The committee adopted an annual budget of $25,700 for Dr. Elliott's fledgling pet project. Dr. Bryan's salary as Director was set at $12,000 per year, and he was offered a modest dwelling allowance as well (Fondren, *Minutes of Dec. 9, 1954* 4). Around this time, Dr. Bryan had already lived in Houston for just over twenty years. Prior to being co-pastor at Houston's First Methodist Church, he served as pastor of St. Paul's United Methodist Church for about ten years. Dr. Elliott had become somewhat acquainted with Dr. Bryan after hearing him give a few sermons at St. Paul's (Elliott, *Birth* 182). Dr. Bryan was a published author, and he received his education from the University of Texas, Southern Methodist University, and the University of Chicago (Bryan, *The Art* 7). He was more than prepared to take the helm at what, at that time, was still being called RAD.

Dr. Bryan and his new board members took Dr. Elliott's challenge very seriously. They wanted to create a program that would blend religious ministry, teaching, research and holistic care of the patients in the Texas Medical Center. Most importantly, the program was to be nondenominational in character and would serve every denomination and faith (Council 2). This blend of Judeo-Christian faiths was important, because the Texas Medical Center was beginning to draw physicians and nurses coming from across the United States and world to train, and those people were a critical part of the community that was to be served by RAD. Additionally, both Christians and Jews were members of the board that founded Dr. Elliott's brainchild; RAD's critical tenet was that their mission would reach everyone from all walks of life. In one of the group's earliest media 1954 news releases, Dr. Bryan said, "It is expected that ministerial students will be brought in for residencies from theological schools in the state and elsewhere and that they will undergo courses and clinical training at the postgraduate level" (Council 2). The idea was to create a program that would train theological students in resident clinical practice to help them become better chaplains in hospitals and better pastors in the field. The cooperation between pastors and physicians was a key component of the program.

Wayne Oates, PhD, then-professor of Pastoral Ministry at the Southern Baptist Theological Seminary in Louisville, Kentucky, said at that time, "This program you contemplate in training and service in the Texas Medical Center will be uniquely significant both medically and religiously not only for this city or this state or this nation, but for the whole world" (Council 2). Another 1954 leader in pastoral care, Karl P. Meister, D.D., National Director of the Board of Hospitals and Homes of the Methodist Church, commented that such a development could not be initiated anywhere he knew of except in Houston due to the city's "far-sighted and public-minded citizens" (Council 2). Dr. Meister, who was himself from Chicago, added that because of its magnificent facilities and leadership, the Texas Medical Center was also a key component to the successful development of this project.

Their positive words of encouragement, and those of so many others, provided the inspiration that Dr. Bryan needed to keep moving forward. One of Dr. Bryan's first tasks was to assemble the deans from the five major Texas theological seminaries and get their approval. These institutions were Southwestern Baptist Theological Seminary, Texas Christian University, The Episcopal Theological Seminary of the Southwest, Southern Methodist University, and The Austin Presbyterian Theological Seminary (Bryan, *Arrangements* 1). Dr. Bryan asked these deans to serve on an Advisory Committee to assist in the program's creation, and he drafted a set of arrangements. Under the new arrangements, theological students would be trained and supervised by a qualified faculty. RAD asked that their work be accepted within the framework of the Pastoral Care department of each seminary and considered as residency work with academic credit granted. The seminaries were also asked to provide scholarships and fellowships for the seminary students doing work for RAD in keeping with their own institution's policies. Finally, the seminaries were to carefully select and recommend prospective students who would then be interviewed by the program's staff; the final acceptance of each student into the program would be made by RAD. The main purpose continued

18

to be very clear: to work together as a cooperative program to develop the healing team of doctor, nurse and minister (Bryan, *Arrangements* 1-3).

Dr. Bryan also studied similar programs in other parts of the United States. He quickly called upon Dr. Meister, who had some 150 hospitals and homes under his direction around the country at that time. He personally met with Rev. Dr. Olin E. Oeschger, an associate of Dr. Meister, to gather additional data. He also garnered sound advice from Rev. Dr. Granger E. Westberg, who was then Chaplain of the University of Chicago Hospitals and Clinics. Dr. Bryan traveled to states as far away as New York and North Carolina to visit other experts in the field, all in an effort to gather as much information as possible to make his program a resounding success. In a personal letter to Dr. Westberg, dated January 1955, Dr. Bryan eagerly wrote: "The program in which you gave us such valuable counsel has finally materialized. The Council of Churches is sponsoring the formation of a religious activities program in the Texas Medical Center. I have been selected as the director. I have been asked to secure data from various institutional projects throughout the United States, out of which we will develop a post-graduate residency program for theological students in cooperation with the theological schools of Texas. In the not too distance future, I would like to visit you and others in the Chicago area who could give us counsel in this matter" (Bryan, *Program* 1). Dr. Bryan's extensive research and personal travels to visit other organizations around the country helped him hone in on a specific mission for RAD, and his passion for his new job was contagious.

On January 5, 1955, RAD announced at one of its first board meetings that they had already secured a $15,000 donation from the West Foundation. This generous amount represented half of the organization's projected budget for the whole year. Dr. Bryan later noted the critical nature of this gift, saying that without the initial donation from the West Foundation, the Institute would have taken many more years to get started. It also was announced that The National Bank of Commerce, where Jessie

H. Jones served as President, would do business with the new program. Temporary office space on the first floor of the Jesse H. Jones Library Building in the Texas Medical Center was chosen, and Houston Architect Cameron Fairchild was selected to handle the renovations for the new location. It was determined that the organization would reside there until a freestanding center could be built in the future. Dr. Bryan was encouraged by the board to continue examining and visiting other similar institutions for direction (Fondren, *Minutes of Jan. 5, 1955* 4). It was not long before dozens of letters of encouragement poured into Dr. Bryan's office from residents of Houston and beyond; many, it seems, were interested in the pioneering venture being created in the Texas Medical Center.

In the spring of 1955, a committee was appointed to prepare papers for the incorporation of RAD's new name as The Institute of Religion. On May 4, 1955, the legal charter of the Institute of Religion was signed and filed in the Office of the Secretary of State at the capitol in Austin, Texas. The filing fee was just ten dollars for a term of fifty years, making the non-denominational organization a non-profit group in the State of Texas. The thirteen founding board members were listed on the charter, and each one signed the paperwork (Muldrow 1-8). These Houston philanthropists and leaders were: Milton A. Backlund, Julia A. Bertner, Ella F. Fondren, Earl C. Hankamer, John T. Jones, Jr., Charles L. King, Virgil E. Lowder, Otis Massey, Latimer Murfee, Thomas W. Sumners, Howard T. Tellepsen, Wesley W. West, and E.H. Westmoreland.

The Institute of Religion was now official, and soon more, much-needed checks arrived. In addition to the West Foundation's substantial gift of $15,000, the Fondren Foundation provided $10,000 in seed funds. Smaller, but no less important, donations of $1,000 were received from The Captain Edward Ewing Barrow Foundation and the Oldham Little Church Foundation, to name a few. The Moorman Foundation in Quincey, Illinois, gave another generous $5,000 donation. Dr. Bryan hired a small staff, and two professors were also brought on board: LeRoy G.

Kerney, B.D. (teaching pastoral care) and Samuel Southard, Th.D. (teaching religion and health). Twelve ministerial students officially enrolled that summer to take those first-ever Institute courses, which focused on the sensitive dynamics of pastoral care (Institute, *Dimensions Summer 1966* 1).

A ceremony to observe the formal opening and dedication of the Institute of Religion was planned for May 8, 1956 at the Jesse H. Jones Library Building Auditorium. Presiding at the event was Otis Massey, the Institute's first Chairman of the Board of Trustees, and, of course, Dr. Bryan, the founding director. Some 165 guests showed up to hear the Chancellor of Southern Methodist University, Umphrey Lee, PhD, give the keynote address. One interesting guest speaker at the dedication was Rev. Charlie Shedd, who was then the pastor of Houston's Memorial Drive Presbyterian Church. Today Dr. Shedd is a world-renowned author of more than forty inspirational books such as *Letters to Philip* and *Letters to Karen* (Charlie 1). Yet another special guest at the dedication that night was Bishop A. Frank Smith, a Methodist church leader and resident bishop of the Houston-San Antonio area Methodist churches. During his years in Houston, Bishop Smith also was an influential trustee of Methodist Hospital in the Texas Medical Center (Spellmann 1). Two days after the Institute's dedication ceremony, Bishop Smith hand-wrote Dr. Bryan a personal letter. "I have seen a lot of occasions connected with institutions, but I have never seen anything anywhere that was as perfect in setting and execution as your program and dinner last Tuesday evening," he scrawled on a piece of stationery from a Dallas hotel. He continued: "I expected it to be such, with you in back of it. I was not surprised, but I was happy and proud ... what you have shared there will be talked about all over the religious and medical worlds" (A.F. Smith 1). Bishop Smith was correct in his prediction, and leaders throughout the state and the country also heralded their support.

The Right Rev. John E. Hines, Episcopal Bishop of Texas, was unable to attend the dedication, so instead he sent a Western Union telegram on May 5, 1956, stating: "Congratulations to the trustees of the

Institute of Religion. This forward step should be most constructive in the effective training of men of religion and of medicine alike to help people to a better life" (Hines 1). Another telegram arrived from Rabbi Robert I. Kahn of Congregation Emanu El in Houston, who wrote: "Our congregation joins me in prayers for God's choicest blessings on this magnificent endeavor for service and leadership to the community and to all mankind" (Kahn 1). And Dr. Westberg, whom Dr. Bryan had leaned on early in the planning for advice, also wrote, "You can be certain that we here at the University of Chicago rejoice with you that the Texas Medical Center is calling attention to the importance of the relationship between religion and health in such a magnificent way" (Westberg, *Formal* 1). There was certainly a buzz of praise for the new Institute of Religion, with many calling it a milestone in theological education.

By October of 1956, Dr. Bryan was proudly bragging about the first group of students who completed the summer semester of Clinical Pastoral Training at the Institute of Religion. "All but four of these are now taking advanced graduate study during the fall term and continuing into the spring semester," he wrote in a personal letter to founding board members and donors Mr. and Mrs. W.W. Fondren. "We have much reason to be proud of this group of young men. As you know, we also conducted classes in religion and medicine for 52 medical students and over 100 nursing students" (Bryan, *Thankful* 1). Dr. Bryan and the other founders were right to be delighted with the fast progress that had occurred in just two short years.

CHAPTER TWO

BREAKING NEW GROUND

*"Health is a state of complete physical, mental
and social well-being, and not merely the absence of
disease or infirmity." – World Health Organization, 1948*

By now the Institute of Religion was being legitimately promoted in print publications distributed by the Texas Medical Center, Inc. A 1950s black-and-white brochure described the Institute as having been "established to conduct a clinical training program in pastoral care of the sick and afflicted for ministerial, medical and nursing students and for ministers, doctors and nurses. The Institute is affiliated with five theological seminaries of Texas and with Baylor University College of Medicine." Likewise, at a December 1956 Institute board meeting, Dr. Elliott announced, "The Medical Center looks upon the Institute of Religion as a basic part of the overall plan" (Fondren, *Minutes of Dec. 14, 1956* 1). Later, in 1958, Dr. Elliott again sang its praises, stating, "The stock of the Institute [of Religion] has gone up and up and up. The entire Medical Center feels that the Institute is carrying on a very high level of educational needs" (Fondren, *Minutes of Jan. 20 1958* 6-7). The Institute's reputation was becoming better known, and there was a buzz about its work.

International attention was noted. Ian McIntosh of London, England was a student at the Institute of Religion in October 1959. He attended a board meeting where he stated his appreciation for the opportunity to study in Houston and talked of his experiences at the Institute. McIntosh explained to the Board of Trustees that there was no practical training of any kind for ministers in England at that time. He said the academic training in his home country was excellent, but "the practical clinical experience is non-existent there." He said he hoped to try to establish this type of work in England, but knew he would face many obstacles, particularly because "less than ten percent of the people in England actively participate in church worship" (Fondren, *Minutes of Oct. 16 1959* 1-2). The board was excited to hear such a glowing first-hand example of the value that the young Institute of Religion was bringing to the Texas Medical Center and to places far beyond its Texas borders.

Talk soon turned to a new location that was granted to the Institute of Religion: a spot of land perfectly set right in the heart of the Texas Medical Center grounds on the corner of Bertner and Wilkins boulevards. Dr. Bryan pointed out that it would be the first of its kind; nothing like it existed in any other medical centers, and he wanted it to be a symbol to the world that vital religion was the heart of healing and health (Fondren, *Minutes of May 15, 1959* 1). The board chose one of its trustees, Eddy C. Scurlock, to chair the Building Committee for this great endeavor. Scurlock, who was fairly new to the board, was a local oil industry tycoon, entrepreneur, millionaire and philanthropist (Who's Who 1). The new four-story building was estimated to cost $600,000 to construct. Capital funds for the building were largely made possible by several grants: $200,000 from the M.D. Anderson Foundation; $100,000 from the Fondren Foundation; and $100,000 from Houston Endowment, Inc., which was the foundation established by Jesse H. Jones. The contractor was Linbeck Construction Company and the architect was John H. Freeman, Jr. (Institute, *Houston Endowment Grant* 1). The new site was designed to provide class and assembly rooms, an outpatient clinic for counseling, library facilities, and offices for faculty and staff. The building also would house the mechanical and power equipment for the new adjoining Texas Woman's University College of Nursing, which already was under construction (Institute, *First Structure* 1).

The new facility was going to be just the backdrop the Institute of Religion needed to continue its vision of training ministers to better work with doctors and nurses in the fields of religion and health. The organization was now four years old, and it had already had a total of 724 students enrolled in the courses it offered. The student body was made up of medical, nursing and ministerial students, as well as pastors. Its inaugural course, called "Religion and Medicine," was the first of its kind ever offered in any medical school, begun in a small classroom at Baylor College of Medicine. Clinical work was conducted at Houston's Hermann Hospital, M.D. Anderson Hospital, Methodist Hospital, Memorial Hospital, the Texas Institute for Rehabilitation and Research, and the Veteran's Administration Hospital. Ministerial students of the Institute served as Chaplain Interns at those medical facilities and already had made over 75,000 visits to patients. Additionally, in 1959, the Rockefeller Foundation provided $10,000 to establish a significant research program called "Religion and the Cancer and Heart Patient" (Institute, *First Structure* 2). To the Rockefeller Foundation grant, the M.D. Anderson Foundation added an additional $5,000 to support this innovative, four-year clinical study of the mental attitudes of heart and cancer patients (Elliot, *Birth* 177).

On December 3, 1959, groundbreaking ceremonies were held, and E. Vincent Askey, M.D., president of the American Medical Association, gave the main speech. Another speaker, Leigh J. Crozier, M.D., director of Hermann Hospital, said, "The Institute of Religion in the midst of a great medical center shows us that religion is a dominant factor in the lives of men and women dedicated to advancing medical science and patient care" (Crozier 1). Texas Medical Center President Leland Anderson added, "While teaching, the Institute is doing real research, seeking to improve the spiritual outlook of all hospital patients. Thus, the Institute of Religion means a great deal to every other institution in the Medical Center" (Anderson 1). Hundreds of people came out for the groundbreaking occasion, and there was an excitement about the possibilities that this new structure would create.

Time, the country's first weekly news magazine, learned what the Institute was doing in Houston and interviewed Dr. Bryan. In the December 14, 1959 issue, *Time* provided national media coverage for the Institute, citing the groundbreaking and its impact on the nation as a whole. The article said it was becoming a major trend for medical schools to train ministers in hospital procedure and for seminaries to stress chaplain service to the sick. According to the article, "Protestant, Catholic and Jewish clergymen lectured to the medical students [at the Institute of Religion] on the details of their faiths so that future doctors might collaborate in aiding the spiritual as well as the mental and physical health of their patients." Dr. Bryan was quoted in *Time* as calling what they teach "spiritual therapy," which he described as treating the whole person: mentally, physically and spiritually (Luce 60). This was major recognition for a Texas organization that was still just under five years old.

Exactly one year after the *Time* magazine publicity, in December of 1960, an Open House welcomed visitors to the newly finished building. A large bronze plaque bearing the names of the current board members was purchased and still hangs in the Institute lobby to this day. In expressing his appreciation for the grants that made the new building possible, Dr. Bryan said, "A group of men here in the Texas Medical Center are treating patients with a new kind of medicine. They are ministering to the soul. They are chaplain interns from the Institute of Religion, learning to provide the sick with pastoral care. Man's enemy is not alone the microbe, but also himself. Thus, the concept of healing the whole person—spiritually, as well as mentally and physically—is accomplished" (Elliot, *Birth* 182). That same year, the Council of Southwestern Theological Schools entered into an agreement with the Institute to provide supervised Clinical Pastoral Education (CPE) for its theological students. Four units of CPE training was and still is required to become a certified chaplain with the Association of Professional Chaplains. From 1955 until the mid-1970s, most chaplains trained at the Texas Medical Center were based at the Institute of Religion (T. Smith 2).

Basically, CPE students met at the Institute each morning for lectures, training seminars and such; then they fanned out to their assigned hospitals in the afternoon to do their pastoral care work. Rev. Julian Byrd, a 1957 graduate of Duke Divinity School in North Carolina, moved all the way from Florida to Houston to take a pastoral care internship at the Institute and became part of the Institute's second graduating class. Rev. Byrd clearly remembers one of his afternoon clinical assignments at the Texas Medical Center: "The original Hermann Hospital was built in 1925, without air conditioning or private rooms, so most of my work was done with patients on the wards with ceiling fans trying to cool things down. It was quite different than today's world in the hospital" (Byrd, *Interview* 4). Rev. Byrd's joining the Institute, and other graduate students like himself, represented a growing movement to professionalize chaplaincy across the country at that time. It was directly linked to the Institute's first mission and Dr. Bryan's vision of being a service center for ministers and physicians in training and hopefully becoming one of the significant research centers in America in the field of Pastoral Care (Institute, *What Is the Institute* 2). Houston resident Ted Smith, D.Min., a long-time expert in the field of hospital chaplaincy, remembers that even in its infancy, the Institute had national appeal, and even international appeal, drawing people from all over the world (T. Smith 4). A case in point is that the U.S. Air Force Department of Chaplaincy saw the potential and in 1966 designated the Institute of Religion as their CPE training center for chaplains (Institute, *Dimensions Summer 1966* 2).

Monetary donations continued to bolster the Institute during the 1960s. The Moody Foundation contributed $15,000, and an executive of Gulf Oil, Madison Farnsworth, gave 100 shares of Gulf Oil Corp. stock to the Institute. In March 1965, friends of Wichita, Texas oilman and philanthropist J.S. Birdwell honored him with an $80,000 gift to the Institute of Religion. The amount represented $1,000 per year for each year of Birdwell's life, given in honor of his eightieth birthday; the generous gift established the Birdwell Library of Religion at the still-rather-new Institute building (Institute, *Dimensions Fall 1965* 2).

The Fondren Foundation gave $50,000 in the form of Standard Oil stock shares during the mid-1960s. Ella Fondren, who was a founding board member, had been a long-time supporter of the Institute. Her late husband, Walter W. Fondren, Sr., who died in 1939, helped form the Humble Oil and Refining Company, which is now Exxon USA. Mrs. Fondren served as the Institute's first Secretary for the Board of Trustees and continued in that role for seventeen years, from 1955 to 1972. In 1966, Mrs. Fondren gave the Institute forty-five acres of unencumbered, valuable land adjoining the Houston International Airport. Ten years later, in 1976, the Institute was able to sell the airport land to the City of Houston, garnering over $450,000 (Weingarten, *Board Minutes of Feb. 5, 1976* 4). Mrs. Fondren died in 1982, just one month short of her 102nd birthday (Ella Fondren, *The New York Times Obituaries*).

Another early board member, Eddy Scurlock, created an endowment of approximately $1.5 million for the Institute in 1966, which to this day remains the largest gift ever given to the Institute (Walzel 6). That endowment fund has grown to about two million dollars today and continues to provide regular income to the Institute (Walzel 6). Scurlock remained a generous supporter of the Institute for many years, serving as Treasurer of the Board of Trustees for several years and as a board member for over a decade. His family foundation, called The Scurlock Foundation, was chartered in Houston in 1954; this was the same year that the Institute of Religion was developed by Dr. Elliott.

The Institute was growing, gaining credibility and attracting attention from around the country. Granger Westberg, the same University of Chicago professor who had once counseled Dr. Bryan about starting up such an institute, moved from Chicago to Houston to take a faculty position as Dean of the Institute of Religion. Dr. Westberg also was named Professor of Religion and Medicine at Baylor College of Medicine (Institute, *Dimensions Fall 1965* 2). He was a good fit. Dr. Westberg had already spent a lifetime trying to deepen the relationship between ministers and doctors, and he was considered a pioneer in the interrelationship of religion and medicine. He was already the author of two books on the subject: *Minister and Doctor Meet* (1961), and the bestseller *Good Grief* (1962), which is still in print today, hails a 50th Anniversary Edition, and is called "a timeless classic" (Westberg, *Good Grief* 7).

It was now 1965, which marked the tenth anniversary of the Institute of Religion, and a quarterly newsletter called *Dimensions* was created to help spread the word. Rev. Julian Byrd, who by now had graduated from the Institute and had become a chaplain supervisor, was hired as Registrar and Alumni Secretary for the Institute and editor of its *Dimensions* newsletter. He fondly remembers those days: "We would have people who might only give us twenty-five dollars each year, but we'd put them on our newsletter mailing list. We had a ladies' group of volunteers from churches who would help get out mailings, put the address labels and stamps on our mailings. They were just invaluable, there were so many people helping us out, and it was really fun to be a part of that" (Byrd, *Interview* 8). The following year, in 1966, more than 300 ministers, and medical and nursing students took courses at the Institute, which Dr. Bryan proudly noted was the largest enrollment numbers to date. Likewise, over sixty ministers sought enrollment that summer; applications came from the U.S., India, Canada, Australia, Hong Kong, and Germany (Fondren, *Minutes of March 17, 1966* 3). Of those sixty applicants, thirty-eight were accepted into the program; this number was an increase over that first summer when only twelve students enrolled (Institute, *Dimensions Summer 1966* 1).

CHAPTER THREE

CHANGE IS IN THE AIR

*"Health is a state of complete harmony
of the body, mind and spirit. When one is free
from physical disabilities and mental distractions,
the gates of the soul open." – B.K.S. Iyengar*

After thirteen years of dedicated leadership, Dr. Bryan retired as head of the Institute in mid-1967, but he continued to have an office there, still came to work daily, and, according to Rev. Byrd, "spent his days out trying to raise money for the Institute" (Byrd, *Interview* 7). Sadly, less than a year after retiring and just one month after attending an Institute board meeting, Dr. Bryan passed away in April 1968. It was an unsteady time in the United States. Martin Luther King, Jr. was assassinated the same month that Dr. Bryan died, and U.S. Senator Robert F. Kennedy also was assassinated in the summer of 1968. On September 10, 1968, another long-time Institute supporter, Otis Massey, who served as the very first Chairman of the Board of Trustees, died, too. The Institute of Religion seemed to reflect what was happening all over the country and soon implemented changes of its own.

After Dr. Bryan's retirement, the Institute called Rev. Thompson L. Shannon, PhD, of California, to start as its new President/Director. When Dr. Shannon took the reigns in 1968, he decided a new name was in order; and so, the Institute of Religion officially was changed in the bylaws to the Institute of Religion and Human Development, a moniker that would stick until 1975 (Fondren, *Minutes of Oct. 29, 1968*). The title of the original *Dimensions* newsletter also changed and now was called *The Institute of Religion News*. Additionally, around this time, the Institute became a full member of the Council of Southwestern Theological Schools, which is still today a group of seminaries and affiliates in the Southwest that cooperate in various joint activities (Perkins). Dr. Shannon had the idea that he would try to turn the Institute of Religion and Human Development into a degree-granting institute. To accomplish this goal, which in the end was never fully realized, he hired several PhDs in pastoral counseling to the faculty and created a branch called "The Counseling Center" (Sunderland 3).

Dr. Shannon also brought up the idea of medical ethics as a viable direction for the Institute. In March of 1968, the Institute, along with Rice University, co-sponsored a medical ethics conference called "Ethics in Medicine and Technology." It was recognized as one of the first major conferences on medical ethics in the world (Verhey, *Institute* 2). Some of the top leaders in the field of that time were invited to teach the four-day seminar: Dr. Joseph Fletcher, director of the American Society for Christian Ethics; Margaret Mead, PhD, a leading world cultural anthropologist; Emmanuel Mesthene, PhD, philosopher and social scientist; Robert F. Drinan, S.J., D.T., an internationally recognized authority on abortion and the law; Paul Ramsey, PhD, another medicine and ethics authority; and Helmut Thielicke, PhD, one of the world's great preacher-theologians and a giant in the post-war theological revival in Germany (R. Smith 1). It was a progressive move for the Institute to make in 1968; this time in the world marked the birth of the field of bioethics, and these well-known religious thinkers came to Houston from all over to give their personal talks on the subject (Meilaender). Twenty-five years later, in 1993, the Institute of Religion would again host an "Ethics in Medicine and Technology" conference to remember and celebrate the same occasion that was begun decades before.

Funds continued to come in during the early 1970s. The Zale Foundation of Dallas donated $52,000 for a two-year project called "Human Values in Medical Education." The Sid W. Richardson Foundation donated $50,000, and the Rockefeller Brothers Fund gave $15,000, with both gifts earmarked for the Institute's work in medical ethics. The Department of Community Medicine at Baylor College of Medicine rented space on the third floor of the Institute of Religion building, which netted $20,000 per year in revenue. Baylor also rented space on the fourth floor to set up a Learning Resource Center, which brought in another $20,000 per year for the Institute (Weingarten, *Minutes of Oct. 23, 1973* 1-6).

Harry S. Lipscomb, M.D. was a prominent director of Baylor College of Medicine's Department of Biochemistry, and he also was the Chairman of the Institute's Board at that time. At a 1970s board meeting, Dr. Lipscomb announced, "Something great is happening at the Institute. A new spirit seems to have come about. The faculty is pulling together, and new affiliations and understandings are being worked out between the hospitals" (Weingarten, *Minutes of May 22, 1973* 2). Incidentally, Dr. Lipscomb later joined what was to become the faculty of the College of Medicine at Texas A&M University in College Station, where he was named Professor Emeritus (Harry 1). It was an exciting time for the organization, a time of energy, growth and leadership. However, by 1972, Dr. Shannon was granted a sabbatical leave for personal reasons, and he and his wife eventually moved to Portland, Oregon where he retired.

For a short time from 1972 to 1974, Kenneth L. Vaux, M.Div., D.Th., served as Acting Director of the Institute. He received his Doctor of Theology degree in 1968 from the University of Hamburg, which was and still is one of Germany's largest universities (University). Today Dr. Vaux is professor of theological ethics at Garrett-Evangelical Theological Seminary in Evanston, Illinois. Under Dr. Vaux, the Institute continued to grow in stature as a leader in medical ethics. For many years the heart and soul of the Institute had been to serve as a training ground in Clinical Pastoral Education. Over time, however, the hospitals throughout the Texas Medical Center began to hire their own CPE supervisors and train their own chaplains; likewise, area medical schools began providing their own education in religion and medicine. The original initiative of the Institute was gradually being taken over by other organizations, which can be seen as a compliment but at the time left a distinct hole (Outler 2).

The Rev. Dr. Ted Smith, who was training as a chaplain resident at M.D. Anderson around that time, explains the result: "That really pulled a big chunk out of what the Institute was doing in terms of its identity, and also its daily operation, and so, as a result, its faculty began to shrink in size" (T. Smith 4). Gradually, the Institute of Religion was no longer playing a primary role in the pastoral care programs, which it had once operated and controlled (Verhey, *Institute* 2). Board member David Stitt, D.D. commented that he was proud of the Institute's position at that time. At a mid-1970s board meeting, he said, "The Institute has made many contributions over the past twenty years. As a result, many hospitals and seminaries have their own ongoing chaplaincy program. For a moment, it looks as if the Institute has worked itself out of a job; however, there is still much to be done" (Weingarten, *Minutes of Feb. 5, 1976* 7). Ted Smith and many others now speculate that due to losing the CPE training piece, medical ethics began to emerge as a distinct discipline for the Institute as it was searching for a new mission (T. Smith 4-5).

It didn't take long for its ethics programs to gain attention. *The Encyclopedia of Bioethics*, originally published in 1979, called Houston's Institute of Religion in the Texas Medical Center the first major institution devoted to medical ethics in the United States (Jonsen 1000). Dr. Vaux helped set up a nine-month residency program designed to equip individuals for leadership in the field of medical ethics, and a limited number of stipends were available for medical school faculty, ethicists and campus ministers. Additionally, a 1974 newsletter published under Dr. Vaux touted a rather new-sounding mission: To be a resource to the theological and ethical needs of pastors, laymen and health professionals (Vaux, *Report* 1).

In the fall of 1974, the Institute was pleased to hire Rev. Julian Byrd as its next President/Director to fill the spot that Dr. Vaux had temporarily held in an interim capacity for the past two years. At that time, Rev. Byrd had spent the last sixteen years running a chaplaincy program at M.D. Anderson, and prior to that, he received training at the Institute of

Religion and served as its registrar and newsletter editor. Rev. Byrd commented, "My own personal experience was that it was exciting to be the Institute's president; it was very different than the clinical work I had been doing with patients, medical staff, medical students, theological students and seminary graduates" (Byrd, *Interview* 9). Signaling a definite end of an era, Rev. Byrd's secretary, Helen Riddle, retired in December 1974 after twenty years of service to the Institute. She began on the Institute's very first day of business as secretary to Dr. Bryan and faithfully served various other directors for two decades (Vaux, *Report* 1). And a year later, in 1975, Rev. Byrd announced that the Board of Trustees had wisely acted to officially change the organization's name back to The Institute of Religion, which was its original chartered name created by the founders. As Rev. Byrd aptly put it, "If we accept the position that religion has to do with all of life, that it should not be thought of as only applicable to a segment of life having to do with personal piety and formal worship, then the addition [of Human Development to the title] was redundant anyway" (Byrd, *From the Director* 1). Rev. Byrd continued as President of the Institute until 1976.

At the peak of the 1970s, the Institute was still receiving donations and serving its community. Then, in June of 1976, the sixteen-year-old Institute building barely escaped major flooding when terrible thunderstorms hit Houston. Many other parts of the Texas Medical Center, however, were ravaged; over ten inches of rain fell in just six hours, thirteen inches of rain impacted the Braes Bayou near the medical center, and there were eight drowning deaths (Significant). At that time, it was considered "the worse flood ever to hit the area," a phrase that was to remain true for the next twenty-five years (Wendler). This flooding reminded the Institute staff of a previous storm, Hurricane Carla, which hit the Texas coastline back in 1961. Carla did considerable damage to the nearby Texas Woman's University building. The hurricane also caused considerable damage by downing 150 trees in the Texas Medical Center, which created a rather devastated-looking appearance for the sprawling campus for a few years to come (Elliott, *Birth* 191).

Rev. Byrd left the Institute in 1976, moved with his family back to Florida, but soon returned to the Texas Medical Center to develop a chaplaincy program at Hermann Hospital. These were his roots, hospital chaplaincy, and Rev. Byrd felt he was finally back doing what he was originally trained to do. During his ten years at Hermann Hospital, he used his contacts to solicit students from the Institute of Religion from varied denominations and faiths to work as chaplains; it was a win-win situation (Byrd, *Interview* 8-9). During Rev. Byrd's tenure at the Institute, he had become friends with a pastor named Rev. Ron H. Sunderland, Ed.D., who in 1966 had moved to the United States from Australia with his wife and four children in tow. Rev. Sunderland was a student of the Institute, and later Rev. Byrd hired him to develop seminars and academic programs in clinical pastoral education. This relationship would prove to be advantageous, because Rev. Sunderland was the obvious choice for Rev. Byrd's replacement and seamlessly began as the next President/Director of the Institute of Religion in 1976.

The Institute's work in bioethics was still getting attention during the latter part of the decade. In December of 1976, Jerome Berryman, J.D., D.Min, D.D., an Episcopal priest who was a fellow of the Institute at the time, attended a Bioethics Conference in Dallas, which attracted some 600 participants. Dr. Berryman reported back to the Board of Trustees: "The Institute's name, its faculty, and its work in medical ethics was mentioned again and again in the most supportive and gratifying terms. The Institute is being identified as the only center in the State of Texas where this sort of conversation is taking place, other than in conferences such as the one in Dallas" (Weingarten, *Minutes of Dec. 15, 1976* 1-6). The trustees and staff of the Institute were proud to hear Dr. Berryman's positive report on their work and reputation. The following year, in 1977, the Institute asked Dr. Berryman to develop a ministry to children called "The Children's Center" to function throughout the Texas Medical Center. Rev.

Sunderland explained that for years it had been assumed that pastoral care ministers could work as well with children as they could with adults; but over time, it was felt that this might have been an unreasonable expectation. "There are obviously some unique things that happen with children and their parents that do not happen with adult patients," Rev. Sunderland said (Weingarten, *Minutes of Feb. 16, 1977* 4). Dr. Berryman's program, which promoted pastoral care of children in hospitals, was well received, and he continued to work with the Institute until 1984 (Berryman 2).

About this same time, two special women joined the organization's Board of Trustees during the mid-1970s and made their presence known in a very positive way. Loise Henderson Wessendorff, a native Houstonian, was a civic leader, a member of the Junior League, and one of the founders of the Texas Institute of Child Psychiatry. She was also no stranger to the Institute of Religion; Mrs. Wessendorff's family had funded the first floor of the Institute's building in honor of her late father, Robert Wilson Henderson (Institute, *Newsletter, Nov. 1974* 7). Mrs. Wessendorf then used her influence to get her good friend, Carolyn Clarke, interested in the workings of the Institute of Religion. Mrs. Clarke, who was president of the Garden Club of Houston and also a Junior League member, joined the Board of Trustees as well. As Mrs. Clarke, who is still an active board member to this day, tells it: "There wouldn't be an Institute if it wasn't for Loise Wessendorff!" (Clarke, *Interview* 11). Indeed, these ladies, along with many of their friends, formed an auxiliary group called The Women of the Institute (WOI) in 1975, which assisted the Institute in its fundraising endeavors. In 2015, the year of the Institute's sixtieth anniversary, Mrs. Clarke boasted more total years on the board than any other member.

The Institute was infused with new life and new leadership throughout the 1970s. Near the end of the decade, the Institute's 1977 annual budget was hovering at approximately $300,000. A year later, in 1978, the Trustees increased that amount when they adopted a new budget of almost $500,000. The Institute offered workshops and courses on a regular basis, which helped spread information to the community about the Institute's good work. They also held various black-tie benefit dinners to raise funds, which helped Rev. Sunderland in his quest to eliminate some debt that the Institute had accrued over the years. It was no secret that securing funds for the organization had always proven to be a challenge. Dr. Elliott explained this dilemma in his book, *The Birth of the Texas Medical Center*: "Funds could be accumulated, though not as readily as they might have been for illnesses like heart disease or cancer. Through the years, difficulties would arise [for the Institute] when funds were sought for operating expenses, research and teaching. The Institute was not an organized church. It had no congregation on which it could depend for support, so its funds had to come from gifts and grants" (Elliott, *Birth* 181-182). Despite this problem, Rev. Sunderland was determined to boost the bank account reserves during his tenure, and he says that within about four years, the organization's finances gradually began to stabilize (Sunderland 2).

⌁— CHAPTER FOUR —⌁
MEDICAL ETHICS AND IDENTITY ISSUES

"The part can never be well unless the whole is well." – Plato

On April 27, 1980, the Institute of Religion celebrated its twenty-fifth anniversary with an afternoon Open House at its 1129 Wilkins location in the heart of the Texas Medical Center. The honored guest was Rachel M. Bryan, widow of the late founder Dawson Bryan. By now the Institute, still under Rev. Sunderland's leadership, was proudly boasting: "Each week over 100 students—clergy, physicians, and nurses—attend classes at the Institute" (Institute, *Newsletter Nov. 1980* 1). Not only that, but for the first time since the Institute's founding in 1955, all teaching programs were now open to any applicants from the community instead of to only a select group of clergy and healthcare providers.

In October 1980, Albert C. Outler, PhD, visited the Institute for a two-day consultation and then wrote a "Consultants Report for Long-Range Planning." Outler, who lived from 1908-1989, was a Methodist theologian and philosopher and was seen as a key figure in the twentieth century ecumenical movement (Albert 1). He was impressed by the magnitude and complexity of the Texas Medical Center itself, and he highlighted the significance of the Institute of Religion as a "heartening symbol of a positive commitment to the primacy of the human reality" (Outler 2). He was reminded of a claim made by Dr. Bryan some twenty-five years earlier that "this [Medical Center] is the most challenging congregation in Houston and the most neglected." Outler recounted Dr. Bryan's original vision of the Institute as a service center for ministers and physicians in training, where their effectiveness in dealing with the personal and spiritual needs of patients and their families could be significantly enhanced. However, because the local hospitals and medical schools had taken over much of this training, it was time to reinvigorate the mission of the Institute of Religion. Outler noted that the hospitals' and schools' adoption of this training aspect should be applauded as "heartening evidence of the Institute's impact on the Medical Center at large" (Outler 2-10). In other words, imitation is a high form of flattery, but the organization perhaps needed to seek a new focus.

Meanwhile, around this time, the Institute was fortunate to have Jim Walzel, a native of Rosenberg, Texas who worked in the natural gas industry, join the Board of Trustees. Walzel was instrumental in procuring the Kathryn Murfee Endowment for the Institute of Religion. Latimer Murfee was a prominent Houston lawyer, a member of St. Paul's United Methodist Church, and an original founder of the Institute of Religion. He died in 1983, leaving his estate to the Kathryn Murfee Endowment; from about 1984 through 2008, the endowment made an annual gift to the Institute. In 2009, Walzel, who was a trustee for the Murfee Endowment, along with the two other trustees, decided to dissolve and distribute the endowment, resulting in a final, very significant $300,000 unrestricted gift to be used by the Institute as it should choose to further its mission. Walzel also personally donated $50,000 to the Institute in February of 2008. Later, he would go on to serve as Chairman of the ISH's Board of Trustees, from 2009 to 2011, and he continues to be a very strong presence on the board to this day (Walzel 7).

The gift from the Kathryn Murfee Endowment, and other new developments, marked the beginning of some of that reinvigoration that Albert Outler and others at the Institute were hoping for. One vast undertaking occurred in the summer of 1982, when The Center for Medical Ethics was created with a formal joint agreement between Baylor College of Medicine, Rice University, and the Institute of Religion. The three partnering organizations hired professor Baruch Brody, PhD, an expert in the growing field of medical ethics, to be the Center's Director. Additionally, the Center for Medical Ethics occupied a portion of the top floor of the Institute of Religion building. The Institute agreed to pay the salary of Earl Shelp, PhD, a colleague of Rev. Sunderland's, who joined the Center as an instructor of medical ethics (Brody 1).

Not long thereafter, however, Rev. Sunderland and Dr. Shelp both decided to leave the Institute of Religion to develop their own program called Foundation for Interfaith Research and Ministry (FIRM), an educational non-profit organization which helps congregations equip volunteers to provide assistance to individuals and families challenged by chronic illness or disability (Shelp). This program was later re-named Interfaith Care Partners. Another expert named B. Andrew Lustig, PhD was hired to replace Dr. Shelp as the Institute's academic professor at the Center for Medical Ethics. Dr. Lustig was highly qualified due to his training in religion and science, theological ethics and bioethics; he also set up programming for the Institute of Religion as another aspect of his job. Dr. Lustig continues in the field as the Holmes Rolston III Professor of Religion and Science at Davidson College in North Carolina (B. Andrew Lustig).

Some thirty years later, Dr. Brody still leads the Center for Medical Ethics at Baylor College of Medicine, and he is also Baylor's Leon Jaworski Professor of Biomedical Ethics. Additionally, he is the Andrew Mellow Professor of Humanities in the department of philosophy at Rice University. According to Dr. Brody, "Andy Lustig eventually left the Center to administer a grant at Rice University, and the Institute was not in a financial position at that time to hire a replacement for him, so the relationship between the Institute and the Center came to a halt" (Brody 2). He says the Center continued to rent space on the fourth floor from the Institute of Religion, as it had always done, so they became tenants of the Institute rather than a group sponsored partially by the Institute.

With Rev. Sunderland's unexpected resignation in 1982, and with the end of the short-lived role as a partner of the Center for Medical Ethics, the Institute again found itself in need of a new direction. The Institute needed leadership, so it called Rev. David Stitt, D.D., who had formerly served as a Chairman of the Board of Trustees, to fill the role as Interim Director.

Dr. Stitt was a former pastor of Houston's Bellaire Presbyterian Church and a former president of the Austin Presbyterian Theological Seminary. He served the Institute very well as an Interim Director from 1983 to 1985.

The work of the Institute continued to advance during the mid-1980s. Carolyn Clarke, who had joined the Board of Trustees back in the 1970s, and still remains an active member, saw a distinct need at the Institute building site. She put her own talents and the skills of her other Garden Club friends to work. Mrs. Clarke recalls, "The grounds around the Institute of Religion were just a Frisbee field and an ugly path between Baylor and Methodist. I asked my Garden Club if they could put a few plantings there, and instead, they came back and said they would raise the money to install a lovely garden." The Garden Club of Houston, under Mrs. Clarke's direction, raised $350,000; of that amount, a $75,000 donation came from the family of Dawson Bryan, and a fountain was built in his name as a memorial to him (Clarke, *Interview* 2). In January of 1984, the Plaza was one of thirteen projects recognized as winners in the 17th Annual Environmental Improvement Awards Competition, which was co-sponsored by the Houston-Gulf Coast chapter of the American Society of Landscape Architects, the Houston Municipal Art Commission, and the Houston chapter of the American Institute of Architects. The beautiful new outdoor space was cited as being "an oasis of green space in the high-tech, high-pressure Texas Medical Center" (Institute, *Plaza Wins*). A few months later, in May of 1984, the Plaza was officially dedicated. Special thanks were given to Carolyn Clarke for her monumental role and initiative on the project, and all donors to the project were honored as a permanent feature at the site. Some ten years later, in 1994, the park was added to a national collection of noteworthy American parks and gardens in the archives of the Smithsonian Institute in Washington, D.C., an honor shared in Houston by Bayou Bend Gardens and Mercer Arboretum and Botanic Gardens (Clarke, *Slides* 1). Most of the gardens and the fountain named for Dr. Dawson Bryan still remain to this day.

Mrs. Clarke, who is now in her nineties, considers the garden implementation to be one of her most important contributions to the Institute.

Despite so many positive efforts, Dr. Brody and others recall that during this time, the Institute was actually facing what many have referred to as an identity crisis. Dr. Brody explains what he thinks was happening: "The first two enterprises of the Institute of Religion—chaplaincy training and developing medical ethics—were great successes. In fact, each of those missions was so effective that they spawned programs that are still going on today very successfully. All it meant though was that the relevant institutions over time took them over. So, by the mid-eighties, the Institute basically faced an identity problem. You know, it's hard to raise money when you can't explain what your purpose is" (Brody 4). It appeared that whenever the Institute had a tangible mission that made sense, the organization was able to make a real contribution to the community at large. Therefore, it was time to address the Institute's purpose and vision once again.

The Rev. J. Robert "Bob" Nelson, D.Theol., D.D., who hailed from Boston University School of Theology, was named the new President of the Institute of Religion in January of 1985, a position he would fill for the next seven years. Dr. Nelson, an ordained Methodist minister, became involved in the emerging field of bioethics while at Boston University; it was a new field that related theological understanding to the science of genetics and medical technology. Dr. Nelson's son, Eric Nelson, once explained in a *Boston Globe* newspaper article that his father "discerned before many others the urgent need for theologians to address the issues that came with the explosion of technological medical situations" (Negri 5). Dr. Nelson's new ideas and vision would soon breathe new life into the struggling Institute.

During his tenure at the Institute of Religion, Dr. Nelson hired a dynamic woman named Betsy Garlington Striegler as Development Director; she was later promoted to Administrator, and she served the Institute from 1990 to 2000. Today, Betsy speaks fondly of the late Dr. Nelson, who died in 2004 at age 84. She recalled during an interview:

"He was an extraordinary man and really had great vision, and his passion was genetics. He was probably one of the first directors that was social enough to get out there with a group to raise big money" (Striegler 8). Shortly after Dr. Nelson arrived, long-time trustee R.A. "Al" Parker died at the age of seventy-two after twenty-two years on the Board, and six of those years were spent as Chairman of the Board of Trustees. To honor this devoted man, the Institute created the "Al Parker Memorial Lectures," which remained in the forefront of Institute activities for many years.

New endeavors were being developed while Dr. Nelson was President, some that still continue to this day as major projects of the Institute. One such undertaking was the creation of a nursing program, which started out as monthly sack luncheons and nurses' retreats. Today, that program has grown by leaps and bounds, and the Nursing Conference, which is usually held each October, draws approximately 150 registrants annually. Gwen Sherwood, PhD, R.N., FAAN, a former board member who is now Associate Dean of Academic Affairs and Professor at University of North Carolina's School of Nursing in Chapel Hill, is credited with helping Betsy Striegler get the Institute's Nursing Conference on its feet (Striegler 11). They also brought in Susan Cooley King, PhD, R.N., a pediatric nurse-practitioner and daughter of Denton Cooley, M.D., a world-renowned heart surgeon and founder of the Texas Heart Institute, to assist with the creation of the nursing program. Sherwood returned to Houston in 2010 to speak at the Institute's annual Nursing Conference. Today, the Nursing Conference is funded in part by Houston's John P. McGovern Foundation. In 2010, board member AnneMarie Wallace established an award that celebrated "Spirituality in Nursing" in memory of her mother, Emma Josephine Loffelholz McMorris. Emma McMorris was a vibrant nurse for many years, but at the young age of thirty-five, she lost her life to breast cancer just one month after diagnosis in 1958. "My mother's presence was one of amazing, gentle grace that filled my soul and created lasting sacred moments that began a life-long yearning for

God," AnneMarie says. Each year, the collaborating hospitals and nursing schools choose a student from their institution to receive the trophy. The Nursing Conference is one of AnneMarie's favorite ISH events, as she appreciates hearing the powerful narratives from the nurses. She is humbled and proud to leave the legacy of this award to honor her mother—an award that recognizes the spiritual nuances in the profession of nursing.

Also in the mid-1980s, under Dr. Nelson's leadership, board member Loise Wessendorff passionately urged the Institute to develop an annual conference that would combine the topics of psychiatry and religion. With Mrs. Wessendorf's help and financial support, the Institute began hosting what today is known as the Psychotherapy and Faith Conference. Throughout Dr. Nelson's term, many nationally recognized leaders came to speak at the Psychotherapy and Faith Conferences, such as: Methodist bishop and theologian William Willimon; psychiatrist and author Gerald May, M.D.; Harvard Medical School psychiatry professor George E. Vaillant, M.D.; celebrated psychoanalyst Ethel Person, M.D.; and mind/body medicine pioneer Herbert Benson, M.D.

Long-time board member James W. Lomax, II, M.D., who is a Professor and Associate Chair at Baylor College of Medicine's Department of Psychiatry and Behavioral Sciences, was on the first planning committee with Mrs. Wessendorff when the Psychotherapy and Faith Conference originally was developed over twenty years ago. Dr. Lomax laughingly remembers Mrs. Wessendorff's personal vision for her pet project: "Loise's language is that psychiatrists and preachers don't talk to each other enough and I want them to" (Lomax 4). Loise Wessendorff passed away in 2008, but her early legacy at the Institute as a founder of the Psychotherapy and Faith Conference continues. Today, her son, Joe D. Robinson, is a board member at the Institute for Spirituality and Health.

The conference has grown exponentially over the years. In 2010, the Psychotherapy and Faith Conference notably celebrated its twentieth anniversary at St. Paul's United Methodist Church with 270 attendees.

The diverse audience was made up of physicians, psychiatrists, psychologists, social workers, nurses and other healthcare givers, and the Psychotherapy and Faith Conference is one of the Institute's biggest projects (Lomax 1). In 2013, the Hope and Healing Center at St. Martin's Episcopal Church joined the Institute to co-host the event, along with Baylor College of Medicine and the Menninger Clinic. Today the event draws more than 300 attendees and remains one of the most important events the Institute puts on each year.

Much-needed funds began to arrive under Dr. Nelson's leadership. In 1986, the H.A. and Isabel Elkins Foundation awarded the Institute with a $100,000 grant; the M.D. Anderson Foundation gave $10,000; and Houston Endowment, Inc. was annually giving the Institute $30,000 (Institute, *Donations* 3). In 1991, the U.S. Department of Energy granted $33,136 for the Institute's project on "Genetics, Religion and Ethics."

The Institute celebrated various important honorees and events throughout the late eighties and early nineties. In 1988, the James F. Mitchell Foundation named James H. "Red" Duke, M.D., "Surgeon of the Year," and the Institute's Board of Trustees honored him for his achievements at a "Caring Spirit Tribute" dinner they hosted at the Houston Country Club. Dr. Duke has been a faculty member at Houston's University of Texas Medical School since 1972, and he is known nationally for his syndicated television spot called "Dr. Red Duke's Health Reports." The Institute of Religion's annual "Caring Spirit Tribute" dinners continued for many years and honored dozens of Houston philanthropists and leaders.

Then, in March of 1990, "An Evening of Celebration" highlighted the Institute's thirty-fifth anniversary. The four distinguished honorees that night were Mr. and Mrs. Roy M. Huffington, Robert D. Moreton, M.D., and the late professor Albert C. Outler, PhD. Social events like this helped the Institute of Religion create awareness throughout the community about their mission. The organization's *New Horizons* newsletter was being mailed to 10,000 people, and four church denominations were enclosing copies of the newsletters in their general mailings (Selig, *Minutes of Sept. 19, 1990* 1).

That same year, in 1990, the Hyman J. Schachtel Memorial Symposium began as part of the Institute's Forum Lecture Series to bring Jewish philosophers and theologians in for lectures and seminars. Rabbi Schachtel (1907-1990) was chief rabbi of Congregation Beth Israel in Houston from 1943 to 1975, and he continued there as rabbi-at-large for the remainder of his life. Rabbi Schachtel joined the Institute of Religion's Board of Trustees in the late 1970s, and he faithfully served on the Board for over ten years. He worked for interfaith understanding throughout the community, and the Institute's Hyman J. Schachtel Memorial Symposium continued in his honor for twenty-five years (Harris 1).

Over the years, other rabbis from Congregation Beth Israel, such as Rabbi Samuel Karff, D.H.L. and Rabbi David A. Lyon, M.H.L., followed in the footsteps of their mentor Rabbi Schachtel, and both men have continued his tradition of bringing a Jewish presence to the Board of Trustees of the Institute. Rabbi Karff served as Beth Israel's chief rabbi from 1975 to 1999; Rabbi Lyon took over in 2004 and is still the chief rabbi at Congregation Beth Israel (Our History 1). Says Rabbi Lyon: "Rabbi Schachtel's name is still equated with a lot of interfaith work in the community, and many bridges were built between Jews and Christians because of him" (Lyon 1). The influence and deliberate work of Rabbi Schachtel still is regularly discussed at the Institute more than two decades after his death.

Also, in March of 1990, the Institute of Religion held a three-day conference on "Genetics, Religion and Ethics" at the University of Texas M.D. Anderson Cancer Center. Some 125 participants attended, and the talks mainly focused on issues regarding mapping the human genome, which was a timely, front-line topic of the era. In fact, about six months after the Institute's conference, the U.S. Department of Energy and the National Institutes of Health began what would become a thirteen-year effort called the U.S. Human Genome Project (Human 1).

However, in the midst of all the progress that was happening at the Institute of Religion, a tragedy struck in April of 1991, when a woman shot Dr. Nelson while he was at work (Striegler 4). Fortunately, Betsy Striegler and other staff members were there to quickly call an ambulance, and Dr. Nelson survived the attack. In 1992, the year following the shooting, Dr. Nelson retired as head of the Institute due to poor health conditions that were caused by the gunshot wound.

Dr. Frederick C. Elliott, the first Executive Director of the Texas Medical Center. Photo courtesy of Texas Medical Center.

Dawson Bryan, D.D., the first Director of the Institute of Religion, which began in 1955. Photo courtesy of St. Paul's United Methodist Church.

CGN HSO19 PD=HOUSTON TEX MAY 5 1017AMC=
DR DAWSON BRYAN=,
    JESSE JONES LIBRARY MED CENTER DLR MAY 8TH=

CONGRATULATIONS TO THE TRUSTEES OF THE INSTITUTE OF
RELIGION, THIS FORWARD STEP SHOULD BE MOST CONSTRUCTIVE IN
THE EFFECTIVE TRAINING OF MEN OF RELIGION AND OF MEDICINE
ALIKE TO HELP PEOPLE TO A BETTER LIFE SORRY NOT TO BE
PRESENT=
    THE RIGHT REV JOHN E HINES BISHOP OF TEXAS=

Letters and telegrams—like these two, which are dated May of 1956—poured in to congratulate the founders of the Institute of Religion for their new endeavor.

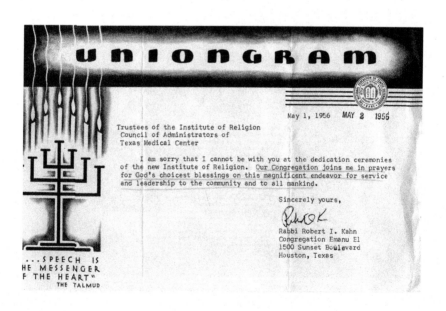

50

Ella Fondren was a founding board member and served as secretary of the Board of Trustees for seventeen years. The Fondren Foundation gave seed funds to help start the Institute of Religion and provided strong financial support for many years. Photo Courtesy of St. Paul's United Methodist Church.

Eddy C. Scurlock, an early board member, was a local oil industry tycoon and a long-time supporter of the Institute. He created a $1.5 million endowment which remains the largest gift ever given to the Institute. Photo courtesy of the Scurlock Foundation.

THE INSTITUTE of RELIGION
Texas Medical Center
Houston, Texas

JESSE H. JONES LIBRARY BUILDING

A ceremony

OBSERVING THE FORMAL OPENING

and

DEDICATION OF THE INSTITUTE OF RELIGION

in the

AUDITORIUM OF THE JESSE H. JONES LIBRARY BUILDING

8:00 P.M., Tuesday   May 8, 1956

A formal opening was held on May 8, 1956 to dedicate the new offices of the Institute of Religion at the Jesse H. Jones Library Building.

Aerial view of the Texas Medical Center with downtown Houston in the background. Photo courtesy of Texas Medical Center.

52

*An early rendition of the Institute
of Religion building, which was
completed in 1960.
Photo from the ISH archives.*

*The first Institute of Religion building, built in the heart
of the Texas Medical Center, opened in 1960 on the
corner of Bertner and Wilkins boulevards.
Photo from the ISH archives.*

*This bronze plaque bears the names of the board members in
1960, the year the Institute of Religion building opened. It still
hangs in the lobby of the Institute for Spirituality and Health.*

53

Loise Henderson Wessendorff joined the board in the 1970s, and years later, developing the Institute's Psychotherapy and Faith Conference became her passion. Photo courtesy of the Henderson-Wessendorff Foundation.

James W. Lomax, II, M.D. of Baylor College of Medicine, is a long-time board member who worked with Loise Wessendorff in the early years to create the Psychotherapy and Faith Conference. Today it is one of the Institute's largest events, attracting over 270 attendees annually. Photo courtesy of the Henderson-Wessendorff Foundation.

Carolyn Clarke has been active on the Board of Trustees since the 1970s, has served as a past Board Chairman, and today, she boasts more years on the board than any other member.

The Garden Club of Houston, under Carolyn Clarke's direction, created the fountain and award-winning gardens around the Institute of Religion building in the 1980s. Photo from the ISH archives.

55

Hyman J. Schachtel was chief rabbi of Congregation Beth Israel in Houston for over thirty years, and he was an active board member for more than ten years. The Institute continued the Hyman J. Schachtel Memorial Symposium in his honor for twenty-five years. Photo courtesy of Congregation Beth Israel.

John E. Fellers, M.Div., D.D., was Executive Director of the Institute from 1995 to 2006.

John K. Graham, M.D., D.Min., was named President/CEO of the Institute for Spirituality and Health in 2010.

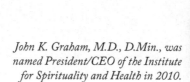

The current Board of Trustees at the Institute for Spirituality and Health include:
Clockwise from top left: Alan Craft; Rabbi David Lyon; Susan Josey; John Kimball Kehoe, DBA; Anne Koci, RN, PhD, APRN-BC, WHNP; James Walzel; Venugopal Menon, MD; Bart Fehr, JD (Legal Counsel); John K. Graham, MD, DMin; Laurence Payne; Zishan Samiuddin, MD; George Anderson; Fr. Donald S. Nesti, CSSp; Mary Katharine Roff, MD; James M. Booth; Richard E. Wainerdi, PhD; Nancy Gordon; James Lomax, MD; Poldi Tschirch, PhD; Jim Bankston, DMin; Carolyn M. Clarke; Bonnie Weekley; Robert Kidd, MDiv; AnneMarie Wallace; Robert Hesse, PhD; Cynthia Craft.
Not pictured: John D. Hawkins, Rabbi Samuel Karff, Barbara M. Kirsch, Joe D. Robinson, Barbara Schachtel-Green, Rev. Tommy Williams.

57

Rabbi Samuel E. Karff was the recipient of the Institute's 2014 "Caring Heart Award," presented at the Gathering of Friends luncheon.
He is an Emeritus board member of the Institute for Spirituality and Health.

In 2011, world-renowned Glen O. Gabbard, M.D., spoke to a packed crowd at the Institute's annual Psychotherapy and Faith Conference. Dr. Gabbard is a Professor of Psychiatry at SUNY Upstate Medical University in Syracuse, New York, a Clinical Professor of Psychiatry at Baylor College of Medicine in Houston, and a training and supervising analyst at the Center for Psychoanalytic Studies. He is also in private practice at Houston's Gabbard Center, and has authored and edited multiple books and scientific papers. Photo from the ISH archives.

The Institute's dedicated staff members are, from left to right:
Stuart Nelson, M.A., Vice President; John K. Graham, M.D., D.Min., President/CEO;
David Cregg, Research and Congregational Outreach Coordinator; Jerri Doctor, Manager
of Operations; Susana McCollom, Employee Enrichment Program Director and Workplace
Chaplaincy; Mark McCrummen, Financial Officer; Cyrus Wirls, Program Manager;
Jeff Sokoloff, Vice President for Advancement. Not pictured: Lex Gillan, Adjunct Faculty.

Medical school students from Baylor College of Medicine receive yoga training from Lex Gillan
at the Institute for Spirituality and Health.

59

Dr. John Graham spoke to a large audience at the 2011 Texas Children's Hospital Conference on Spirituality in Pediatrics. Photo by Allen Kramer.

Today the Institute for Spirituality and Health is located at 8100 Greenbriar and enjoys its close proximity to the Texas Medical Center in Houston.

⟨~ CHAPTER FIVE ~⟩

FROM THE NINETIES TO THE MILLENNIUM

*"The physician should not treat the disease but the patient
who is suffering from it." — Maimonides*

A search soon began to find a replacement for Dr. Nelson, and Allen Verhey, B.D., PhD, served as Director of the Institute for the next three years, from 1992 to 1995. Prior to moving to Houston, Dr. Verhey was the Blekkink Professor of Religion at Hope College in Michigan for ten years, and his work focused largely on the application of Christian ethics, especially in the areas of medicine and health. He says the committee chose him because "my interest in robustly religious reflection on medical ethics seemed to have won the approval of the Board in my interviews with them concerning my vision of the Institute" (Verhey, *Interview* 1). Like his predecessor, Dr. Verhey nurtured the Nursing Program and the Psychotherapy and Faith Conference, invited popular speakers, and continued his work in medical ethics. While Dr. Verhey considered his time at the Institute to have been "fruitful" and "full of meaningful work," he soon discovered that he missed teaching in the classroom. So after just a few years, Dr. Verhey left the Institute; he taught for over thirty years in the religion department at Michigan's Hope College before finishing his career as the Robert Earl Cushman Professor of Christian Theology at Duke Divinity School in North Carolina. Dr. Verhey continued to teach and write until six weeks before he died in 2014 after a long struggle with Amyloidosis.

After Dr. Verhey's tenure, John E. Fellers, M.Div., D.D., was then selected to serve as Executive Director of the Institute, and he held the position for eleven years from 1995 to 2006. Dr. Fellers studied at the University of Houston, the Candler School of Theology at Emory University, and the University of Edinburgh, and he also held an honorary doctorate from Wiley College in Texas. He was also no stranger to the Institute; Dr. Fellers was previously on the Board of Trustees for six years while serving as pastor at St. Paul's United Methodist Church in Houston. To this day, it is traditional that whoever is the current pastor of St. Paul's is invited to serve as an Institute board member. Dr. Fellers had left Texas briefly to serve as a pastor at two different Methodist churches in Louisiana; one of the churches was First Methodist Church in Shreveport, Louisiana, which at the time was the largest Protestant church in the state. Dr. Fellers returned to Houston when he was asked to head up the Institute of Religion (Institute, *John Fellers* 1).

Dr. Fellers once wrote, "The one thing that has remained constant is our founders' conviction that a religious presence is needed at the heart of one of the world's greatest medical centers. It is exciting for all of us to be working together to prepare the Institute for a new century of service at life's most crucial intersection, the place where soul and healing meet" (Institute, *John Fellers* 1). His vision was to draw the Institute closer to local churches and synagogues while maintaining its scholarly vocation as a teaching and research organization. Just six months into office, Dr. Fellers was already pursuing the idea of making the Institute a catalyst for Congregational Health Ministry in the Houston area. He was quoted in 1995 as saying: "I hope the Institute can become a center for Congregational Health Ministry in the 1990s, just as it was a center for Clinical Pastoral Education in the 1950s and 1960s" (Institute, *John Fellers* 1). Dr. Fellers said that Congregational Health Ministry was more than parish nurses or health coordinators; he said it also involves affirming healthy lifestyles, establishing support groups, dealing with ethical and moral issues surrounding medical treatment, and targeting health programs for all age groups.

Consistent with this approach, Dr. Fellers brought his vision of parish nursing to this region of the country in 1998 by wisely hiring Dr. Karen Hahn, PhD, R.N., A.P.N. Dr. Hahn explains that the idea of parish nursing was first developed during the 1970s in Chicago, and the idea began to grow throughout the 1980s across the country. She herself worked with the International Parish Nurse Resource Center (IPNRC) to become trained as a Parish Nurse Coordinator, a Chaplain, and also as a Spiritual Director. The IPNRC is a large organization that works with nurses and communities as they explore ways to incorporate parish nursing into their faith tradition (About 1). Describing her work at that time, Dr. Hahn says, "The interreligious faith and health alliance, which we had formed, identified that one of the basic needs for faith-based community outreach in this region was to have stronger coalition-based social service agencies where basic needs could be met. People needed food. They had to have a place to go for food. If they needed clothes, they needed help with that. If they needed rent and utility assistance, they had to have someplace to go" (Hahn 3). This undertaking spoke volumes to Dr. Fellers, and throughout his tenure at the Institute, he made parish nursing one of his primary focuses under the guidance of Dr. Hahn.

Eventually Dr. Hahn's project received grant funding and began to function independently in 2005; it separated from the Institute and was named the Center for Faith and Health Initiatives, where Dr. Hahn still serves as Executive Director. She says the coalition has over thirty-five different churches, health and social service providers, and educational organizations that have been involved for more than ten years. She explains, "The whole emphasis is on companioning and walking with faith communities in their journey for holistic health. So these relationships are kind of like extended family, especially when you are working with the smaller churches" (Hahn 9). Today, Dr. Hahn credits Dr. Fellers and the Institute as a whole for getting her life's work off the ground.

The work of the Institute was going well until June 8 and 9, 2001, when Tropical Storm Allison caused another major flood in Houston and throughout the entire Texas Medical Center. It had been twenty-five years since the last severe medical center flood, and this one wreaked havoc that had never been seen before. The Institute of Religion building at 1129 Wilkins, in the heart of the Texas Medical Center, was flooded and damaged beyond repair. Precious documents and files were lost in the storm that was cited as dropping the highest level of rainfall ever received in the Texas Medical Center (Wendler). More than thirty-five inches of rain fell over a three-day period, causing nearly two billion dollars in damage to the Texas Medical Center and making the whole area inaccessible for at least nine hours (Gilchriest). A total of forty-one deaths are directly related to the heavy rain, flooding, tornadoes, and high surf generated by Tropical Storm Allison; twenty-three of those deaths were in Texas alone (Stewart 1). Thanks to a ninety-minute warning from Rice University's Flood Alert System, some lives and property at the Texas Medical Center were saved, but the Institute's beloved "home" was ruined.

Jim Walzel remembers the resulting wreckage vividly: "The flood did so much damage to our building that it was going to be hugely expensive to patch it back up." He explains that Methodist Hospital wanted the flood-devastated space, so they struck a deal with the Institute of Religion. In exchange for their ruined building, the Institute was offered free office space at a new location owned by the hospital on the second floor of 8100 Greenbriar, the same location where it still is housed today. Methodist Hospital also agreed to pay the Institute $15,000 per month to rent the old building for the next 100 years, which Walzel says does provide a "safety net financially, because we have that guaranteed income" (Walzel 6). Eventually the old, water-damaged building was torn down.

The Institute's new Greenbriar location gave way to a new name. In 2003, the organization began calling itself the Institute of Religion and Health. It revised its mission: To advance the integration of religion, health and healing in the Texas Medical Center and the larger community. Also, in 2003, Dr. Fellers hired a dedicated woman named Jerri Doctor as the Institute's new Manager of Operations. Following the flood, Jerri assisted Dr. Fellers in the daunting task of moving the Institute offices to the Greenbriar building. Today, she continues to manage the daily activities of the office with a smile, and her vast knowledge of people throughout the Texas Medical Center makes her an invaluable asset to the organization (Graham, *Interview* 14).

In 2006, Dr. Fellers retired, and he died the following year in July of 2007. The Institute hosts the John Fellers Lecture in his honor. The Rev. Dr. L. James "Jim" Bankston, D.Min., the current pastor of St. Paul's United Methodist Church and an Institute board member, explains: "Dr. Fellers gave such great leadership and had such a wonderful spirit, was such an academician and such a spiritual person all at the same time that the current directors have wanted to honor his memory with a lectureship that would offer remarks within the field" (Karff, *Paradigms* 1). In April 2011, Rabbi Sam Karff gave the keynote address at the John Fellers Lecture, which was held in the Rio Grande Room at The Methodist Hospital. Rabbi Karff, a longtime board member, was chairman of the personnel committee that originally invited Dr. Fellers to head up the Institute. Rabbi Karff said to the packed audience at Methodist Hospital that day, "John truly believed in the importance of reaching out and of interfaith dialogue and of mutual respect. He did so much to advance the cause of our Institute" (Karff, *Paradigms* 4). Jerri Doctor fondly recalls her years working for Dr. Fellers: "He was just the dearest man and just the best boss, and I have so many fond memories of him. So it was very hard for me when he passed away" (Doctor 3). Dr. Fellers worked at the Institute for eleven years, so far surpassed in time served only by the first Institute President, Dr. Bryan, who served for twelve years.

The Institute needed to find a replacement for Dr. Fellers, who had served as its leader for more than a decade. By this time, the spirit of the United States had changed following the tragic terrorist attacks of September 11, 2001, and the nation was now at war in Afghanistan and Iraq. Jim Walzel explains that when Dr. Fellers left his position, he strongly encouraged the Institute to find a medical doctor as his replacement, because he thought this would be a beneficial change for the organization. Walzel says, "Methodist Hospital was setting up a Palliative Care Unit, and at the same time, we were having conversations with them that we'd like to have a doctor come in and head up the Institute. So we made a deal with Methodist Hospital that when they hired someone, that physician would work part-time at each organization" (Walzel 8). This part-time arrangement was useful, because it would allow the Institute to creatively fund a physician's salary requirements, which were typically higher than what a former pastor might expect to earn. Without this arrangement with Methodist Hospital, Walzel says that hiring a medical doctor would have probably been impossible at that time for the Institute.

In 2006, James D. "Jim" Duffy, M.D. was hired by Methodist Hospital to work part-time for their organization; and at the same time, Dr. Duffy was named President of the Institute of Religion and Health. Dr. Duffy was the first Buddhist to serve as President of the organization, and the board also was pleased to finally have a medical doctor in the headship role for the very first time.

Under Dr. Duffy's leadership, on December 13, 2006, the Institute rang in its fiftieth anniversary celebration with a musical called "An Evening of Sacred Sound Recognizing the Spirit of Healing," held at Rice University's Duncan Recital Hall. The Institute honored the family of founding board member Howard Tellepsen at that special, milestone event by presenting them the "Carolyn Clarke Caring Spirit Award." Howard Tellepsen, who died in 2000, had attended the very first planning meeting that Dr. Elliott held on December 9, 1954, and he generously gave his time and resources to the Institute for many years. Another presentation made that night was to Sir John Templeton, who was awarded the "John Templeton International Spirit of Healing Award" (Duffy).

Two years later, in 2008, Dr. Duffy decided to leave Methodist Hospital to take a new position at M.D. Anderson Cancer Center, which also led to the end of his tenure at the Institute. M.D. Anderson needed him to work for their organization on a full-time basis, so he was no longer able to split his time between two organizations (Walzel 11). So with Dr. Duffy's departure, the Institute began making plans to find a replacement.

Change was happening everywhere at this time. The United States elected its first African-American President, Barack Obama, and "change" became a common thread throughout his campaign. Apple Inc. began selling its ultra-thin MacBook Air computer, baby boomers were about to retire, and a global recession was in the works (Nolen 1).

In the midst of these worldwide transformations, in 2008, the Institute itself made a final name change: The Institute for Spirituality and Health, a title that remains today. The Board of Trustees made the decision to change the title because they felt that the word "spirituality" embraced more than just religion (Graham, *Interview* 14). The Institute's mission, however, remained the same as the founders had always intended: To increase knowledge of and sensitivity to the role that spirituality plays in health and in healing, a message that today is fortified by more than 3,000 articles in medical literature (Graham, *Recapping* 1).

Another medical doctor was hired as President of the Institute, and from 2008 to 2010, Richard "Dick" Materson, M.D., was next to fill the leadership role. Dr. Materson was a private physical medicine and rehabilitation physician for many years, and he also held various academic and leadership positions at Baylor College of Medicine and throughout the Texas Medical Center. He already had served as the Institute's Chairman of the Board for two years, so he was an easy shift for the organization. However, his health had been poor, and a physical handicap had confined him to a wheelchair for many years. Dr. Materson's untimely death in February of 2010 too soon left the Institute for Spirituality and Health without a director once again.

CHAPTER SIX

THE INSTITUTE TODAY

"The story of the Institute of Religion is a story of faith at its beginnings and in its continuings." – Dr. Allen Verhey

In March 2010, John K. Graham, M.D., D.Min, was named President/CEO of the Institute for Spirituality and Health. The Rev. Dr. Graham had already been a board member for six years, so he was a seamless transition after the passing of Dr. Materson. Formerly a board-certified plastic surgeon, Dr. Graham became an Episcopal priest in 1994 and served at St. Martin's Episcopal Church in Houston for many years. Dr. Graham remembers the call he received from Jim Walzel, who was then-Chairman of the Board of Trustees, asking if he would replace Dr. Materson as President/CEO of the Institute. Dr. Graham says, "I think I almost immediately said yes. I really felt like maybe I could make a difference because I'm both a physician and a priest" (Graham, *Interview* 1). Board Member Nancy Gordon agrees: "Being a physician and ordained member of the clergy, I think, is a key element. It is just perfect, and everything is coming full circle again. Dr. Materson got the focus back for us. And Dr. Graham has honed in even more. Our focus now is crystal clear" (Gordon 1). The blend of medical doctor and minister was certainly a unique combination the Institute had never had in a leader up until this point, and the board was excited about the possibilities.

One of Dr. Graham's first initiatives was to implement Grand Rounds in the hospitals, which was well-received, well-attended and appreciated by many people. Many medical students attended the Grand Rounds and lectures, fulfilling one of the Institute's goals: to educate medical students and residents in the spiritual aspects of patient care (Graham, *Recapping* 1). Baylor College of Medicine students also come to the Institute as part of their Longitudinal Ambulatory Community Experience program, called L.A.C.E. for short, which exposes students to primary care practices and to community health services. Dr. Graham also began hosting a Thursday afternoon lecture series that was held at the Institute offices and featured various speakers.

In the summer of 2010, Dr. Graham spent a week at Duke University School of Medicine where he attended a class called "Research in Spirituality and Health," taught by Harold Koenig, M.D. Dr. Koenig is the co-author of *Handbook of Religion and Health* (2012), an in-depth record of the research that has been done in this field over the past thirty-five years. The workshop, attended by forty-three students from around the world, provided an overview of the research that has been done and encouraged students to engage in their own research. Dr. Graham returned from his studies enthusiastic about having the Institute engage in spirituality and health research (Graham, *Interview* 14).

In September of 2010, Dr. Graham hired Meagan Alley, a Rice University graduate, to survey the spiritual practices of physicians who are members of the Harris County Medical Society. The results of the year-long survey were very interesting, with 81 percent of physicians seeing the practice of medicine as a calling. When asked whether they felt the influence of religion and spirituality on health was generally positive or negative, 82.7 percent said "generally positive," 12 percent said "equally positive and negative," and only 1.8 percent said "generally negative." When asked whether they believe in God or believe that another supernatural being ever intervenes in patients' health, 53 percent of the physicians surveyed said yes, 28 percent said no, and 18 percent were undecided. In response to the question: "Is it appropriate to discuss religious and spiritual issues with patients," 52.6 percent said, "it's always or usually appropriate," while 30 percent said, "it's sometimes appropriate and sometimes inappropriate." Only 5 percent said, "it's always inappropriate" (Graham, *Recapping* 1). Dr. Graham says that in the United States, 95 percent of people will say they believe in God, and over half of them are praying every day in some way. He adds, "And almost everyone, including atheists, prays if they have an extreme crisis" (Graham, *Interview* 3). The results of the survey have proven to be a valuable tool when communicating with medical students and when giving talks in religious settings. Meagan Alley moved to Maryland to pursue a master's degree at Johns Hopkins University, and the results of her extensive physician survey are still being used, examined and updated at the Institute. The data has been used in presentations at the Conference on Medicine and Religion in Chicago, Illinois in 2014 and in Cambridge, Massachusetts in 2015.

Another important initiative of the Institute was the addition of Kenneth I. Pargament, PhD, who served from 2011 to 2013 as a Distinguished Scholar in Residence. Dr. Pargament is the author of two major textbooks: *Spiritually Integrated Psychotherapy* (2011), and also *The Psychology of Religion and Coping* (2001), a highly cited book on spirituality and health regarding the area of coping. A professor of psychology at Bowling Green State University in Ohio, Dr. Pargament was on sabbatical leave while serving as the Institute's Distinguished Scholar in Residence. Dr. Pargament spoke of the uniqueness of the Institute for Spirituality and Health in the Texas Medical Center and throughout the country. He explains, "I think the ISH is a real pioneer in this area. In the last twenty to thirty years, there has been an upsurge in spirituality and health both at the research scientific side and at the practice side. But the Institute was doing this for years; they had this vision decades before it was anything popular or even trendy" (Pargament 1). Dr. Pargament unequivocally says the Institute is doing unique work, unlike that of any other place in the United States or elsewhere. Today Pargament periodically returns to Houston to speak at Institute-related conferences and continues to collaborate with his colleagues at the Texas Medical Center.

One of Dr. Graham's other early initiatives was that for the first time in decades, the Institute for Spirituality and Health was now actively being an important gathering place for chaplains to come together. "The chaplains from the different hospitals realize that they are now more isolated in their own hospitals, and they don't get together enough, so now they are gathering at our building periodically," Dr. Graham said (Graham, *Interview* 5). Chaplains met to work on two key areas: chaplaincy continuing education and training, and research to provide evidence-based validation of the work they do in hospitals. The Institute is the umbrella organization that is making this happen. The Institute also collaborates with hospitals and institutions to develop programs and presentations about medicine and spirituality. Among these are: Rice University, St. Luke's Episcopal Health Charities, The Menninger Clinic, Baylor College of Medicine, The University of Texas Medical School at Houston, The McGovern Center for Humanities and Ethics, St. Luke's Episcopal Hospital, Houston Methodist Hospital, M.D. Anderson Cancer Center, St. Joseph Medical Center, Memorial Hermann Medical Center, Texas Children's Hospital, Houston Methodist Hospital Research Institute, the Texas Medical Center, as well as numerous churches and civic groups. In the coming years, the Institute will continue its collaboration with a greater number of hospitals and institutions throughout the Houston region (Graham, *Interview* 6).

Rabbi David Lyon, M.H.L., Senior Rabbi at Congregation Beth Israel, became Chairman of the Board of Trustees in 2011 and served for two years. He enjoyed the new ventures that Dr. Graham, Dr. Pargament and others brought to the Institute. During his time as Chairman, Rabbi Lyon commented, "John Graham is such a soulful, spiritual, honest man, and his drive helped us get back on track, doing what we are supposed to be doing. And then, inviting Ken Pargament to work with the ISH is a remarkable opportunity for us to stretch our wings and extend well into the Medical Center and well beyond it, too. Dr. Pargament feels, and I'm glad that he does, that we can be local, we can be regional, and we can also be international. We are really a fertile ground, bursting with potential and opportunity" (Lyon 2). With this momentum gathering at the Institute, Dr. Graham knew the Institute was poised to enter another phase in its continual evolution. Dr. Graham explained in 2011, "Today, with Ken Pargament as our Distinguished Scholar in Residence, we are focusing on research in the area of spirituality and health. One arm of our research will be to document through evidence-based studies the positive effect chaplains have in the hospital setting." He said that the Institute hoped to offer chaplains post-graduate study to help prepare them for the dramatic changes that will take place in healthcare over the next century. Dr. Graham also envisioned that the Institute could offer education for laymen and laywomen, possibly through a two-year training program that would lead to certification as a Spiritual Health Caregiver (Graham, *Interview* 14).

Dr. Graham elaborated on his early vision for the Institute: "I believe there is a great future for those who are trained to meet the spiritual needs of patients in hospitals, nursing homes, and other healthcare facilities. These institutions will soon be graded by patients on the care they received, and this will determine, in part, the reimbursement institutions receive for services rendered. When that happens, more than ever, healthcare facilities will seek to minister to the whole person—body, soul and spirit. Having people trained to provide that kind of service, alongside seminary-trained chaplains, will be a growing reality" (Graham, *Interview* 13). Dr. Graham, the staff, and many board members saw the Institute for Spirituality and Health evolving yet again in a positive way.

Promoting the progressive work of the Institute was another primary objective Dr. Graham took on soon after taking office. In 2011, a total of $13,000 in monetary gifts from board members Barbara Kirsch, Carolyn Clarke, and Marvin Peterson provided much-needed funds that enabled the Institute to hire a public relations firm. As a result, the Institute was able to upgrade the quality of its mailings and print media, as well as professionally plan for future fundraising banquets. Another generous gift, from David and Bonnie Weekley in 2012, allowed the Institute to receive advice from Sterling Associates, a Houston-based firm that provides consulting services to nonprofit organizations. The Weekleys continue to fund the Sterling Associates contract on an ongoing basis.

Bonnie Weekley, who has served on the Board of Trustees since around 2007, took over as Chairman of the Board in April 2013, replacing Rabbi Lyon. One of her goals is to continue the push to reintroduce the Institute to the other member institutions throughout the Texas Medical Center. "I feel very strongly that we are a new and improved version of the Institute of Religion. I would like all the [medical center] institutions to be able to avail themselves of what we have to offer. I don't want ISH to be a well-kept secret. I want it to be out there, publicized, used and shared," Bonnie says (Weekley 4). In January of 2014, Sterling Associates reported: "The ISH has built a strong reputation in the Texas Medical Center as the primary resource for healthcare providers interested in learning more about the connection between health and spirituality. The board and staff are passionate about the organization's mission, committed to its success, and excited about its future. Staff leadership is forward-thinking and eagerly seeks new and innovative programming opportunities to advance the mission." Also around this time, results from a general survey conducted by the Institute mirrored the glowing reviews of the consultants, with nearly 100 percent of respondents saying they felt the Institute for Spirituality and Health filled an important need in the Houston community.

The Gathering of Friends benefit luncheon was another new endeavor developed by Dr. Graham and his team, and it has become an annual event held each November at River Oaks Country Club. Susan G. Baker, wife of Secretary James A. Baker, III and author of the 2010 autobiography, *Passing it On*, was the guest speaker at the Institute's first Gathering of Friends benefit in 2013. The Favrot Fund donated $10,000 that first year to honor James T. Willerson, M.D. of the Texas Heart Institute. The second year, Gabrielle "Gabby" Giffords and her husband Captain Mark E. Kelly were the featured speakers; they share their story of hope and resilience in their best-selling book *Gabby*, a memoir that has topped multiple best-seller lists. Also at the 2014 Gathering of Friends event, Rabbi Samuel E. Karff and TIRR Memorial Hermann were the recipients of the Caring Heart Award.

Within two short years of its creation, the Gathering of Friends luncheon continues to grow and draws more than 350 guests. Plans are in place to feature Texas Children's Hospital at the 2015 Gathering of Friends luncheon, with a focus on a surgery that separated conjoined twins in February 2015.

In his early years as President, Dr. Graham predicted that in the coming decade, the organization's evolution would focus on two complimentary disciplines: research and education. Dr. Graham's vision has proven correct. In 2012, Stuart C. Nelson, M.A., joined the Institute as a project manager and was promoted to Vice President the following year. Stuart graduated from Rice University with majors in cognitive science, religious studies and psychology; he earned a master's degree in religious studies from University of California-Santa Barbara. Stuart explains that a third discipline of the Institute is direct services, which adds to the research and education components of which Dr. Graham spoke. For example, ISH partners with The Women's Home, a non-profit agency that helps women in crisis regain their self-esteem and dignity, empowering them to return to society as productive, self-sufficient individuals. The Institute is helping The Women's Home form a spiritual care program for their clients, most of whom have experienced homelessness because of mental illness, abuse or addiction. The Institute also works with Bo's Place (grief recovery), The Jung Center of Houston, the Hope and Healing Center, and numerous other non-profits throughout Houston (Nelson 1-3). The Institute hosted a "Non-Profit Summit" in May 2015, where almost forty non-profit organizations gathered at the Richard Wainerdi Wellness Center to network and hear informative speakers. Lisa Miller, a professor of psychology and education at Columbia University, was the featured speaker.

Another example of the Institute's direct services is the launch of The Meditation Station, which Stuart says is a collaborative project with Dawn Mountain Center for Tibetan Buddhism. *Tricycle* magazine's Fall 2014 issue featured the venture, which is the country's first pop-up meditation hall—a portable contemplative environment designed to bring meditation to people wherever they are (Get 26). "It can be deployed around the city, and the idea is that you can set up the Meditation Station and it provides a sacred space, if you will, for people to go and meditate," Stuart explains. The lightweight design features a menu of guided meditations and can be brought to parks, festivals, conventions, community centers, offices or even hospitals (Nelson 3). The Institute also began hosting a weekly Bereavement Support Group in 2013 for individuals who are grieving the loss or anticipated loss of a loved one. The group is sponsored by the Departments of Spiritual Care and Palliative Care at Houston Methodist Hospital, as well as The Institute for Spirituality and Health.

The University of Chicago's Annual Conference on Medicine and Religion is another major undertaking the Institute joined to co-sponsor in 2014 (in Chicago, Illinois) and 2015 (in Cambridge, Massachusetts). The conference, which began in 2012, is a leading forum for discourse and scholarship at the intersection of medicine and religion. It exists to enable health professionals and scholars to gain a deeper and more practical understanding of how religion relates to the practice of medicine, with particular attention to the Abrahamic faith traditions of Judaism, Christianity and Islam. In March of 2016, the Institute for Spirituality and Health will host the event in Houston.

Building on the "new and improved" outlook mentioned by Chair Bonnie Weekley, the Institute sought to better reflect its interfaith mission by adding two new board members: Zishan Samiuddin, M.D., representing the Islamic faith; and Venugopal Menon, M.D., representing the Hindu tradition. Also, in 2014, the staff continued to expand under Dr. Graham's tenure as President. Susana McCollom, who had already been an ISH adjunct faculty member for about a year, was hired full-time as Director of Employee Enrichment and Workplace Chaplaincy. As a trained chaplain, Susana did her clinical pastoral education at New York Presbyterian Hospital; she earned a B.A. from the University of Texas, an M.A. in Sociology from the University of Houston, and an M.A. in Theology from

Washington Theological Union. "I want to position the ISH as a leader in workplace spirituality, because it's about the human spirit and about different expressions of spirituality," Susana says of her work with organizations throughout the community (McCollom 2). She also is working to build up the Institute's Spanish-speaking component. David Cregg, a University of Texas graduate who has written two theses on the psychology of religion, joined the Institute staff in 2014 as the Research and Congregational Outreach Coordinator. He divides his time doing academic research and congregational outreach. On one research project, Cregg has examined the relationship between death, anxiety and religion; on a second project, he has collaborated with a team of researchers from New York and Boston to look at the neural correlates of meditation. For congregational outreach, Cregg visits different congregations to raise awareness of the Institute's presence around Houston and to find ways that the Institute can be a resource for churches, synagogues and mosques. Cregg will leave in August 2015 in order to attend graduate school, but the impressive work he began at the Institute will continue. Jeff Sokoloff fills another newly created position as the Vice President for Advancement, where he seeks to identify new audiences, build collaborations with other institutions and organizations, and provide leadership in fund development. Cyrus Wirls, a Rice University graduate with a B.A. in Cognitive Sciences and Mathematics, joined the Institute as Program Manager. Lex Gillan, who has been with the Institute since 1974, continues to bring his yoga and meditation services to the organization.

The ongoing work of the growing staff and board has built favorable impressions throughout the community, and funding has increased as a result. The Fondren Foundation, which in the mid-1950s provided much-needed seed funds to help start the Institute, donated $150,000 in September of 2012. The following year, the generous donation from the Fondren Foundation was the initial cornerstone contribution that created a Permanent Endowment Fund to strengthen the long-term financial goals of the Institute. In 2014, Alan and Cynthia Craft donated $100,000 of their personal funds, with plans to make this a recurring annual donation; they also intend to leave a portion of their estate to the Institute. "Both Cynthia and I have picked certain things out of the Bible, like feeding the hungry, and that is what we have spent our charitable life doing," says Alan. The Crafts explain that they have both been touched by illness in different ways, so the connection between spirituality and health has become important to them. Adds Cynthia: "When ISH offers mind-body experiences to doctors or to potential doctors, or to nurses or to anyone in the health profession, the way I see it is they're offering a connection that has more substance than what you can learn from a textbook" (Craft 5-7). The David and Bonnie Weekley Family Foundation gave $25,000 in 2012, $165,000 in 2013, and $25,000 in 2014; they also underwrote consulting help from Sterling Associates. During 2014 and 2015, other greatly-appreciated contributions also flowed in: $100,000 from Memorial Hermann Hospital; $25,000 from Texas Children's Hospital; $25,000 from the Henderson-Wessendorff Foundation; and $25,000 from Regina Rogers of Beaumont, Texas.

On May 4, 2015—exactly sixty years from the day the early founders signed their Texas charter on May 4, 1955—the Institute for Spirituality and Health celebrated its sixtieth anniversary with an Open House at the Greenbriar location. Board Chairman Bonnie Weekley called the sixth-decade anniversary a sort of "family reunion" where the early foundations or offspring of the original founders back in the 1950s could come together. The Institute hired consultant Blaise R. Fallon, J.D., M.B.A., founder of Fallon Philanthropy Advisors, to introduce a major gift fundraising initiative in 2015—the first of its kind since its founding. Said Fallon: "The sixtieth anniversary for an organization is like the seasons of life. You're beginning to reflect upon your youth and the people who helped you out and made you grow and made you what you are today. We're taking a look back historically at the organizations and individuals who were instrumental in being the catalyst for growth for the Institute for Spirituality and Health." An anniversary planning committee was developed and hosted various events throughout the year in recognition of the six decades of service and growth the Institute experienced in the Texas Medical Center. Dr. Graham explains, "I see the future as an opportunity to fulfill our mission to increase knowledge of and sensitivity to the role that spirituality plays in health and in healing," (Graham, *Interview* 13). It's a unique mission that the board members and staff are committed to fulfilling.

So, it is important to look forward. But it is also important to look back and see that the Institute for Spirituality and Health began at the initiative of the Texas Medical Center, namely due to the vision and dream of one individual, Dr. Frederick Elliott. This is the Institute's first and fundamental constituency: the doctors, the nurses, administrators, employees, and patients of the Texas Medical Center (Verhey, *Director's Report* 2). It has been said that the Institute could not have begun without the support of churches and synagogues, and it cannot continue without the interest and loyalty of communities of faith and their members.

In 1976, as Dr. Elliott was retiring, it is written that he looked down Bertner Avenue and saw the Institute of Religion building, which was then located in the middle of the Texas Medical Center. He said, "It rounds out the total purpose for our Medical Center. That is, for the care of all phases of man—religious, mental and physical" (Elliott, Birth 199). Dr. Elliott died in 1986. He was a visionary, and the impact of his life's work will be felt by millions of people for decades to come. At the Institute for Spirituality and Health today, that is certainly true.

Has the Institute fulfilled the initial charge given to its founders some sixty years ago? Yes, but their work is not finished. The challenge to bring spirituality into medicine will continue as long as the Texas Medical Center is still around, and as long as Houston's two medical schools keep training men and women to enter the practice of medicine. The challenge must be renewed in every generation, and that continues to happen today through the staff, board, faculty, and the foundations and individuals who have financially supported the Institute for Spirituality and Health.

✿— APPENDIX —✿

The following is a list of six study questions that were submitted to the author in 2013 by a reviewing committee of graduate school professors at Louisiana State University in Shreveport, followed by Cathey Nickell's answers.

Study Question 1:

As you note, the Institute has proven very adaptive to changing its mission (from Chaplaincy training, to Bioethics, etc.) in the rapidly changing fields of healthcare and medical research (and the attendant ethical issues involved). So what is next? Rather than just adapting to the times, what specific areas of focus do you see developing for the Institute?

Author's Answer:

The Institute for Spirituality and Health will probably always continue its tradition of adapting to the times and reinventing itself so as to always be relevant in any given moment. Healthcare is a fluid field, not stagnant, and the Institute has learned to acclimate to that fact. One new focus currently developing for the Institute is that of biotechnology. Dr. Arthur Levine, Senior Vice Chancellor for the Health Sciences at the University of Pittsburgh, defines biotechnology as "the use of living organisms to produce engineered products that can modify health or the environment; it is a set of biological techniques developed through basic research (molecular, cell and structural biology) and now applied to product development."

Modern biotechnology began just over one hundred years ago, and due to its rapid growth in medicine, the healthcare industry is feeling the pressure to become more specialized than ever before. For example, at the Texas Medical Center, Baylor College of Medicine has established the Human Genome Sequencing Center, a field in its infancy now, but one that will have a great impact on medicine in the near future. Another example is Rice University's BioScience Research Collaborative, which works hand-in-hand with other Texas Medical Center institutions. This group has entered the exciting field of nanotechnology, promising to create "nanobots," DNA robots that find and target cells for medication and can be injected into the bloodstream of patients to cure certain diseases. Finally, surgeons worldwide are now being taught robotic surgical techniques that are becoming the standard level of treatment for patients. Physicians will need specialized training in these fields in order to keep up with the rapidly changing advances.

Each of these advances, and many more, are challenging physicians and other healthcare providers in ways that have not been seen before. The implications include an increased level of stress for physicians, pressure to keep up with colleagues, and also the fact that focusing on biotechnology could adversely affect the traditional doctor-patient relationship. The Institute for Spirituality and Health believes that physicians and nurses will need specialized training to help them maintain their balance between their professional and personal life. It is an opportunity for the Institute to provide new guidance and training for medical students, nursing students, and also for physicians/nurses currently in practice.

Study Question 2:

In a culturally diverse community like Houston, you rightly note the importance of interfaith collaboration in the Institute. Over most of its existence the Institute has primarily been identified with Christian/Jewish efforts. How will the Institute continue its efforts involving Islamic and non-Western religions like Buddhism, Hinduism, etc.?

Author's Answer:

Dr. Graham has made an effort to develop relationships with Muslim, Buddhist and Hindu groups in the Houston area. He regularly attends lectures at the Institute of Interfaith Dialog, a Muslim Group that seeks to promote mutual understanding, respect and cooperation among people of diverse faiths and culture. Dr. Graham also appeared on a panel at another Muslim Mosque to further dialogue between the Houston organizations. Dr. Graham and his wife, Pat, have eaten a Ramadan meals with Muslim families and they have invited them to eat in their Christian home, as well. Additionally, in 2010, Pat herself traveled with a Muslim group to Turkey to learn more about their Sunni/Sufi faith and culture, and she was able to bring her knowledge and experiences back to the Institute.

In September of 2013, Dr. Graham and Stuart Nelson, ISH Vice President, traveled together to New York to attend a Garrison Institute event, "Contemplation, Collaboration and Change." This was an American-Buddhist organization and signals the Institute's ongoing interest in forming strong relationships with people of all faiths. The Institute also has conducted numerous panel discussions that have included Christian, Jewish and Muslim speakers, and Dr. Graham recently spoke at a Hare Krishna Temple in Houston. The emphasis on becoming a truly multi-faith organization is a central focus of the ISH, and the organization continues to bring in people of all faiths to sit as members of the Board of Trustees.

Study Question 3:

In chapter six, you report that Dr. Ken Pargament "unequivocally says the Institute is doing unique work, unlike that of any other place in the United States or elsewhere." You cite a number of other publications and reports on spirituality and medicine elsewhere in the country, so in your opinion, what makes the Institute's work unique?

Author's Answer:

The Institute for Spirituality and Health in Houston is unique for several reasons. First of all, there are only five or six similar "spirituality and health" organizations at this time in the nation. In addition to the ISH, the other main such institutes include: (1) George Washington Institute for Spirituality and Health, which is located at a medical school in Washington, D.C.; (2) Spirituality and Health Institute at Santa Clara University in California, which is linked to the Jesuit faith; (3) The William Blevins Institute for Spirituality and Mental Health at Carson-Newman University in Tennessee, a Christian school; (4) Center for Spirituality and Health at the University of Florida in Gainesville; (5) Research Institute for Spirituality and Health, which is not in the U.S., but rather is a network for Switzerland and Europe; and most recently, (6) Nevada Institute for Spirituality and Health in Las Vegas, which just opened in January 2013, and actually toured the Houston ISH and used it as the primary model for its own creation and development.

These other organizations are housed within an academic institution and, frequently, are part of the Department of Psychiatry within a medical school. Thus, the ISH is unique in that it is the only freestanding Institute without the restrictions that can occur when under the influence of an academic program where funding may be limited. The non-profit ISH has no such constraints and may seek funding directly for its programs. Additionally, being independent, the Institute is able to reach out to all hospitals in the region and beyond without the concern of disloyalty. This is not the case for those programs which must further the cause of the specific organization to which they belong and which are generally forced to comply with the goals and mission of their governing organization. The Institute for Spirituality and Health also does not answer to a specific religious denomination, which means it is fully able to reach out to all individuals of all faiths, thus fulfilling one of its primary missions.

Study Question 4:

You say that the Institute is working on "evidence-based validation" of the work it is doing. Can you describe what some of this evidence, or validation, might be?

Author's Answer:

Evidence-based research is research that utilizes the scientific method to minimize bias in interpretation of results. It is research that is not dependent on anecdotal reports of individual cases. Instead, validation of this type of work requires double-blind studies and efforts to recognize and minimize confounders, which may skew results, leading to false and misleading conclusions. For example, one of the Institute's current efforts has been to study the work that chaplains do in the hospital setting to determine if there is a measurable benefit to having chaplains see patients. Another example: the Institute evaluates medical students before and after they attend an ISH lecture on spirituality in patient care to determine if they enlarged their understanding of the material presented. Additionally, in 2010, a graduate student hired by the Institute conducted a yearlong study to survey the spiritual practices of physicians who were members of the Harris County Medical Society. The Institute has broadly shared her results with various organizations throughout the Texas Medical Center and at national conferences; these results also are being used as teaching-tools in the area medical and nursing schools.

Study Question 5:

You make mention that one current goal of the Institute is to prepare chaplains in post-graduate study for the changes that will come in healthcare over the next fifty years. What specific challenges do you think the coming decades might bring for these students as they enter health care ministry?

Author's Answer:

As stated in the answer to the first study question, advances in modern biotechnology will be dramatic over the coming fifty years. Foundational research in genome therapy, nanotherapy and robotic surgery are a few examples of the changes that the healthcare industry expects in the decades ahead. These advances will offer the exciting opportunity to heal diseases, previously seen as impossible. However, it will require a very different training for medical students, and the physician of the future may not look very much like the beloved family doctor of the past. The challenge is to embrace the new technology and not lose the ability to deliver compassionate care within the doctor-patient relationship.

Study Question 6:

I have just a point of curiosity about the Board of Trustee's addition of the word "spirituality" to the Institute's name to reflect terminology that embraces "more than just religion." Can you explain this a little further?

Author's Answer:

The word "religion" comes from the Latin word *ligare*, which means, "to bind." The term typically refers to the beliefs, practices, rituals and worldviews that bind a particular group of people together. World religions share many aspects, such as "The Golden Rule," but each community of faith has practices that are distinctive to their own faith system. In 2008, the Institute's Board of Trustees voted to change the organization's name in order to encompass more beliefs and to welcome more individuals into their mission.

The Institute believes people are spiritual beings and that healthcare should strive to treat the whole person—that is, the bio-psychosocial and spiritual aspects of what it means to be fully human. Spirituality includes all of life, not just a person's religion or beliefs. Spirituality includes one's connection to nature, to the arts, to family and friends, and to the creatures of this world, including our pets. Spirituality also includes one's connection with the transcendent mystery that many call "God." The Institute embraces the fact that a person can be quite spiritual and yet not be part of a particular religion.

CHRONOLOGY OF
THE BOARD OF TRUSTEES: *

1955-1958:

Chairman: Otis Massey

Vice Chairman: Wesley West

Secretary: Ella Fondren

Treasurer: Earl C. Hankamer

Office Secretary & Assistant Treasurer: Helen Manning

Other Board Members: Milton Backlund; Mrs. E.R. Barrow; Juila Bertner; Warren Dale; Thomas C. Evans; Mrs. Walter Goldston; John T. Jones, Jr.; Charles L. King; Virgil E. Lowder; Latimer Murfee; Mrs. C.E. Naylor; Eddy C. Scurlock; Thomas W. Sumners; Howard T. Tellepsen; E.H. Westmoreland.

1959-1961:

Chairman: Latimer Murfee

Vice Chairman: Earl C. Hankamer

Secretary: Ella Fondren

Treasurer: Eddy C. Scurlock

Other Board Members: Martha Backlund; Mrs. E.R. Barrow; Warren J. Dale; Thomas C. Evans; Madison Farnsworth; William G. Farrington; Mrs. Walter Goldston; John T. Jones, Jr.; Charles L. King; Otis Massey; Lewis H. McAdow; Mrs. C.E. Naylor; J. Newton Rayzor; Dean J. Milton Richardson; David L. Stitt; Howard Tellepsen; E.H. Westmoreland.

1962-1965:

Chairman: Eddy C. Scurlock

Vice Chairman: William G. Farrington

Secretary: Ella Fondren

Treasurer: Madison Farnsworth

Other Board Members: Martha Backlund; Thomas C. Evans; Lewis McAdow; Latimer Murfee; Al Parker; Mrs. C.E. Naylor; Dean J. Milton Richardson; David L. Stitt.

1966-1970:

Chairman: R.A. "Al" Parker
Vice Chairman: John F. Lynch
Secretary: Ella Fondren
Treasurer: E.J. Mosher
Acting Secretary: Helen Riddle
Other Board Members: Rex G. Baker; Martha Backlund; William G. Farrington; John Wm. Lancaster; Lewis McAdow; Eddy C. Scurlock.

1971-1972:

Chairman: R.A. "Al" Parker
Vice Chairman: Rueben W. Askanase
Secretaries: Ella Fondren; Andre A. Crispin
Treasurer: C.R. Williams
Acting Secretary: Helen Riddle
Honorary Trustee: Mrs. Dawson C. Bryan
Life Member Trustees: Mrs. Edward R. Barrow; Ella Fondren; Lewis H. McAdow; J. Milton Richardson; E.H. Westmoreland.
Other Board Members: Martha Backlund; Rex G. Baker, Jr.; John de Menil; Bernard Farfel; John Hill; John Wm. Lancaster; Harry S. Lip-scomb; John F. Lynch; Edward Mosher; Latimer Murfee; Levi C. Olan; Albert C. Outler; J. Milton Richardson; John L. Roach; Hampton C. Robinson; Pierre Schlumberger; Eddy C. Scurlock; Weldon H. Smith; Bernard Weingarten; John Wildenthal.

1973:

Chairman: Harry Lipscomb

Vice Chairman: Reuben W. Askanase

Secretary: Andre A. Crispin

Treasurer: C.R. Williams

Other Board Members: Martha Backlund; Rex G. Baker, Jr.; John de Menil; Bernard Farfel; John Hill; John Wm. Lancaster; Harry S. Lipscomb; John F. Lynch; Edward Mosher; Latimer Murfee; Levi C. Olan; Albert C. Outler; J. Milton Richardson; John L. Roach; Hampton C. Robinson; Pierre Schlumberger; Eddy C. Scurlock; Weldon H. Smith; Bernard Weingarten; John Wildenthal.

1974:

Chairman: Harry Lipscomb

Vice Chairman: John Wildenthal

Secretary: Bernard Weingarten

Treasurer: C.R. Williams

Counselor: Pierre M. Schlumberger

Other Board Members: Bernard Weingarten; David Stitt; Earl C. Calkins; Kenneth Chafin; Loise Wessendorff.

1975-1977:

Chairman: Earl C. Calkins

Vice Chairperson: Patsy Arcidiacono

Secretary: Bernard Weingarten

Treasurer: James Hargrove

Honorary Board Member: Mrs. Dawson Bryan

Life Members: Lewis McAdow; Ella Fondren; Latimer Murfee; Milton Richardson; John Roach; E.H. Westmoreland.

Other Board Members: David Bybee; Kenneth Chafin; Harry Chavanne; Carolyn Clarke; Charles Rebstock Gregg; J. Daniel Joyce; A. Scott Kelso;

Harry Lipscomb; Frank Metyko; David Mumford; Levi C. Olan; Albert C. Outler; R.A. "Al" Parker; Edwin Peterman; Edward P. Randall; H.C. Robinson; Judson Robinson, Sr.; Hyman J. Schachtel; Eddy C. Scurlock; Kenneth Shamblin; David Stitt; Eleanor Tinsley; Leon Weiner; Loise Wessendorff; John Wildenthal; Bernard Weingarten.

1978:

Chairman: David L. Stitt
Vice Chairperson: Carolyn Clarke
Secretary: Eleanor Tinsley
Treasurer: John Wildenthal
Honorary Life Member: Mrs. Dawson C. Bryan
Life Members: Ella Fondren; Lewis McAdow; Latimer Murfee; J. Milton Richardson; John Roach.
Other Board Members: David Bybee; Earl Calkins, Sr.; Kenneth Chafin; Mrs. Kenneth Dobkins; James Hargrove; Daniel Joyce; A. Scott Kelso; Prentis Moore; David Mumford; R.A. "Al" Parker; Edwin Peterman; Canon Puckett; Edward P. Randall; Hyman Schachtel; Eddy Scurlock; Bebe Selig; Jan Van Eys; Bernard Weingarten; Joe C. Wessendorff.

1979:

Chairman: David L. Stitt
Vice Chairperson: Carolyn Clarke
Secretary: Eleanor Tinsley
Treasurer: James W. Hargrove

1980-1985:

Chairperson: Carolyn Clarke
Vice Chairman: Harry Chavanne
Secretary: Bebe Selig; Loise Wessendorff
Treasurer: James W. Hargrove

Other Board Members: Patsy Arcidiacono; Louis T. Austin, Jr.; Warren S. Bellows, Jr.; Roger J. Bulger; J. David Bybee; Earl C. Calkins, Sr.; Kenneth Chafin; Harry Chavanne; Richard Crews; James L. Copeland; Patsy Cravens; Finis A. Crutchfield; Mrs. Kenneth Dobkins; Jack T. Dulworth; John E. Fellers; Gloria Herman; J. Daniel Joyce; Scott Kelso; Carol Lane; David Mumford; Merrill O'Neal; Edward Peterman; Edward Randall; Hyman J. Schachtel; Bebe Selig; Randolph Smith; David L. Stitt; Jan Van Eys; James A. Wharton; John Wildenthal; Jim Walzel; Bernard Weingarten.

1986-1988:
Chairman: David M. Mumford
Vice Chairperson: Carolyn Clarke
Vice President for Development: Bebe Selig
Secretary: Loise Wessendorff
Treasurer: James W. Hargrove
Assistant Treasurer: Gloria Hermann
Life Members: Mrs. Dawson C. Bryan; Lewis H. McAdow; John J. Roach; Hyman J. Schachtel; David Stitt.
Other Board Members: Louis T. Austin, Jr.; Mrs. James L. Bayless; Warren S. Bellows, Jr.; Roger J. Bulger; Earl C. Calkins, Sr.; John B. Carter; Harry Chavanne; Richard Crews; James L. Copeland; Patsy Cravens; Robert J. Cruikshank; Finis A. Crutchfield; Warren Dale; K. Wayne Day; Mrs. Kenneth Dobkins; Jack T. Dulworth; John E. Fellers; Laurens A. Hall; Gloria Herman; Samuel E. Karff; David Mumford; Robert Rakel; Bebe Selig; William L. Turner; Jan Van Eys; James A. Wharton; Jim Walzel.

1989-1991:

Chairman: Jan Van Eys

Vice Chairperson: Carolyn Clarke

Secretary: Bebe Selig

Treasurer: James L. Copeland

Other Board Members: T. Louis Austin, Jr.; Warren S. Bellows, Jr.; Roger J. Bulger; Earl C. Calkins, Sr.; Mrs. John B. Carter, Jr.; Harry J. Chavanne; Patsy Cravens; Robert J. Cruikshank; K. Wayne Day; Mrs. Kenneth Dobkins; Jack T. Dulworth; Charles W. Hall; Laurens A. Hall; James W. Hargrove; Mrs. Carroll R. Hochner; Samuel Karff; Lois Moore; David M. Mumford; Susan Plumb; Robert E. Rakel; John C. Ribble; Mrs. John J. Robinson; Enrique San Pedro; Barbara Schachtel; Carroll Shaddock; Thomas K. Tewell; William L. Turner; Clyde J. Verheyden; Jeffrey H. Walker; Jim Walzel; Loise Wessendorff; Jim Wharton.

1992-1994:

Chairman: Jan Van Eys

Vice Chairperson: Carolyn Clarke

Secretary: Bebe Selig

Treasurer: Carroll Shaddock

Asst. Treasurer: George Rollins

Life Members: Mrs. Dawson C. Bryan; Lewis H. McAdow; David Stitt.

Other Board Members: Waren S. Bellows; Harry J. Chavanne; Robert J. Cruikshank; K. Wayne Day; Richard F. Dini; Jack T. Dulworth; Charles W. Hall; Mrs. Carroll Hochner; Samuel Karff; Lois Moore; David M. Mumford; Susan C. Plumb; Robert E. Rakel; John C. Ribble; Karen Robinson; Barbara Schachtel; Thomas K. Tewell; Emily Tinsley; William L. Turner; Clyde J. Verheyden; Jeffrey H. Walker; Jim Walzel; Loise Wessendorff.

1995:

Chairman: K. Wayne Day

Vice Chairman: Jan Van Eys

Secretary: Carolyn Clarke

Treasurer: Carroll Shaddock

Other Board Members: Waren S. Bellows; Harry J. Chavanne; Robert J. Cruikshank; Richard F. Dini; Jack T. Dulworth; Charles W. Hall; Samuel Karff; Lois Moore; David M. Mumford; Susan C. Plumb; Robert E. Rakel; Karen Robinson; Barbara Schachtel; Bebe Selig; Emily Tinsley; William L. Turner; Clyde J. Verheyden; Jim Walzel; Loise Wessendorff.

1995-1996:

Chairperson: Carolyn Clarke

Treasurer: Carroll Shaddock

Other Board Members: Jim Bankston; Warren Bellows; Harry Chavanne; Robert Cruikshank; Richard F. Dini; Jack Dulworth; Paul F. Feiler; Charles W. Hall; Joanne Hook; Samuel Karff; Jim Lomax; Lois Moore; David Mumford; Robert Rakel; Karen Robinson; Barbara Schachtel; Bebe Selig; Dean Walter Taylor; Kittsie Thomas; Emily Tinsley; William Turner; Clyde Verheyden; Jim Walzel; Loise Wessendorff.

1997-1998:

Chairman: William Turner

Vice Chairperson: Bebe Selig

Secretary: Joanne Hook; Emily Tinsley

Treasurer: Jim Walzel

Acting Secretary: Betsy Garlington

1999:

Chairperson: Bebe Selig
Vice Chairman: Jim Bankston
Secretary: Emily Tinsley
Treasurer: Jim Walzel

2000-2004:

Chairman: Jim Bankston
Vice Chairperson: Barbara Schachtel
Secretary: Emily Tinsley
Treasurer: Jim Walzel
Other Board Members: Carolyn Clarke; Harry Chavanne; Samuel Crocker; Richard Dini; John Fellers; Betsy Garlington; John Hawkins; Samuel Karff; Jim Lomax; Richard Materson; Robert Newell; David Peterson; Marvin Peterson; Suzanne Sachnowitz; Gwen Sherwood; Kittsie Thomas; Roy Walter; Dan Wilford.

2005-2006:

Chairperson: Betsy Garlington Striegler
Vice Chairman: Jim Walzel
Secretary: Barbara Schachtel
Treasurer: John D. Hawkins
Other Board Members: Jim Bankston; Carolyn Clarke; K. Wayne Day; Richard Dini; Jim Duffy; John K. Graham; Samuel Karff; Jim Lomax; Richard Materson; David Peterson; Marvin Peterson; Suzanne Sachnowitz; Pamela Triolo; Roy Walter.

2007-2008:

Chairman: Richard Materson
Vice Chairman: Jim Walzel
Secretary: Barbara Schachtel

Treasurers: John D. Hawkins; Barbara Kirsch

Assistant Treasurer: Jim Bankston

Other Board Members: Sam Axelrad; Carolyn Clarke; K. Wayne Day; Richard Dini; Jim Duffy; Gary Freeman; Thomas Horvath; Subroto Gangopadhyay; Nancy Gordon; John K. Graham; Susan Josey; Samuel Karff; Ray Khoury; Basheer Khumawala; Barbara Kirsch; Jim Lomax; David Lyon; Dick Materson; Faber McMullen; Charles Millikan; Marvin Peterson; Dwight Ramsey; Suzanne Sachnowitz Syme; Renae Schumann; Kevin Trautnner; Kent Wallace; Roy Walter; Elizabeth Young; Bonnie Weekley.

2009:

Chairman: Jim Walzel

Vice Chairman: John K. Graham

Secretary: Bonnie Weekley

Treasurer: Barbara Kirsch

Legal Counsel: Marvin Peterson

2010:

Chairman: Jim Walzel

Vice Chairman: David Lyon

Secretary: Bonnie Weekley

Treasurer: Barbara Kirsch

Other Board Members: Andy Achenbaum; Jim Bankston; Anthony Brown; Carolyn Clarke; Subroto Gangopadhyay; Anne Gill; Nancy Gordon; John K. Graham (Ex Officio); John Hawkins; Robert Hesse; Thomas Horvath; Susan Josey; Samuel Karff; Raymond Khoury; Basheer Khumawala; Jim Lomax; David Lyon; Charles Millikan; Laurence J. Payne; Marvin Peterson; Barbara Schachtel-Green; Renae Schumann; AnneMarie Wallace; Roy A. Walter.

2011-2012:

Chairman: David Lyon

Vice Chairman: Robert Hesse

Secretary: Bonnie Weekley

Treasurer: Susan Josey

Other Board Members: Jim Bankston; Anthony Brown; Carolyn Clarke; Anne Gill; Nancy Gordon; John K. Graham (Ex Officio); John D. Hawkins; Thomas Horvath; Gary Jones; Samuel Karff; J. Kimball Kehoe; Basheer M. Khumawala; Barbara Kirsch; Anne Koci; Jim Lomax; Charles R. Millikan; Donald S. Nesti; Laurence J. Payne; Marvin Peterson; Joe D. Robinson; Mary Katharine Roff; Barbara Schachtel-Green; Poldi Tschirch; AnneMarie Wallace; Roy A. Walter; Jim Walzel.

2012-2013:

Chairman: Rabbi David Lyon

Vice Chairman: Robert Hesse

Secretary: Bonnie Weekley

Treasurer: Susan Josey

Counsel: Marvin Peterson

Other Board Members: Jim Bankston; Anthony Brown; Carolyn Clarke; Anne Gill; Nancy Gordon; John K. Graham (Ex Officio); John Hawkins; Thomas Horvath; Gary Jones; Samuel Karff; John "Kim" Kehoe; Basheer Khumawala; Barbara Kirsch; Anne Koci; Jim Lomax; Charles Millikan; Donald S. Nesti; Laurence J. Payne; Joe D. Robinson; Mary Katharine Roff; Poldi Tschirch; Barbara Schachtel-Green; Richard Wainerdi; AnneMarie Wallace; Roy Walter; Jim Walzel.

2013-2014:

Chairperson: Bonnie Weekley

Vice Chairman: Robert Hesse

Secretary: John "Kim" Kehoe

Co-Treasurers: Barbara Kirsch; Joe D. Robinson

Counsel: Marvin Peterson

Other Board Members: Jim Bankston; James Booth; Carolyn Clarke; Anne Gill; Nancy Gordon; John K. Graham (Ex Officio); John Hawkins; Thomas Horvath; Gary Jones; Susan Josey; Samuel Karff; Bob Kidd; Anne Koci; Jim Lomax; David Lyon; Donald S. Nesti; Laurence J. Payne; Mary Katharine Roff; Barbara Schachtel-Green; Poldi Tschirch; Richard Wainerdi; AnneMarie Wallace; Jim Walzel; Tommy Williams.

2014-2015:

Chairperson: Bonnie Weekley

Vice Chairman: Robert Hesse

Secretary: John "Kim" Kehoe

Treasurer: James Booth

Counsel: Bart Fehr

Other Board Members: George Anderson; Jim Bankston; Carolyn Clarke; Alan Craft; Cynthia Craft; Nancy Gordon; John K. Graham (Ex Officio); John Hawkins; Susan Josey; Samuel Karff; Bob Kidd; Barbara Kirsch; Anne Koci; Jim Lomax; David Lyon; Venugopal Menon; Donald S. Nesti; Laurence J. Payne; Joe D. Robinson; Mary Katharine Roff; Zishan Samiuddin; Barbara Schachtel-Green; Richard Wainerdi; AnneMarie Wallace; Jim Walzel; Tommy Williams.

* The ISH apologizes if any names were inadvertently omitted.

CHRONOLOGY OF THE
PRESIDENT/CEO

Dawson C. Bryan, D.D.	1955 – 1967
Thompson Shannon, Ph.D., D.D.	1967 – 1972
Kenneth L. Vaux, M.Div., D.Th. (Interim)	1972 – 1974
Rev. Julian Byrd	1974 – 1976
Rev. Ron H. Sunderland, Ed.D.	1976 – 1982
David Stitt, D.D.	1983 – 1985
J. Robert "Bob" Nelson, D.Theol., D.D.	1985 – 1992
Allen D. Verhey, B.D., Ph.D.	1992 – 1995
John E. Fellers, M.Div., D.D.	1995 – 2006
James D. "Jim" Duffy, M.D.	2006 – 2008
Richard "Dick" Materson, M.D.	2008 – 2010
John K. Graham, M.D., D.Min.	2010 – present

Members of the Adjunct Faculty are appointed because of their interest in the mission of the Institute for Spirituality and Health. They are prominently recognized in their academic field of study. Throughout the year, members of the Adjunct Faculty serve as lecturers at ISH events both at the Institute and throughout the Texas Medical Center.

W. Andrew Achenbaum, Ph.D., U.S. historian and author of at least five books, including *Older Americans, Vital Communities*; Professor of History and Social Work at University of Houston.

Jon G. Allen, Ph.D., holds the Helen Malsin Palley Chair in Mental Health Research; Professor of Psychiatry in the Menninger Research Department of Psychiatry and Behavioral Sciences at the Baylor College of Medicine.

Harvey Aronson, Ph.D., a licensed therapist in private practice; meditation teacher and translator with many years of involvement in Buddhist studies and meditation; founding director of Dawn Mountain.

Anthony E. Brown, M.D., M.P.H., an Assistant Professor of Family and Community Medicine at Baylor College of Medicine.

Eduardo Bruera, M.D., holds the F. T. McGraw Chair in the Treatment of Cancer at The University of Texas M.D. Anderson Cancer Center, and is the Chair of the Department of Palliative Care and Rehabilitation Medicine.

Nathan Carlin, Ph.D., Associate Professor of Medical Humanities in the McGovern Center for Humanities and Ethics at the University of

Texas Health Science Center, and holds an appointment in the Department of Family and Community Medicine at UT Medical School.

Thomas R. Cole, Ph.D., the Beth and Toby Grossman Professor and Director of the McGovern Center for Humanities and Ethics at the University of Texas Health Science Center; Professor of Humanities in the Department of Religious Studies at Rice University.

Lex Gillan, ERYT, practitioner and teacher of yoga and meditation for nearly 40 years.

Thelma Jean Goodrich, Ph.D., faculty member at the Houston Galveston Family Therapy Institute and Advisory Council of the McGovern Center for Health, Humanities and the Human Spirit at University of Texas Medical School at Houston.

Harvey L. Gordon, M.D., Clinical Professor of Urology and Professor of Biomedical Ethics at Baylor College of Medicine.

Karen Hahn, Ph.D., R.N., A.P.N., founder and Executive Director of the Center for Faith and Health Initiatives, an interfaith community health agency.

Robert J. Hesse, Ph.D., Co-founder and President of Contemplative Outreach Network, Inc.; visiting instructor at Rice University and Pontifical University Rome, and adjunct professor at University of St. Thomas; Vice Chairman of the Institute for Spirituality and Health.

Samuel E. Karff, D.H.L., Rabbi Emeritus of Congregation Beth Israel; Associate Director of the McGovern Center for Humanities and Ethics at the University of Texas Health Science Center; visiting professor in the Department of Family Medicine at the University of Texas Medical School in Houston.

Anne Carolyn Klein, Ph.D., Professor of Religious Studies at Rice University, and founding director and resident teacher at Dawn Mountain.

Jeffrey J. Kripal, Ph.D., J. Newton Rayzor Professor and Chair of Religious Studies at Rice University.

Sheila LoboPrabhu, M.D., Associate Professor of Psychiatry at Baylor College of Medicine.

James Lomax, M.D., Ph.D., Associate Chairman and Director of Educational Programs in the Department of Psychiatry at Baylor College of Medicine.

Susana McCollom, Employee Enrichment Program Director and Workplace Chaplaincy at the Institute for Spirituality and Health.

Kenneth Pargament, Ph.D., Professor of Clinical Psychology at Bowling Green State University.

Michael Winters, Ph.D., Psychologist in private practice in Houston.

Bing You, M.D., L.Ac., D.A.A.P.M., teacher in Acupuncture, Tui-na, Qi-Gong and Tai-chi Sword at Chengdu University of Traditional Chinese Medicine in Sichuan, China; active lecturer at Rice University, University of Houston, and Memorial Hermann Wellness Institute; has a clinical practice specializing in sports injury and pain management with a secondary specialty in internal medicine disorders.

✑— REFERENCES —✑

"About Parish Nursing." International Parish Nurse Resource Center. *IPNRC.* Web. 18 Jan. 2012. <http://www.parishnurses.org/InternationalParishNurseResourceCenter>.

Anderson, Leland. "What the Institute of Religion Means to the Medical Center." *Groundbreaking for the New Institute of Religion Building.* Texas Medical Center, Houston, TX. 3 Dec. 1959. Speech.

"Albert C. Outler." *Theopedia.com.* Biblical Christianity, 19 Mar. 2007. Web. 02 Dec. 2010. <http://www.theopedia.com/Albert_C._Outler>.

"B. Andrew Lustig." Davidson College. *Davidson.edu,* 2010. Web. 3 May 2011. <http://www3.davidson.edu/cms/x6032.xml>.

Berryman, Jerome W. "Dr. Director Jerome W. Berryman." *Educators.* Web. 16 Oct. 2013. <http://www.rpi.se/pdfer/Educators/023.Vita.Berryman%20-%20Long.pdf.>

Brody, Baruch A. Personal Interview. 03 May 2011.

Bryan, Dawson C. *An Evaluation of Problems, Responsibilities, Opportunities of Religious Activities and Recommendations for the Formation of An Institute of Religion in the Texas Medical Center.* Rep. Houston, TX, 1954. Print.

---. *Arrangements Between The Institute of Religion and The Theological Seminaries.* Rep. Houston, TX: Institute of Religion, 1954. Print.

---. *The Art of Illustrating Sermons.* Nashville, TN: Cokesbury, 1938. Print.

---. "Program Has Finally Materialized." Letter to Dr. Granger Westberg. 8 Jan. 1955. MS. Institute for Spirituality and Health, Houston, TX.

---. "Thankful for Your Interest." Letter to Mr. and Mrs. W.W. Fondren. 26 Oct. 1956. MS. Institute for Spirituality and Health, Houston, TX.

---. "Welcome to This Historic Occasion." *Groundbreaking for the New Institute of Religion Building.* Texas Medical Center, Houston, TX. 3 Dec. 1959. Speech.

Byrd, Julian. "From the Director." *The Institute of Religion.* Vol. 2, No. 2 (Sept. 1975): 1-4. Print.

---. Personal Interview. 01 Feb. 2011.

"Charlie Shedd Institute of Clinical Theology." *Richmont.edu.* Richmont Graduate University, 2008. Web. 15 Sept. 2011. <http://www.psy.edu/charlie-shedd-institute-forclinical-theology>.

Clarke, Carolyn. Personal Interview. 15 Dec. 2010.

---. "Slides for Institute of Religion Park." Letter to Dr. Richard E. Wainerdi. 06 Apr. 1994. MS. Institute for Spirituality and Health, Houston, TX.

Council of Churches of Greater Houston. Rev. Virgil E. Lowder, Executive Director. *Dr. Dawson Bryan Appointed Director of the Institute of Religion.* Houston, TX: Council of Churches of Greater Houston, 1954. Print.

Craft, Alan and Cynthia. Personal Interview. 28 Feb. 2015.

Cregg, David. Telephone Interview. 03 March 2015.

Crozier, Leigh J. "What the Institute of Religion Means to the Hospitals." *Groundbreaking for the New Institute of Religion Building.* Texas Medical Center, Houston, TX. 3 Dec. 1959. Speech.

"Denton A. Cooley, M.D.: 100,000 Hearts." *Texas Heart Institute.* Web. 23 Jan. 2012. <http://www.texasheartinstitute.org/AboutUs/History/A_Surgeons_Memoir.cfm>.

Doctor, Jerri. Personal Interview. 08 March 2011.

"Dr. Shannon Retires." *The Institute of Religion and Human Development.* Vol. 1, No. 3 (Aug. 1974): 1-8. Print.

Duffy, James D., comp. An Evening of Sacred Sound: Celebrating Fifty Years. Houston, TX: Institute for Religion and Health, 2006. Print.

"Ella Fondren, Whose Husband Was Involved in Exxon's Start." *The New York Times Obituaries.* 05 May 1982. Web. 23 Jan. 2012. <http://www.nytimes.com/1982/05/05/obituaries/ella-fondren-whose-husband-was-involved-in-exxon-s-start.html>.

Elliott, Frederick C. *The Birth of the Texas Medical Center: a Personal Account.* Ed. William Henry Kellar. College Station: Texas A & M UP, 2004. Print.

Fallon, Blaise. Telephone Interview. 26 Feb. 2015.

Fondren, Ella F., comp. *Minutes of the Meeting of the Committee on Religious Activities Development in the Texas Medical Center.* 9 Dec. 1954. Board secretary's transcription of board meeting minutes. Houston, TX.

---. *Minutes of the Meeting of the Committee on Religious Activities Development in the Texas Medical Center.* 5 Jan. 1955. Board secretary's transcription of board meeting minutes. Houston, TX.

---. *Minutes of the Meeting of the Board of Trustees.* 14 Dec. 1956. Board secretary's transcription of board meeting minutes. Houston, TX.

---. *Minutes of the Meeting of the Board of Trustees.* 20 Jan. 1958. Board secretary's transcription of board meeting minutes. Houston, TX.

---. *Minutes of the Meeting of the Board of Trustees.* 15 May 1959. Board secretary's transcription of board meeting minutes. Houston, TX.

---. *Minutes of the Meeting of the Board of Trustees.* 16 Oct. 1959. Board secretary's transcription of board meeting minutes. Houston, TX.

---. *Minutes of the Meeting of the Board of Trustees.* 17 March 1966. Board secretary's transcription of board meeting minutes. Houston, TX.

---. *Minutes of the Meeting of the Board of Trustees.* 29 Oct. 1968. Board secretary's transcription of board meeting minutes. Houston, TX.

"Get Meditating, Houston!" *Tricycle: The Buddhist Review.* Fall 2014: 26-27. Print.

Gilchriest, Linda, and Ronda Wendler. "Tropical Storm Allison Tenth Anniversary This Month." *TexasMedicalCenter.org.* Texas Medical Center, 1 June 2011. Web. 4 Sept. 2011. <http://www.texasmedicalcenter.org/root/en/TMCServices/News/2011/06-01/Tropical+Storm+Allison+10th+Anniversary+this+Month.html>.

Gordon, Nancy. Personal Interview. 12 May 2011.

Graham, John. "The Institute for Spirituality and Health: Recapping 2011, Eagerly Anticipating 2012." *Texas Medical Center News.* (1 Dec. 2011): 15. Print.

---. Personal Interview. 15 Oct. 2011.

---. Telephone Interview. 03 Feb. 2015.

Hahn, Karen. Personal Interview. 21 April 2011.

Hanson, Eric. "Ex-secretary Indicted in Wounding of Boss." *Houston Chronicle.* 02 Nov. 1991, Star ed., sec. A: 1-2. Print.

Harris, Phyllis. "Hyman Judah Schachtel." *Handbook of Texas Online.* Texas State Historical Association, 03 December, 2011.
<http://www.tshaonline.org/handbook/online/articles/fsc83>.

"Harry Shepherd Lipscomb." *The Bryan-College Station Eagle.* Legacy.com, 19 May 2010. Web. 20 Feb. 2012. <http://www.legacy.com/obituaries/theeagle/obituary.aspx?n=harry-shepherd-lipscomb&pid=142873670>.

Hines, John E. "Congratulations." Letter to Dr. Dawson C. Bryan. 5 May 1956. MS. The Institute for Spirituality and Health, Houston, TX.

"History of 'In God We Trust'" About the Treasury. U.S. Department of the Treasury, Apr. 2011. Web. 19 Oct. 2013.

"Human Genome Project Information." *Oak Ridge National Laboratory.* U.S. Department of Energy, 25 July 2011. Web. 05 Dec. 2011.
<http://www.ornl.gov/sci/techresources/Human_Genome/home.shtml>.

Institute of Religion. Ed. Julian Byrd. *Dimensions.* Vol. 1, No. 1 (Fall 1965): 1-4. Print.

Institute of Religion. Ed. Julian Byrd. *Dimensions.* Vol. 1, No. 3 (Summer 1966): 1-6. Print.

Institute of Religion. "Donations." *New Horizons.* Vol. 13, No. 1 (Feb. 1986): 1-4. Print.

Institute of Religion. First Structure of its Kind at the Texas Medical Center. Houston: 11 Oct. 1959. Print.

Institute of Religion. Groundbreaking Ceremonies for New Building. Houston, TX: 29 Nov. 1959. Print.

Institute of Religion. Houston Endowment Grant. Houston, TX: 26 Feb. 1960. Print.

Institute of Religion. *Institute of Religion and Human Development Newsletter.* Vol. 1, No. 4 (Nov. 1974): 1-8. Print.

Institute of Religion. "John Fellers Named New Executive Director." *New Horizons.* Vol. 23, No. 1 (Fall 1995). Print.

Institute of Religion. *The Institute of Religion Newsletter.* Vol. 7, No. 2 (Apr. 1980): 1-4. Print.

Institute of Religion. *The Institute of Religion Newsletter.* Vol. 7, No. 9 (Nov. 1980): 1-4. Print.

Institute of Religion. "Institute Plaza Wins Award." *New Horizons.* Vol. 11, No. 1 (Jan. 1984). Print.

Institute of Religion. What Is the Institute of Religion? Houston, TX: Institute of Religion, 1955. Print.

Jonsen, Albert. "History of Medical Ethics in the 20th Century." *Encyclopedia of Bioethics.* Ed. Stephen Garrard Post. Vol. 3. New York: Macmillan Reference USA, 2004. 1000. Print.

Josey, Susan. Personal Interview. 12 May 2011.

Kahn, Robert I. "Cannot Attend." Letter to Trustees of the Institute of Religion. 1 May 1956. MS. Institute for Spirituality and Health, Houston, TX.

Karff, Samuel E. Personal Interview. 14 Dec. 2010.

---. "Paradigms of Medical Practice and Education." The John E. Fellers Symposium. Institute for Spirituality and Health. The Methodist Hospital, Houston, TX. 06 April 2011. Keynote speech.

Lammers, Stephen E., and Allen Verhey. *On Moral Medicine: Theological Perspectives in Medical Ethics.* Grand Rapids, MI: William B. Eerdmans Pub., 1998. Print.
Lomax, James. Personal Interview. 10 March 2011.

Luce, Henry R., ed. "The Healing Team." *Time: The Weekly Newsmagazine.* 14 Dec. 1959: 60. Print.

Lyon, David. Personal Interview. 20 April 2011.

McCollom, Susana. Telephone Interview. 27 Feb. 2015.

Meilaender, Gilbert. "Religion in a Public Voice." *First Things*. Ed. Allen Verhey. The Institute on Religion and Public Life, Dec. 1996. Web. 01 Nov. 2011. <http://www.firstthings.com/article/2007/11/003-religion-in-a-public-voice-32>.

Muldrow, A. M., comp. *Charter of the Institute of Religion*. 4 May 1955. Document. Office of the Secretary of State, Texas, Austin.

Negri, Gloria. "J. Robert Nelson, Theologian and BU Professor, Dean." *The Boston Globe*. 13 July 2004, sec. B: 5. Print.

Nelson, Stuart. Personal Interview. 27 Jan. 2015.

Nolen, Jim. "What Happened to the Economy in 2008?" *McCombs TODAY*. Web. 18 Jan. 2012. <http://mccombstoday.org/2009/01/nolen-what-happened-to-the-economy-in-2008>."

Our History." Congregation Beth Israel. Congregation Beth Israel. Web. 23 Jan. 2012. <http://www.beth-israel.org/about-us/our-history>.

Outler, Albert. *A Consultant's Report to the Long-range Planning Committee*. Rep. Houston, TX, 1980. Print.

Pargament, Kenneth. Personal Interview. 07 April 2011.

"Perkins School of Theology." *SMU.edu*. Southern Methodist University, 2011. Web. 21 Aug. 2011. <http://smu.edu/catalogs/graduate/perkins/continue.asp#council>.

Peterson, David. *A Tale of Two Communities: Healthcare and Spirituality*. Rep. Houston, TX, 2003. Print.

Selig, Bebe, comp. *Minutes of the Meeting of the Board of Trustees*. 19 Sept. 1990. Board secretary's transcription of board meeting minutes. Houston, TX.

Shelp, Earl, and Ron Sunderland. *InterfaithCarePartners.org*. 2011. Web. 04 Sept. 2011. <http://www.interfaithcarepartners.org/index.php/page/c/history/>.

"Significant Houston Area Floods." *WxResearch.org*. Weather Research Center, 2007. Web. 02 Sept. 2011. <http://www.wxresearch.com/almanac/houflood.html>.

Smith, A. Frank . "Dedication Ceremony." Letter to Dr. Dawson C. Bryan. 10 May 1956. MS. Institute for Spirituality and Health, Houston, TX.

Smith, Robert. "Helmut Thielicke: Between Pulpit and Lectern." *Crosswalk.com.* Christian Living Resources, 01 July 2009. Web. 01 Nov. 2011. <http://www.crosswalk.com/church/pastors-or-leadership/helmut-thielicke-between-pulpit-and-lectern-11605343.html>.

Smith, Ted. Personal Interview. 2 Dec. 2010.

Sokoloff, Jeff. Personal Interview. 27 Jan. 2015.

Spellmann, Norman W. "Angie Frank Smith." *Handbook of Texas Online.* Texas State Historical Association. Web. 18 Jan. 2012. <http://www.tshaonline.org/handbook/online/articles/fsm14>.

Stewart, Stacy R. "Tropical Cyclone Report: Tropical Storm Allison." National Hurricane Center. 28 Nov. 2001. Web. 19 Jan. 2012. <http://www.nhc.noaa.gov/2001allison.html>.

Striegler, Betsy Garlington. Personal Interview. 04 May 2011.

Sunderland, Ron. Personal Interview. 14 Dec. 2010.

"University of Hamburg." *Universität Hamburg.* 22 Sept. 2011. Web. 24 Sept. 2011. <http://www.uni-hamburg.de/index_e.html>.

Vaux, Kenneth L. "Examining the Interfaith Aspects of the Presidential Campaign with Rev. Dr. Ken Vaux." *TheRavenFoundation.org.* The Raven Foundation, 12 Nov. 2008. Web. 21 Sept. 2011. <http://www.ravenfoundation.org/resources/examining-the-interfaith-aspects-of-the-presidential-campaign-with-reverend-doctor-ken-vaux?print=1>.

---. *Ministry on the Edge: Reflections of an Interfaith Pioneer, Civil Rights Advocate, and the First Bioethicist.* Eugene, Or.: Wipf & Stock, 2010. Print.

---. "Report from the Acting Director." *The Institute of Religion and Human Development.* Vol. 1, No. 1 (Jan. 1974): 1-4. Print.

Verhey, Allen. Telephone Interview. 04 May 2011.

---. *Institute of Religion: Director's Report.* Rep. Houston, TX, 1992. Print.

Wallace, AnneMarie. Telephone Interview. 10 March 2015.

Walzel, James. Personal Interview. 11 Feb. 2011.

Weekley, Bonnie. Telephone Interview. 25 Feb. 2015.

Weingarten, Bernard, comp. *Minutes of the Meeting of the Board of Trustees.* 22 May 1973. Board secretary's transcription of board meeting minutes. Houston, TX.

---. *Minutes of the Meeting of the Board of Trustees.* 23 Oct. 1973. Board secretary's transcription of board meeting minutes. Houston, TX.

---. *Minutes of the Meeting of the Board of Trustees.* 05 Feb. 1976. Board secretary's transcription of board meeting minutes. Houston, TX.

---. *Minutes of the Meeting of the Board of Trustees.* 15 Dec. 1976. Board secretary's transcription of board meeting minutes. Houston, TX.

---. *Minutes of the Meeting of the Board of Trustees.* 16 Feb. 1977. Board secretary's transcription of board meeting minutes. Houston, TX.

Wendler, Ronda. "Early Flood Warning System Online." *Texas Medical Center News Online.* Texas Medical Center, Inc., 15 Aug. 2001. Web. 14 Aug. 2011. <http://www.tmc.edu/tmcnews/08_15_01/page_02.html>.

Westberg, Granger E. "Formal Dedication." Letter to Dr. Dawson Bryan. 27 Apr. 1956. MS. Institute for Spirituality and Health, Houston, TX.

---. *Good Grief: a Constructive Approach to the Problem of Loss.* Melbourne: Joint Board of Christian Education of Australia and New Zealand, 1962. Print.

Wilburn, Gene. "Dr. Frederick Chesley Elliott." *Houston Chronicle.* 17 May, 1959. Print.

"What Happened in 1955." *Thepeoplehistory.com.* The People History, 2011. Web. 01 Sept. 2011. http://www.thepeoplehistory.com/1955.html>.

"Who's Who: Eddy C. Scurlock." *HoustonHistory.com: 175 Years of Historic Houston.* HoustonHistory.com, 1999. Web. 21 Aug. 2011.

❧ INDEX ❧

Alley, Meagan, 70-71

Anderson, George, 57

Anderson, Leland, 25

Askey, E. Vincent, 25

Backlund, Milton, 16, 20

Baker, James A., III, 74

Baker, Susan G., 74

Bankston, L. James "Jim", 7, 57, 65

Barrow, Captain Edward Ewing, 20

Benson, Herbert, 45

Berryman, Jerome, 36-37

Bertner, Julia, 16, 20

Birdwell, J.S., 28

Booth, James M., 57

Bo's Place, 75

Brody, Baruch, 7, 40-43

Bryan, Dawson, 16-31, 39, 42, 49

Bryan, Rachel M., 39

Byrd, Julian, 7, 27, 29, 31, 34-36

Center for Medical Ethics, 40-41

Cooley, Denton, 13, 44

Clarke, Carolyn, 7, 37, 42-43, 55, 57, 66, 73

Craft, Alan, 57, 77-78

Craft, Cynthia, 57, 77-78

Cregg, David, 59, 77

Crozier, Leigh, 25

David and Bonnie Weekley Family Foundation, 78

Dawn Mountain Center for Tibetan Buddhism, 75-76

DeBakey, Michael, 13

Doctor, Jerri, 7-8, 59, 64-65

Drinan, Robert F., 32

Duffy, James D. "Jim", 66-67

Duke, James. H. "Red", 13, 46

Elliott, Frederick C., 15, 16, 23, 28, 38, 49, 66, 79

Fallon, Blaise R., 78

Fairchild, Cameron, 20

Farnsworth, Madison, 28

Favrot Fund, 74

Fehr, Bart, 57

Fellers, John E., 13, 56, 61-65

Fletcher, Joseph, 32

Flood of 1961 (see Hurricane Carla)

Flood of 1976, 35

Flood of 2001 (See Tropical StormAllison)

Fondren Foundation, 20, 24, 28, 51, 77

Fondren, Ella, 16, 20, 21, 28, 51

Fondren, Walter W., Sr., 22, 28

Freeman, John H., Jr., 24

Gabbard, Glen O., 58

Garden Club of Houston, 37, 42, 55

Garlington, Betsy (see Striegler, Betsy)

Giffords, Gabrielle "Gabby", 74

Gillan, Lex, 59, 77

Gordon, Nancy, 7, 57, 69

Graham, John K., 7, 14, 56, 57, 59, 60, 69-76, 79, 83

Graham, Pat, 8, 83

H.A. and Isabel Elkins Foundation, 46

Hahn, Karen, 7, 62-63

Hankamer, Earl C., 16, 20

Hawkins, John D., 57

Heath, Frank, 11

Henderson, Robert Wilson, 37

Henderson-Wessendorff Foundation, 54, 78

Hesse, Robert, 57

Hines, John E., 21, 50

Hope and Healing Center, 46, 75

Houston Endowment, Inc., 13, 24, 46

Houston International Airport, 28

Huffington, Roy M., 46

Hurricane Carla (1961), 35

James F. Mitchell Foundation, 46

Jones, Jesse H., 19-20, 24, 52

Jones, John, Jr., 20

Josey, Susan, 7, 57

Jung Center of Houston, The, 75

Kahn, Robert I., 22, 50

Karff, Samuel, 7, 47, 57, 58, 65, 74

Kathryn Murfee Endowment, 40

Kehoe, John Kimball, 57

Kelly, Mark E., 74

Kelsey, Mavis P., Sr., 16

Kerney, LeRoy, 20-21

Kidd, Robert "Bob", 57

King, Charles L., 16, 20

King, Susan Cooley, 44

Kirsch, Barbara, 57, 73

Koci, Anne, 57

Koenig, Harold, 12, 13, 70

Larson, David, 13

Lee, Umphrey, 21

Levine, Arthur, 81

Levin, Jeff, 12

Lipscomb, Harry, 33

Lomax, James W., II, 7, 45, 54, 57

Lowder, Virgil, 16, 20

Lustig, B. Andrew, 41

Lyon, David A., 7, 47, 57, 72

Massey, Otis, 16, 20, 21, 31

Materson, Richard "Dick", 67, 69

May, Gerald, 45

McCollom, Susana, 59, 76-77

McCrummen, Mark, 59

McCullough, Michael, 13

McIntosh, Ian, 23-24

McMorris, Emma Josephine Loffelholz, 44-45

M.D. Anderson Foundation, 24, 25, 46

Mead, Margaret, 32

Meditation Station, 75-76

Meister, Karl, 18, 19

Menon, Venugopal, 57, 76

Mesthene, Emmanuel, 32

Miller, Lisa, 75

Moody Foundation, 27

Moorman Foundation, 20

Moreton, Robert D., 46

Murfee Endowment (see Kathryn Murfee Endowment)

Murfee, Latimer, 16, 20, 40

Nelson, Eric, 43

Nelson, J. Robert "Bob", 43-48, 61

Nelson, Stuart C., 7, 59, 75-76, 83

Nesti, Father Donald S., 57

Nickell, Cathey Graham, 8, 81, 115

Nursing Conference, 44-45

Oates, Wayne, 18

Oeschger, Olin, 19

Oldham Little Church Foundation, 20

Outler, Albert, 39-40, 46

Parker, R.A. "Al", 44

Pargament, Kenneth I., 7, 12, 71-73, 83

Payne, Laurence, 57

Person, Ethel, 45

Peterson, Marvin, 73

Psychotherapy and Faith Conference, 45-46, 54, 58

Ramsey, Paul, 32

Riddle, Helen, 35

Robinson, Joe D., 45, 57

Rockefeller Brothers Fund, 32

Rockefeller Foundation, 25

Roff, Mary Katharine, 57

Rogers, Regina, 78

Samiuddin, Zishan, 57, 76

Schachtel-Green, Barbara, 57

Schachtel, Hyman J., 13, 47, 56

Scurlock Foundation, 28, 51

Scurlock, Eddy C., 24, 28, 51

Shannon, Thompson L., 31-33

Shedd, Charlie, 13, 21

Shelp, Earl, 41

Sherwood, Gwen, 44

Sid W. Richardson Foundation, 32

Smith, Angie Frank, 21

Smith, Ted, 7, 27, 34

Sokoloff, Jeff, 59, 77

Southard, Samuel, 21

Sterling Associates, 73, 78

Stitt, David, 34, 41-42

Striegler, Betsy Garlington, 7, 43-44, 48

Sumners, Thomas, 20

Sunderland, Ron H., 7, 36-38, 39, 41

Tellepsen, Howard, 16, 20, 66

Templeton, Sir John, 66

Thielicke, Helmut, 32

Time magazine, 26

Tricycle magazine, 75-76

Tropical Storm Allison (2001), 63

Tschirch, Poldi, 57

U.S. Human Genome Project, 47

Vaillant, George E., 45

Vaux, Kenneth L., 33-34

Verhey, Allen, 7, 61, 69

Wainerdi, Richard E., 57, 75

Wallace, AnneMarie, 44-45, 57

Walzel, Jim, 7, 40, 57, 64-66, 69

Weekley, Bonnie, 7, 57, 73, 74, 76, 78

Weekley, David, 73, 78

Wessendorff, Loise Henderson, 37, 45, 54

West Foundation, 19-20

West, Wesley, 16, 20

Westberg, Granger E., 19, 22, 29

Westmoreland, E.H., 20

Willerson, James T., 74

Williams, Tommy, 57

Willimon, William, 45

Wirls, Cyrus, 59, 77

Women's Home, The, 75

Zale Foundation, 32

The Institute for Spirituality and Health depends on contributions from the community to accomplish its goals and to achieve ongoing success. We are a registered 501(c)(3) non-profit organization. We are grateful for your tax-deductible donation.

For more information, please contact us at:

THE INSTITUTE FOR SPIRITUALITY AND HEALTH
at the Texas Medical Center
8100 Greenbriar, Suite. 220
Houston, TX 77054

713.797.0600

www.ish-tmc.org

Cathey Graham Nickell has spent her life writing, and this book became her first published work. The original 2012 edition of *Uniting Faith, Medicine and Healthcare: A 57-Year History of The Institute for Spirituality and Health at the Texas Medical Center* was a project that took more than a year to complete. Cathey conducted numerous personal interviews with long-time supporters of the Institute. She searched through volumes of board minutes, newsletters, special event programs, books, documents and various Internet resources in an effort to compile a chronological historical record of the organization's years from 1955 to 2012. She spearheaded a project in 2015 to update and reprint the book to commemorate the Institute's 60th anniversary.

Cathey was raised in Shreveport, Louisiana and relocated to Houston, Texas in 1998. She earned her Bachelor of Arts degree in Journalism and Marketing/Management from Baylor University in 1985. She completed a Master of Arts degree from Louisiana State University-Shreveport in 2013. While living in Shreveport, Cathey was a reporter for *The Shreveport Times*, a freelance writer for *Forum Magazine*, and later worked in the public relations field at Schumpert Medical Center, Louisiana State University-Shreveport and Columbia Highland Hospital. In Houston, she worked as a development publications writer for Baylor College of Medicine. Since that time, she has enjoyed being a state-at-home mother, volunteer and freelance writer. In 2015, Cathey wrote and published her first children's picture book titled *Arthur Zarr's Amazing Art Car*. She continues to write and is a member of the Houston Writers Guild, the Society of Children's Book Writers and Illustrators, and the **Association of** Writers and Writing Programs. Cathey lives in Houston, Texas with her husband and family.

CPSIA information can be obtained
at www.ICGtesting.com
Printed in the USA
LVOW04*2226221115

463641LV00016B/31/P

9 780692 426135

THE
IRRESISTIBLE
URGE TO FALL FOR
YOUR ENEMY

THE

IRRESISTIBLE
URGE TO FALL FOR
YOUR ENEMY

BOOK I OF THE DEARLY BELOATHED DUOLOGY

BRIGITTE KNIGHTLEY

ACE
NEW YORK

ACE

Published by Berkley

An imprint of Penguin Random House LLC

1745 Broadway, New York, NY 10019

penguinrandomhouse.com

ACE is a registered trademark and the A colophon is a trademark of Penguin Random House LLC.

Book design by Daniel Brount

Endpaper art by Nikita Jobson

Export edition ISBN: 9780593956731

Library of Congress Cataloging-in-Publication Data

Names: Knightley, Brigitte, author.
Title: The irresistible urge to fall for your enemy / Brigitte Knightley.
Description: New York : Ace, 2025. | Series: Dearly beloathed
Identifiers: LCCN 2024043322 (print) | LCCN 2024043323 (ebook) |
ISBN 9780593819456 (hardcover) | ISBN 9780593819470 (ebook)
Subjects: LCGFT: Romance fiction. | Fantasy fiction. | Novels.
Classification: LCC PS3611.N569 I77 2025 (print) | LCC PS3611.N569 (ebook) |
DDC 813/.6--dc23/eng/20241210
LC record available at https://lccn.loc.gov/2024043322
LC ebook record available at https://lccn.loc.gov/2024043323

Printed in the United States of America
1st Printing

The authorized representative in the EU for product safety and compliance is
Penguin Random House Ireland, Morrison Chambers, 32 Nassau Street,
Dublin D02 YH68, Ireland, https://eu-contact.penguin.ie.

Pspsps.

Glossary

DEOFOL

From Old English (OE) *dēofol*, "devil." Animal familiars used for communication, companionship, and counsel. Deofol are not chosen; they manifest early in childhood as a juvenile form of the animal in question and grow alongside the child. Their physical form may be nebulous or detailed, depending on the summoner's control of seith.

PLATT'S POX

Named after Epilotte Platt, a Haelan who first described the disease during an outbreak a century before this story begins. Platt's Pox is a viral infectious disease characterised by large, weeping sores. It most frequently occurs in children between the ages of one and twelve. Encephalopathy is a serious, and unfortunately common, complication, requiring Haelan intervention to reverse.

SEITH

From Old Norse *seiðr*, "magic"—though Aurienne Fairhrim would tell us that any magic, studied thoroughly enough, is science. Everyone can use seith for basic applications such as summoning their deofol, using a waystone, or powering up seith capacitors. Advanced study of seith requires initiation into an Order; mastery requires a tācn.

GLOSSARY

TĀCN

From OE *tācn*, "sign, symbol, evidence." A brand seared into the palms of full members of a given Order. The branding mechanism opens their seith system to the world and allows exponentially greater flow and manipulation of seith.

THE TĪENDOMS

From OE *tīen*, "ten," + *dōm*, "jurisdiction." The collective name for ten petty kingdoms vying for control of an archipelago in the North Atlantic Ocean. The porosity of the borders between the Tīendoms depends on the political climate; when war looms, as it frequently does, waystones are shut down and borders are closed.

WAYSTONES

From OE *weg*, "road, path; freedom of movement," + stone. Waystones are tall, rune-engraved menhirs placed along a network of ley lines called the waystone graticule. They are the most common means of travel in the Tīendoms. They are frequently found next to pubs, which are responsible for the upkeep of the waystones. The waystone graticule is controlled and managed by the Leyfarer Order.

CONTENT NOTES

The Irresistible Urge to Fall for Your Enemy is an enemies-to-lovers romantasy featuring an assassin and a healer. It contains elements that may not be suitable for all readers, including graphic violence, on-page torture, on-page deaths of minor characters, swearing, brief sexual content, medical content including fictional diseases affecting adults and children, and depictions of sick children in a hospital-like setting. Please read with care.

For further information on the Orders and a pronunciation guide, please refer to pages 361 and 367, respectively. Finally, this novel is set in an alternate UK. British English is used throughout.

The Tiendoms

THE

IRRESISTIBLE

URGE TO FALL FOR

YOUR ENEMY

IRRESISTIBLE BASTARD MEETS IMMOVABLE BITCH

Osric

It wasn't until Aurienne Fairhrim that Osric learned eye contact could hit like a knife. She stood, upright and austere, in the confines of a daguerreotype, pinning him with black-bright eyes.

"Her?" asked Osric.

"Yes, sir," said Physicker Fordyce.

"Must it be her?"

"You really haven't a choice, sir."

Osric dropped the daguerreotype. It landed on his desk, from which vantage the woman's penetrating gaze found a new victim and perforated the ceiling. Also ornamenting Osric's desk unpleasantly were Aurienne Fairhrim's curriculum vitae and a list of publications verging on the infinite.

"She's one of the Haelan," said Osric. "Her Order won't work with mine. She'll refuse as a matter of principle."

"She may, sir," said Physicker Fordyce. "You asked us who *could* heal you—not who would."

"Don't be cheeky."

"No disrespect meant, sir," said Fordyce. "The Haelan Order's members are matchless healers, and Aurienne Fairhrim is herself unsurpassed among them. She's a phenomenon when it comes to the seith system. If she declines—"

"Of course she'll decline; she's a Haelan."

"—then Physicker Shuttleworth and I will do our utmost to slow the degeneration."

"How long have I got left?" asked Osric.

Fordyce glanced at his colleague. Osric waited for the latter to say something of use, but Physicker Shuttleworth merely looked frightened, had a panicky spasm, and choked on his own saliva.

Fordyce found his courage among his colleague's sputters. "It's difficult to predict with any sort of accuracy."

"Answer me," said Osric.

"At our best guess, three or four months before your abilities begin to dwindle significantly, sir," said Fordyce.

"Dwindle significantly," repeated Osric.

"Yes, sir," said Fordyce.

"I'm going to lose my seith."

"That is, unfortunately, one of the likely outcomes, sir."

"I can't lose my seith," said Osric. "You know what I am."

Yes, the physickers knew; it was why they were on the verge of pissing themselves. They both nevertheless confirmed it with vigorous nods towards Osric's boots.

"You're a member of the Fyren Order, sir," said Shuttleworth. "P-perhaps you could envisage an early retirement?"

A brutally stupid question to which Osric replied, "Do you know how Fyren are retired?"

"Er—no, sir."

"Death."

"Ah."

"Bit of a problem, isn't it?"

"Yes, sir."

"I must say, this outcome is a disappointment, given what I paid the two of you," said Osric.

"Your illness is—really, it's quite unfortunate—not treatable, per se," said Fordyce. "It's a degenerative condition with no known cure."

"The Haelan are the greatest healers alive," said Shuttleworth, who had recovered from his suffocation to blind Osric with this luminous insight.

"Aurienne Fairhrim really is your best option, sir," said Fordyce. "If anyone can help you, it's her."

"She's my only option, if you and your colleague are to be believed."

"Erm—yes."

Having concluded that the physickers would be of no further use, Osric dismissed them. "I'm sure I can count on your discretion with respect to my condition."

The physickers stammered out a few yeses.

"My steward will see you out," said Osric. "Give us a moment."

Fordyce and Shuttleworth bowed low before exiting Osric's study. They placed their hats upon their useless heads and scuttled out towards the reception room.

Osric called for his steward. "Mrs. Parson?"

Mrs. Parson and her white-streaked bun popped round the door-post. "Yes, sir?"

"See to it that neither of those physickers remembers this visit."

"Of course."

Osric held the daguerreotype of Aurienne Fairhrim up for Mrs. Parson's inspection. "Here's my apparent saviour. What do you think?"

Mrs. Parson grasped about at her bosom until she found her spectacles. She perched them on her nose and peered at the image. "She looks lovely."

"She looks like a means to an end," said Osric.

3

Mrs. Parson tapped Fairhrim's high-necked white dress. "One of the Haelan?"

"Yes. Sanctimonious to the core, no doubt. Aurienne Fairhrim is her name."

Mrs. Parson eyed Osric over her spectacles. "If she's a Haelan, she won't help you."

"Obviously," said Osric. "However, she is, apparently, a Phenomenon. And I'm in need of a Phenomenon, Parson. How shall I convince her to assist?" He turned to a looking glass, inspected the finest cheekbones in the Tīendoms, and said, "Seduction?"

"I don't think you'd manage it," said Parson.

"You offend me, madam."

Mrs. Parson, who was annoyingly sensible, said, "She's a Haelan. She'd sooner walk into the Thames than help you. Perhaps we can equip you with a plan B. And a plan C."

"*B* for *Blackmail*, *C* for *Coercion*?"

"Amusing, sir," said Mrs. Parson, though she did not look amused.

"Very well," said Osric. "Equip me. Do a spot of investigating on Aurienne Fairhrim. Find me a bit of leverage. Bribing, extortion, threats to life and limb—you know. The usual."

"Very good, sir," said Mrs. Parson.

"That's sorted, then. After you've seen our guests out, could you fetch my daggers for tonight's sparring session? The Moulineaux pair, if you would."

"Of course, sir."

Mrs. Parson left. Osric flexed his hands. The numbness was spreading; it had started at the nape of his neck and now followed his seith system down, past his shoulders, and, in prickling tingles, into his fingers. Osric had thought little of it until he'd begun to notice corresponding fluxes in the flow of his seith, at which point he had summoned the physickers. Their diagnosis lay heavy upon him: seith degeneration. In common parlance, seith rot.

Would it be wiser to make up some excuse to avoid this evening's spar with his fellow Fyren? He never missed a spar. It might raise questions, and Osric couldn't afford to raise questions at this rather delicate juncture.

Mrs. Parson brought him his daggers. Osric strapped them on, plastered a roguish grin across his face, and went to the waystone.

He supposed it couldn't hurt to go. With the numbness spreading as it was, it literally couldn't hurt.

IT TOOK MRS. PARSON A FEW DAYS TO RETURN TO OSRIC WITH THE RE-sults of her investigation on Aurienne Fairhrim. Osric considered himself an expert when it came to intelligence gathering, but Mrs. Parson, with her network of serving girls and charwomen, was a force in her own right.

She knocked on the door to Osric's study with a conspiratorial air. Osric waved her in.

"Findings on Aurienne Fairhrim." Mrs. Parson pulled a wodge of paper out of her apron. "My half grand-aunt's daughter's third cousin works in the Haelan kitchens."

Osric did not attempt to work out Mrs. Parson's genealogical Möbius strip. He fanned the papers out on his desk. "And? What have we discovered? Has Fairhrim got any family we can use? Any debts we can acquire? Kidnap? The situation is growing desperate."

"There is some family," said Mrs. Parson. "Father from the Danelaw, mother from Tamazgha. Both presently in London. No debts to speak of; she's rather well-off. Kidnap would, of course, always be an option."

"A classic," said Osric.

"May I tell you what I think?" asked Mrs. Parson.

"Say on."

"Given the nature of the task, you might prefer her to be cooperative," said Mrs. Parson. "I've discovered that the Haelan Order is in pursuit of funding. They're seeking a substantial amount for one of their research endeavours. You've heard of the Platt's Pox outbreak?"

"Vaguely," said Osric. "I don't keep up with street urchins and their diseases."

"This particular disease may offer scope for you to strong-arm a Haelan into healing you," said Mrs. Parson.

"Bless the pestilent children, then," said Osric. "What's the required amount?"

"Twenty million thrymsas."

"Bugger me sideways."

"As I said, sir—substantial. The Haelan are in discussion with funding councils and the kings and queens of all of the Tīendoms in pursuit of the capital, but they've met little success. It seems everyone shares your apathy towards the street urchins, the poor things. But if you were to offer the amount, perhaps Haelan Fairhrim could be persuaded to set aside her natural antagonism to one of your Order."

"Bribery it is," said Osric. "Good shout."

Mrs. Parson looked doubtful. "Do your coffers hold twenty million?"

"I didn't say we were actually paying her."

"Ah."

"Proceed with the offer. Let me know how you get on."

Instead of trotting off to accomplish her task, however, Mrs. Parson remained in front of Osric's desk. "If I may make another suggestion, sir?"

"What is it?"

"Aurienne Fairhrim is well protected." Mrs. Parson shuffled through the documents until she came to a series of floor plans. "She lives in the Haelan fortress at Swanstone. She has rooms in the compound itself. To further complicate matters, Swanstone is patrolled by Wardens."

"Wardens? I *hate* Wardens. Colossal bell-ends, every one. Why have they got Wardens at Swanstone?"

"I'm told the Haelan and Warden Orders have some sort of agreement," said Mrs. Parson. "Healing for protection, and vice versa."

"How many Wardens have they got at Swanstone?" asked Osric.

"Three or four at any given time."

"That's a bloody inconvenience." Osric observed the map of Swanstone's grounds. "I see now that approaching Fairhrim with this bribe might require someone with a particular skill set."

Mrs. Parson nodded. "A bit of skulduggery wouldn't go amiss."

"One of my specialties, as it happens."

"Quite."

"Right," said Osric. "Where's my cloak? I'm off to bribe. And if Fairhrim refuses, I shall proceed with kidnap."

"A classic, sir."

"What's the nearest waystone to this Haelan fortress?"

"Closest pub is the Publish or Perish."

"Excellent."

Cloaked up, gloves on, and hair attractively tousled, Osric set off to the waystone.

AT SWANSTONE, DUGGERY WAS SKULLED.

The Haelan Order was headquartered on an island at the frigid arse-end of the Danelaw. The white fortress of Swanstone, with its snow-tipped battlements, seemed to scowl defiance at Osric as he approached. Mrs. Parson was correct: Aurienne Fairhrim was well protected. She and her Order were literally ensconced in ivory towers.

Osric waited until dusk began to lengthen shadows before making his approach. The fortress itself worried him less than the Wardens.

Infiltration was one thing; infiltration with Wardens present was another. Their Order specialised in defence and the violent dismemberment of intruders. They were an exceptional foe for a naughty Fyren here to bribe a Haelan.

However: Osric was exceptional, too.

He took the shadow-way up the ramparts and tucked himself between the wings of an enormous stone swan to observe. He spotted the hulking figures of Wardens—two of them below, two upon the ramparts with him—gleaming in armour. There were also a dozen Swanstone guards on patrol. One of the Wardens on the ramparts had her lightshield on, bright between the chinks in her armour. A shadow-walker like Osric wouldn't be able to get within stabbing distance of her.

But today—rare thing—Osric had no intentions of stabbing anyone. He was here to play nice.

A few white-clad Haelan crossed the courtyard below. To Osric's eye, the entire place suffered from an extreme of the aseptic: dry, functional, pure. Even the snow, arranged in fine lines by the wind, seemed intentional in its placement, and sanitised.

Below the snow, the courtyard gleamed with protective wards. Thick, glowing lines of the Wardens' seith crisscrossed the flagstones as they patrolled.

Osric watched the Wardens pace out their rounds for an hour before venturing forth. Then, taking exquisite care to avoid the shifting wards, he melted into the darkness at the foot of a battlement, and glided from shadow to shadow until he had made it into the fortress proper.

It took him two hours, but he triggered no wards, and didn't kill anyone.

Champion.

Mrs. Parson's pilfered floor plans informed Osric that Fairhrim's office was in the lofty north tower. He traversed the fortress to find it, passing a nursery crammed with crusty, crying infants, and a large room whose sole purpose seemed to be the collection of children's corpses.

Couldn't they bury them? Morbid sorts, these Haelan.

No—there was audible groaning—the children weren't quite dead. A group of Haelan bustled past Osric into the room. None of them was the unsmiling woman from the daguerreotype. He carried on down the corridor from shadow to shadow, evading the occasional guard as he went, pleased every time that it was a mere man, and not another Warden.

At length, a placard informed Osric that he had reached the Centre for Seith Research. A promising place to be, given his condition. There was a sick ward here, as well as examination rooms full of ominous-looking apparatus. While most of Swanstone seemed still dependent on gas, these rooms were fitted with electricity and diverse seith-powered contraptions.

There were less corpsey patients in this sector, which was encouraging.

A waiting room gave onto examination rooms. Along the wall was a painted mural of bubbles entitled *Did you know?* Each bubble contained a factoid for the edification of those waiting. Osric read the bubbles as he passed:

> Early in our history, *seith* was a collective term for powers ranging from protective warding to battle magicks.

> Everyone has a seith system. It is composed of specialised structures (seith channels and nodes) that run alongside your nervous system.

> Seith has many uses. In day-to-day life, you probably use it to send deofols or use waystones. Specialised study allows us to manipulate seith for more complex applications, such as healing.

Those who wish to achieve these levels of manipulation must earn a tācn. A tācn is a brand seared into your palm that opens your seith system to the world. Tācn are earned by members of an Order after many years of study.

Overusing seith comes with a Cost. How one's Cost is determined is still under study. Current research suggests that it is an amplification of certain physiological or genetic predispositions.

Outside Fairhrim's office door was a desk at which sat an owlish little man clattering upon a brass writing ball. He was in Osric's way, but Osric did not kill him. He wished to make a decent first impression on Fairhrim, after all, and so he merely concussed the man and tucked him neatly under his own desk.

Fairhrim's office was locked. Osric removed his glove and pressed his left palm to the lock. His tācn glowed red as he pushed his seith into it, reading the shadows within as he picked it. Child's play, obviously. After a few soft clicks, the door opened.

Aurienne Fairhrim was not within. Osric therefore made himself at home.

Fairhrim's furnishings were as austere as the rest of Swanstone, an unpleasant mix of functional and sparse. Osric chose a chair. The chair forced him into a straight-backed pose instead of his usual sprawl; he found himself sitting like some sort of spod eagerly awaiting Teacher's arrival.

On his right stood a bookcase bursting with tomes with such encouraging titles as *Crushing It: Rehabilitation of Seith Channel Com-*

pression Injuries and *Seith Fibre Ruptures and Avulsions: Protocols for Clinical Treatment* and *Reversible Interruption of Seith Flow: An In Vitro Study* and *Seith Channel Transection Injuries.*

An auspicious collection, given what he was here for. Good to see that Fairhrim was studious.

Then, with a whispered "Ah," Osric noticed that the works had all been authored by Fairhrim herself.

On Osric's left, a series of slender windows swept upwards, following the curve of the tower. Fairhrim might've had a view of the sea, but the windows were thickened by ice, and let in light rather than scenery.

Posters of individuals with various layers of skin and muscle peeled off decorated the walls. Osric had flayed a few people in the course of his career—his clients had to pay an additional fee for the service; it was messy work—but Fairhrim appeared to have her own sort of expertise in the field.

Adding to this jolly decor was a skeleton that grinned at Osric from a back corner. Thin copper wires, representing, he supposed, the seith system, wound through and around the skeleton's dusty bones. A pair of pink heart-shaped sunglasses rested upon its skull.

The sharp *clack-clack* of footsteps echoed in the corridor. Osric positioned his hood so that his face was in shadow (if he had to sit like a spod, he would, at least, look sinister while he did it) and settled into his chair to wait.

He did not wait long. The door opened and a woman entered the office, if an irritated tornado could be said to enter an office.

It was Aurienne Fairhrim. The daguerreotype had captured her features—the light brown complexion and black eyes; the dark hair pulled into a bun—but not her height, or the haughtiness in her bearing.

She radiated restrained aggravation as she strode in. Gleaming wing-shaped epaulettes at her shoulders confirmed her rank as a fully fledged Haelan. She was clad in her Order's whites—a dress rustling with heavy skirts, fastened with a double row of buttons all the way up to the throat. In her arms she juggled a tumbling vortex of items: a satchel, documents, multipacks of lancets, and, most incongruously of all, an enormous sack of onions.

Fairhrim spotted Osric. Instead of looking surprised at his intrusion, she grew even more irritated. There was no stammered enquiry about who Osric was, or how he had got in, or what he wanted.

Rather, Fairhrim said, "A bit early, aren't we?"

She marched up to Osric and dropped the sack of onions into his lap. "Erm," said Osric.

Fairhrim dusted onion peels from her palms. They fell on Osric's newly shined boots. She snatched his gloved hand in her bare one and gave it a brisk shake.

"Haelan Fairhrim," she said. "But you must call me Aurienne. Pleasure. Welcome to our hallowed halls, et cetera. I hope we won't be sending too much business your way, but, well . . . the occasional loss is unavoidable. I know you're inundated with the Pox cases. I'll strive to keep my unit's contributions to a minimum. And yes—I told the family that you lot hardly use onions anymore, but they were insistent. They hadn't any other form of payment. Hopefully you can find some use for them. If nothing else, soup, I suppose."

This speech was delivered with a voice curt and precise. Having decided that the conversation was over, Fairhrim gestured towards the door with the snap of a wrist. "I won't keep you longer. It was nice to meet you. Wes hāl—be well."

She seated herself at her desk, arranged her skirts round her feet, and, with a mutter of "Bloody admin," began to sort through paperwork.

Osric was annoyed; the onions had spoiled his aura of menace.

"I'm not here for onions," said Osric.

Fairhrim looked up, surprised, apparently, that he was still there. "No?"

"No."

"Aren't you the new undertaker?" asked Fairhrim.

"Actually, I'm—" began Osric.

Fairhrim was—there was no other word for it—attacked by a piece of paper.

She stabbed it into submission with an ink pen. "Sorry. We've an Ingenaut in residence at Swanstone—a brilliant member of a brilliant Order, of course, but some of her inventions work too well. She made the charts sentient. They get aggressive when you're behind. You were saying . . . ?"

"I'm not the new undertaker."

Fairhrim was only half listening; she was wrestling the squirming paper. "Oh? Are you sure? You rather look like an undertaker. Or is it embalmer? Mortician? You must tell me the preferred term."

"I'm here for healing," said Osric.

"Healing?"

"Yes. Specifically from you."

This felt, to Osric, like the right moment to begin to intrigue her. He pushed his hood back a little, so that she could see a bit of the Face. He tilted his head so that his cheekbone caught the light. His cleft chin clefted majestically.

Who wouldn't want to heal this?

Fairhrim, as it transpired. Unaffected by this opening display, she said, with a dismissive wave, "If you're participating in one of my Centre's studies, go back down to reception. They'll sort you out."

Reception? *Reception?*

Osric had been too subtle, obviously.

In the midst of her wave, Fairhrim paused. "Hang on—how did you get in here? I thought you'd been let in because you were the undertaker."

"I let myself in," said Osric.

"Did you, indeed?" Fairhrim was unimpressed by this feat. "Well, you can't just barge in and expect a healing. We're selective about who we take on at Swanstone. This isn't a hospital. It's a research institute. You've got to go through the proper channels."

"I won't go through the proper channels," said Osric, "because no one else must know of this. It's got to be our little secret."

He hit her with a grin (devilish) and a wink (suggestive).

For the first time since she'd arrived, Fairhrim looked at Osric—really looked at him, you know, undistracted by onions and violent bits of paper. But it wasn't the smile or the wink that captivated her. Her eyes travelled up his cloak, carefully devoid of emblems or marks. They moved to the heavy signet ring on his right hand and lingered on his black gloves.

Now she grew suspicious. Now she realised something was amiss.

"Can I count on you?" asked Osric, accompanied by a raised eyebrow (sportive).

Fairhrim's expression turned inhospitable. Osric decided not to further fatigue his eyebrows; there would be no more seductive sallies here. Her type was, evidently, not dark and dangerous. He knew a lost cause when he saw one, and Aurienne Fairhrim was a lost cause.

"Right," said Osric, slapping his knees. "On to plan B."

"Plan B?" asked Fairhrim.

"I've heard that your Order is seeking funding," said Osric. "I may have a contribution to offer."

"Oh? You'll have to speak with Lambert, two floors down. He heads Charity and Donations."

"I'm specifically interested in supporting your Order's work on Platt's Pox."

Again Fairhrim's eyes sought Osric's gloves. "Your interest delights me, of course, but, as I said, Charity and Donations would be your starting point. Paediatric diseases aren't my area anyway." Her gaze flicked towards the door. "How *did* you get in here? Where is Quincey?"

"Who?"

"My assistant."

"Assistant? A tripping hazard, rather," said Osric. "He's napping."

Fairhrim edged one hand to the left of her desk, which informed Osric that there was an alarm mechanism there.

"Don't press the panic button, Haelan Fairhrim," said Osric. "I'd rather things didn't get messy."

Fairhrim stilled. "That sounds like a threat."

"It is."

"Who are you and what do you want?"

"We could've got to this point much sooner if you hadn't mucked about with the onions," said Osric. Also if he hadn't mucked about with attempting to flirt with her, but he preferred not to take responsibility for things. "As I said, I want healing."

"What you'll get is a broken coccyx, when the Wardens throw you out," said Fairhrim.

Now that she had confirmed that something was amiss, Fairhrim did not appear frightened. She appeared, on the contrary, freshly annoyed. Did all of the Haelan have such poor self-preservation instincts, or was she particularly dim?

"Do you think I heal every impostor undertaker who wanders into my office?" asked Fairhrim.

"You will with this one," said Osric. "I'm going to help you cure your precious Pox."

The aggressive chart on Fairhrim's desk twitched back to life. She slapped it. "We're not curing it. We're looking to immunise against it."

"Right. Whatever. I wish to buy your services—and your discretion—with a donation. I know your Order's negotiations with the usual funding agencies haven't been successful."

Fairhrim pressed her lips into a narrow line. "They haven't been successful to date. We've only just begun to make submissions to the various bodies. These things take time."

Osric waved away her technicalities. "Wouldn't you rather have the money now? Get started? Cure the guttersnipes?"

"Immunise, not cure," said Fairhrim. "And I'm not a physicker-for-hire. There are hundreds of those in London alone. Why don't you go to one of them with your gold?"

"I've been told I need your particular expertise."

"By who?"

"Physickers-for-hire."

"Which ones?"

"Fordyce and Shuttleworth."

Fairhrim gave a snobbish little tut. "That's the best money can buy, is it?"

"They came highly recommended."

"And what have they diagnosed you with?" asked Fairhrim. Her eyes swept over Osric in a once-over, as though she might work out his affliction by sight alone.

"That's for you to discover," said Osric. "Do you want the funding or not? It's a simple proposal. You heal me. You tell nobody. I'm offering twenty million."

Fairhrim's gaze settled on Osric's gloves. "Show me your palms."

"No," said Osric, given that she would find the Fyren tācn on his left palm objectionable.

"Then my answer is also no."

Osric sighed. "I'd rather not have to kidnap you. That would be a bother."

"Oh?" Fairhrim sat up, if it was possible, even straighter. "You're going to kidnap me, are you?"

"Yes. *And* not give you the money."

Fairhrim's right hand twitched. On her palm, the tācn of the Haelan Order glowed: a white swan. "You're rather bold if you think you can kidnap me."

"You're rather stupid if you think I can't."

"Who *are* you?"

"Someone in desperate need of your help."

There was scepticism in the set of Fairhrim's mouth. "That would've been more moving if you hadn't just threatened to kidnap me. Show me your palms."

"No."

"You want me to heal you, but you won't show me your palms?"

"Correct."

"If you're hiding them, it's because you know I'll refuse to heal you."

"Precisely," said Osric.

Fairhrim's hand inched towards the panic button again.

"Don't," said Osric. "You'll be sentencing whoever comes to a violent death."

"You think you can take on the Wardens?" asked Fairhrim.

Osric did not—not one-on-one, anyway—but he said, "Do you really want to gamble with their lives?"

"Leave," said Fairhrim.

"I'm leaving with either an agreement between the two of us . . . or you, stuffed into the bag of onions. You decide."

"I don't even know what's wrong with you," said Fairhrim. "Even if I were to agree—which I won't—I don't know if I could heal you."

"I'm asking you to try."

"Can I run some diagnostics?" asked Fairhrim.

"No. Agreement first."

"It must be bad."

"It is."

"Fatal?"

"For all intents and purposes."

"What if I can't heal you?" asked Fairhrim.

"I'll die. And perhaps I'll take you with me," said Osric.

"Wonderful."

"Am I persuading you?"

"Persuasion would require an iota of something like charm."

This vexed Osric. "I'm not charming?"

"No," said Fairhrim. "You follow one of the Dusken Paths. I won't help you. And you stink of onions."

"The onions are *your* fault. Don't do it to help me; do it to help the Poxies. Think of all the suffering you could alleviate."

"Prevent, rather."

"Whatever."

Fairhrim studied him. Osric had to admire her composure. There were no tears or trembles. Her only real emotion was contempt when her gaze drifted to his gloves, now that she knew he wasn't a follower of the Bright Paths. The question at present was whether the temptation of the gold—or the weight of his threats—would outweigh her aversion.

He hoped it would. She seemed a logical sort of creature.

"You're calm about all this," said Osric.

"I'm trained to keep a cool head in times of crisis," said Fairhrim. "Though my subjects are usually haemorrhaging blood rather than absurdities."

Osric had already suspected that he didn't like Fairhrim. That was now confirmed.

His patience with the negotiations ran out.

"Kidnap it is," said Osric. He rose, poured the onions onto the floor, and flapped the empty sack at Fairhrim. "Get in."

Fairhrim's scoff was interrupted by the door bursting open.

A second meteorological phenomenon entered the room. This one was a small storm.

"I am *sick* of tickling Research and Innovation's balls," said the storm.

It was an old Haelan, Black, white haired, crackling with anger.

Fairhrim leapt to her feet. Her haughtiness gave way to nervous servility. Osric was piqued; she looked more fearful now than she had at any point during their conversation.

Fairhrim folded into a low bow, a hand on her heart. "Haelan Xanthe."

Haelan Xanthe surged into the room upon a cloud of white Haelan robes. In her fist was a crumpled letter, which she shook in Fairhrim's direction. "A rejection from those muppets at the Research and Innovation Council."

"Oh no," said Fairhrim.

"Oh yes," said Xanthe. From her broad tones, Osric surmised that she was from Strathclyde. "On the most spurious of grounds. Our proposal doesn't line up with their funding programme's priorities, apparently. Have you ever heard such bollocks? We are literally in the throes of an outbreak. We've been asked to resubmit next cycle. I've half a mind to infect Woolwich with the Pox. Perhaps then he'll understand what we're about. Cultivate a bit of empathy among the scabs. Pity it only affects children—"

Xanthe cut herself off, sniffed the air, and asked, "Why do I smell onions?"

Looking about to find the source of the pong, she noticed Osric. Her eyes travelled down his cloak to the mess of bulbs at his feet.

"Who's this, then?" she asked. "The new undertaker?"

"No," answered Osric. "I am not the bloody undertaker. You're interrupting a negotiation session, Gran-gran, so if you wouldn't mind—"

"A negotiation? For what?" Xanthe turned to Fairhrim. "Did this man just call me *Gran-gran*?"

Fairhrim looked, if you please, embarrassed. "I'm so sorry. No idea who he is. He's got in somehow. He tried to bribe me for a healing. And now he's threatening kidnap with, honestly, grotesque ineptitude. The Wardens will make short work of him."

"Ask them not to damage him too much," said Xanthe, eyeing Osric as though he were a slab of meat. "We could use another corpse in the anatomy lab. We're running low on adult males."

"I will," said Fairhrim. "At least he'll be of some use to the world."

"I *beg* your pardon," said Osric.

Fairhrim ignored him. She turned back to Xanthe. "Have you told Élodie the news yet?"

"Not yet. She's going to be gutted. I won't be able to convince the other Heads to dig further into our reserves to support her. I simply don't understand—back-to-back rejections from five agencies in the midst of a crisis such as this one, and the Heads of the Tīendoms all sitting idle."

The two Haelan continued their little chat, and Osric—well, Osric had never felt so unimportant in his life. Mrs. Parson might have warned him that the Haelan were lunatics who prioritised administrative matters over their imminent deaths.

"Hello? Hi? I'm still here," said Osric, waving at Fairhrim over Xanthe's shoulder. "Still going to kidnap you, too. And now I'll have to kill this old dear for what she's witnessed. I hope you're happy."

"Kill *me*?" said Xanthe.

Xanthe threw her head back and cackled. Fairhrim stared at Osric with her eyebrows at her hairline.

"Bit of an idiot, is he?" asked Xanthe.

"So I've gathered from our brief acquaintance," said Fairhrim.

Osric, miffed, wondered whether he ought to kill them both for this show of disrespect.

The Haelan continued their discussion as though he weren't there.

"What was the bribe, out of curiosity?" asked Xanthe.

"Twenty million," said Fairhrim. "In support of Élodie's proposal, actually."

"Twenty million? Woden's balls."

"No idea of its provenance, of course." One of Fairhrim's silver epaulettes rose as she shrugged. "Or whether it even exists."

"Tempting, in light of this," said Xanthe, holding up the rejection letter. Her wrinkles rearranged themselves into an exceptionally shrewd expression.

"He won't show me his hands," said Fairhrim.

"Ah," said Xanthe. "He's too sane to be a Dreor, but too stupid to be a Fyren, surely. Perhaps one of the Agannor? No. He would've already possessed one of us."

"Regardless, I would never," said Fairhrim.

Xanthe rolled the rejection letter into a tube, which she tapped against her mouth. "If he really *did* have the money, though . . ."

"He's a walker of the Dusken Paths," said Fairhrim.

Xanthe waved her hand towards Fairhrim in a dismissive gesture almost identical to the one Fairhrim had used with Osric.

Fairhrim blinked an incredulous blink. "Haelan Xanthe, *surely* you aren't considering—"

Xanthe turned to Osric, who was delighted to finally exist again.

"Have you got all twenty million in gold?" asked Xanthe, enunciating with particular care, as though speaking with an imbecile.

Osric set aside his vexation in the face of this lifeline. "Yes."

"Really?" said Xanthe. "Fuck me. I should switch Orders."

She cackled. Fairhrim, who apparently found nothing funny, stared.

"You can have it in our vaults by Friday?" asked Xanthe.

"Yes," said Osric again.

"Why did you come to Haelan Fairhrim specifically?" asked Xanthe.

"I was told she specialises in the seith system."

"That she does."

"I'm told she's a Phenomenon."

"No one better." Xanthe came to stand in front of Osric. The old Haelan was small, bowed about the shoulders, absurdly wrinkled in the face. She studied him with a kind of pity. "So it's your seith that troubles you. Poor thing."

The adjective startled Osric. It had never been applied to him before: he was not poor.

"I understand your desperation," continued Xanthe. "Aurienne would be the specialist you need."

"I *don't* specialise in healing walkers of the Dusken Paths, however," interjected Fairhrim.

"Is he one?" asked Xanthe. "We can't say. We haven't seen his hands."

"Because he's refused to show them to us," said Fairhrim.

"Excellent." Xanthe nodded. "Plausible deniability."

Fairhrim sputtered. "With all respect—"

"We won't have to keep fondling the pendulous balls of the granting agencies this way," said Xanthe.

"But—"

Xanthe tapped Fairhrim on the forehead with the rolled-up letter. "I had to wade hip deep through dying children to get here, Aurienne. Don't let's be precious about twenty million in gold."

"Healing one of his kind is against everything we stand for," said Fairhrim.

"Oh, I agree. It'll be difficult for you."

"Difficult for *her*?" cut in Osric. "What about me? I'm the one who's sick."

Xanthe turned to Osric with something of her previous storminess. "Yes, her. She'll be the one sullying herself. Now, if you're serious, let's discuss terms. You'll deposit twenty million thrymsas in the Haelan vault by close of play Friday, in the form of an anonymous donation to the Pox fund. Once our bookkeepers have examined the gold for any jiggery-pokery, Aurienne will heal you to the best of her ability."

"Haelan Xanthe, this is *most* irregular—" began Fairhrim, but Xanthe looked at her, and Fairhrim closed her mouth with a snap.

"My only stipulation is that no one must know," said Osric.

Xanthe made an impatient gesture. "Obviously. We also have a vested interest in keeping this sort of unsavoury arrangement discreet."

"Then we have a deal," said Osric.

Fairhrim looked on in tight-lipped silence.

"Aurienne is more than capable of taking care of herself," said Xanthe. "But I should tell you, if she comes to harm in the course of treating you, I will kill you myself."

Osric wanted to laugh at this preposterous old lady. However, as Xanthe held his gaze, he felt something of her seith. It was as though a small dry hand had given his gravestone a friendly pat.

He did not, to the best of his knowledge, have a gravestone.

"Understood," said Osric.

"Only half as stupid as you look." Xanthe tore up the rejection letter and scattered it on the floor, among the onions. "Right. I await news of a substantial donation of unknown origins on Friday. In the meantime, I've got lives to save. I'll leave you two to work out the details. Mind you be good."

Osric wasn't certain who that last instruction was directed towards—it couldn't have been aimed at him, surely. He was never good.

Xanthe swept towards the door. Fairhrim sank into another of those hand-on-heart bows as she left.

Silence fell. Osric rearranged his cloak. Fairhrim regarded him with absolute disdain.

"Pleased to have this sorted," said Osric.

"Get out," said Fairhrim.

"Don't be so angry. You're doing it for the Poxies."

"I'm doing it because Haelan Xanthe told me to," said Fairhrim.

"I'll send you my deofol with further instructions for our first session."

"I'm the Haelan. I'm the one who will be sending instructions."

"Have you got suggestions for a neutral meeting place?" asked Osric. "I don't want to come back here. Wardens are a pain in the arse to avoid."

"I haven't at the minute," said Fairhrim. "You've just sprung the request upon me."

"Well, *I* do. Watch for my deofol. Oh—speaking of—link with me."

"Excuse me?" said Fairhrim.

It *was* a bit forward to ask to link tācn. It was something reserved for friends and family, so that their deofol—seith familiars—could travel from one tācn to another to deliver messages. Fairhrim, however, was looking at Osric as though he had suggested the most foul of depravities.

"We can sever the link as soon as you've healed me," said Osric.

Fairhrim's cold stare grew calculating. At length, she said, "Fine."

Linking required tācn-to-tācn contact. Osric therefore removed his glove. Fairhrim's jaw tightened as he confirmed her suspicions; it was his left glove that was coming off. Only those who walked the Dusken Paths had their tācn on their left palms.

Osric held up his hand, revealing the hellhound's skull that adorned it—the tācn of the Fyren Order. Normally, the sight of this tācn struck terror. It was a harbinger of a very immediate, violent death.

Fairhrim offended Osric by being disgusted instead of afraid—as though, in lieu of his open palm, he had presented her with an open nappy, used, and asked her to touch it.

"You're a shadow-walking coward-for-hire," said Fairhrim.

"Yes."

"Vile," said Fairhrim.

She nevertheless reached her right hand towards Osric. They brushed their tācn together. The wing of the Haelan Order's swan touched the fang of the Fyren Order's hellhound. They pushed out their seith and learned each other's signature. Fairhrim's seith was cool, restrained, and felt like glass. Osric's deofol would now be able to find her directly to bear his messages; her deofol would likewise be able to find him. (He wondered what form her deofol would take. Something prickly, he wagered. A scorpion, probably.)

They pulled their palms apart. Fairhrim held her hand away from herself, as one would after having touched something filthy.

There was a knock at the door. "Haelan Fairhrim?"

Osric slipped behind the door and gestured at Fairhrim to open it, with a whispered injunction to not do anything stupid.

Fairhrim opened the door. Through the crack at the hinges, Osric saw a black-clad cadaver of a man. There was a powerful whiff of formalin.

The man shook Fairhrim's hand and said, "Hello. I'm the new undertaker. I'm here about the onions?"

UPON HIS RETURN TO THE FAMILY SEAT AT ROSEFELL HALL, OSRIC WAS accosted by Mrs. Parson.

"Well, sir?" she asked. "What news?"

"Good news, I think," said Osric. "Some pettifogging, but I suppose that was to be expected. She'll do it."

"Bless her."

"No. Don't bless her. She is singularly disagreeable; I don't like her at all. Also, there is a hiccough."

"Oh?"

"We've got to deposit that twenty million in gold by the end of the week."

"That won't be a problem," said Mrs. Parson. "We've just received a heap of beautifully forged thrymsas from Beckenham."

"They can't be forged," said Osric. "We'll have to cough up real coin. The Haelan are already suspicious. I can't risk delaying this—or having them withdraw from the agreement."

Mrs. Parson was wide-eyed. "But . . . you haven't got twenty million in gold."

"I know. You'll have to sell the triptych, and *The Milkmaid*. The de Beauveau, too. It hurts me to part with them, but it can't be helped. Talk to Sacramore. I suppose we can't sell *The Eaters* yet?"

"Far too hot. You just acquired it two months ago."

"Right. Can't exactly flog it down the pub, then. Sell whatever other bits and bobs we need to to reach the twenty-million mark. It's to be offered as an anonymous donation to the Haelan Order, directed to the Pox fund. Can I leave the arrangements to you?"

Mrs. Parson nodded, but her eyes remained wide. "Twenty million. This is . . . this is a sizable portion of your fortune."

"We will, obviously, be stealing it back."

Mrs. Parson looked relieved. "Oh! Very good, sir."

AURIENNE WISHES DEATH
UPON HER NEW PATIENT

Aurienne

It was hard, being perfect in an imperfect world, but Aurienne managed. If she had a flaw, it was that she was the Best, and she knew she was the Best. Some called it arrogance. She called it competence untainted by performative humility.

But if she was the Best—as brilliant as she was beautiful, a researcher unparalleled, a friend cherished, a daughter beloved, a lover sometimes (Did anyone truly deserve her? Frankly, no)—why, pray, had she just been asked to care for the Worst? Tasked to heal a Fyren, of all the foul things in the world?

The Fyren had had the gall to leave her his card. It was black, edged in gold, and proclaimed in an elegant script:

Osric Mordaunt.
Art. Acquisitions. Assassinations.
By appointment only.

The card was perfumed, which offended Aurienne more than the assassination appointments: Swanstone was a scent-free establishment.

She stepped out of her office and into the corridor, where she found poor Quincey in an unconscious heap under his desk. Once revived, Quincey remembered nothing of what had happened to him and decided that he must have fallen over. Aurienne healed his concussion and did not correct him.

It was tempting for Aurienne to conclude that Xanthe had lost the plot—that her mentor's genius (and she was a genius, unrivalled in her field—peerless) had finally tilted into madness. However, as Aurienne tripped her way through halls heaped with victims of the Pox, she was forced to conclude that Xanthe wasn't mad. Xanthe was an opportunist reacting to indifferent funding councils and apathetic monarchs. If the Fyren did come through with the gold—well, who was Aurienne to refuse?

A grey-robed apprentice sprinted past Aurienne and gasped, "Ward Fourteen—they're asking for all available Haelan. Can you come?"

He was gone before Aurienne could answer. Aurienne pivoted and made for Ward 14. Honestly, the Fyren was only the newest complication in a day already bursting with them. And Aurienne was good at dealing with complications. She was good at dealing with everything.

She joined her harried colleagues in the temporary Platt's Pox ward. Breage—the Paediatrics matron, usually imperturbable—was wild-eyed and breathless. Aurienne was assigned to four beds and poured her seith into children at the brink of brain death.

A dishevelled deofol materialised in the ward. It took the shape of an osprey, her feathers all askew. Aurienne recognised the deofol as Lorelei's, the head of Paediatrics.

"Twenty new arrivals at the waystone," said the deofol. "We're drowning. Who can come?"

The six Haelan at work in the ward, each retrieved from their specialisations to lend their tācn here, looked up from their charges.

"Twenty?" gasped Aurienne.

"Stop bloody admitting them," said Cath, the head of Trauma and Acute Care. "Someone throw something at the bird."

"Kindly don't harm the messenger," said the deofol, pulling her wings in close.

"This isn't a hospital," said one of the Haelan from Haematology. "We simply haven't the capacity."

Élodie, pulled in from Virology, said, "The hospitals are full. There's nowhere else for them to go."

The deofol nodded. "Infected children are being rounded up and dumped at the Publish or Perish. The Wardens are helping load them up in carts to bring them in. You should see the waystone. Absolute nightmare."

One of the Haelan from Biostatistics dragged a desperate hand across his face. "Gods. I shouldn't be here. I should be running models on this disease. Working out transmission dynamics. Forecasting. Élodie should be in the lab, not here."

"Keep healing," snapped Cath, bustling past him to the next bed. "You can save thirty lives in the time it takes a physicker to save one."

"The Heads will work out resource allocations when they've had a minute to breathe," said Aurienne. "I can't believe the virulence."

"It makes no sense," said Élodie, kneeling at the side of a listless, scab-ridden girl. "There were only a hundred cases a fortnight ago."

Aurienne saw signs of her exhausted colleagues' approaching their seith limits; their Costs were making themselves known. Élodie's jaw was beginning to lock. Biostatistics was starting to bleed from the mouth. Haematology was hobbling as though hit by arthritis in both knees. Cath was lucky—her Cost was hair loss; it was why she kept her head shaved. As for Aurienne, her hands were chapping—a minor issue while she was fresh, but the more she used her seith, the more the wounds deepened, until they painfully exposed her metacarpals and phalanges.

"Where are the Heads?" asked a Haelan from Endocrinology, utterly out of her element among the children. "Where is our leadership?"

"Xanthe and Abercorn are at the waystone," said the deofol, "draining their seith dry. Prendergast has gone to the king of the Danelaw to squeeze support out of him."

Aurienne pressed her tācn to the forehead of an unconscious little boy. "I'll go to the waystone. At the very least, I'll be on hand for seith transfers."

"Don't drain yourself in the process," called Cath.

"I won't," said Aurienne.

And she didn't. No one controlled their seith like Aurienne Fairhrim.

THE NEXT FEW DAYS BLED INTO ONE ANOTHER AS THE POX OUTBREAK raged on. Every Haelan's research was suspended. Platt's Pox couldn't be contracted by adults, but any apprentice Haelan young enough to be at risk was confined to Cygnet House. The waystone at the Publish or Perish continued its wretched deliveries; infected children were drawn up to Swanstone by the cartload.

There was no further news from the Fyren for the rest of the week. Aurienne cherished conflicting hopes. On the one hand, she wished that he would do as he had promised and bestow a desperately needed windfall upon her Order to get the Pox under control. On the other, she hoped that he had gone and died.

At five o'clock on Friday, shouts of joy echoed through Swanstone's halls. The handful of Haelan not on rounds gathered at Charity and Donations to find the usually staid Lambert dancing about with his secretary; the Haelan Order had just received an extraordinary anonymous donation in support of the Platt's Pox inoculation.

Élodie, the lead researcher on the inoculation, was in a state of teary shock. She trembled in the arms of Cath, who peppered her with kisses, and then threw herself around Aurienne's neck. The room was all delight and laughter. Aurienne managed a brittle smile as Élodie sobbed into her shoulder. The money was wonderful; its provenance was not. Speculations, diverse and fanciful, were made on the identity of the donor: One of the kings or queens of the Tīendoms? Some millionaire who had lost a child to the Pox? The gods themselves?

No one speculated that it might've come from a Fyren, of course. That would be too fantastical. The idea simply did not occur.

"We're so lucky," said Cath.

Élodie dashed away tears. "Frīa's blessings on this donor."

"A good and generous soul," said Lambert.

"I should like to sh-shake their hand," sniffed Élodie.

"I should like to kiss them on the mouth," said Cath.

Aurienne said nothing, because, you know.

Haelan Xanthe made an appearance, partook in the general hugging, and, when no one was looking, gave Aurienne an apologetic pat on the shoulder. Aurienne left Charity and Donations bitterly resigned to healing a Fyren for a—rather worthwhile, it had to be said—bribe.

As she entered her office, her tācn tingled. A deofol was incoming and requesting permission to take form. She recognised the sly, smoky seith; it was the Fyren's deofol.

Aurienne locked the door and held her tācn towards the floor. Something dark and sinuous materialised next to her. The Fyren's deofol took the shape of a wolfish shadow, ill-defined save for a sharp double line of white teeth.

"You've received the funds?" asked the deofol in a dusky hiss.

"Yes," said Aurienne. "All seems to be in order."

"Excellent." The deofol's disembodied grin floated upwards until it was at Aurienne's eye level. "We've found a place to meet. Take a waystone to the Gogmagog."

"What sort of place?" asked Aurienne.

"A meeting sort of place," said the teeth, uselessly.

"Tell your master that I require an aseptic environment," said Aurienne. "And it must be well ventilated."

A golden eye appeared over the teeth. "I shall be sure to inform him of your preferences."

"Specifications, not preferences," said Aurienne.

A shrug rippled through the deofol. "Be at the Gogmagog at midnight."

"Midnight?"

"The best time for mischief," said the deofol.

"That's far too late. I rise at four for my first rounds."

"Have a nap, then."

"A nap? You think I've got time for naps? We're in the middle of a Pox outbreak, you impertinent—"

But Aurienne was speaking to nothing. The deofol had melted into shadow and disappeared.

Midnight came round. Aurienne, tired and irritated (she had not had the nap), packed her Haelan satchel. She descended snowy steps into Swanstone's courtyard, from whence she made her way to the portcullis.

The Wardens were at their stations, a good head and shoulders taller than the guards. Their closed helmets shone under the moonlight; their wards shimmered across the snow at their feet.

The Haelan Order and the Warden Order had a long-standing, mutually beneficial agreement. The Wardens sent a complement of their best to Swanstone to protect the Haelan, and the Haelan sent a complement of their best to the Warden headquarters at Tintagel Castle to heal any Wardens in need. Aurienne's next rotation at Tintagel's infirmary would be coming up this autumn; she would have to see how to fit that into her many priorities.

She removed a glove and flashed the white glow of her tācn towards the Wardens.

"Late night, Haelan," commented the tallest one as she drew the postern gate. Aurienne recognised her voice—this one was called Verity.

"Indeed," said Aurienne. "Off for a drink. It's been a long day."

"Well deserved," said Verity. "When shall we expect you back?"

"An hour or two, I should think."

Verity inclined her helmet. "Take care of yourself."

"Thank you."

Aurienne passed through the gate with casual salutes from the other Wardens. Feeling like a liar and a criminal, she crossed the moat and went over the long bridge that connected Swanstone to the mainland. The fortress had originally been built on a peninsula, but the sea had long ago reclaimed the narrow isthmus. Fitful waves roiled far beneath Aurienne's feet as she walked.

In the quaint village of Swanstone-on-Sea, Aurienne passed low sod-and-stone houses and arrived at the Publish or Perish. At this late hour, the pub's waystone was, thankfully, devoid of travellers and new batches of sick children.

The usual etiquette when using a waystone was to have a drink at the connected pub—or, when one hadn't the time, such as when skulking off to meet a Fyren, to leave payment upon the windowsill. Aurienne, unfortunately in the latter category, left a coin upon the ledge.

She held her tācn to the ancient standing stone and pressed seith into the runes that spelled out the Gogmagog. She took a steadying breath as she did so; she hated waystone travel. It was discomposing in a literal sense. One's molecules ought to stay together, not be splayed into a ley line. The alternative, however, was endless journeying by carriage, and so Aurienne braved the waystone graticule, even if every plunge into it turned her stomach.

The waystone glowed into life, flashed *Mind the gap*—Aurienne minded the gap very much—and whisked her into a ley line.

The particles that made up Aurienne reconvened at the waystone just outside the Gogmagog. She pressed one hand against the stone for balance and the other, with her tācn aglow with seith, to her forehead to stem her queasiness.

The Gogmagog was set among desolate, snowcapped hills. A lonely gas lamp was the only source of light. The pub's windows were dark. Aurienne left a coin on the sill and peered about, given the high probability that a Fyren was lurking nearby.

"You're punctual," came the voice of the Fyren. "Good."

Yes: there he was. Lurking. That was what his sort did. Lurk, and murder innocents for money.

Deeming his remark on punctuality too jejune to merit a response, Aurienne said nothing. She could make out only bits of him among the shadows: the tip of a boot, the snow-sodden bottom of a cloak, the edge of a black hood.

Unfortunately, he was chatty, and was determined to inflict his conversation upon her. "I'd thought you might be cheeky and bring a Warden," he said.

"I'm sure they would've been enchanted to meet you, but no. I don't typically double-cross those with whom I've made agreements."

"Charming habit," said Mordaunt. "You don't look remotely nervous."

"I'm never nervous," said Aurienne. It wasn't boastful; it was true. "Where are we going?"

"Up," said Mordaunt, with a gesture towards the hill.

After more than fifteen hours on her feet that day, Aurienne wasn't overkeen on the walk. She let Mordaunt take the lead and break a path for her in the snow. Their steps grew ponderous as they climbed higher and the snow deepened. Their trails added long veins to the white hillside. After a few minutes of this exertion, their breath streamed behind them in plumes. The February wind grew lazy as they climbed; it opted to pass through them, rather than around.

Their objective seemed to be a half-collapsed structure at the top of the hill. It was a barn, Aurienne realised as they approached. A literal barn. Was this a joke?

Mordaunt held the door open for her with vast gallantry, as though he were ushering her into the most fashionable assembly room in London.

"You needn't look so cross," said Mordaunt.

"I specified an aseptic environment," said Aurienne, stepping over broken flagstones. "How do you expect me to heal you if you can't follow the simplest of instructions?"

"It's perfectly clean," said Mordaunt. "There hasn't been a cow here in months—present company excepted."

So he was a Fyren *and* an arsehole. What luck.

The barn wasn't perfectly clean, by the by. There was a heap of steaming excrement right in front of Aurienne, and it could talk.

This vulgar aside she kept confined, naturally, to her thoughts.

"Does the ventilation meet your standards at least?" asked Mordaunt. The wind whipped at his hood as he posed the question.

Aurienne caught a glimpse of a close-lipped smile bisected by a scar.

Brilliant. The arsehole thought he was funny, on top of everything else.

"I need a proper consulting room," said Aurienne. "Or did you intend to sit in the trough to be examined?"

"Make do," said Mordaunt. "I thought you were meant to be exceptional."

"In normal working conditions," said Aurienne. "Not in a derelict barn, in a blizzard, at midnight."

The Fyren drew the door shut, which cut out the worst of the wind. He pulled a lantern out of his cloak, lit it, and sat upon the mouldy remains of a bale of hay. "There are too many eyes in normal working conditions. Can we begin?"

Aurienne had managed her seith carefully in the wards to ensure that she would have enough left for tonight. It disgusted her to waste such a precious thing on one of this man's ilk. Now that it was time to use it, it felt like squandering—like throwing away something dear on someone utterly unworthy.

THE IRRESISTIBLE URGE TO FALL FOR YOUR ENEMY

However, preliminary diagnostics would be a first step towards understanding what was ailing the Fyren. With any luck, he was well on his way to a horrid, drawn-out death.

"Diagnostics, then," said Aurienne. She removed her cloak and gloves.

The Fyren did not follow suit. He kept his hood up, so that all Aurienne could see was that scarred, sarcastic mouth. The rest of his face was shadow.

The shadow looked at her and said, "The sullying begins."

It was an attempt at flippancy, but the tension in his shoulders gave the lie to it. Mordaunt was not at ease.

After disinfecting her hands, Aurienne held her palm towards him and gathered her seith to her tācn. Its white light joined the yellow of the lantern.

She waited for the Fyren to free up a patch of skin for her to proceed, but he merely sat there.

"What are you waiting for?" asked Aurienne.

"What are *you* waiting for?" came Mordaunt's response, both wary and annoyed.

"This requires contact," said Aurienne, holding her tācn at him. "Obviously."

"Oh," said Mordaunt.

"If you can bear to shed the cloak-and-dagger look for a minute, kindly undo this," said Aurienne, with a gesture to Mordaunt's neckline. "Clavicle or chest works best for general diagnostics."

Mordaunt suffered the hardship with evident irritation. He undid the clasp of his cloak and began to work at the cravat and collar underneath.

His hood fell back, exposing silver-white hair, winsomely tousled, and pale skin. His features, Aurienne decided, suited him: insolent (the grey eyes) and sardonic (the cut of the eyebrows, the mouth). The various scars that pitted his face weren't surprising, given his profession. They added something savage to a countenance that was otherwise patrician.

The sardonic mouth said, "Rude to stare."

"Assessment requires observation," said Aurienne. "Or would you like me to attempt it blindfolded?"

Mordaunt looked as though he had a retort ready, but decided to hold his tongue. He pulled his shirt open and exposed a bit of his chest to Aurienne.

Aurienne had touched a great many unpleasant things in the course of her career—secretions, purulent exudates, effusions of every description—but none were as loathsome as a Fyren.

As she pressed her tācn to the Fyren's skin, his brows pulled together. He twitched under her touch. She could feel the tension in him—a desire to recoil, a disgust. He didn't want to be touched by her as much as she didn't want to touch him. Aurienne was pleased that they were jointly suffering in this regard.

Her preliminary diagnostics resulted in unsurprising findings: evidence of many years' worth of physical trauma, mostly healed; an epithelium crisscrossed by scar tissue; a high heart rate; elevated cortisol and adrenaline.

The scarring was something. The man was branded by years of fights. She could confirm that he had never been worked on by a Haelan. None of her Order would've left such a war zone behind.

Her attention was drawn to a mess at Mordaunt's cervical spine. Burst fractures, poorly healed, had compromised his seith system, which was now headed towards putrefaction. He was indeed on his way to a horrid, drawn-out death.

No. Mordaunt was a Fyren. A drawn-out death wasn't on the cards. A Fyren without his seith was useless. His own kind would make short work of him well before the disease did.

Which meant one less killer for hire terrorising the populace. Excellent.

Aurienne flicked diagnostic images into being. They floated, pallid white, between her and the Fyren.

She pointed at the largest image. "Tell me about the bodged surgery at your neck. Was it done in a bush?"

"Yes. Literally. Field medic."

"What happened?"

"A training injury."

"Oh? Does training involve being bludgeoned by a sledgehammer?"

"A maul, rather."

"Barbaric," said Aurienne.

Mordaunt shrugged. "Valuable lessons were learned."

"I thought those brutish training methods had been outlawed by the Peace Accords," said Aurienne.

"I'll let you advise my warchief of that. She'd be delighted to hear your input."

"How long since the initial injury?" asked Aurienne.

"A few months."

"And you've only just begun to feel the impact on your seith?"

"Yes. Fluctuations in the past weeks. I've had the best physickers available look at it—save for your Order's precious experts, of course."

"They've already told you the fractures at your neck didn't heal as they should've? And that the injury damaged your seith system?"

"Yes. They said it's seith rot."

"It is. An advanced case." Aurienne touched at the diagnostic image, illuminating parts of it in brighter white. "Fascinating. And incurable."

In the glow of the diagnostic schema, Mordaunt's jaw clenched. "The physickers said you'd be able to help."

"You were lied to," said Aurienne. "I suppose they fancied keeping their heads, given your Order's reputation, so they threw you the most tentative of lifelines and scurried away. Seith degeneration isn't curable."

"They said you dabbled in the Old Ways," said Mordaunt.

Aurienne held back a scoff. Was that what this was about? Was that stupid venture still haunting her? Ridiculous.

"No one dabbles in the Old Ways," said Aurienne. "I've got—I had—an interest in some folklore, nothing more."

"They said you presented something at one of the universities."

Aurienne made a note to find Fordyce and Shuttleworth and make them suffer for their idiocy. "I didn't present anything. I discussed the most nascent of ideas, informally, with colleagues. Did Fordyce and Shuttleworth mention that this was ten years ago?"

"Ten *years*?"

"Yes. It was nothing but a flight of fancy, when I was an inexperienced Haelan only just starting out. I didn't even have a working hypothesis. I abandoned the idea long ago. We're talking about fairy tales."

"What was the flight of fancy?" asked Mordaunt.

"An integration of the Old Ways into modern healing practice. If it's the Old Ways you're interested in, I can give you a list of thirty academics far more versed in them than I. You can go kidnap them."

"Are they looking at applications for curing seith rot?"

"No," said Aurienne. "And neither am I. It was nothing but a thought experiment. An intellectual exercise. A scholarly fantasy at best. Are you seriously telling me you'd subject yourself to an unproven course of treatment informed by the worst parts of folk medicine and wishful thinking?"

A person of moderate intelligence would say no in response to this dire assessment. An imbecile would say yes.

"Yes," said Mordaunt.

Aurienne pursed her lips in the face of this unsurprising confirmation. "Our agreement was for me to heal you to the best of my ability—which does not, I assure you, mean the clinical application of fairy tales."

"What can you do, then?" asked Mordaunt.

"Based on what I've seen tonight—this was only preliminary imaging, mind—your seith system is hanging on by a thread. It's like a disintegrating candle being held up by its wick. You're suffering from a degenerative condition with limited treatment protocols. Normally, I would suggest seith debridement—"

"Seith what?"

"Debridement. The removal of the nonviable tissues—the seith channels and nodes that are already dead—in the hopes of stemming the progress of the disease. In a case as extensive as yours, it would disrupt your channels completely, and you'd no longer be able to use your seith at all."

Mordaunt's mouth was set in an unhappy line. "Not an option, then, is it?"

"It is for most," said Aurienne. "Losing your seith should be the least of your worries. The degeneration won't stop there. It'll progressively affect your nervous system, then your circulatory system. Did the physickers not tell you? This disease is fatal. Are your limbs numb?"

"They didn't—it's *what*? Yes, they are."

"Torpraxia." Aurienne nodded. "It's already too late for debridement."

Mordaunt ran an agitated hand through his hair. "Too late? I'm just going to die? What can I do?"

"Put your affairs in order," said Aurienne.

"Your bedside manner could use some work."

"Something about being coerced into healing a Fyren erodes my sympathy," said Aurienne. "Also, there's no bed. I can buy you a bit of time. I can't say how much."

"I don't want bought time," said Mordaunt. "I don't want to slow the inevitable. I want to reverse the rot."

"Can't be done," said Aurienne. "What's dead is dead."

"The Old Ways hypothesis."

"Unviable."

"Do it."

"I practise evidence-based healing. You're asking me to attempt something on the basis of misplaced hope."

"And your research."

Aurienne, with additional slowness given that Mordaunt was so thick, repeated: "It wasn't research. It wasn't a hypothesis. It was a young Haelan's daydream."

"Apply your daydream to me, then."

"It won't work."

"Have you tried it?" asked Mordaunt.

"No," said Aurienne.

"So you haven't any *evidence* that it won't work."

Mordaunt sat back in satisfaction, as though he had just committed a masterful rhetorical stroke. Aurienne pressed a fingertip to the bridge of her nose.

However. The man's fixation on this worthless course of treatment presented an opportunity. It wouldn't work. He would die. Her Order already had his money.

Aurienne stared at the Fyren and pondered the sacrifice of her professional ethics in light of these excellent outcomes.

Mordaunt cocked his head at her. There was smugness in it. He thought he had argued her into a corner.

Perhaps the most painful part of this ordeal would be dealing with the man's stupidity.

"Fine," said Aurienne.

"Fine?" repeated Mordaunt.

"Yes. I'll do it."

Mordaunt, suspicious, asked, "Why did you change your mind?"

"Your argument was so thoughtful. So well reflected."

Mordaunt tapped a gloved finger against a thigh. "Was that sarcasm?"

Aurienne waved the query away. "If we're going to do this, I need to examine you properly, with the right instruments—and *not* in a byre."

"Where, then?" asked Mordaunt. "We can't be seen."

"So you've said. How have you kept the physickers silent?"

"My steward is adept at the brewing of paramnesiac teas," said

Mordaunt. "Though, given their exaggeration of your research, I'm wondering if I oughtn't have killed the physickers outright."

"Please don't. We've already got a dearth of physickers."

Mordaunt did not look as though he was considering Aurienne's wishes in this matter. He replaced his collar and knotted his cravat. His gestures were oddly elegant, the movements of a sophisticate, rather than a murderer. Everything about him was polished, actually—his clothes, his mannerisms, his speech. And then there were the scars— and the profession—marring it all. Strange contradictions.

Aurienne didn't care enough about him to ponder them further.

"My Order hosts clinics in rural areas," said Aurienne. "I should be able to find a quiet facility that isn't knee-deep in manure."

"You exaggerate," said Mordaunt. "This was ankle-deep at worst. No Wardens at these clinics?"

"I'm usually accompanied by, at the very least, a Swanstone guard when out in the community. Xanthe and I will concoct a pretext for me to go alone."

Mordaunt drew his hood over his head and became the thing of shadow again. The sight of his cloaked silhouette, so knavish, so Dusken, sparked fresh animosity in Aurienne.

In a patronising tone, of the sort one might take with one's domestic staff, Mordaunt said, "See that you do. I expect your deofol shortly."

This served only to reaffirm Aurienne's opinion that he was not only a hateful Fyren but also a monumental twat.

"It won't be shortly," said Aurienne. "You've asked me to apply a hypothesis that doesn't exist to cure a condition that can't be cured. I'm going to spend hours sorting through archival material to piece together whatever I preserved of that project, and even more hours preparing some sort of treatment protocol based entirely on fairy stories. You'll hear from me when you hear from me."

Mordaunt made no indication that he had been chastened. Instead, he gave Aurienne a bow, and said, "I await your deofol at your pleasure, then."

"I can assure you there is no pleasure involved," said Aurienne.

"I do agree with you there," said Mordaunt.

AURIENNE'S NEXT MEETING WITH XANTHE BEGAN WITH A REQUEST FOR an update on Mordaunt, whom Xanthe had taken to calling Onion Boy.

"That's what he wants you to do?" said Xanthe when Aurienne had explained the substance of her exchanges with the Fyren. "Heal seith rot? Who does he think you are? The goddess Frīa herself? I thought he merely had a blocked node, or something else nice and treatable."

"His degeneration is extensive," said Aurienne. "And, of course, he's a Fyren, so he's rejected all the usual management protocols, because the loss of his seith represents the loss of his livelihood and his life."

"You told him it was impossible?"

Aurienne nodded. "Repeatedly. Unfortunately, he got wind of an old investigation of mine. Do you remember my work on the Monafyll Stone?"

Xanthe clasped her hands before her. "I *do* recall that project. One of your first forays as a principal investigator after earning your Haelan wings. I always thought it was a pity you'd abandoned that line of enquiry. There was something hopeful about it. Quaint."

"Disastrous, rather," said Aurienne. "An impossible dataset, a methodology best described as madness, experimental design so poor that I would've been rejected by every board from here to Pednathise Head, zero reproducibility—anyway, that's what he wants me to try on him."

"The man is bonkers." Xanthe's mouth, so wrinkled that it almost disappeared into itself, widened as she cackled.

"He's drowning and he's clutching at straws," said Aurienne.

"Onion Boy, the Eternal Optimist."

"I'll go through the motions and let the thing follow its inevitable course. His seith will stop flowing in a matter of months. The neuro-degeneration has already set in."

Xanthe observed Aurienne with something thoughtful in her black eyes. "That is one means of proceeding."

"What's the alternative?" asked Aurienne.

"Giving this a real go. Don't just go through the motions. This is ideal from an experimental perspective, isn't it? You can test your idea completely off the books, without passing it through any of the usual bureaus or research ethics boards, on a willing subject who is entirely disposable."

"But—but the research ethics boards exist for a reason—"

"He's a desperate Fyren, and you've just said you're going to let him die. Are research ethics really a part of the equation?"

A fair point, really, and so Aurienne tried a different tack: "Right— but there's also a reason I'd abandoned the idea. It's not sound science. It's not viable. It was a fantasy."

"It wasn't viable then," said Xanthe. "You've got ten years of experience as a researcher under your belt now."

"Ten years doesn't change the fact that this will literally involve sitting next to rivers at the full moon and saturating him with my seith."

"That's the methodology?"

"That's it."

"Not ideal," said Xanthe. "But if you discover that we can effect miraculous cures by sitting in the muck next to a river at the full moon, you'll be well on your way to an early retirement."

"I don't want an early retirement," said Aurienne.

"Aurienne?"

"Yes?"

"The man has paid us twenty million thrymsas for the privilege of having you apply your unviable fantasy to his case. Give it to him. It's his dying wish."

There was an undercurrent of command in Xanthe's otherwise casual tone. The time for argument was over.

Aurienne bowed her head. "Yes, Haelan Xanthe."

"Now, go put the *re* in *research*, and try, try again."

Onion Boy, His Travails and Misfortunes

Osric

It took the Haelan a week to give Osric a sign of life. His tācn tingled with the arrival of her deofol while he was ensconced in an armchair that wasn't his, wiping blood that wasn't his off a knife that also wasn't his.

He had just murdered a little Wessexian lordling at the behest of one of the Kentish queen's men. Most people wished for peace among the perpetually skirmishing Tīendoms; the Fyren Order prayed for war. It was far more lucrative.

Osric recognised Fairhrim's glassy, cold seith immediately. He flashed his tācn at the ground, and her deofol came through. It took the form of a white, red-eyed creature unlike anything Osric had ever seen before. It looked like someone had a vague idea of what cats, foxes, and weasels looked like, and lumped them all together into one animal.

Most deofols were nebulous creatures of seith. Not so with Fairhrim's. She had (rather impressively, it had to be said) rendered every whisker and hair on the thing.

The deofol floated past the corpse at Osric's feet with a critical sort of sniff and said, "You're the Fyren, then."

Not only was Fairhrim's seith control such that she could render whiskers; it was so powerful that her deofol had physical weight. Osric learned this when the creature leapt into his lap and found his bladder with all four paws in a single concussive blow.

"You pointy-footed bugger," gasped Osric.

"That's a messy kill," said the deofol, jutting its chin towards the body.

"My client wished to send a message," said Osric.

"Was the message *I don't know where the jugular is and had to stab him twelve times to find it*?" asked the deofol.

So Fairhrim's deofol was as irritating as she was. No surprises there.

"When I want a—a cat-weasel's opinion on my work, I'll ask for it," said Osric.

"I'm a genet," said the cat-weasel. "An albino genet. Aurienne was right. You *are* stupid."

"Insult me again and I'll have your head."

"You'd be in possession of at least twice the amount of brains, then," said the deofol. "Perhaps I should let you. It would be the charitable thing."

If the creature hadn't been made of seith, Osric would've snatched it by the scruff of its neck, but he couldn't snatch it any more than he could grab Fairhrim's seith.

"Aurienne has found a place for you to meet," said the deofol. "Take a waystone to the Princess and the Fool in Hessilhead. You'll see signs for a clinic for acute buttock folliculitis."

"A clinic for what?"

"Spotty bums," said the deofol. "Follow the signs. Aurienne will be there."

"When?"

"Now," said the deofol.

"Now?" repeated Osric. "I'm in the middle of something."

"Now," said the deofol again. "She won't wait for you."

It disappeared in a puff of white fur and did not hear Osric's choicest swear words.

Osric, provoked, took the nearest waystone to the designated pub. First, he was at nobody's beck and call, least of all this priggish Haelan's. Second, it was broad daylight, and he hated operating in broad daylight. Third, between the name of the pub and the signs for a clinic for spotty bums that he was now following through this gods-forsaken little hamlet, he rather felt that she was taking the piss.

The villagers puttering about gave Osric startled looks as he stalked through the hamlet's streets, his hood up, his greatcoat flaring behind him.

What part of *my condition mustn't be discovered* hadn't this idiot understood?

He found the final spotty-bum sign and knocked upon the clinic door.

The idiot opened the door.

Fairhrim's greeting consisted of a look. There was a lot in it; she looked at Osric as though he were a wart that had acquired sufficient sentience to knock on doors.

"Are you bloody serious?" asked Osric.

Fairhrim, taken aback by the wart's rudeness, straightened. "Excuse me?"

"Summoning me? In broad daylight? In a public place? I told you that my condition mustn't be discovered."

"It hasn't been discovered," said Fairhrim. "You're hooded up like death personified. And anyone who did see you will think you're suffering from folliculitis."

Osric pointed at one of the overly detailed posters that had haunted his walk. "You had to choose arse acne?"

"To guarantee us privacy," said Fairhrim. She held the door open. "Get in."

Osric stepped into the tired little consultation room. The place was lit with new electric lights far too bright for his liking. There was an examination table against the wall. Miscellaneous medical paraphernalia was scattered about, looking both curative and foreboding, rather like Fairhrim herself.

Her travelling cloak was clasped shut with a silver wing. She removed it to reveal her stiff Haelan dress, high about the neck and impeccably white, save for the sharp silver epaulettes.

"Also," said Osric, removing his own cloak, "I'm not at your beck and call. Don't summon me like this again."

Fairhrim grew rigid. She turned to him and spoke with a false sort of brightness. "Oh? And I'm at yours, am I? You can impose meetings on me, in abandoned barns, at midnight, without offering me any kind of alternative, but meeting during perfectly normal hours under a perfectly well-thought-out pretext in a perfectly suitable location presents difficulties, does it? I showed your schedule the same respect you showed mine; didn't you like it?"

She fixed him with a Look. Osric developed a new understanding of what *gimlet-eyed* meant.

Osric decided not to die on this particular hill. "Perhaps we can each make improvements to our scheduling habits when it comes to the other's calendar."

"A compromise?" asked Fairhrim.

"Yes," said Osric, assuming that this was a positive thing.

It was not. Fairhrim sniffed in Osric's direction, as though manure from the barn still wafted from him. "I've compromised enough just being here today. But, nevertheless, we can compromise. Now, disrobe."

"I—what?"

"Disrobe," repeated Fairhrim. Then, slower: "Remove your clothes. There are gowns in the cupboard. I'll be back in a minute."

She left the room before Osric could make an argument. Nudity in the face of her ongoing animosity felt unwise. But refusal felt—well, pathetic. She was only a Haelan and she was by herself.

Was she by herself? What if she came back with a Warden when he was stark bollock naked? She reeked of hostility.

He would keep his weapons close at hand.

Osric began to undress. This was no small task. After much unclipping, unbelting, and unstrapping, he removed the following inventory from his person: twelve throwing knives, his blaecblade, two backswords, one amputator, and, finally, a dozen syringes and vials containing substances as nasty as they were illegal.

These items he placed upon the examination table with care.

He was less precious about his clothes: waistcoat, shirt, collar, cravat, trousers, underthings, and boots were all tossed towards a chair.

Osric opened the cupboard to discover that the gowns were, judging by their colour and size, intended for little girls, rather than men who liked to cultivate an air of sinister elegance.

He pulled a faded pink thing on, which, when placed over his head, left his dangly bits exposed.

He decided to wrap the gown around his hips like some sort of kilt.

Thus attired, he leaned against a cabinet, looking as suave as one could in a strip of puce-coloured linen, to await Fairhrim's return.

He felt, once again, that Fairhrim was taking the piss. No one took the piss out of Osric Mordaunt with this level of frequency and nonchalance. She was lucky that she was necessary to him at this moment; he would've murdered her for the cheek otherwise.

The Means to an End knocked, and her crisp voice asked, "Ready?"

"Yes," said Osric. Should the Haelan have brought company to attack him while he was naked, he had throwing knives threaded between his fingers.

Fairhrim swept into the room. Her hard eyes passed over Osric and rested on his knife-bristling fists.

"Really?" was her unimpressed comment. "I can assure you that if I'd planned any harm to you, it would've happened already."

Well. That was cocky.

"You've got a high opinion of yourself," said Osric.

"Deserved, I assure you," said Fairhrim. She jutted her chin towards his gown. "That is quite the ensemble."

"Fetching, isn't it?"

"Did you try the adult cupboard?" asked Fairhrim.

"What adult cupboard?" asked Osric.

"The one you're sitting on."

"Oh," said Osric.

(He had not tried the adult cupboard.)

Fairhrim advanced into the room with a critical air that made Osric feel like he was back in the barracks as a young Fyren, awaiting his warchief's inspection.

"We're going to need the examination table, if you wouldn't mind moving this"—Fairhrim made an impatient gesture towards Osric's weapons—"mess of an arsenal."

Osric moved his things under Fairhrim's watchful eye and sat upon the table.

"Is there a single inch of you that isn't covered in scar tissue?" she asked.

Osric looked down at himself—at his chest, decorated by reminders of various blades; at his forearms, ridged by burns; at his shins, scattered with memories of a long-ago explosion.

"There is," said Osric. "A few inches, actually. Under the kilt."

Fairhrim, who had no sense of humour, said aridly, "Spare me further details."

"These scars mark the hazards of my Order," said Osric. "We haven't got fancy Haelan at hand to fix things."

"If your Order wasn't so dead set on the mercenary, my Order might have come to an understanding with yours centuries ago. But we digress."

Fairhrim dragged a large sack out of a wardrobe.

"What's that?" asked Osric.

"Your body bag," said Fairhrim.

So she did have a sense of humour. Dry, though. Very dry.

Osric expressed some doubts that his corpse would fit. Fairhrim pulled the sack open to reveal mysterious contraptions. She excavated one from the bottom and dusted it off. Osric recognised it as a small Curie machine.

She rolled the rickety machine into place next to Osric. Her arm brushed his. It was one thing for people to approach him when they didn't know that he was a Fyren—he was, after all, strikingly good-looking and magnetically charismatic—but when they did know what he was, they stayed well clear. There was no brushing of arms. Except from Fairhrim, who, apparently, feared nothing.

"Right," said Fairhrim. "We'll begin with some imaging. I'd much rather be using our equipment at Swanstone, but, given the circumstances, this will have to do."

"Why are we using machines? Why aren't you doing the, you know?" said Osric, with explanatory mystical gestures.

"Because live diagnostics are extremely seith intensive," said Fairhrim. "I'll be able to examine these images at my leisure—and not waste my seith on the likes of you. Stop talking, and don't move."

She aimed the machine at Osric's neck, which was not a sensation he enjoyed. There was the flash of her tācn as she powered up the machine with a surge of seith into its capacitor. It blinked into life with gleeful whirring. Then came brisk snaps, so close to Osric's throat that he almost flinched.

Fairhrim switched off the lights and projected grainy images from the Curie machine onto a wall. She stood before the images and studied them in silence.

Stillness reigned in the clinic. Osric found himself watching Fairhrim's tall figure with something disgustingly like hope. For a hint that, perhaps, everything wasn't as bad as she had said it was. For an indication that the rot wasn't rot, and that it would be reversible. For a bit of good news.

Fairhrim stood in the pale light with a finger and thumb at her chin. She did not move, save for her eyes, which flicked along the image on the wall. Her brows were drawn together. Her cheekbones were prominent in the dim light.

Her precise voice broke the silence and skewered Osric's hope.

"Pulverised," said Fairhrim.

"What?" said Osric.

"Your cervical spine. And the healing—such as it was—frankly, appalling. They put your bones back together like a child smashing puzzle pieces together. They damaged your seith channels in the process, and the deterioration set in from there. You would've been a candidate for a nodeplasty on the affected seith channels. But no. Instead, we've got this cack-handed mess to deal with. Talk to me about the numbness."

"It's mostly my hands," said Osric. "It's starting to go up my arms. Hasn't had an impact on my dexterity, though."

"Good," said Fairhrim. "Your lovely colleagues haven't noticed anything, then."

"No. I'd be under watch if they had. We cull the weak."

Fairhrim's expression turned sanctimonious. "I don't understand why one would dedicate one's life to so cruel an Order."

"Money," said Osric.

Quite impressive, how Fairhrim could pack all her moral repugnance into a glance.

She wheeled away the Curie machine and swabbed Osric's neck with some pungent liquid. He felt the cold burn of antiseptic.

"Phenol?" asked Osric.

"Hlutoform," said Fairhrim. "A broad-spectrum bactericide, virucide, and fungicide. A colleague of mine developed it for use in her operating theatre. It's used all over the Tīendoms now."

She pulled a second machine from the sack of contraptions. "Franklin diffractor," she explained. "It'll let me examine your seith fibres."

All her machines seemed to enjoy being aimed at vulnerable spots. This one made a sort of chuckling sound as Fairhrim pressed a tubelike protrusion to Osric's bare chest. She attached other bits on long wires to his shoulders, his back, and his knees.

"Don't move," said Fairhrim again, as Osric felt himself about to be lanced at point-blank range by the giggling machine.

On the wall, the pictures of his bones were replaced by a shining network of lines, vaguely in the shape of a man.

Again Fairhrim studied the images in silence, interrupted only by her snapped "Stay still" when Osric dared take in too deep a breath.

And again, Osric found himself studying her as she studied him, looking for a sign that things were not All That Bad.

Fairhrim was quick to ruin it.

"It's bad," said Fairhrim. She pointed to lines that shimmered white. "Intact." She then indicated lines speckled with black. "Damaged by seith degeneration, commonly known as seith rot."

Many of the lines projected onto the wall were black, emanating from a cluster at the base of the figure's neck. It was a sobering sight.

Fairhrim pressed some buttons on the diffractor, which brought the seith fibres into even sharper relief. She measured things with silver instruments and made notes in a chart. "The numbness you're experiencing is called torpraxia. It's what happens when decaying seith fibres interact with your nerves. It's normally more pronounced in extremities."

She ran her finger up and down Osric's limbs, as well as his back and chest, and took note of where his numbness began and ended.

"Can't you simply—simply push a bit of seith into those rotted lines? Like you do when you're healing wounds?" asked Osric.

A stupid question, probably. Yes—confirmed by the look Fairhrim levelled at him.

She gathered together enough small words to explain it to him. "No. We cannot simply *push a bit of seith* into those lines. We are talking about one of the most delicate, and poorly understood, structures in the human body. Unlike in the nervous system, we've never managed to trigger the activation of latent circuits in a degenerating seith system, or the genesis of new channels. There is no plasticity—no regeneration. Grafting attempts fail. Transplants fail. What's dead stays dead."

Fairhrim traced a blackened line on the wall with a fingertip. "There have been hundreds of experimental studies and trials—by me, by my Order before me, by universities, by physickers and chirurgeons. All of them have failed. There is no clinically validated treatment for seith degeneration—only speculative hypotheses, including mine, which I very much regret having shared at this particular moment." Irrelevantly, she added, "Lucky your tācn is on your left palm."

Only walkers of the Dusken Paths had their tācn on their left palms; Osric therefore failed to see why this pleased Fairhrim among her otherwise dismal accounting. "Er—why?"

"Those lines are relatively untouched by the degeneration. It's why you're still able to use your seith. The fluctuations you mentioned will get worse, however." Fairhrim pointed at a place near the figure's armpit. "Your decline will accelerate once these nodes deteriorate."

Osric stared at the figure projected on the wall, crisscrossed with its rotted black lines. Now he tasted sickness; now he tasted the bitterness of despair. He wanted to throw a knife into the figure's head. He wanted to crash the stupid chuckling Franklin diffractor into the floor. He wanted to put a hand to Fairhrim's throat and make her say what he wanted to hear, rather than these terse truths.

He didn't want to die.

"Normally I'd hold your hand and say some gentle things about how difficult this must be to hear," said Fairhrim, "but I'd rather not waste my breath making a Fyren feel better."

There were, at least, no worries about things getting mopey.

"Good," said Osric. "Don't bother. I'm downright cheerful. Because you've got a speculative hypothesis, and you're going to test it out on me, and it's going to work."

Fairhrim gave him a look that was equal parts haughtiness and irritation. "It isn't. It's a waste of time. Given that I won't be able to monitor your progress through regular visits at Swanstone, I'd like to put seith markers in you. Is that all right?"

"Why wouldn't it be all right?"

"It's not a common practice anymore. They're painful to insert. And we have much better instruments to monitor progress now—but you can't exactly visit me at Swanstone daily."

"Do it, then."

"It's going to hurt," said Fairhrim.

"Have you seen my scars?"

"Very well," said Fairhrim. She pressed her tācn to his shoulder. "I'm going to put eight throughout your system."

Her seith flared as she pressed in the first marker. It did, indeed, hurt—a potent, lingering, stinging pain, as of a thick needle jutting into the most tender parts of Osric's seith channels. Eight times, eight deeply unpleasant times, Fairhrim stabbed her markers in. Out of sheer machismo, Osric did not flinch as she worked her way to his forearm, up his back, and down his legs.

He did not complain. He merely perspired.

Fairhrim observed him with mild approval before removing a third contraption from the wardrobe. Osric hoped that she hadn't noticed the bead of sweat trickling down between his shoulder blades.

"Another machine?" asked Osric.

"Yes. I'm going to give you an overview of my speculative hypothesis, so that you understand what foolishness you're asking us to embark on."

"That's a Lovelace engine," said Osric, recognising the newfangled thingy.

"Well done."

"I do pride myself on not being a complete idiot."

"Do you?"

Fairhrim sounded genuinely surprised. Osric fantasised about throttling her for the second time in so many minutes.

Fairhrim pressed her tācn to the engine. It beeped into life. Osric stewed in his annoyance.

The figure on the wall with the rotted seith lines disappeared. It was replaced by a diagram of an oblong, grimy-looking stone adorned with vertical inscriptions.

"You've heard of the Monafyll Stone, of course," said Fairhrim.

"No," said Osric.

Fairhrim blinked at him. On her otherwise imperturbable countenance, it was an expression of astonishment. "I suppose I oughtn't be shocked. It was only the greatest archaeological discovery of the century, but it's got nothing to do with murders or money and therefore wouldn't be of interest to you."

"Thank you," said Osric. "You're growing to understand me."

The prospect of such a rapprochement did not seem to enthuse Fairhrim. "A brief history lesson, then. The Monafyll Stone is believed to be at least five centuries old. At first glance, it appears to be nothing more than a lunar calendar, naming each of the year's full moons. The appellations may be familiar to you; some of the nomenclature is still in use."

Beside the drawing of the Stone, a list appeared:

- Hrímfrost (Hoarfrost) Moon
- Hyngre (Hunger) Moon
- Cúsc (Chaste) Moon
- Hara (Hare) Moon
- Blædnes (Blooming) Moon
- Begbéam (Bramble) Moon

- Hunig (Honey) Moon
- Thunor (Thunder) Moon
- Bédríp (Harvest) Moon
- Meodu (Mead) Moon
- Gnyrn (Mourning) Moon
- Endeláf (Last) Moon

"Scholars aren't in agreement on the Monafyll Stone's purpose, but they do agree that it's more than just a lunar chart. You notice these marks?" Fairhrim pointed at divots on the outside edge of the Stone.

"A worm?" hazarded Osric. "A chicken?"

"A serpent and a swan," said Fairhrim. "And these—herbs, a pestle, a potion, and, here at the bottom, a healing hand. Typical healing iconography—but it's unusual to find it superimposed on a lunar calendar. The number seven is marked in several places. Scholars have suggested that this depicts some kind of healing path, or pilgrimage, or ritual, to be followed at the full moon."

"So it *is* about the Old Ways," said Osric. "Have we got to dance about in henges?"

There was hauteur in the tilt of Fairhrim's chin. "If it were that simple to achieve wonder cures, don't you think everyone would be doing it?"

"What are those lines?" asked Osric, pointing at curling marks carved along the moons down the Stone's centre.

"Possibly decorative elements. Possibly natural erosion. Possibly an unknown variant of a dead language. One philologist has proposed that it may be one of the fairy tongues." Fairhrim looked as though the notion offended her. "Of course, that idea isn't well received by academics. Ultimately, whatever this Stone represented—if it was, indeed, a heretofore undiscovered mode of healing—has been lost to time. We have no directions other than the list of moons and these healing motifs. Ten years ago, an enterprising young Haelan decided to explore the matter further—unfortunately."

"Fortunately," corrected Osric.

Fairhrim did not agree, as evinced by her pinched nostrils. She tapped at the Lovelace engine. The Monafyll Stone disappeared. What followed was a rapid-fire sequence of images: pages from books, lines of poetry, snippets of fairy stories, scrawls on birch bark, transcripts of long-ago conversations between long-dead people. Fairhrim flipped through these items with curt commentary; they were all tales of miraculous healings at the full moon.

"All unsubstantiated," Fairhrim hastened to add. "A fine collection of apocrypha, really. But, nevertheless, a considerable number of accounts. Full-moon healings are a recurring motif throughout our history, from our children's stories to our theologies. The Monafyll Stone's discovery was regarded as nothing more than a contribution to this motif by most scholars. Rightfully so. The full moon's alleged potencies have been the subject of enquiry over centuries now, and the results have always been failure. But I—overexcited, naive girl that I was—thought I could do better."

Fairhrim, standing perfectly upright, with her hair compressed into the most severe of buns, and her starchy dress buttoned up to her throat, did not look like she had ever been an overexcited girl in her life.

"The Stone's discovery and its explicit connection between the moons and healing spurred me on to investigate whether or not there was a grain of truth in the miracle tales," she continued. "I wanted to analyse the apocrypha and seek out commonalities. Patterns. Recurrences too strange to be coincidence."

"And? Did you find those things?" asked Osric.

A shallow sigh escaped Fairhrim. "I found problems. Acquiring all of these sources, and translating them where necessary, cost a fortune, of course."

"I'm involved now. Cost is no longer a factor," said Osric—generously, he thought.

Fairhrim did not agree. Judging by the clench of her jaw, she thought it, on the contrary, unseemly. "Do you simply buy or kill your way out of every difficulty life presents you?"

"I use the resources at my disposal," said Osric. "You should, too."

"Resources as blood drenched as yours cross certain ethical bounds."

"Your ethical bounds keep you so confined, it's a wonder you can move."

"I don't know how *you* move, given the weight of your sins."

They glared at each other. Fairhrim was all edges: dark eyes piercing, lips pressed thin.

She said, "Shall we return to the topic at hand?"

Osric said, "Let's."

Fairhrim continued her explanation in a clipped voice. "I'm not one for qualitative analyses but I hadn't any choice with this particular dataset, if I can be so bold as to call this hotchpotch that. I began to capture and code anything that seemed even marginally relevant—names, places, times, seasons, ailments, demographics—and created this monster."

Now projected onto the wall was an enormous diagram segmented by tables within tables, and arrows and labels, and large red question marks scattered about. The healers purported to have brought about the full-moon cures were a varied lot: wisewomen, Druids, witches, alchemists, physickers, fairy folk, the gods themselves. The places were equally varied: barrows, wells, crossroads, hill forts, death roads, mountaintops, ponds, islands, doorways, spirit-ways. The diagram also captured moments—sunrise and sunset, high noon, midnight—season, weather, and, finally, which of the twelve full moons was in the sky, if the source indicated it at all. The diagram was populated to bursting with data on probabilities, scales assessing the validity of the sources, odds ratios, recurrences, confidence intervals, and replicability.

If this was only the beginning, it was massively impressive, though Osric would rather eat his puce gown than say so to Fairhrim.

She herself, however, did not seem to think so. She swept a disdainful hand towards the data. "The only meaningful thing I was able to draw from the mess was the importance of place, and the importance of time, for these alleged healings. And the most irritating part is that I needn't have gone to all this trouble, because the importance of those things is reiterated time and time again in any children's book, or folktale, or fairy story."

Fairhrim pulled an actual children's book out of her satchel and thrust it in Osric's direction as though it were a weapon. She snapped it open and leafed through it, her finger pressing into the soft, fanciful illustrations as she went. "Thin places. Between places. Places where the stitches between our world and the Otherworld fray. Crossroads. Places at the edges of things."

She came to a painting of a sunrise. "And times at the edges, too. Dusk or dawn. Or moments between things—between the calm and the storm, between tidal shifts, between winter and spring. And, of course, the common factor is the full moon, which is when all of the most spectacular of these alleged healings occur—but, for all we know, it's merely a storytelling flourish."

"The Stone, though," said Osric. "That's real."

"The Monafyll Stone is far more likely to be capturing belief than a real, observable phenomenon," said Fairhrim. "I need you to understand the high likelihood of failure if we pursue this so-called course of treatment."

"Call it an experiment," offered Osric.

His suggestion was not well received. "This poorly conceived enquiry is not an *experiment*. It's an embarrassment. A credibility killer. A career ender—working illicitly with a Fyren notwithstanding. It's a disgrace to this."

Fairhrim held up her tācn. She stared at the swan on her palm as though she were betraying it. "If we had the luxury of a thousand full moons, and a thousand subjects, and a thousand Haelan to heal them, and we could tweak the variables at our leisure, then, perhaps, we could call it an experiment. We can't call it anything but an—an exploratory foray. The variables at play are truly staggering. Reproducibility is low to nil."

Fairhrim's tense shoulders dropped a fraction of an inch, which was, Osric supposed, her best demonstration of despondency. "I told you that this was nothing but a thought experiment. I was curious. I analysed the available data. But, as they say, rubbish in, rubbish out. Looking back now, I'm shocked that I even entertained it for so long. It was doomed to begin with. Some things can't be healed."

"But you're meant to be a seith-system Phenomenon," said Osric. "A genius."

Fairhrim gave him a cool look that informed him that he had offended her. "I am. I can deal with seith lesions, blockages, burst microchannels, wholesale severances. I can heal all seven classes of peripheral seith-fibre injuries. No one can reverse seith rot. But I told you I'd try, so I'll try. We'll follow the Old Ways. We'll go to the places where the boundaries are thin. We'll find in-between times. And I will try to heal you. And if there's a grain of truth in those old tales, perhaps we'll find it."

Osric never learned. There it was again: the flutter of hope, bouncing up past his heart into his throat.

"Where do we begin?"

Fairhrim switched off the Lovelace engine. "I've got a short list of locations—a very short list. Few accounts provide enough geographic detail to allow us to find specific places and retrace the steps of the healers. We'll begin there. I'd much rather proceed with a plan in mind for all twelve moons, but I think, given the advanced state of your condition, we've got no choice but to be rather more ad hoc about it."

Fairhrim looked pained, as though she had never before been ad hoc about anything and it hurt her to be so now.

She consulted a chart. "The next full moon is six days hence. Let's meet then. Waystone at the Shaggy Chimera, five thirty. Unless you've got a murder in the diary?"

This final question was posed with a blandly naive look, which only added to its piquancy.

"I can reschedule the murder," said Osric.

Fairhrim appeared to have views on this. However, her attention was drawn to her tācn. She held her palm up, and the arrival of a deofol interrupted any opining. The deofol took the form of a strange-looking salamander.

"What *is* that?" asked Osric.

"An axolotl," said Fairhrim.

The shabby, wrinkled deofol perched upon Fairhrim's shoulder. "Hello, dear," it croaked. "You're wanted at Swanstone, quick as you can. An entire orphanage was hit with the Pox."

Fairhrim leapt towards her satchel and began to pack it. "On my way."

The axolotl observed Osric with a beady black eye.

"Hello, Onion Boy," said the axolotl. "Nice tutu."

"It's a kilt," said Osric.

But the axolotl had disappeared, leaving Osric speaking to thin air.

"I would've called it a loincloth," said Fairhrim, whose opinion Osric had certainly not asked for, either.

"That was Xanthe's deofol, I assume?" asked Osric. "Looks as moth-eaten as she is."

"Moth-eaten?" repeated Fairhrim. "How dare you? Xanthe is over two hundred years old—"

"How? Did she forget to die?"

"—and you aren't in any shape to insult anyone's physique, I can assure you."

"*Excuse* me?"

Fairhrim made for the door. "I've got to go. I've got real patients to take care of."

Osric made a shooing motion. "Good. Go look after your invalids."

Fairhrim pivoted. "Invalids? You're the most invalid of them all. I've never dealt with such a congenitally weak intellect."

"Watch your insolence. I've cut out tongues for lesser insults."

"You've just insulted me, my patients, and Xanthe, in so many seconds, and *I'm* the insolent one? If anyone should have a glossectomy, it's you, and I would gladly volunteer to perform it."

"A what?"

But Fairhrim was gone. The door snapped closed behind her.

Osric scowled at it, then threw a knife into it for good measure.

What a pity this Haelan was of use to him. She'd be far more tolerable dead.

4

AURIENNE SUFFERS IN NATURE

Aurienne

In addition to managing a Fyren and his irrational expectations, Aurienne was responsible for Swanstone's Centre for Seith Research. She had been bullied into the directorship six months ago by the Heads of her Order in spite of her protestations. Like any researcher worth her salt, Aurienne had outright refused the position, preferring to continue her pursuits in the lab—the noble advancement of knowledge, etc. And, also, she would rather die than do anything involving so much admin.

However, when old Haelan Whiffleby had retired last autumn, the Heads identified Aurienne as his logical successor, because she was ruthlessly organised, always had Things Under Control, and, additionally, everyone was a bit frightened of her. Aurienne argued that these were not leadership qualities, that she was a researcher above all, and also, as previously indicated, she would rather die than deal with admin. A silence had followed this pronouncement, after which the Heads had looked at one another, and Abercorn had said, fine, they would appoint

Murbock-Biddle as Director. This was a distressing suggestion, given that Murbock-Biddle was a cretin. In the face of this underhanded tactic, Aurienne had accepted the directorship and inherited Whiffleby's quarters at the top of the north tower, furnished largely with spiders and spores of mould.

She had also inherited his quotidian serving of problems. Today, an assortment of perfectly resourceful Haelan, suddenly bereft of all *débrouillardise*, approached her with the following issues: There was a leak in the ceiling of Lab 5 and what should they do? They were low on tissue culture media and would she approve another order and please sign these forms to bypass the procurement process because they would be out by tomorrow otherwise? Would she permit a subscription to the following periodicals, which were not relevant to seith research but nevertheless seemed interesting? The chromatography refrigerator wasn't working, and also could they institute a policy on allergens in the Centre because someone almost died because someone else ate a shrimp?

Aurienne's lab was a raft of sanity among the sea of admin. That was where she repaired to—not to say, fled to—presently. Loose hair was not permitted in the lab; she twisted her plait into a bun transversed with a bone curette and instructed it to stay there. (Sometimes her hair obeyed and sometimes it didn't. Life was full of such anxieties.)

She strode into the lab to find a group of apprentices observing a pair of senior apprentices working on her current study. Tentative title: *Evaluating Peripheral Seith Channel Trauma: A Histological Approach.* Not snappy, but eminently informative, which was the greater goal.

The apprentices in their dark grey robes clustered in an anxious knot at the end of a workbench, observing the two older ones. Corinne and Nym were on the cusp of earning their wings, so close to coming into their Haelan whites that their robes were of the palest silver.

Corinne was hunched over a microscope, calling out findings to Nym. "Specimen three: microrupture. Specimen four: episeithial tear.

Specimen five: microrupture. Specimen six: loss of undulation. Specimen seven: episeithial stretch—er, or tear. Oh, Haelan Fairhrim, you're here—what do you think?"

Aurienne peered into the microscope. "At least one seith fibre terminates in a gap. It's a tear. Line up to have a look, you lot."

Thus addressed, the apprentices shuffled into a nervous queue to peer at the specimen.

Corinne scribbled out a note. "The zone of transition between stretch and rupture is so narrow."

"It is," said Aurienne. "That's why six paragraphs of our methodology lay out our quantification process."

The apprentices dispersed and Corinne returned to her place at the microscope. "Specimen eight: microrupture. Specimen nine: loss of undulation. Specimen ten . . ."

When Corinne and Nym had finished, Aurienne ran through their findings. "I'd like you to examine the relationship between the micro-architectural ruptures and injury severity grades. Use Wilcomb's correlation with Hall's correction."

"Yes, Haelan Fairhrim," said Corinne and Nym.

"Have you remarked this interesting pattern of minimal injury to the episeithium and periseithium under acute stretch conditions?" asked Aurienne.

"Erm—no," said Corinne.

"Make a note of it," said Aurienne. She turned to the young apprentices. "You've observed this study from the beginning. Any thoughts on limitations we ought to highlight?"

The apprentices shrank away from her until they hit the worktop, where they coagulated into a petrified blob.

"There are loads worth mentioning," said Aurienne encouragingly, and suggesting, she hoped, that she ascribed their silence to a surfeit of ideas rather than a dearth.

The coagulated apprentices were incapable of voicing opinions on limitations, focusing their efforts instead on looking exactly like young owls. Aurienne turned her enquiring gaze to Corinne and Nym, and it was their turn to coagulate.

"Erm—perhaps I would suggest that our stretch test doesn't accurately mimic real-life injury scenarios," suggested Nym. Nym had the peculiar quality of being always uncertain and yet always right. "Also, we've focused the study on seith fibres extracted from forearms. Seith fibres from other areas may have different biomechanics."

"Very good," said Aurienne. "Include those. I'd also like you to add the boilerplate about any histologic evaluation risking artefacts from handling the tissue. Also indicate that the seith fibres were not in a living organism when subjected to the injury—which, as we know, affects elastance."

While Nym and Corinne scribbled, Aurienne dismissed the younger apprentices. They bowed vigorously with their hands on their hearts and scuttled out.

"How are you two progressing on seith transfers?" asked Aurienne. "I'd like to move on to cadaver workshops in the autumn; I'll have to make the arrangements soon."

"Not well," said Nym.

"I blew up a cantaloupe," said Corinne.

"You've been doing daily practice?" asked Aurienne.

"Yes," said Corinne. (Nym nodded and looked tearful.)

"You mustn't be discouraged," said Aurienne. "You haven't yet got your tācn. Few of us can achieve the required level of seith control without one. I want you both to have a break. No more practice. Two weeks off. We'll start fresh from the basics afterwards."

"Yes, Haelan Fairhrim," came Corinne and Nym's relieved responses. They made their bows and left.

So much for the rational portion of Aurienne's day. Now for the mad portion: tonight was the full moon, and it was time to meet the Fyren.

AURIENNE TOOK A WAYSTONE TO THE SHAGGY CHIMERA FOR THE EVE-
ning's rendezvous. The pub had long shut down; its door swung in the
breeze, accompanied by forlorn squeaking.

A hirsute chimera wound its way across the pub's faded sign, which
had lost several letters, and advised Aurienne thus:

SHAG

HIM

Aurienne received the instruction with hostility.

In the continuing comedy of errors that was her life, she squelched off
into the muck at the edge of the nearby pool, and waited for a murderer.

Her data for March's full moon—when the tales were good enough
to specify—favoured the edges of pools or ponds when it came to place
(eighty-nine percent), and sunset when it came to time (seventy-seven
percent). This particular pool, the Wasdale fairy pool, had been mentioned by name in a work of Cumbrian theology: some archdruid had
managed to cure an ovate of the black fever with nothing but a touch
and a push of seith right where Aurienne stood. It had happened two
centuries ago, on the day of the Cúsc moon, as the sun set.

A lovely tale. Not at all sound science, however, and Aurienne,
hanging about among quagwort and frogbit, felt like a fool. A frazzled,
slightly moist fool.

But it was the day of the Cúsc moon, and the sun was beginning to
dip, and, fool that she was, she would be giving the thing a real go, per
Xanthe's instructions. How had she gone from her lab's rigorous science
to this? She must take care not to injure herself due to methodological
whiplash. (Limitations in the current study: Everyone Has Gone Mad.)

Time ticked on. The Fyren was late, which was, somehow, not a surprise.

Finally, there was movement near the waystone across the pond, and there he was: the murderer.

Spring had sprung in floods of mud. The Fyren picked his way through it with obvious disgust. Aurienne watched his progress without advising him that a path ran the other way round the pool.

The Haelan maxim was *Harm to none*, but private fantasies couldn't be policed, and Aurienne indulged in one involving the Fyren slipping and drowning, and thus putting an end to both of their miseries.

He was regrettably sure-footed.

Mordaunt did not bother to greet Aurienne but rather carried on a muttered commentary as he squelched towards her: "Why isn't there a road? Has anyone been here since the fall of Byzantium? This is gooier than Woden's eye socket."

More whinging than Aurienne had expected from a Fyren. Weren't they meant to be rugged killers? This specimen had the fortitude of wet quiche.

Though the weather was fine, Mordaunt kept his hood up. Aurienne had no objections. She knew what lay underneath—a caustic eye and a vexatious mouth—and missed the sight of neither.

Mordaunt plucked down his cowl, sniffed in her direction, and said, "You smell like death."

"I've been experimenting on seith fibres extracted from human cadavers," said Aurienne.

"I knew it," said Mordaunt, followed by the lofty pronouncement: "I have an extraordinary sense of smell."

It seemed too facile to point out that, indeed, this seemed to be the only sense he had.

"Is that blood?" asked Aurienne.

"Just a bit of battle sweat," said Mordaunt.

"Yours?" asked Aurienne, with a moderate effort to keep the hope from her voice.

"No," scoffed Mordaunt. "What a stupid question."

"Is it? You've taken a few stabs in the course of your career. I've seen the evidence."

Mordaunt waved a hand. "Memories of bygone days. I'm nigh untouchable now. My mark today did make a stabbing attempt—but he only had a spoon."

"A spoon?"

"He was eating yoghurt," said Mordaunt, by way of explanation.

"You—you killed someone while they were eating yoghurt?" asked Aurienne.

"Yes. It was good yoghurt, too."

"You *ate* the yoghurt?"

"After he was dead, yes. He'd hardly touched it. What? What's the matter? Have you mistaken me for someone respectable?"

"Have you any sense of honour whatsoever?"

"No," said Mordaunt. "Anyway, I came here for a healing, not an assessment of my morals. Can we get on with it?"

Aurienne stared at Mordaunt. The shadow under the hood stared back at her.

He was well on his way to dying. There would be one less of him in the world. It would all work out in the end.

It was time to continue this farce of a healing exercise.

Aurienne made a curt gesture to their surroundings. "So—a thin place."

"Does it feel thin to you?" asked Mordaunt.

Aurienne looked around. The sun glinted on the pool. Water gurgled down a smallish waterfall at its far end. Swallows dipped and swooped. Tender grass peeped from black earth. A fat bumblebee investigated her bun.

"No," said Aurienne. "It feels ordinary."

"I thought so, too," said Mordaunt.

"We're here because a fragment of Cumbrian theology mentions a wondrous healing on this very spot, two hundred years ago, at sunset on the day of the Cúsc moon. It's one of few sources that offered the triumvirate of time, place, and moon, and so here we are."

"I trust the Cumbrian theologists," said Mordaunt.

"I don't," said Aurienne. "A few pages later, their recommended remedy for wet gangrene is to suck it out of the affected appendage."

"Wet gangrene?" repeated Mordaunt.

"Yes."

"Sucking?"

"Yes." Aurienne enumerated a few examples for his edification. "Fingers. Toes. A penis, in one unusual instance."

Mordaunt stiffened. "I will vomit yoghurt on you if you continue."

"I would've thought you'd have a strong stomach for this sort of thing: gore and viscera and assorted nastiness."

"Gore, yes; viscera, yes. Gangrene gobjobs, however, are not part of my repertoire."

They waited for the sun to set. The first midges of spring discovered them. Aurienne and Mordaunt swatted them away.

The sun sank a bit lower. Aurienne stood still; Mordaunt shifted from foot to restless foot. Approximately a billion midges deployed their next sortie and decided to hover at nostril height. Aurienne and Mordaunt twitched and slapped at them. The midges left again.

They watched the dance of the swallows.

Suddenly, Mordaunt looked as though he'd experienced a Thought.

"What?" asked Aurienne.

Mordaunt pushed the toe of his boot into the mud and drew out some lines.

"Fancy a game of noughts and crosses?" he asked.

Aurienne stared at him. After the lapse of a suitably lengthy silence to convey how inane she thought this question was, she said, "No."

Mordaunt shrugged and began to play noughts and crosses against himself.

The sun sank a little more. A breeze played across the pool and sent ripples dancing around the reeds. The smell of last autumn's rotting plant matter wafted up from damp earth.

Mordaunt stalemated himself.

The midges came for round three and were beaten back again.

Mordaunt began some impatient pacing along the pool's edge.

The sun reached the skyline at the far end of the field. Finally, the light gentled, softened, and turned golden.

"Hood and neckcloth off," said Aurienne, sanitising her hands.

Mordaunt did as he was told immediately. An improvement from the last time. Good: Aurienne did not like repeating herself.

Under his scars, the Fyren had arranged his features into something neutral, bordering on indifferent. This was belied by the expectant flicking of his gaze from the pool to the setting sun. He really had some level of hope.

The hum of the fat bumblebees quieted. A warbler sang its soul into one last song. The swallows netted the softening skies and faded into gathering dusk. Stillness reigned.

Aurienne, fool that she was, strained her senses for some kind of change as the sun set and they reached the moment between day and night. A shift in the winds, perhaps, or a distant Druidic chanting, or the portentous flight of a murder of crows.

None of these things happened, of course. Everything remained perfectly ordinary.

Mordaunt had removed his neckcloth. There was something of entreaty in his manner, in the way he clasped it between his joined hands, in the way he bowed his pale head as Aurienne came near.

He was tall, but she was tall, too, and found the back of his neck an easy reach. Setting aside her disgust at wasting seith on so vile a creature again, she pressed her tācn to his skin.

Like the rest of him, the skin at Mordaunt's nape was marred. On the diagonal, Aurienne felt the ropiness of a long ridge of scar tissue—the mark of a whip, if she were to guess. Then there was the messiness where the maul had hit him to create the injury that had so damaged his seith system.

Her tācn glowed white between her fingers as she summoned her seith. Mordaunt stood rigid, tense, anticipatory.

Aurienne followed her seith into him and travelled the damaged lines of his seith channels. Deep into his seith system she pushed, through his brachial line into the intercostal, into the subcostal, into the lumbar, and down into the sacral plexus. She lingered longest where the degeneration had set in, at splitting myelin sheaths and deteriorating nodes, along seith channels that were little more than necrotised furrows.

The sun hovered at the edge of the horizon and was, for a moment, both under it and over it, and, for a moment, it was neither day nor night.

The earth tilted. The sun found its vanishing point.

And Aurienne's seith—and all her years of experience, and her finesse, and her control—did nothing at all.

She withdrew from Mordaunt and blinked herself back into the world, into an evening of pale violet.

The full moon had risen.

Mordaunt rubbed at the back of his neck. "Should I feel—different?"

"It didn't work," said Aurienne flatly.

Failure—and embarrassment at having tried something as stupid as this—made her callous. She'd been right. Nothing to be found here but a loss of time and temper.

"It was just like every other attempt at healing seith rot," said Aurienne. "You can't bring dead things back to life."

Mordaunt's jaw was clenched. He had done worse than her: he had hoped in earnest, and his disappointment was all the harsher. He tied his neckcloth on and drew his hood over his head. Now only his mouth was visible, pulled down in a bitter line.

"You thought it'd be that easy?" asked Aurienne.

"With the right combination of place and time and Haelan, I was foolish enough to cherish a hope."

"This process is going to involve a lot of trial and error," said Aurienne. "Mostly error. You'd better get used to it."

Mordaunt was distraught and sulky. To be fair to him—not that he deserved fairness, but Aurienne could be generous—he was going to die.

"Mightn't we make another attempt tonight?" asked Mordaunt. "While the moon is full?"

"The data favours sunset as the best time for this particular moon," said Aurienne. "Anything else will be a waste of time. Not that this wasn't already a waste of time."

"Surely twenty million thrymsas buys me a measly second attempt," said Mordaunt. "Indulge me with one more imposition on your time."

"And squander my seith again? I think not. We can both find better ways to spend the evening."

Aurienne turned towards the waystone, intent on regaining Swanstone and leaving Mordaunt to his doomed hopes.

Gloved fingers caught her sleeve.

Mordaunt, abandoning, with evident pain, all dignity, said, "Please."

Above them hung the full moon—ghastly, beautiful, uplit by the dead sun.

A solitary raven made an arcing trajectory across the sky.

Xanthe had told Aurienne to give the thing a real go.

She had enough seith.

In the face of her unyielding silence, Mordaunt salvaged the shreds of his dignity; his face closed, his earnestness disappeared. He pulled his cowl over his face, became a thing of shadow, and turned away.

Aurienne rustled about in her satchel and pulled out a notebook. "I detest operating in this improvisatory manner"—Mordaunt pivoted—"just titting about the countryside without a plan—"

Mordaunt, seized with sudden liveliness, leapt to Aurienne's side. "Let's tit about. I *love* titting about."

He crowded Aurienne and her notebook, and tried to read over her shoulder.

Aurienne held her notes to her chest until he backed away. "The entire point of my research was to be *systematic* about aligning thin places with in-between moments. About following the data. However, in the face of your insistence, and in the absence of the chance to devise an actual plan—"

Mordaunt asked, with energy, "Where shall we go?"

"My inventory of specific Cúsc moon locations is paltry," said Aurienne. "This pond was my best option. The next best was the most feeble of sources—a single line in an old Dyfedian ballad mentions hot springs that were curative at the Cúsc moon."

"Which hot springs?"

Aurienne consulted her list. "Er . . . it simply said 'the waters at Kentigern.'"

"Let's go," said Mordaunt, striding towards the waystone.

"We don't even know if the springs still exist."

"We're going to find out. I don't know how many full moons I've got left. Come on. Stop dawdling."

The suggestion that Aurienne, of all people, would ever dawdle was as impertinent as it was ridiculous. She picked her way through the wet grass to the other edge of the pond—the one with the path—and beat Mordaunt to the waystone. She waited for him there, bursting with restrained disdain.

Mordaunt, as he approached from the other side, looked preoccupied—but this time, it wasn't because of the mud.

"If I lose my seith, I won't even be able to use waystones anymore."

"Correct," said Aurienne.

"Fuck," said Mordaunt.

Aurienne offered no sympathy.

"You're pitiless with your truths," said Mordaunt.

"You'd prefer the comfort of lies?" asked Aurienne.

This gave Mordaunt pause. "No," he said at length. "There's something stirring about these sincere cruelties of yours."

"Cruelty is your domain, not mine."

Aurienne tugged a well-worn map of the waystone graticule out of her satchel and found the town of Kentigern. "The closest pub will be the Randy Unicorn."

Mordaunt did a double take at her. "The Randy?"

"Yes."

"Ah," said Mordaunt. There was something significant in the syllable. Something amused in its delivery, too.

"What?" asked Aurienne.

"Nothing. Let's go."

Aurienne knew very well that it wasn't nothing, but she didn't wish to give him the satisfaction of her curiosity. They removed their gloves to press their tācn to the waystone. Mordaunt's tācn flared an ugly red. Aurienne despised the sight of the thing. How many had died by that hellhound's ruddy glow? How many innocents?

She looked away, repulsed. Her palm found cool stone. Her own tācn glowed white between her fingers. The waystone awoke. *Mind the gap* flashed. Aurienne and Mordaunt were dragged into the ley line and hurtled towards Kentigern.

The pond dreamed on under the quiet sky.

THEY QUARREL AGAIN

Aurienne

Aurienne had expected Kentigern to be a pretty sort of spa town, something like Bath or Brightbridge Wells. Instead, the waystone spat them into being in an alley that felt markedly seedy.

The sign for the Randy Unicorn swung overhead. Aurienne, peering at the creature in the twilight, could confirm that the unicorn was, indeed, randy. The artist had not been coy about it.

In front of them was the door to the Unicorn, lit on either side by red lanterns. This was not merely a public house, then—this was a brothel.

Two buxom women in low-cut dresses trotted out, and taught Aurienne the real meaning of titting about.

"I suppose we should ask where the hot springs are," said Aurienne.

"I know exactly where they are," said Mordaunt.

"Where?"

"In there," said Mordaunt, pointing at the Randy Unicorn.

"What?"

"They've got really excellent baths. I suppose that's what's left of your long-ago hot springs."

"You've been here?"

"A few times. Best brothel in Dyfed."

Aurienne stared at the door with concern. Under the erect unicorn curled the words *Come one, come all.*

"Don't be frightened," said Mordaunt. "The ladies won't bite, unless you pay them to."

"I'm not frightened of *the ladies*," said Aurienne, stiffening at the very suggestion. "I work with *the ladies* regularly."

"You do?"

"Yes, and they're lovely. My Order runs drop-ins for them. What frightens me is the possibility of being recognised in the company of a Fyren."

"Well, then, put your hood up. Hide your dress. And—slouch a bit, or something. Stop looking so much like a hoity-toity Haelan."

Aurienne (who was not hoity-toity and who found excellent posture to be a virtue) pulled her hood high and arranged her travelling cloak so that it covered her Haelan whites. "And you?"

Mordaunt's answer was cut off by a group of figures exiting the Unicorn. They were all, like him, clad in black, and exuding a general air of villainy.

"Never mind," said Aurienne, given that Mordaunt would fit right into the general miasma of disrepute.

Mordaunt held the door for Aurienne. They entered a foyer, at the front of which was a small shop selling sex toys, contraceptives, enema kits (on offer: a free jar of Laxadaisical, the Carefree Laxative), and novelty sweets (penis lollies, clitoris liquorice).

The foyer was crowded with counters, each of which served different . . . well, Aurienne would call them specialties, based on the signs above them. Behind each counter was a corridor, presumably leading to rooms where these activities took place.

Aurienne squinted at the raunchy signs in the penumbra: this way for women seeking women, this way for women seeking men, this way for whips and chains, this way for groups, this way for—inanimate objects?

Absorbed by a picture of a man vigorously penetrating a boot, Aurienne bumped into a counter. This one was adorned with a painting of a pie.

"Hiya," said the naked, muscular man behind it. "How can we inseminate you today?"

"Erm," said Aurienne, articulately.

Mordaunt seized her by the elbow and pulled her away.

"Sorry, mate," he said to the naked man. "Wrong counter."

The man nodded in friendly understanding. He had the largest penis that Aurienne had ever seen. It nodded, too. Mordaunt steered Aurienne towards the rightmost corridor. The penis all but waved goodbye at them.

"We're here for the baths, not your breeding kink," said Mordaunt.

"That man was remarkably well-endowed," said Aurienne.

"They call him the Clydesdale. Since he's so fascinated you, you can go have a play with him, but only after we've done the healing. Business first."

"Thank you, but no," said Aurienne.

"No?"

"Two words for you: bruised cervix." Aurienne, still watching the Clydesdale over her shoulder, asked, "What do you suppose he does with it when it's not erect?"

"Drapes it round his neck, like a feather boa," said Mordaunt.

He dropped coins into an attendant's hand. "Two tickets for the baths, please."

They proceeded towards the baths by descending a steep stairway leading into a sort of underground spa. Steam rooms and massage rooms opened up on either side of them.

They came across a small group watching a show. The show consisted of a man performing autofellatio. Aurienne had to pause to admire the man's spinal flexion.

"*That* is some impressive lumbar sagittal mobility," said Aurienne.

The man uncorked himself with a pop and said, "Thank you."

Mordaunt stared at Aurienne with a raised eyebrow, but led her onwards without comment.

The air grew steamier as they descended into the bowels of the Unicorn. Finally, they came to a low-ceilinged room lined with curtained-off rooms.

Aurienne assumed that these were for more sex things—privacy booths, perhaps?

However, an attendant came her way, gave her a white towel, and drew her towards one of the booths. Another attendant did the same with Mordaunt.

Aurienne's attendant saw her confusion and offered an explanation: "Oh—is it your first time here? You've got to shower before entering the baths. There's a basket for your clothes. The towel is only for modesty purposes. Please don't take it into the water."

The attendant pulled open the curtain to reveal a shower, which she switched on for Aurienne.

Aurienne glanced at Mordaunt to see how he was taking this turn of affairs. She caught a twist of amusement across his scarred lips before he disappeared behind his own curtain. So he thought this was funny, did he? He was having a grand time, was he? That was fine. She would soon be putting a damper on his mood with another failed healing. Let the Fyren enjoy himself while he could; he was a dead man walking.

Her mood bolstered by the thought of Mordaunt's inevitable demise, Aurienne showered. She tucked her telltale Haelan dress and satchel at the very bottom of the basket and passed it to the attendant.

Aurienne exited the shower wrapped in the Modesty Purposes

towel. It offered the barest covering of tit and arse. The amiable attendant offered her a hooked stick with various protrusions, which she said
was for trigger-point massages. Aurienne took it, grateful to have something to hold to hide the tācn on her palm.

Mordaunt waited for her at the entrance of the baths, dripping wet
and wrapped in his own towel.

Aurienne was no stranger to communal bathing, which was the norm
at Swanstone. The prospect of a shared soak with a Fyren, however, was
as novel as it was unattractive. She knew, rationally, that his moral deg-
radation couldn't leech into the waters and infect her, but the notion of
stewing together was nevertheless repugnant.

Mordaunt asked how he looked. Aurienne didn't answer, given that
he was addressing a large looking glass, for whose benefit he ran his
fingers through his wet hair and adjusted his towel lower on his hips.
However, she discovered that the query had been directed at her when
he turned to her and said, "Hello?"

Aurienne swept a look of assessment his way. The Fyren's state of
undress revealed agreeable proportions: a well-developed chest, shapely
calves, lines from shoulder to foot suggesting grace and athleticism. But
he dripped with moral obscenities as well as water, and Aurienne would
not be contributing to his smugness by conceding any of it. He was a
Fine Specimen in the way an abscess might be a Fine Specimen; the
best, most shapely, most beautiful abscess in the world still brimmed
with foulness and ought to be incised and drained.

As her kindly attendant was passing by, Aurienne opted for civility
and said that Mordaunt was Not Objectionable.

"Not objectionable?" repeated Mordaunt. *"Not objectionable?"*

She had vexed the Abscess, who remarked, ulceratively, that she
looked like a lost water diviner with her stupid stick, before leading the
way towards the baths.

Aurienne studied the scars that bisected his back amid lean muscle.

Harm to none aside, if one were to add to the tapestry, most of the lines required to spell *TWAT* were already there; it wanted only two diagonals.

The baths consisted of five pools scattered among natural rock formations. The area was lit with sputtering gas lamps. Steam hovered over the water, accompanied by a whiff of sulphur. The air was hard to breathe; Aurienne's lungs felt as though they were filling with moisture. Her hair, pinned into its usual bun, came to life and sprang curious tendrils out to palpate the atmosphere.

Here and there, through the steam, she could make out the heads of other patrons, bobbing in the water.

An attendant pointed at a sign as they walked in:

NO SEX IN THE BATHS.
PLEASE KEEP YOUR SECRETIONS TO YOURSELF.

As they passed the sign, Aurienne saw a handwritten addition below it, which someone had attempted to scrub out. It remained faintly legible: *No one wants to swim in your jizz, Scrope.*

Then, below that: *Too late.*

Aurienne shuddered.

Mordaunt led the way to one of the farthest pools, empty save for a couple at one end, having a cuddle under an attendant's watchful eye.

"Right," said Mordaunt, "this'll do."

Without further warning, he removed his towel. Aurienne was able to look away before receiving yet another eyeful of unsolicited penis. Aurienne enjoyed penises and vulvas equally, but penises seemed, as a general rule, more prone to unasked-for exposures, which was too bad, because they weren't as pretty as vulvas—except, perhaps, for the glossy candied ones in the shop upstairs.

Mordaunt splashed into the water and said, "Fuck me, that's hot."

Between the Fyren, the heat, and Scrope's sperm, Aurienne didn't wish to make such a wholehearted plunge. She opted to sit on the edge of the bath, Modesty Towel held firmly around the important bits, and test the water with a tentative foot.

"Aren't you coming in?" asked Mordaunt, from somewhere behind a cloud of steam.

"This is boiling," said Aurienne.

"Don't be a coward," said Mordaunt.

"I'll faint."

"Was the healer in the water with the healee in the ballad?"

"The account didn't specify; it merely indicated that the waters were curative at the March full moon. And even if it did specify, I wouldn't get in. I don't want to swim in Scrope's semen. Enjoy your little marinade in the pathogen soup."

"Coward."

"The water is unusually milky; you must concede that."

"Surely you aren't suggesting that Scrope's loads are so vast, he's filled five pools with them?"

"Did you *see* the Clydesdale? Anything is possible."

Mordaunt made a strangled sound of aggravation. He disappeared into the steam for a while, apparently doing a few laps to work off his irritation.

When he came back, he asked, "Does this feel like a thin place to you?"

"No," said Aurienne. "I've literally never breathed so thick an atmosphere."

"Me neither," said Mordaunt. "Give it a go anyway."

He rose out of the water and backed towards Aurienne until he was within her reach. He positioned himself strategically so that she was out of view of the attendant and the other couple in the pool.

Aurienne stared at the white nexus of scar tissue at the base of his neck with annoyance. She had already wasted seith once on him today. Additionally, she was breaking protocol by not sanitising her hands, but her hlutoform was in the basket, along with the rest of her belongings.

"Hello?" prompted Mordaunt.

"I should be using this seith to help someone worth it," said Aurienne.

"I'm worth twenty million thrymsas and a Pox cure," said Mordaunt.

"It's an inoculation, not a cure," said Aurienne. With many furtive looks around her, she activated her tācn. Somewhere above them, the Cúsc moon glowed. Her palm met the Fyren's wet skin. Once again, she pushed her seith into him. Once again, she felt the deadness in the extremities of his seith system and the slow-creeping decay through the rest.

And once again, her seith could do nothing. What was dead stayed dead.

She pulled out.

She didn't need to tell Mordaunt that nothing had happened. He knew. His quiet *fuck* dissipated into the haze around them.

"I told you to expect failure," said Aurienne.

Mordaunt faced her. Steam condensed upon his face and clung to the stubble at his jawline. "There's something in your hypothesis. There's something in that Stone, too."

"There might be. But the Something could take years to establish. The right conjunction of time and place and—and who knows what other factors could be at play, that were simply not captured in the old accounts? For your immediate purposes, the Monafyll Stone is a dead end."

"What was the name of the philologist?" asked Mordaunt. "The one who translated the unknown language on the Stone?"

"*Disgraced* philologist," corrected Aurienne. "*Claimed* to have translated. His name was Widdershins. His findings were retracted. He lost his position as a professor. He was put out to pasture. I can assure you that pursuing that line of enquiry is an even bigger waste of time."

Aurienne wiped droplets from her face. "I'll have another look at the data. I'm nursing an idea that certain times and places may be more powerful than others. Or perhaps there's a cumulative effect if you've got enough factors layered upon one another—the right place, the right time, the right weather, the right moon. I don't know. It's difficult to establish patterns when the stories only provide one or two circumstantial details—details which may themselves have shifted in the telling and retelling."

Mordaunt looked pouty among the billowing steam.

Aurienne hadn't the time or inclination to mollycoddle. "Don't sulk. I've been up front about the absurdity of this endeavour from the beginning."

"I'm not sulking," said Mordaunt, sulkily.

"I told you this ad hoc approach wouldn't do," said Aurienne. "I'll send word when I've worked out the next best conjunction, for April's full moon. In the meantime, keep a firm grip on your expectations."

"You can lecture me about firm grips when you can manage one on your towel."

Aurienne looked down to discover that a breast had almost escaped confinement. She pushed the offender back into place.

Mordaunt's sulkiness made way to smugness. Aurienne was overcome by a desire to step on his head and drown him.

The couple at the other end of the bath left and Aurienne and Mordaunt were able to give vent to their feelings. Mordaunt said that what Aurienne really wanted was a more Elastic Spirit; she was an unbearable combination of high-handed and small-minded. Aurienne said thank you; she would consult him next time she needed advice from an Abscess with inferior hair. Mordaunt, vexed, said, how dare she, when her bun looked like a perfect onion? Aurienne informed him, by the by, that she would never again offer a second healing at the full moon, and that he would be lucky if she showed up at all. Mordaunt said that he had paid for her services, and was she certain she wanted to make an enemy of him? Aurienne retorted, as though they weren't enemies already? Mordaunt asked if she would stop waving her crook at him like a distraught Bo-Peep. Aurienne dropped her stick into his hands and declared that she was leaving. Mordaunt asked what he was meant to do with this stupid hook, other than strangle her with it. Aurienne said he could use it to hang himself if he wished.

These warm goodbyes exchanged, they parted.

Osric Wishes
to Murder a Child

Osric

The Fyren Order took a rather more nomadic approach to headquartering than the Haelan. They shifted their base of operations every few months, which meant that Osric got to visit truly charming parts of the Tīendoms. Tonight, he strode down an alley lit by sputtering grease lamps in the picturesque town of Shanksby in Strathclyde, taking in the local sights (a rat nibbling upon a severed human head) and smells (piss, suffering).

Osric spared the severed head a quick glance to see if he knew whose it was—he did not—and proceeded among buildings in various stages of decomposition. His objective came into view at last: a long-abandoned pharmacy with boarded-up windows. The crude carving of hellhound fangs on its peeling door marked it as the current location of the Fyren HQ.

The sign above the pharmacy had lost a letter, and now proclaimed, with no less accuracy:

HARMACY

BLOODLETTING SERVICES AVAILABLE.

The bell on the door gurgled a sickly jingle as Osric pushed it open. His nostrils were met with the acridity of decaying materia medica. In the dimness around him stood rows and rows of amber glass bottles, some broken, some whole, their dusty labels fading away in the gloom. Remains of the pharmacist's trade were scattered about on the floor: disintegrating prescription ledgers, a brass scale, smashed.

Behind the counter stood a slender man balancing a rapier upon the point of a finger. It was the dainty Sacramore, the Fyren Order's second-in-command—small, oversensitive to draughts, and an absolutely deadly swordsman.

"Osric, darling, lovely to see you," said Sacramore.

"Who lost his melon?" asked Osric, with respect to the orphaned head outside.

"Some lordling or other," said Sacramore. "Offended Tristane by trying to negotiate. Threatened to report our location to the Strathclydian king. And Tristane, pure soul that she is, wished to save the king the trouble of beheading him. The rest is here." Sacramore nudged at something below the counter with a satin slipper. "I'm meant to dispose of him, but, honestly, he's making a decent footrest."

The footrest oozed a rivulet of blood towards Osric, who side-stepped it to approach the counter.

"Have you got anything for me?" asked Sacramore, who was not only an excellent fencer but also an excellent fence.

Osric clattered a handful of precious stones onto the counter, stolen after dispatching his latest mark.

Sacramore didn't even bother to prod at the gems; he determined their value, apparently, by sound alone. He peered at Osric like a disappointed magpie. "Why are you wasting my time with trinkets, darling?"

"I'll take whatever you can get for them," said Osric.

"*Tss*," said Sacramore. "Bit short on cash, are we?"

Osric, who had just paid twenty million thrymsas for the privilege of being called an "Abscess with inferior hair," said bitterly, "A little."

Sacramore brushed the gems out of view with a disgusted sweep of his handkerchief, as though Osric had just done a poo on the counter. He jutted his chin towards the signet ring on Osric's right hand. "That would go for a pretty pile, if you ever wanted to part with it."

"It's not for sale," said Osric.

"Let's have a look at it anyway," said Sacramore, pressing a loupe to his eye.

Osric slid the heavy gold ring off his glove.

"Bloodstone, eh?" asked Sacramore.

"From Rùm."

"Intaglio of a hound rampant. Lovely rose motif." Sacramore held the ring upon the flat of his palm. "Heavy gauge. Eighteen carats. Shank attractively ornate. I like the scrollwork. Rather worn down—a few centuries' worth of use, eh?" Sacramore returned the ring to Osric. "If you found the right buyer, you could have a fair bit of pocket money."

Osric replaced the ring. "No buyer could pay what it cost me."

Sacramore, his loupe still pressed against his eye, tutted at Osric. "Dramatic boy. What's a little patricide among friends?"

"Is Tristane in?" asked Osric.

Sacramore twirled his rapier towards a corridor behind the counter. "*Madame* awaits. Do be careful."

"Why? What am I in for?"

"Nothing. Proceed."

"What sort of mood is she in?"

"Quixotic," said Sacramore.

"I'm serious," said Osric.

"Canescent."

"Sacramore."

"You mustn't say my name in such commanding tones," said Sacramore. "You'll give me the vapours."

Osric placed his hand over Sacramore's on the counter and made deep and intimate eye contact. "You know how much I depend on you."

Sacramore fanned himself with his kerchief and said coyly, "You beguiling bastard."

"Tell me."

"Can't blow the gaff."

"Can you blow other things?"

"Osric," gasped Sacramore.

"*I* can."

"You're being rather cheeky for someone within immediate kissing range," said Sacramore.

Osric swept his thumb over Sacramore's knuckles and dropped his gaze towards his mouth.

"You've stopped talking and it's making me nervous," said Sacramore.

"Not everything can be said with words," said Osric. "That's why we invented longing looks."

"Oh, behave."

"Tell me."

Sacramore caved with a sigh. "Noldo just came out of there shaking like a shitting dog."

"Really? Why?"

"No idea. I only hope you haven't done anything to incur Madame's displeasure."

"Of course not," said Osric, who would obviously never dream of gallivanting about with a member of an enemy Order, etc.

"Then you haven't anything to worry about," said Sacramore. "I dare say you'll be fine."

Osric raised Sacramore's hand to his mouth, pressed a kiss on it, made Sacramore's knees buckle, and proceeded down the corridor. Among old boxes lining the hall, there lay a massive, scummy tub letting off a foetid reek. The water within—more gunge than water—wriggled with thousands upon thousands of leeches. By what quirk of nature were the creatures still alive? Osric peered over the edge of the tub to find the answer: they were feasting upon themselves.

Interesting.

He came to the door of the pharmacist's office and knocked.

"Entrez," came Tristane's voice.

Osric *entrez*'d.

Tristane was such a fabled figure in the Fyren legendarium that it still shocked Osric to find her doing regular human things, such as eating a Cornish pasty.

"Sit," said Tristane, around a mouthful of crust.

Her green eyes followed Osric as he found a seat in the gloom; she liked to keep things dark in her war room. The only light emanated from the flickering glow of a Lovelace engine.

Tristane was Osric's warchief, a revered Fyren with, it was rumoured, over three thousand kills to her name. She had the most geometrically correct hair that Osric had ever seen and was particularly frightening because she was French.

"Pornish pasty," said Tristane, pushing a basket of pasties towards Osric. "Owing to them being shaped like penises. Leofric brought them in."

"Of course it was Leofric," said Osric, helping himself to a cock. (Leofric was his sometimes partner. Also a consummate sex pest.)

"You've taken care of the Painswick merchant?" asked Tristane.

"I have," said Osric. "Dismembered and left on display in the window, as requested."

"Excellent. Your steward can collect payment at the Dog's Bollocks.

Are you looking for another job, or would you like some time off to en-joy the fruits of your labour?"

"What else have you got?"

Tristane slid an envelope towards Osric. "A grievance between gen-tlemen. London. Our regular fee for the killing, with a fifty percent bonus if you make it look accidental."

Osric took the envelope. "Done."

"The client has indicated that a drowning would be preferred, but they leave the final decision to you." Tristane scribbled a note to herself, then asked, "How are things otherwise?"

The question put Osric on alert; Tristane didn't do chitchat.

"Fine," lied Osric. "Why do you ask?"

"You weren't in on Thursday," said Tristane. "I'd wanted to intro-duce you to the new recruits. Did you forget?"

Tristane fixed Osric with a sedulous eye. Osric's mouth went dry around his pasty.

"Shit," said Osric.

"*Effectivement*," said Tristane.

"Sorry. I had another thing come up."

"Was the thing that came up your penis?"

"I beg your pardon?"

Tristane sat back in her chair. The perfect isosceles triangle that was her hair swung with the movement, then settled back into its sharp black angles. "You were seen at the Randy Unicorn. Was there some emergency? You were overdue for a ball massage, perhaps?"

"Ah," said Osric. "Yes. The Randy. I *was* there. You're right. All my apologies—I forgot that I had another commitment."

Tristane studied Osric in silence. Lying came easily to him, how-ever, and he met her gaze with a look that conveyed that he was sheepish due to a poorly scheduled rub and tug—and not that he had missed her event because he had biffed off to hot springs at the full moon with a

Haelan in the harebrained pursuit of a cure for an incurable disease that would kill him if Tristane didn't.

"Sorry," said Osric again, producing an abashed grimace for good measure.

Osric rarely displeased Tristane. She therefore compartmentalised her annoyance and did not further probe his ill-timed testicular massages.

She returned to the subject of the new recruits. "A promising lot. With them trained up, I don't think it'll be possible for the Dreor to ever catch up with our numbers again."

Osric whistled. "They really haven't managed to replenish their ranks since the Winter War."

"No. As far as I'm concerned, they're functionally extinct. I've always said they're too selective as an Order. There are only so many individuals with the right build, the right propensities, and the right . . . mind."

"Or lack thereof."

"Exactly," said Tristane. "However, I can't be too smug. We'll be losing one of our number soon."

"Oh?"

"Noldovite."

"What about him?"

"Our dear Noldo has failed a mission." Tristane rapped long black-painted nails on the desk, in a way that suggested that, at this moment, Noldo wasn't particularly dear; in fact, she would like to press those nails into his jugular.

"Ah," said Osric. "He's getting on a bit, isn't he? Perhaps too old for fieldwork?"

"If only it was old age," said Tristane. "The reality is far worse: it appears that he's developed a conscience."

"No," gasped Osric.

"A malady that strikes the best of us," said Tristane. "He decided that the mark, and I quote, 'didn't seem to deserve being murdered.'"

"*Deserve?*" repeated Osric, scandalised. "We don't arbitrate. We execute."

"I know. Can you imagine if we all fannied about, hemming and hawing about deservedness? This is an equal opportunity Order. No judgement. Only results." Tristane shook her head; her triangle of hair swayed in alarm. "It appears that Noldo's grasp of this key part of our *philosophie* has weakened."

Osric tutted. "He's practically gone rogue."

"His target for the assignment has now gone into hiding," said Tristane. "I had to refund the client, which was mortifying, as you can imagine. We don't do refunds. We're the Fyren Order, not Murder Mart."

"What are you going to do with Noldo?"

"I might've carried out a tācn excision—I *am* fond of him; he's always served the Order well—but, given that he hadn't solid enough kidneys to complete the most basic of jobs, and made the Order look incompetent in the process . . ."

Tristane had the charming habit of translating French idioms directly into English; Osric was generally too frightened of her to request clarification. He took Noldo's feeble kidneys in stride and asked, "Do you want me to take care of him?"

"No," said Tristane. "I'll do it myself. He deserves that much."

"Be careful. He's wicked with that blaecblade."

Tristane gave Osric an indulgent smile. Her eyes became crescent moons above her cheeks. "Thank you, but . . . few are more wicked than me."

"Will you tell the others?"

"Only when I've got the body. I'll bring it here to burn. It isn't worthy of our tācn, even in death." Tristane sighed, then grew businesslike again. "I expect you here tonight to meet our new recruits. Mind you don't forget."

"Of course," said Osric, bowing. "I do apologise about last week. It won't happen again."

"Keep your cock under control, Mordaunt."

Then, in a threatening sort of way, she took a large bite out of a penis pasty.

Osric took that as his cue to leave.

Back in the leech reek of the corridor, he crossed two other Fyren coming in to meet Tristane: Lady Windermere and Brythe. Lady Windermere, her whip at her hip and a dancer's grace in her stride, always put Osric in mind of an elegant praying mantis—in stark contrast to Brythe, who was a graceless brute.

Lady Windermere winked at Osric. Brythe was occupied in dragging along a hapless prisoner. His maul was strapped into his belt—the same maul, incidentally, that was responsible for Osric's training injury a few months ago.

Pulverised your cervical spine, came Fairhrim's precise voice as Brythe neared. *Barbaric.*

Osric, who had never held a particular rancour towards Brythe for the injury, now found himself macerating in it. That maul had resulted in complications. In Osric having to crawl to an enemy Order and empty his coffers into theirs for a minuscule chance at healing Brythe's blunder. And he couldn't even ask for justice, because revealing the extent of the damage would put him in his Order's crosshairs for a cull.

It was therefore tempting to push his dagger into Brythe's too-thick chest.

"You all right, Mordaunt?" asked Lady Windermere. "You've a gleam in your eye."

"Mordaunt?" Brythe turned around with a grin. He slapped Osric on the shoulder and almost propelled him into the wall. "My man. As great a blackguard as ever was damned. All right?"

"Good to see you both," said Osric, trying to look less killy. (Lady Windermere had sensitive antennae about that sort of thing.)

Lady Windermere gave him a curious look, but seemed to detect no ill intentions. She tilted her chin towards their prisoner. "Just back from a stakeout."

"Took days," said Brythe. "Bored the arsehole off me." He tugged a rope, and his unfortunate prisoner tripped and flopped towards him. "But we've got our man in for his interrogation."

"Bit whiffy in here, isn't it?" said Lady Windermere.

Osric indicated the tub. "That'll be the leeches."

Lady Windermere approached the tub and observed the slow roil of the leeches. "Poor things."

"I know," said Osric. "They must be starved."

Osric looked at Lady Windermere. Lady Windermere looked at Brythe. Brythe tilted his head in the direction of the prisoner.

"Soften him up before he meets Tristane?" asked Lady Windermere.

"I reckon that's a good idea," said Brythe.

Brythe pulled the sack off the prisoner's head and pushed him towards the tub. The man screeched into his gag at the sight of the starving, wriggling goo beneath him. Just as things were about to get interesting—Osric was keen on animal welfare—his tācn tingled.

Fairhrim's deofol was asking to come through.

"I'll leave you two to it," said Osric. "Let me know how you get on. This is all rather innovative."

Brythe seized the prisoner by the hair and plunged his head into the tub. There was a high-pitched, bubbly gurgle.

"We'll share our notes," called Lady Windermere over the splashing.

Osric exited the Harmacy, blowing a kiss to Sacramore (returned with a girlish flourish) as he left.

He shadow-walked to a nearby roof. His tācn buzzed insistently at him; Fairhrim's deofol had absolutely no patience.

As usual, and because Fairhrim was a show-off, the albino genet gleamed into existence with every whisker and hair rendered in extraordinary detail.

"Finally," said the deofol as it materialised.

"What do you want?" asked Osric.

"I'm here to convey a message." The deofol floated to Osric's eye level. "Aurienne spent the past week conducting inferential statistical analyses."

"Maths?"

"Yes."

"That does strike me as her sort of hobby."

The deofol bristled at Osric. "It wasn't for *fun*. You're to keep your diary clear the night of the Hara moon. Meet Aurienne at the waystone at the Rummy Thing. Ten o'clock at night."

"She's found something promising, has she?" asked Osric.

"More promising than bathing in spunk." The deofol wrinkled its muzzle. "Did it make your skin smooth, at least?"

"As a baby's bum."

"Like your brain, then."

Osric aimed a cuff at the deofol, but it went right through the creature.

"Aurienne did say you were slow," tutted the deofol. "I had assumed she meant that metaphorically."

It disappeared. Osric could not have said, at that moment, whether the deofol or its mistress was more aggravating.

MARCH SNIFFLED AND SNEEZED TO ITS RAINY, MISERABLE END. OSRIC heard nothing further from Fairhrim for the remainder of the month, which was excellent, because he couldn't stand her. However, after weeks had passed in silence, and brought with them nothing but the advancement of the rot, he found himself hoping that Fairhrim would grace his tācn with her seith again. He wished she would make some spectacular discovery and her deofol would materialise and throw insults at him while delivering the good news.

She did not; it did not. In this sense, both continued to provoke him.

Osric dealt with his anxieties by thieving his way through the finest galleries in the Tīendoms and murdering minor members of the peerage.

"Perhaps," he suggested to Mrs. Parson when the silence drew overlong, "Fairhrim has died."

Mrs. Parson gave him one of those half-pitying, half-affectionate looks that sometimes escaped her, as though she weren't his steward but rather a tolerant aunt. "She's told you what you need to know. You can't expect a Haelan to keep up a frequent correspondence with a Fyren."

They were eating in the kitchens. Well, Osric was eating. Mrs. Parson was attempting to make apricot jam, but the stoned apricots kept disappearing before they could make their way into the pot.

"I've got the address you were looking for," said Mrs. Parson, plucking a bit of paper out of her apron and passing it to Osric, who hovered behind her. "You're meeting Haelan Fairhrim tomorrow night?"

"Yes. Ten o'clock at the Rummy Thing, somewhere in Kent."

Mrs. Parson, who had been measuring sugar, spilled a bit of it and tutted to herself.

"It's the Hara moon tomorrow," said Osric. "I didn't know moons had names. Did you?"

"Learned them from my mother long ago," said Mrs. Parson. "Haelan Fairhrim surprises me. Her sort don't keep to the Old Ways."

"She doesn't. She's hostile about it. I'm never sure whether she's going to heal me or knee me in the spuds." Osric flung himself into a chair. "I don't like any of this. I don't like needing her."

"She's your only hope," said Mrs. Parson.

"*Aegri somnia*, that's what she is. A sick man's dream."

Osric's tācn tingled, but it was not the restrained coolness of Fairhrim's seith. It was, on the contrary, lively, demanding, and sharp. He held up his palm. Tristane's deofol gleamed into existence above Mrs. Parson's cutting board.

Tristane's deofol was a polecat—a violently irritable creature normally, but today she was in an unusual good mood. "Hullo. What's all this? Are you making jam?"

"Trying to," said Mrs. Parson. "Apricot."

"Lovely," said the polecat. "*Un délice.* Sunshine on toast."

"To what do we owe the pleasure of your company?" asked Osric.

"Tristane has finally caught Noldo," said the polecat, with a delighted spin in midair.

"Oh, bravo," said Osric.

"The burning will take place tomorrow at sunset," said the polecat. "All Fyren are expected to attend. Meet at the Dog's Bollocks."

"I'll be there," said Osric. "Give Tristane my felicitations."

The polecat gleefully flashed her fangs and said, *"Avec plaisir,"* then spun upon herself and disappeared.

"Putrid luck for Noldo," said Osric.

"That's just before you're meeting the Haelan," said Mrs. Parson.

"It is," said Osric. "Do you think she'll notice if I smell like Fyren flambé?"

ALL LEVITY ASIDE, WATCHING NOLDO'S CORPSE BURN WAS A SOBER REminder of the Fyren Order's ruthless willingness to cull those who no longer served its purposes. Osric left for the Rummy Thing as soon as he was able, accompanied by a new sense of urgency to heal his failing seith system, as well as a whiff of burnt flesh.

The Rummy Thing was, indeed, a rummy thing. In the long shadows of the April evening it looked more like a shack than a pub, suffocated by ferns, leaning against the waystone in a weary sort of way. The waystone was also unusual—it was almost perfectly round, with a hole right through the middle.

The pub was surrounded by trees, from which an upright figure detached herself and advanced, iceberg-like, towards Osric. Fairhrim had hidden her Haelan whites under a blue travelling cloak. The cloak did little to camouflage everything else that made Fairhrim Fairhrim, however—the sharp cheekbones, the superior tilt of her chin, the disdainful set of her mouth.

Most people were charmed by Osric—or, if they knew what he was, terrified of him. Fairhrim was neither. She approached with the grim determination of a soldier setting off to war.

Osric found himself almost looking forward to their inevitable skirmish. There was, after all, something curative in the drawing of blood.

"You're late," said Fairhrim. She sniffed in his direction. "I smell burning."

"Just a corpse," said Osric, shaking out his greatcoat. "Lingers a bit."

Fairhrim's condemnation came in the form of pursed lips, which remained pursed as Osric rearranged his coat.

"Are you waiting for a kiss?" asked Osric. "It was a Fyren, if that makes you feel better."

He waited for Fairhrim to assimilate this information. She assimilated. The pursedness disappeared. "I suppose that *is* good news. Why were you burning one of your own?"

"He was naughty," said Osric.

"You're all naughty."

"He betrayed one of my Order's most fundamental tenets."

Fairhrim asked, with asperity: "Isn't that what you're doing as we speak?"

"Yes."

"Will you be next, then?" enquired Fairhrim, with an offensive amount of anticipation.

"Not if you do what I paid you to do," said Osric.

"You paid for something impossible. Do you think I might attend the burning when this endeavour inevitably fails?"

"It won't fail," said Osric, wishing he were as convinced as he sounded.

Fairhrim stepped up to Osric and peered into his face. Osric did not move so she wouldn't win.

"Obstinacy and hope," said Fairhrim. "What a foolish combination."

"I prefer strong-willed," said Osric.

"I'll mention that in your eulogy when I attend your farewell barbecue."

"There will be no farewell barbecue."

"All right," said Fairhrim in the tone one takes with a stupid idiot whom one no longer cares to argue with. "How's your seith? Any changes since last month?"

"The fluctuations are getting worse. The numbness has spread."

"You're still able to use it, which is the good news." Fairhrim's eyes slid over him. So penetrating was her gaze that Osric felt she might actually slice him open and have a look within. "I've got just enough seith for our healing attempt. I decided to put my faith in the maths, even if everything about this course of treatment is naive, uncontrolled, and suboptimal. I've put together a plan for today based on what seem to be the most successful parameters linked to the Hara moon. I have little confidence that it will work, of course, but we only have so many full moons—and I've only got so much seith."

Fairhrim snapped her hand in the direction of a bridleway. "Let's talk as we go. We've got a bit of a walk."

Osric followed her along the path. "Where are we going?"

"Along the South Downs," said Fairhrim. "This place has the full repertoire—it's on the cusp between earth and sea, it's got a long history of unexplained phenomena at the Hara moon, and it's positively studded with ancient barrows."

"Barrows?"

"Burial mounds."

"We like barrows?"

"We do. Barrowlands are good—they're places between the living and the dead, between us and eternity. The maths concurs, insofar as it can."

This last part was said as though Fairhrim pitied the maths—as though she had put it through something unbefitting of maths and felt sorry for it.

"And, of course," she continued, "we're also on a temporal cusp at this time of year—moving from winter into spring. We'll be attempting the healing at midnight."

"How far up are we going?" asked Osric.

"Only an hour or so of walking, I should think," said Fairhrim. "This area is Hedgewitch territory, by the way. Let's mind our step—and our manners."

"I'm not worried about a few outlaw witches," said Osric.

Fairhrim froze him with a look.

"What?" asked Osric. "They just putter about in ditches, growing mushrooms and things."

"Not that I needed further confirmation that you're an idiot, but that was another data point."

"I *beg* your pardon," said Osric, with rather less of the *beg* and more of the intent to decapitate.

"Have you ever met a Hedgewitch?" asked Fairhrim, unfazed by his intents, murderous or otherwise.

"No," said Osric.

"Keep a civil tongue in your head if we run into one," said Fairhrim, which was rich of her. "They've got even less regard for the law than you—and they consider men a nuisance."

Fairhrim eyed Osric as though he were as prime a specimen of a nuisance man as had ever walked the earth.

"How can anyone have less regard for the law than me?" asked Osric, offended.

"To you, it's a thing to break. To them, it simply doesn't exist."

Osric pondered this philosophical difference in silence. The moon-dappled woods fell behind. Black downlands opened up before them in rolling hills.

Both Fairhrim and Osric held up their tācn in the dark. Fairhrim was lighting her way with hers; it cast a white shimmer upon the path straight and narrow. Meanwhile, Osric used shadows to navigate; his seith mapped contours and profiles, cracks in the earth, the shape of ivy clambering over stone. There was a lovely irony to their respective way-finding: her light created a blind spot for him, and his shadows were inscrutable darkness to her; opposite topographies guided them up the same path.

They came to a crossroads marked by two signposts. One pointed left and said *Over Here*, and the other pointed right and said *Over There*.

"Practical," said Osric.

Fairhrim followed the sign for Over There.

They came to another sign, which said *Ignore This One*. The next said *Notice: Sign Not in Use*.

Fairhrim seemed unperturbed. In Osric's opinion, however, the Hedgewitches ought to leave off making signs and focus on their mushrooms.

Now they came to a sign that pointed up and said *Down*.

"Really?" said Osric.

They climbed up the Down.

Which upset him.

Osric smelled crushed thyme and fescue in Fairhrim's wake. Underfoot, the soil grew thin. Chalk gleamed through it like bone.

They went through a kissing gate. No kisses were forthcoming.

Thorny, wind-tortured shrubs grew along the path and threatened to draw blood from the careless traveller. "Sea buckthorn," explained Fairhrim as they passed, adding that its berries were a good source of vitamin C. Osric had not asked for this information and did not care.

The air around them hummed with mosquitoes and meadow grasshoppers.

Osric heard a minuscule, croaky voice say, "Ugly boots."

He stopped and looked around. There was nobody there.

Fairhrim, too, stopped. "Did you say something?"

"No," said Osric.

"Never mind," said Fairhrim, though she looked unsettled.

She turned and went on, picking her way along the path with narrow, precise steps.

"Hair up so tight, she can't even close her eyes," came a croaky voice again, this time from the other side of the path.

Osric, his blaecblade in hand, whipped around.

There was nothing there save wind-stunted thistles, blowing in the breeze.

Fairhrim stared at the spot where the voice had come from. "That wasn't you?"

Osric had many talents, but ventriloquism was not one of them. "No."

"Why's he so slouchy?" came another raspy voice, from somewhere behind them. "Posture like a damp croissant."

"She's got a rod up her arse; dunno what's better," replied another. "She's so . . . perpendicular."

"The face on him, though . . ."

"Like a burst sofa."

"Look at her eyes."

"Contents of a portaloo."

"And his nose?"

"A boil, rather."

Then a new voice chimed in: "Don't let them bother you."

Osric and Fairhrim turned to find a dirty little girl sitting on a stile. Her black hair caught the moonlight. Her clothes were sack-like and held in place by buckles at the elbow and the knee. She swung muddy bare feet as she looked at them. They stared back.

"Sorry—don't let who bother us?" asked Fairhrim.

"The critique crickets," said the child. There was a purple flower hanging from her lips; she chewed upon its stem. "What are you doing here?"

Fairhrim's fingers found Osric's forearm and squeezed a warning before he could open his mouth. He therefore did not tell the little girl to fuck off with her questions.

"We're looking for somewhere to do a bit of healing," said Fairhrim.

The child pointed a grimy finger to the top of the Downs. "That's a good Somewhere."

"Thank you," said Fairhrim.

"It can be dangerous," said the child.

"Oh?"

"The veil is thin up there. Don't fall through." The flower twirled between smirking lips. "Small chance of that, though."

"Why do you say that?" asked Fairhrim.

"You lot are never able to cross," said the child, with a cavalier gesture towards Osric and Fairhrim. (This was said as though Osric and Fairhrim were Like, which they were decidedly not.)

"You can't even see," continued the child. "You look and you behold nothing."

Having made this impressive, vaguely insulting pronouncement, the child pushed herself off the stile and skipped down the path.

"Wait!" called Fairhrim.

But the child was gone. Grass danced in the wind where she had stepped.

Osric had little patience for enigmatic children who disappeared mysteriously. He was going to throttle answers out of the little twit. "Let's go after her and—"

"No," interjected Fairhrim. "Whatever you were about to say, don't say it out loud."

"Was that a Hedgewitch?"

"A newling, perhaps." Fairhrim looked serious. "If it was, you won't find her."

Osric took the statement as a challenge. It vexed him that the child had appeared before them so silently and disappeared so easily. Even the best Fyren shadow-walkers couldn't pull off that sort of feat. He wanted an Explanation.

He had done three jobs that day and was running rather low on seith, but he nevertheless pulled off his glove and awoke his tācn. He felt about in the shadows in the direction where the child had vanished. First he pushed his seith out fifty feet, and found nothing, and then a hundred feet, and found nothing, and then he flooded it out past two hundred feet (his Cost made itself known; his right eye went blurry)—and he found still nothing. The child was gone.

Fairhrim, who had been watching his investigation in haughty silence, said, "I told you."

"I believe I'd like to learn more about Hedgewitches," said Osric. Which was as close as he would come to admitting that Fairhrim had been right.

"Good luck," said Fairhrim. "There's a reason you think all they're good for is wading about in ditches."

"What do you mean?"

"They're safer if everyone believes they're useless. No one bothers them. At one point in our history, they were relentlessly persecuted. They've never forgotten."

"And how do you know so much about them?"

"I knew one once." Fairhrim touched her neck, and for a moment she looked wistful—sad, even—and then her face closed again.

Osric turned his attention back to the stile. There wasn't a single bent blade of grass, or a single disturbed pebble, where the girl had been kicking her feet. Of the flower she'd been chewing on, a leaf and a single petal remained.

"Harebell," said Fairhrim, observing the petal. "Also known as fairy thimble."

"You say that as though it's significant."

"There are claims about its properties. Undocumented, of course—"

Fairhrim interrupted herself with a double take at Osric. "Your eye. It's gone white."

"My Cost."

Fairhrim, who had briefly looked concerned, said, "Ah," and regained her impassivity.

She continued up the footpath. Osric found himself breaking a sweat as they climbed. The crickets began to chirp again, and turned their attention to the shape of Fairhrim's bun ("Frizzy turnip") and Osric's body odour ("Chimney and armpit").

The commentary faded as Osric and Fairhrim climbed. Which was good, because Osric wanted to laugh, but he didn't want to laugh with Fairhrim, because that would be chummy, and they weren't chums.

He stole a glance at her. Her lips were pressed together harder than usual, and twitched when one of the crickets called him a mithering wanker.

They reached the top of the Downs.

"Well," said Osric, panting, "we are definitely Somewhere."

"Right," said Fairhrim. She, too, was breathless. She pointed her hands in opposite directions. "Sky above, earth below. The living and the dead. The present and the past. Winter turning to spring. And the Hara moon presiding over it all."

"Sounds potent," said Osric.

"Let's give it a go."

Osric pulled off his cloak and collar. Fairhrim dropped her satchel and removed her cloak. She consulted her pocket watch as midnight neared. The acrid, too-clean scent of hlutoform reached Osric's nostrils as she spread it over her hands.

They waited. The pocket watch ticked to eleven fifty-nine. Two moon-gazey hares loped dreamily along cropped turf. The wind picked up. Fairhrim, with her white dress gusting around her, stood like a bride at some wild altar. Fescue and thistle danced upon barrows. The sea murmured a song that seemed melancholy.

They stood on the border between death and life; they stood on the bones of kings.

At ten seconds to midnight, Fairhrim tugged down the back of Osric's shirt to expose his nape. This was the third time they were attempting this, and he had learned what to expect. There was the moment of silence when Fairhrim did nothing but study the back of his neck. Then came the brush of her palm and the shudder in the air when she activated her tācn. He felt the reluctance in her touch, her desire to flinch away, the force of her will keeping her hand against his skin.

As for Osric, he loathed having people behind him, and his own instincts desired him to pull away from this vulnerable position—but it was Fairhrim, so it was all right. Frankly, he could think of very few in his acquaintance whom he trusted more than her to stand behind him with a hand at his neck.

Strange thought, that.

Fairhrim's cool palm pressed against his skin. Her seith, too, was cool. As during her previous attempts, Osric found himself impressed by her control over it. He would never tell her, of course—she was arrogant enough as it was—but he had never encountered such masterful command over seith. And as before, it felt salutary to have her seith flow through him. It was Goodness itself coursing into his system.

The moon hung above them, hard, pitted, bone white. And Osric, under Fairhrim's palm, stood motionless in this place between sea and earth and winter and spring and the living and the dead, and he hoped. A translucent cloud passed the moon; the landscape grew insubstantial and twinkled unsteadily between pearl and black. In the stillness, the pace of time felt altered. A minute passed like an hour. The horizon felt wider.

Fairhrim followed Osric's seith system to the very tips of his fingers, lingered there for an optimistic moment, and retreated.

There was an afterglow that came with her seith, even after she'd pulled her hand away. A humming through him, a burnishing.

But it wasn't the healing Osric needed. He felt exactly the same as before. Once again, nothing had happened.

He was an idiot for insisting on this load of absolute malarkey. And she was an idiot for humouring him.

"Fuck," said Osric.

Fairhrim's exasperated sigh feathered the back of his neck. That surprised him; she was so convinced that this wouldn't work that another failure should've been expected. Why the sigh of frustration? What other outcome was she anticipating?

Also surprising: how intimate it was to feel Fairhrim's breath against his skin. Bit tingly. Bit pleasurable.

Bit disturbing. Nothing about Fairhrim was pleasurable.

For a moment they stood in silence made companionable by their mutual disappointment. But Osric didn't want companionship. He wanted results.

He ignited war again between them by saying, accusatorily, "This isn't bloody working."

"Really?" came Fairhrim's tart response. "Isn't it? I hadn't noticed."

From the safety of renewed war (oxymoronic; it was fine), Osric replaced his collar.

Fairhrim left him to his dressing and paced. Her steps were quickened by aggravation. "I'm missing something."

"Well, there's a rather critical clue you refused to examine further," said Osric.

Fairhrim turned. Her skirts whipped around her ankles before settling back into their crisp vertical lines. "A *critical clue*? Please— enlighten me."

"The writing on the Monafyll Stone. The bits in the fairy tongue."

Fairhrim stared at Osric. Tension ran down the line of her jaw. "The hallucinations of a discredited philologist about a language that doesn't exist? That's my missing clue? Brilliant."

"Why not? Our current approach clearly isn't the answer."

Fairhrim resumed the brusque back-and-forth. Osric expected a cutting refusal and prepared to launch his own barbs—only Fairhrim, to his vast surprise, ended up agreeing with him.

"Why not, indeed?" said Fairhrim.

Osric felt that stumbling feeling—you know the one, when you're aggressively climbing stairs and the top stair is simply not there because you've already hit the landing.

"This entire treatment plan is predicated on nothing but fantasy," continued Fairhrim. "Why not indulge further? Lean into the ridiculousness of the whole idea?"

"I'll remind you that this ridiculousness is my only hope of survival," said Osric.

"Against expert advice to the contrary," said Fairhrim, like the pitiless creature she was.

Osric produced a piece of paper, upon which an address was written in Mrs. Parson's tidy cursive, and gave it to Fairhrim. "We're going to go find the discredited philologist."

"What?"

"Tonight. It won't involve using up your precious seith. Have you anything better to do?"

"Thousands of better things." Fairhrim read Mrs. Parson's note with a raised eyebrow. "Nether Wallop?"

"Ooh," said Osric. "My favourite game: is it a place or is it a kink?"

"This is going to be a waste of time. Widdershins was already a fringe sort of professor before he went off the deep end. He's absolutely barmy. I told you—his findings were retracted. His doctorate was revoked. He hasn't any scholarly credibility."

"I don't care about scholarly credibility," said Osric. "We'll shake him up. Get some answers. See how they fit into the rest of the apocrypha."

"He might not want to talk to us."

"I'll make him talk," said Osric.

"How?" asked Fairhrim, like the naive thing she was.

"Trust me."

"Trust *you*?" repeated Fairhrim. "Absolutely not. Make him talk? Is your plan to torture the man?"

"Yes."

"No."

"Yes."

"Have you no compassion?" asked Fairhrim.

"I'm not burdened with it, no."

"I categorically object to torture."

"Do you, really? It had escaped my notice," said Osric, before sauntering away.

"Mordaunt," snapped Fairhrim, and she made his name sound so pejorative, it delighted him.

They bickered about the merits of torturing dotty old professors all the way down the Downs. Osric said that he was the expert here and that he would appreciate it if Fairhrim reserved her pointy opinions for her own areas of specialisation. Fairhrim said she was going to review the literature on the efficacy of torture and sharpen her pointy opinions further, and then puncture him with them. Osric asked why she must be so obstreperous. Fairhrim asked when would he stop being a Menace to Society. Osric called her a Self-Righteous Plague. She called him a Foppish Crouton.

The night air was full of the hum of insects, but the critique crickets did not offer fresh insult, perhaps because Osric and Fairhrim were doing such an excellent job by themselves.

They returned to the waystone and the lean-to that passed for a pub. Instead of striding up to the waystone, as Osric had expected, Fairhrim walked towards the Rummy Thing.

"You can't be serious," said Osric. "We've got things to do."

"It's bad form to use their waystone to come all the way out here and not even leave a coin," said Fairhrim.

She left a coin on the windowsill and made Osric leave one, too.

The Plague and the Crouton pressed their tācn to the waystone and went to Nether Wallop.

THE VICISSITUDES OF HATE

Osric

Osric and Fairhrim materialised in Nether Wallop (pub: the Tiddly-wink) and found it to be a pretty country village. They hailed a woman herding sleepy, fat sheep with an enquiry about Widdershins.

"You want the old professor?" The woman pointed down a country lane. "That way. The burnt-down place. Good luck to you."

"Why the luck?" asked Osric.

"He's Away, isn't he?" said the shepherdess.

"Er—so he's not there?"

"No," said the shepherdess, as though Osric was being thick. "He's Away. He's there, of course—but he's not."

"He's there but he's not?"

"Pixie-led, you know," said the shepherdess.

"Pixie-led?" repeated Fairhrim.

"Fairy-struck," said the shepherdess.

In the face of Fairhrim's and Osric's blank stares, she apparently concluded that she was dealing with two fully licensed cretins, and gave up. She bimbled off with her charges, muttering that any one of her sheep had more brains than the two of them combined.

The country lane led them to an old, burnt shell of a cottage just outside the village proper. Osric knocked upon the sooty door.

"Do we address him as Professor?" asked Fairhrim. "He's not one anymore, not really, after the fiasco about the fairy tongues. I suppose it's just Widdershins. Mr. Widdershins. Let me talk, as we agreed. Don't threaten him."

"As *we* agreed? I never agreed," said Osric.

"You did. You said *All right.*"

"I said *All right, your approach confirms that you know nothing about intelligence gathering.* Not *All right, let's proceed with your amateur plan.*"

"*My* amateur plan? We should be looking for his old publications in archives to see if we can find a copy of the retracted piece about the Stone, not shaking him down in his own home in the middle of the night. This is *your* amateur plan."

"I know you enjoy snuffling about in dust for hours on end, but *I'd* rather go to the source."

"Your techniques are out-of-date and needlessly cruel."

"Your way involves a century of research, which is time I simply don't have."

"If you've got so little time, then why are we going on wild-goose chases instead of following the data?"

"*The data* has had three chances to prove itself and has failed every time."

"I told you, that's the nature of this kind of experiment—which *you* insisted on pursuing."

"I thought you said it wasn't an experiment."

There was the clearing of a throat.

Osric and Fairhrim looked up to find a round, bald man at the door.

The man had a colander on his head, which did not immediately inspire confidence.

Fairhrim resumed her usual impassivity. She took in the colander with the mere twitch of an eyebrow. "Forgive us for disturbing you at this late hour. We're looking for Mr. Widdershins."

"I'm *Mr.* Widdershins," said the man, with an angry sort of emphasis on the *Mr.* "What d'you want?"

"We've got a few questions about the Monafyll Stone," said Fairhrim. "We're conducting a bit of an investigation."

"An investigation, is it?" asked Widdershins. His anger faded. He looked at a spot somewhere above Fairhrim's head, and said, "From the Latin *vestigium*, a footprint or trace."

Fairhrim took the unsolicited etymology in stride. "Yes. Precisely."

Widdershins blinked and came back to his tetchy self. "And what are your qualifications, pray? Are you runologists?"

"No."

"Philologists? Dialectologists? Etymologists? Semioticians? Archaeologists?"

"Erm—I'm a Haelan," said Fairhrim.

Widdershins made an unimpressed moue. Fairhrim looked offended.

"If the Stone had an injury, I'm sure she would appreciate that." Widdershins turned to Osric. "And you, sir, of the jism white eye?"

This reference to Osric's Cost might have earned the man a punctured lung, only Fairhrim was there, and would doubtless raise objections.

"I'm an Interested Observer," said Osric, instead of Assassin-for-Hire.

"An Observer?" repeated Widdershins. "With half the usual amount of eyes? Like Woden, did you give your right eye so your left could See?"

"Never mind about my . . . companion's . . . eyes," said Fairhrim.

"You published something on the Monafyll Stone some time ago, but it was retracted, and we'd like to get our hands on a copy—"

"It was retracted, yes," cut in Widdershins. "Do you know what else was retracted? My funding. My position. My reputation. My *doctorate*. That paper ended me. That is the nature of the academy, you know. You mustn't go too far beyond the bounds of the Accepted. You may lose everything."

Fairhrim grew grave. "I am aware."

Osric felt a wave of accusation wash over him, because it was his fault she was straying beyond the bounds of the Accepted.

"Why, then, is a Haelan looking into the Monafyll Stone?" asked Widdershins. "It's nothing but an archaeological bagatelle for your sort, isn't it? Or are you intent on running your career directly into a shitpit?"

"Personal curiosity," said Fairhrim.

Widdershins studied her as though she were a mysterious bit of text to decipher. Then he said, "I'll give you two silly plums some advice. Hard-earned advice."

He waved Fairhrim and Osric towards him. They approached. Osric could see Widdershins' single remaining hair, white, escaping from a hole in the colander.

Widdershins gestured them in farther. They leaned in even more.

"Fuck off," said Widdershins, loudly, spraying them both with spittle.

He slammed the door shut.

Fairhrim stared at the door. She wiped a fingertip below her eye. A knife danced across Osric's knuckles.

They heard another door open and close, this time round the back of the cottage. Osric and Fairhrim looked at each other, then cut through a bed of stringy lavender to reach the back garden.

There was a creek behind the cottage, towards which Widdershins was presently wandering, clad in a set of waders. He stripped off his shirt and stepped into the moonlit creek, his colander still on his head.

"He hasn't got any nipples," noticed Osric. To Widdershins, he called, "Why haven't you got any nipples?"

"You can't just ask people why they haven't got nipples," said Fairhrim.

"Lost them in the fire," said Widdershins.

He splashed about in the creek.

"Mr. Widdershins, what are you doing?" asked Fairhrim. There was concern in the question.

"Tadpoling. *Obviously.*"

"It's the middle of the night," said Fairhrim.

"Best time for it. Also, fuck off."

"We want a copy of your article; then we'll gladly fuck off," said Osric. "Have you still got one?"

"It doesn't exist anymore," said Widdershins, splashing about. "Burnt everything."

"Then what did it say?" asked Fairhrim. "What were your findings on the Stone?"

Widdershins ignored them.

"Leave off the pollywogs and answer the questions," said Osric.

Widdershins' expression went vacant again. "*Pollywogs.* From *poll*, head, and *wiglen*, wiggle. A wiggling head."

"You suspected that the language on the Stone was a fairy tongue," pressed Fairhrim. "Had you managed to translate it?"

Widdershins addressed a point next to her shoulder. "*Translate.* From the Latin *transferre*, a carrying across. There is also the Greek version, *metaphrasis*. A speaking across—as these things do, you know; they speak to us from across the gulfs of time and tongues long forgot."

Widdershins removed the colander from his head and plunged it into the creek.

Osric lost his patience. "If this dotard gives us one more bloody etymology—"

"*Dotard*," said Widdershins. "From Middle Dutch *doten*, to be foolish. *Ard* indicates a particular quality, usually pejorative. And so we also have *drunkard* and *coward* and *dullard* and *laggard*." Widdershins' dreamy gaze refocused. He looked Osric dead in the eye. "And, of course, *bastard*, but you're well acquainted with that one, boy, being such a stellar example yourself."

Osric turned to Fairhrim and said, informatively: "I'm a cock hair away from murdering this man."

"I'm not familiar with that unit of measurement," said Widdershins. He, too, turned to Fairhrim. "How imminent is my demise? What's the length of a standard cock hair?"

Osric was interested in Fairhrim's answer—she probably had a cock-hair almanac with data and averages and things—but she did not respond to the query. She brushed past Osric and stood on the bank of the creek. "If we could return to the translation—"

"I've caught one," said Widdershins. He showed Fairhrim the colander, in which a tadpole wiggled.

"Very nice," said Fairhrim. "Lovely tadpole. But to return to your article—what if we use your findings and prove that you were right?"

"Oh? And how will you do that?" asked Widdershins. "Summon a fairy to corroborate?"

"If you'd tell me what you thought the Stone said—"

"She didn't say. She may have *conveyed*, in the most abstract of senses."

"Right, what it—she—conveyed. The healing ritual—the pattern. If I was to discover that there was some truth to it—that you weren't wrong, or deluded, or barmy—we could undo some of the misfortunes you've suffered. Reverse the retraction. Have you reinstated as a professor."

Widdershins said, "You poor, stupid creature," but it wasn't clear whether this was addressed to Fairhrim or the tadpole. "I've got a bucket for you."

Fairhrim stood irresolute for a moment before asking, "Sorry?"

Widdershins jerked his round chin towards the back of the garden. "In the shed. That's my contribution to your reckless endeavour, if you're so hell-bent on tainting your credibility with this pursuit."

"I can assure you that I'm not. However"—an eloquent look was cast towards Osric—"circumstances are such that I haven't a choice in the matter."

"The galvanised bucket, then," said Widdershins. "You may keep it. Drown your sorrows therein when this inevitably ends in tears."

Widdershins waded farther into the creek and disappeared under the long fronds of the willow trees that edged it. "Galvanised," came his voice as he went, soft and dreamy again. "From *Galvani*, surname of an eighteenth-century professor—made the legs of dead frogs twitch."

Fairhrim watched him go. There was a vertical line between her contracted brows. "Am I going to end up like him?"

"What? Completely nutty?" asked Osric.

"Discredited." Fairhrim bit her lip. "Stripped of everything that matters."

"We needn't worry until you start splashing about in puddles looking for tadpoles," said Osric.

"You're not funny."

"And you're not barmy. Stop worrying."

"I'm not barmy *yet*. I fear that time spent with you pushes me closer to that edge."

"Hah," said Osric, because this was, once again, rich of her. "Let's go find this bucket."

They stepped through Widdershins' overgrown garden to find a dilapidated shed. There, among broken spades and torn wellies and mildew and rust, stood the bucket. It was filled with a dozen large, grey-white, crumbly pieces of—something. Chalk?

Osric would've liked to be the first to work it out, but of course Fairhrim beat him to it.

She knelt next to the bucket and pulled out one of the bits. She ran her fingers over its faint markings.

"A plaster cast of the Stone," she said.

She pulled more pieces out of the bucket and set them out on the floor. By the time Osric had processed her intentions, knelt down beside her, and begun to study the puzzle, she had finished piecing the bits together.

The Monafyll Stone's cast, about six feet long, lay in its fragmented length before them.

"How are you so quick?" asked Osric.

"I've stared at pictures of the Stone for hours," said Fairhrim. "Oh—look."

Here and there along the pieces, small notes were pinned, written in a slanted hand.

"Widdershins' translation notes," said Fairhrim, groping about for her satchel. "Preliminary, I suppose. Read them to me, would you? Begin at the top, there."

She pulled her notebook from her satchel. Osric had seen the hideous thing before—it was bound with a bright pink spiral and featured a fuchsia cat.

Osric read the fragmented bits of translation. "'Children of the moon. Faerydom. Cure for all evil'—with three question marks; I don't think he was confident about that one."

"Right," said Fairhrim, glancing up from her writing. "And then?"

"'Beginnings of dawns and ends of evenings.' Erm. Then he gets into the lunar calendar proper. 'Hrímfrost Moon—January—Exile. Hyngre Moon—February—Light streaming . . .'"

Fairhrim took notes as he went, resulting in a table drawn in an illegible hand. ("What is this?" asked Osric. "Is that meant to be a number? Five or three? Fouve? Threeve?")

1. Hrímfrost (Hoarfrost) Moon	exile
2. Hyngre (Hunger) Moon	light streaming
3. Cúsc (Chaste) Moon	dream-laden (?)
4. Hara (Hare) Moon	. . . look through the shinbone of a hare . . .
5. Blædnes (Blooming) Moon	. . . blackened sun at land's end
6. Begbéam (Bramble) Moon	Running waters cross (?)
7. Hunig (Honey) Moon	rainbow (???)
8. Thunor (Thunder) Moon	waves draw you under
9. Bédríp (Harvest) Moon	that hidden abode
10. Meodu (Mead) Moon	the grey path (?), the dim kingdom
11. Gnyrn (Mourning) Moon	light and shadow among leaves
12. Endeláf (Last) Moon	shadow-quenched

"I had hoped for rather more precise instructions," said Osric. "This isn't much to go on."

"No," said Fairhrim. "It's *loads* to go on."

"Is it?"

"Well—pretending that it's correct, of course," said Fairhrim. "I can use some of these to validate the worst of my speculations. I've no idea how Widdershins went about translating this, though. As far as I understand, this is a language isolate. There are no cognates—no linguistic relationships with any known tongue. I suppose he wasn't able to explain it to his colleagues' satisfaction, either."

"Perhaps the tadpoles told him."

Fairhrim was engrossed in her notebook. "But this is progress. We can make something approaching a plan. These translations will help us prune potential locations considerably. Look at the Blædnes moon—now we know we're looking for a cliff, or a beach—an edge of some sort, anyway. I can run through my tables and have a tidy-out."

"D'you think a 'cure for all evil' includes seith rot?" asked Osric.

Fairhrim looked up from where she knelt. "If this treatment was a cure for evil, it would be fatal to you."

"*Oi.*"

"So, either way, we may never find out." Fairhrim placed the plaster pieces back into their bucket.

"You're taking the bucket?" asked Osric.

"Yes. To catch my tears, or whatever Widdershins said, when this affair inevitably goes awry." She hoisted the bucket against her hip. "I'm going. I'll contact you before the next lunation, so that we can proceed with this . . . lunacy."

"Horrid pun," said Osric. "And this affair won't go awry."

Fairhrim gave her notebook an exasperated wiggle in Osric's direction. "This isn't science. This isn't medicine. This is absolute pie-in-the-sky, whimsical, pipe-dream, cloud-cuckoo-land *fantasy*. And it will go awry, because everything about it is awry."

"It's going to work, or we'll both perish miserably."

Osric saw that he had offended his Means to an End, and that she was looking particularly Mean. "*You'll* perish miserably. I'll go on with my life as I did before, happy and Fyren-free."

And, just like that, they were back in the skirmish. They exited the shed. A fractious wind picked up; it flipped Osric's hair around and plucked a curling strand out of Fairhrim's bun.

"You'll fix me or die with me," said Osric.

"Oh? It's threats now, is it?"

"It's a thing called incentivisation."

"My only incentive here is a direct order from Haelan Xanthe, and it's the only reason I haven't tossed you to the Wardens."

"Perhaps you should; I'd rather be dismembered than deal with such an uptight little fusspot."

"Perhaps I will—it'd be a relief to no longer suffer such a useless ganglion of a man."

"Ganglion?" repeated Osric.

"Fusspot?" said Fairhrim.

They glared at each other, Osric with vast distaste, so that she understood that she was the world's most trying woman, and Fairhrim with raw opprobrium, which made it clear that she thought him deficient in brains as well as morals.

Fairhrim was unafraid, violently unafraid, daring him to continue. They stood close. That was the thing about war: every clash, every battle, brought each nearer and nearer to the other. Their breaths intermingled, passed thresholds their lips would never cross. The wrongness of it was almost erotic.

There was a flush across Fairhrim's cheeks. Osric felt himself swallow. Suddenly, the eye was not satisfied with seeing; suddenly, the mouth wished to taste.

No more breaths were exchanged, because neither of them breathed. The scarred moon hung above them. Its light fell softly upon blushing cheeks, softly on the strand of hair that clung to Fairhrim's lip. Her gaze was darkly brilliant. The wind sent dry lavender petals around them like chaff.

Fairhrim, with a blink, drew back. She recovered her usual impassivity, but there was something brittle about it. She whirled her cloak around herself, threw Osric a final glare, and strode away without a parting word.

Osric let her disappear down the road before following her to the waystone. He took his time; he had a post-Fairhrim malaise he needed to walk off.

There was such witchery in a pair of bright eyes.

Pity they had to be hers.

Noblesse Oblige

Aurienne

Of the four hundred children brought into Swanstone over the course of the Platt's Pox outbreak, the Haelan managed to pull three hundred out of danger. The remaining patients were in Ward 14, formerly the cafeteria, now converted into a ward with a hundred beds. In those beds lay the remaining patients, still in the throes of the brain fever, being kept alive by Haelan dedication and sheer obstinacy.

Emotional regulation was one of Aurienne's fortes, but as the outbreak raged, her preferred strategies—suppression, compartmentalisation—lost their efficacy. During today's shift in Ward 14, a little girl no older than four, scab crusted and delirious, clutched at Aurienne's fingers and brought her to tears. Aurienne glanced about to check that no one was watching, knelt beside the girl's bed, and pressed a hug into her wasted body.

She must carry on. Others needed her. She took a steadying breath—hlutoform and the sickly scent of sickness invaded her mouth—brushed away her tears, gave the girl's hand a final press, and carried on to the next bed. Like a coward, she did not take note of the girl's patient ID; she didn't want to notice her absence if she was gone by the time her next shift rolled around.

Aurienne saw signs of fraying in others, too. Lorelei, the head of Paediatrics, was usually obnoxiously cheerful. Today she was hollow eyed and functioning by rote, and reporting to Xanthe with uncustomary dispassion. Xanthe herself, with whom Aurienne shared the shift, simmered with a low fury. She listened to Lorelei's report as she worked a line of beds. The wrinkled skin at her jowls quivered with the clench of her jaw.

Xanthe was usually explosive. This seething rage troubled Aurienne more than an irritated outburst would have.

Their shift came to its end at seven o'clock in the evening.

"Come," said Xanthe to Aurienne after they had completed their sanitation protocols. "Let's get dinner and eat in my office."

Aurienne and Xanthe made their way to the temporary cafeteria, now housed in a corridor. Aurienne dearly missed the fare at home—tangy salads, her mother's chicken-stuffed briouates, rfissa fragrant with fenugreek—but seith was best regenerated with heavy, calorie-dense foods, and that was what Swanstone's kitchens did best. Upon her tray she heaped butter-soaked mushroom pasties, fatty stew, cheeses, and cream tarts.

Xanthe's office was a pleasant low-ceilinged room on the ground floor of Swanstone's south end. In the daytime it was flooded with sun; in the nighttime it was lit by a wide hearth; at all times there was reliably a kettle singing within. Aurienne cleared a seat for herself on an ottoman partially interred beneath journals on tissue engineering, limb regeneration, and the treatment of end organ failure. Xanthe almost disappeared into the folds of an armchair, her tray upon her bony knees.

"There's fuckery at work," declared Xanthe.

She traded Aurienne a stack of letters for the journal on organ failure.

"What are these?" asked Aurienne.

"I asked colleagues around the Tīendoms to confirm whether any of them had received adequate funding for inoculation development. Four months into this outbreak—thousands of infected children across the Tīendoms—and no one has received anything of substance. Not us, not the universities, not any of the research groups. This in spite of multiple increasingly strident pleas."

"I was prepared to blame incompetence, but I believe we've now moved on to cruelty," said Aurienne. "I suppose it's because the Pox is only affecting the most impoverished children—the ones not 'worth' putting money into?"

Xanthe aggressively bit a pickle. "You'd think that, with ten bloody kings and queens jostling for supremacy round here, there would be at least one for whom *noblesse* would *oblige*?"

"They aren't French enough," said Aurienne.

"That's the problem. We ought to have let the French have their bloody Norman Conquest and be done with it. But no. We beat them back. And now, eight centuries later, here we are, with ten petty kingdoms, and ten clowns in charge, instead of a Noblesse-Obliging Frenchy." Xanthe ate a piece of cheese and added, "We'd have better Brie, too."

Aurienne flicked through the letters from Xanthe's contacts. Each confirmed receipt of the most nominal sums in support of inoculation development.

"The northernmost Tīendoms are the ones with the lowest rates of the Pox—I suppose that explains their lack of interest," said Aurienne, running through the numbers. "The Danelaw and Dyfed contributed something—not much, but something. Kent and Mercia are egregious. They've got some of the highest incidence rates of the Pox and have given the least to anyone."

"Dumnonia, too," said Xanthe. "Clowns. All clowns."

"Clowns with a distinct lack of empathy."

"They wouldn't know empathy if it bit them on the cock."

"What are you going to do?" asked Aurienne.

"Write a strongly worded letter to each clown," said Xanthe. "I've got them ready."

Xanthe wriggled out of her armchair and went to her desk. Beside her silver writing ball was yet another stack of letters. Mysteriously, she also pulled out a sealed test tube in which a clear liquid sloshed.

"Erm . . . what is that?" asked Aurienne.

"A special addition I'm going to include in the letters," said Xanthe. "A sort of postscript."

"A postscript? Labelled *biohazard*?"

"Yes."

"Haelan Xanthe, you can't."

"Can't I? Did you not see those children whose so-called lives we just spent three hours prolonging? And the monarchs throwing an insulting handful of thrymsas their way? And in the meantime, life in their castles goes on—masquerades, dances, banquets?"

"It's awful—it's wretched—but you can't do this. You'd better sit on it."

"I can't sit on it," said Xanthe, wiggling the tube. "I'll get verrucas in my arsehole."

"What?"

"*Ignis papillomavirus*," said Xanthe, tapping the tube. "Don't look at me like that. A few warts won't kill anyone."

"That's—that's an excruciatingly painful condition," said Aurienne.

"So is the Pox."

"Have you spoken to the other Heads about this?"

"Prendergast is a diplomat," said Xanthe, with a dismissive swing of the fire-wart tube. "Sometimes I'm not certain what the difference is between *diplomat* and *doormat*. Three or four letters, but much the same thing. Abercorn is nothing but a fart."

"He is not," said Aurienne. (Abercorn was a highly respected endocrinologist.)

"In this case, he's been just as effective as one."

Aurienne didn't often dare contradict Xanthe, but her mentor's anger was leaking dangerously into vengefulness. She took the stack of letters from Xanthe and found that they were directed to kings and queens and variously addressed as *Dear Feckless Idiot* or *Cretin* or *Absolute Invertebrate*.

"Élodie is working on the inoculation," said Aurienne. "There's an end in sight. If you were to send these and infect everyone with warts— I know, I *know*; they aren't lethal—there would be impacts on our Order."

"We don't owe allegiance to any of the clowns."

"Right, but we *are* in the territory of the king of the Danelaw, who you've addressed as"—Aurienne checked the letter—"an anaemic, inbred, cowardly pig. He could make life difficult for us. He could expel us. You know how long it took us to develop our facilities at Swanstone."

"I could soften it," said Xanthe. "Could simply call him a pig."

But she was, herself, softening. She took the letters from Aurienne's hands. "It did make me feel better to write them."

"I know."

Xanthe's mouth disappeared upon itself as she sucked at her gums. With a brisk gesture, she threw the letters into the fire. "I am two hundred years old, Aurienne. I think my patience is simply wearing thin."

Aurienne watched Xanthe's anger curl and burn in the hearth. She remembered the squeeze of the little girl's hand, and thought of the monarchs in their castles, with their feasts and their dances and their precious children well isolated from the Pox, and part of her wished Xanthe had sent the letters, warts and all.

THERE WAS ONE POSITIVE IN THE DAYS TO COME, WHICH WAS THAT, among all the stressors in Aurienne's life, the one called Osric Mordaunt would be absent for an entire month. May shimmered beautifully before her: four weeks until the Blædnes moon, four weeks of normalcy, four weeks without interactions with the murderous delinquent.

But, obviously, Fate had other plans. Fate, mused Aurienne, liked to take the piss.

This contribution to modern philosophy went unvoiced because Aurienne was trapped behind her desk by Quincey, going through the correspondence pile.

Mordaunt's deofol tingled at her tācn. Fate had given her five days of reprieve before he wedged himself back into her life. Frīa save her. Mordaunt's money did a lot of good at Swanstone; he, however, was of little added value to Aurienne, except in the sense that he caused her to secrete additional cortisol.

As his deofol tingled at her palm for permission to materialise, Aurienne found herself unable to decide what was more harrowing: the prospect of dealing with the Fyren, or Quincey and the Administrative Faff.

This was the price—the curse—of being the Best. Everyone wanted a bit of you.

Aurienne ignored the deofol's request. She didn't owe the Fyren immediate availability. And if it annoyed him to wait, all the better.

Poor Quincey, familiar with Aurienne's distaste for Dreaded Admin, was doing a rapid-fire questioning session. Aurienne was asked to join a miscellany of Committees, Working Groups, and Task Forces, develop curricula for an assortment of universities, assess potential Haelan apprentices, and devote more time to community clinics.

The tingle in Aurienne's tācn disappeared. Mordaunt's deofol had retreated, probably back to its master to report its failure.

"Two referrals for consideration," said Quincey, placing letters in front of Aurienne. "The first, a compression injury resulting in damaged seith channels. The other I think you'll like—seith haemorrhages. The patient is an Ingenaut; she's starting fires every time she stands next to an engine."

"Ask Whitman if he'd take on the compression injury," said Aurienne. "I'll take the haemorrhage case—she sounds like a good candidate for the micro-occlusion trial. Have her transferred to my ward here, though. I'm not wasting time with waystones."

Quincey, pleased that he had guessed correctly, made a note, and proceeded to the next item. "We've also received this." He handed Aurienne a memo. "Every Haelan has been asked to continue to give fifteen hours a week to the Pox ward, given the current crisis. The Heads thank you for your understanding in these challenging times."

Aurienne took the memo, grateful to have been reminded about the challenging times. She might've forgotten about them otherwise.

"Finally, these beasts have been clamouring for your attention." Quincey passed Aurienne a squirming wodge of charts pinned together with vascular clips. "That's me done. You'll tell me if I can do anything to be of help?"

"I will," said Aurienne. "Thank you, Quincey. You're the only reason I haven't quit everything and gone into exile."

Quincey blushed. He had a desperate sort of crush on Aurienne, which he occasionally exhibited by waffling about inane things, which he now, to her chagrin, began to do. He propped himself against her desk in what was probably intended as a debonair lean, and discussed his Friday-night plans, which involved a rhubarb festival and related turf wars.

Aurienne's tācn prickled again; Mordaunt's deofol was back for another attempt. Mordaunt was the lowest form of life, but even the most inutile protozoa was occasionally useful, and so, too, was the Fyren.

"I've got a deofol coming in," said Aurienne. She waved Quincey out. "Good luck with the—the rhubarb mafia. Cartel. Would you shut the door behind you?"

Quincey made his bows and exited. He tried to close the door behind him. Aurienne heard his sputtered objections—"So sorry, you can't go in, she's got a deofol on the way, excuse me, sorry, didn't you hear me?"—then some general sounds of belligerence, and then the Director of Trauma and Acute Care barged in, accompanied by the Haelan Order's top virologist.

Cath's shaved head contrasted sharply with Élodie's exuberance of flaxen curls. It was one of their many contrapositions; Cath loved graveyards and amputations and boxing, while Élodie liked the piano, obscure diseases, and pressing flowers in books. They were perfect for each other.

"Aurienne won't mind; it's just us," said Cath to Quincey with kind reassurance, as though she hadn't just manhandled him into submission. To Aurienne she said, "We've brought snacks."

Élodie, looking drawn and pale, followed Cath in, and laid herself on the floor.

"What are you doing?" asked Aurienne.

Élodie, in her soft French accent, answered, "Coping."

This seemed an excellent mechanism to Aurienne, who abandoned her chair to lay herself beside Élodie, her dress splayed in a neat semicircle. There was, indeed, much to cope with.

Cath joined them on the floor, sitting cross-legged among her snacks (pretzels, cheese cubes, grapes, a large tumbler of tea). She hand-fed Aurienne and Élodie where they lay and called them the most beautiful corpses; they had shrouds and everything.

Haelan could choose how they wore their whites. Aurienne, favouring structure and femininity, tended towards the Order's traditional dresses. Cath's whites today took the form of high-waisted trousers and a long, fitted frock coat, gorgeously cut, which had the effect of making everyone around her look as though they were wearing sacks. Aurienne made a note to visit the Order's robe makers and investigate this option.

All their silver epaulettes, however, were identical; Aurienne, Cath, and Élodie had each earned their tācn at the same time, and each therefore bore ten lines, denoting their ten years as Haelan.

"Have that deofol in," said Élodie, with a gentle touch to Aurienne's arm. "We interrupted."

It repulsed Aurienne to lie to her nearest and dearest, but given that the deofol was a bloody Fyren's, she hadn't a choice. "It's all right. It's only my mum." She opted for a sudden, but tactical, change of subject: "Did you hear that we've been asked to keep up the fifteen hours at Paeds?"

A sigh burst from between Cath's teeth. "I hadn't. Frīa's pointy nips. Can we ask for exceptions? I haven't dared cut my clinic hours, but everything else is in the toilet."

"I got one," said Élodie to the ceiling. "An exception, I mean."

"Well, obviously *you* got one," said Cath.

"Has your team made progress on the inoculation?" asked Aurienne.

Élodie managed a weak smile. "Given the mad time constraints and the feeling that we are somehow responsible for every additional sick child, I'm pleased. We'll be able to roll out an immunisation programme soon. Thank the gods. None of our colleagues at the universities have achieved much at all."

"None?" asked Cath.

"Their labs have been hamstrung, just like we were," said Élodie. "No money, save internal funding. No one has managed to squeeze out anything substantial from any of the research councils or the Tīendoms."

"I heard that from Xanthe," said Aurienne. "It's an embarrassment."

"They've all pivoted to new strategic priorities, apparently," said Élodie, with a vague gesture upwards. "I don't know the politics."

"I wouldn't have thought prolonging mass casualties among children would've been the most politically astute move," mused Aurienne.

"They're the children no one cares about," said Cath.

"One day this will be a case study," said Élodie. She drew bullet points in the air as she planned it. "Vaccine-preventable diseases. Research financing. Socioeconomic variables."

Cath's title suggestion was *A Study in Policymaking by Royal Arse-holes and the Innocents Who Died as a Result.*

"During the last Platt's Pox outbreak, they had an excuse—inoculation hadn't yet been developed," said Élodie. "That was about a hundred years ago."

"What brought the last outbreak to its end?" asked Aurienne.

"Extinction of the host population," said Élodie.

"Gods."

Cath looked grim. "That's a lot of dead children."

"Yes," said Élodie. "The spread was confined to small settlements in Mercia. Lichfield and thereabouts. It was before waystones were in common use, so the virus stayed relatively localised. That's not the case anymore. Borders between Tīendoms are open, unless there's a war."

"And they won't shut down the waystones to prevent the spread now, of course," said Cath. "It would inconvenience too many—and the only ones who are suffering are beggar-children and foundlings."

Cath passed her tea tumbler to Aurienne, who opened it.

Aurienne inhaled fragrant vapours of peppermint. "Lovely, this."

"Have you any mugs?" asked Cath.

"No, but I've got these," said Aurienne, reaching for a clattering box of sterile specimen containers. "Brand-new."

"Grand," said Cath.

Aurienne divided the tea into perfect sixty-millilitre portions, upon which the three Haelan sipped.

Aurienne's tācn tingled again, but heavily, almost painfully. Mordaunt's deofol was insisting *again*. Bristling with repressed annoyance, Aurienne excused herself to the lav.

Down the hall and behind a locked door, she pointed her tācn to the floor and let Mordaunt's deofol through. (It was tempting to aim it at the toilet; she mastered the impulse; *Harm to none* included drowning deofols in the loo, probably.)

Smoky black wisps infested the place and coalesced into a wolfish shape. The white grin of Mordaunt's deofol materialised among the shadows, followed by a pair of golden eyes.

"You'd better have an excellent reason to have pushed like that," said Aurienne. "I've half a mind to sever my link with your master."

The deofol attempted an ingratiating grin, but given that it was all sharp teeth, it had rather the opposite effect. "Greetings, Haelan. How are you? You're looking very well today, if I may say—"

Aurienne, operating on three hours of sleep, two pretzels, and one specimen container of tea, did not harbour delusions in this regard. "You may not. What do you want?"

"So sorry for pressing you," said the deofol, lowering itself to its belly and whisking its smoky tail across the floor in obsequious sweeps. "It's urgent. My master is having—he's having a seith constipation."

"I beg your pardon?"

"He can hardly push it out. It won't come to his tācn. He nearly hadn't enough to send me."

"A blockage?" asked Aurienne.

"I don't know. Can you come?" The deofol resumed its cajoling tail wags. "No one will see you. His steward and groundsman are away."

"You're far more polite when you need something," said Aurienne.

"I know," said the deofol, with more tooth baring. "I'm manipulative like that."

"Where is he?" asked Aurienne.

"The family seat. Rosefell Hall. There's a private waystone. Will you come? Please?"

The deofol was now attempting puppy-dog eyes, but, given that it was a creature of soul-corroding darkness, the endeavour was more per-turbing than anything else.

"Fine," said Aurienne.

"Thank you," breathed the deofol. "I'll tell him you're on the way."

"I'll be there in a bit," said Aurienne. "I've got to wrap up here. Leave. You mustn't be seen."

"Of course," said the deofol, bowing its head low as it faded away. "Thank you, Haelan. He'll be waiting for you."

Aurienne returned to her office to find both Trauma and Virology enjoying a nap on the floor. She let out an envious yawn as she packed her satchel. Thanks to Mordaunt and his newest crisis, her nap would have to wait.

She glided about on tiptoe, gathering her things as Cath and Élodie slept. Her efforts were for naught, however; just as she was snapping her satchel shut, an eruption of shouts echoed from the courtyard below her office.

Aurienne strode to the window, intending to whip it open and berate the culprits—raucous apprentices with the Friday happies off to the pub, probably—but, as she pushed open the window, she saw that the commotion wasn't caused by raucous apprentices. It was the Wardens.

"What on earth?" gasped Aurienne.

She was joined by a bleary-eyed Élodie and a grouchy Cath. They caught the tail end of a fight: the blue glow of the Wardens' tācn (the horned head of an auroch), the glimmer of their trapping wards, and the capture of three or four black-clad figures. The Wardens speared the figures into the ground—who twitched and went still.

On the far side of the courtyard, curious apprentices popped heads round a door. A Warden snapped an order at them; they pivoted and ran back in.

Swanstone guards jogged into the courtyard, bearing torches. By their light, Aurienne could see blood splattered across the flagstones, and the figures of three men and a woman, hooded and cloaked, impaled into the ground.

One of the Wardens lifted a dead man by the scruff of his neck and tore off his hood. His head lolled. Another Warden pulled her spear out of the corpse—or plucked, rather; she made it look effortless, even though she had driven it through the man's spine. The third Warden searched his body, stripping it of clothes as she went, until the dead man was naked, save for the blood running down his middle from the gory hole at his diaphragm.

The Wardens proceeded in this manner with the three other corpses. The first man had fared the best, frankly; the others had fought the trapping wards, and so dropped a limb or two when lifted to be searched.

Aurienne recognised none of the bodies.

Cath made a low whistle. "Fresh organs for Transplant Surg."

"And fodder for the anatomy lab," said Aurienne.

Cath pointed to a severed foot. "Pop a piece of string on that and you've got a mad good-luck charm."

"*Regardez*—the Heads are coming out," said Élodie.

Xanthe's small figure entered the circle of torchlight, along with bald Abercorn and skinny Prendergast.

"What have you discovered?" asked Abercorn, as Aurienne, Cath, and Élodie eavesdropped like naughty apprentices.

"We detected them hours ago, sniffing around the moat," said Verity, the tallest of the Wardens. "Lured them in with spotty warding along the east wall. They were skittish, but eventually came through. Nothing of use on them for identification."

"What are those?" asked Prendergast, indicating a pile near the corpses.

"Incendiary devices," said Verity. "Call your resident Ingenaut. They must be inspected and disarmed."

One of the other Wardens, Haven, held a gleaming dagger to the light. "They were well equipped. This is quality kit. A lot of gold on them, too."

"Any idea what they wanted?" asked Xanthe.

Verity's steel sabaton nudged at a heap of ropes, gloves, and grappling hooks. "They were geared up for an incursion. Not sure to what end. We didn't wish to allow them into Swanstone proper to find out."

"Were they members of any Order?" asked Prendergast.

"No." Haven unfurled the corpses' limp hands. "No tācn."

Xanthe's dry, annoyed voice rang across the courtyard. "Perhaps next time we could try a live capture, so that we might interrogate them?"

Haven turned her helmeted head to Xanthe. "Our command is to kill intruders on sight. You may speak to the Head of our Order if you wish to change the agreement."

Aurienne stiffened at Haven's tone. Élodie produced a small gasp of outrage.

Xanthe was less ruffled than her audience. "Very well. If you're done with the bodies, we'll find a use for them. Thank you for your vigilance tonight."

The Wardens had, at least, the wherewithal to salute her and the other Heads, before stamping off to return to their posts.

Aurienne, Élodie, and Cath settled onto the window ledge to observe the goings-on like the Fates. The bodies were carted away; the blood was mopped up; the clothes were carried off. Felicette, the bespectacled and slightly mad Ingenaut who lived at Swanstone, observed the incendiary devices, then gathered them up in her arms and trotted off like a child with new presents. The three Heads retreated into the fortress, looking grave.

"I wonder what they wanted," said Élodie. "Can't've been the medicinal garden again, not with those bombs. Unless they wanted to destroy it."

Aurienne gasped at the hideous thought.

"We've a healthy vault," said Cath. "Perhaps the bombs were a distraction."

"D'you think they'll let us out?" asked Aurienne. "I'm meant to be going to see—to see my parents tonight."

Another lie because of the Fyren. Disgusting. Resentment fermented within Aurienne like some sort of yeast.

"Must you go, tonight of all nights?" asked Élodie.

"She'll be fine," said Cath. "A Warden will probably escort her to the waystone."

Cath was right. When Aurienne approached Verity at the front gate a quarter of an hour later, she was questioned on the necessity of an outing. Aurienne lied again, yeastily, and was escorted to the waystone at the Publish or Perish.

Verity was on edge. Her helmeted head swept left and right as they crossed the bridge from Swanstone to the village; her spear was loose in her gauntlet; her shoulders were tense even under her pauldrons. Her wards shimmered under her feet.

"Will there be an investigation, or something, to work out who those people were?" asked Aurienne.

Verity's sentences were more terse than usual. "Not by us. We're not here to play detective. You'll have to ask your Heads."

"I'm certain they'll launch one," said Aurienne. "Those weren't run-of-the-mill thieves."

"They weren't. There was money behind them."

"I don't like it."

"Don't worry, Halean." Verity clasped Aurienne's shoulder with a heavy, steel-clad hand. "If more come, they'll meet the same fate. They didn't even have a tācn."

"I suppose few things must really worry you when you're stationed at Swanstone."

"Few."

"What would?"

"The Agannor Order making a move." Verity's helmet took on a thoughtful tilt. "Imagine having to fight your own spear-sister because she's possessed by one of those fiends. Or perhaps an onslaught of Dreor. Unlikely in this day and age."

Aurienne found it interesting that the Fyren Order didn't make Verity's list. Mordaunt would doubtlessly be offended.

"But this is idle talk," said Verity. "The Peace Accords forbid such foulness among the Orders."

"I've never met either an Agannor or a Dreor," said Aurienne.

"Good," said Verity. "I hope you never do. We had a Dreor attack once at Tintagel. It was terrorising the village outside our walls. It took two of us to bring it down. Like fighting a rabid dog, only the dog had plate armour and a scythe, and was bigger even than me."

"What happened?" asked Aurienne.

"We captured it. Dinadan—the Head of the Wardens—convened the other Orders to the Stánrocc to come to an agreement on what to do with the creature. Our position was that the Dreor had committed an act of aggression against the Warden Order and should be executed, in keeping with the Peace Accords. The Bright Paths all voted in favour; the Fyren and Agannor voted against; the Hedgewitches abstained. The Dreor Order didn't send a representative. So the Bright Paths won. When we got back to Tintagel, we got a ward on each of the Dreor's boots and split it in half. Then we burned it. It was laughing the entire time."

"Are they all mad?" asked Aurienne.

"No. They've got different—well, I suppose you could call them ranks. Some take the tācn and carry on as you or I did after we received ours. Some take the tācn and lose their minds. Apparently, the weaker the will, the greater the risk. So I've heard, anyway. I don't know much. One oughtn't know much about the Dusken Paths."

At the Publish or Perish, Aurienne tapped a coin on the window to get the attention of Grette, the publican, and left it on the sill.

Verity stood by as Aurienne pressed seith into the runes for the pub near her parents' home in London.

"Thank you for the escort," said Aurienne. "And the reassurance. I hope the rest of the night is less eventful. Wes hāl—be well."

Verity gave Aurienne a sharp salute as she was drawn into the waystone graticule.

Then it was time for more Mordaunt-inspired fun; upon materialising at the waystone in London, Aurienne ran into one of her parents' neighbours, and had to fabricate another story to make her getaway from him.

She took the waystone to a random pub, and from there was finally able to reach her destination: Rosefell Hall, the Mordaunt family seat.

ROSEFELL HALL

Aurienne

Waystone travel always left Aurienne feeling ill, and back-to-back dips into the waystone graticule made it even worse. It was a foul-tempered ride through the ley line.

The molecules that made Aurienne recongregated at Rosefell Hall, somewhere in Mercia. She felt clandestine, sick, and saturated by her own lies. She pressed her tācn to her forehead to quell her nausea as she took her bearings. She was next to a waystone at the edge of a broad, overgrown gravel drive.

The waning moon, cloud crossed, offered little in terms of light, so Aurienne walked towards the house with her tācn held aloft. The air was thick with the sound of night insects, punctuated by the crunch of her footsteps on the gravel.

Rosefell Hall came into view. The great house loomed black before Aurienne, a wide, rambling structure, with windows boarded up here and there, a roof missing half its shingles, and walls choked with vines.

A weathervane in the shape of a running hound spun, though there was no wind.

Of course this was where the Fyren lived. It looked downright haunted. It was a lair.

Aurienne didn't like vines. Vines were rat ladders.

The house's great front doors were flanked by heraldic greyhounds holding petal-adorned shields. Upon the door hung a tarnished brass knocker in the shape of a sprig of wild roses. Aurienne pounded out three impatient knocks thereon, startling the night insects into silence.

She expected a dramatic opening of the doors, and perhaps a sinister butler, for whom she preemptively formulated a curt request to fetch his wretched master. However, there was no opening, and no butler. Instead, the handles rattled, accompanied by muffled swearing.

At length, Mordaunt's gloved fingertips appeared in a crack between the doors, then his hands, then his face.

"Don't get many visitors, do you?" asked Aurienne. (She did not assist with his struggle.)

Mordaunt looked cross. "You took so long to come, the hinges bloody rusted."

"I was unavoidably delayed. You're lucky I came at all."

Mordaunt did not care enough to ask why she had been delayed, which was fine; Aurienne was reserving that for some upcoming negotiations.

"Use the entrance round the back, by the kitchens, next time," said Mordaunt.

Presumptuous of him to assume there would be a next time, but all right.

Mordaunt managed to drag one door open enough for Aurienne to slip through. "Get in."

He wasn't as well put together as usual. His collar wasn't crisp; his shirt wanted ironing. His gaze was suspicious, bordering on wild. His silver-white hair, normally artfully windswept, was askew.

He jammed the door shut behind her. A bit of plaster fell on Auri-enne. Likewise a spider. Mordaunt brushed both off with a muttered apology for these disagreeable additions to her person.

"I don't care," said Aurienne. "I live in an attic."

She followed Mordaunt into the house. Their footsteps echoed along the cavernous front hall's flagged floor. The windows—those that remained unboarded—were stained with more heraldic greyhounds and roses. Great beams ran across the ceilings, blackened with mould. Candles flickered here and there, shedding little light.

"Do you live alone in this great, empty house?" asked Aurienne.

"Yes," said Mordaunt.

"You're a misanthrope, then?"

"Why do you think I kill people?"

Mordaunt led her out of the front hall and through a series of high-vaulted corridors.

"What happened to your family?" asked Aurienne.

"Killed them all."

"Ah."

"Ate their hearts."

"Oh."

"You believe me?"

"Yes."

"How dare you?"

"I thought you wanted me to trust you," said Aurienne.

"Not when I'm obviously lying," said Mordaunt.

"Where is your family, if you didn't kill them all?"

"Well," conceded Mordaunt, as one caught in a little white lie, "I did kill my father. My mother died of—causes."

"Not natural?"

"No."

On either side of the corridor, dark rooms lay like mausoleums. Elegant furnishings decayed within, encased in their white winding-sheets. Wallpaper peeled. Curtains rotted. Floorboards creaked under their feet. All was faded grandeur.

It pleased Aurienne to see it. Let the Fyren rot.

A mild sneezing fit accompanied this uncharitable thought. Aurienne could not abide dust.

They came now to the back of the house, in an area that seemed a little more lived-in and, happily for Aurienne's sinuses, less dusty. They passed a grand piano, a room walled with portraits, another packed with silver vases and mirrors, and another full of marble sculptures.

"I am a great appreciator of beauty," said Mordaunt. In the face of Aurienne's raised brow, he added, "You look as though you doubt me."

"Killing is the ugliest thing there is."

"One must fund the beauty somehow."

Aurienne made no comment save a judgemental tut. They passed a small armoury glistening with weapons, and a gallery of paintings of dizzying sun-filled landscapes.

"What are those?" asked Aurienne.

"Landscapes."

"As seen in a malarial dream?"

"It's called Impressionism."

They passed a deep alcove. Immured by pink and mauve curtains, the alcove made a peculiar sort of tube.

"Is this meant to look like a colon?" asked Aurienne.

"A colon?" repeated Mordaunt.

Aurienne pointed at the pink frills and folds. "Villi. Mucosa. Sub-mucosa. These pockets make compelling intestinal crypts."

Mordaunt was both pained and offended. "What? No. That was a part of the viewing experience for my beautiful de Beauveau. *Dusk Roses*. I had to sell it."

Aurienne peered into the colon's lumen. There was a bare frame at the end of it. "Why?"

"You," said Mordaunt. The word was potent with accusation.

"Me?"

"Twenty million thrymsas."

"Ah."

"Should've gone with the kidnap," said Mordaunt.

"You were wise not to," said Aurienne.

Mordaunt did not look convinced. Aurienne didn't argue the point. He needn't know what ravages she could've laid on him. *Harm to none* held until it abutted with self-defence, at which point Aurienne could be—well, rather harmful. A Haelan knew exactly how to keep people alive, and conversely, a few interesting ways to cause immediate death. There was a reason the Order's tācn was an Aer.

"Also your fault," said Mordaunt, with a gesture towards an arrangement of live vines, twining around a blank square of wall. "And that one, too," he said, pointing at a trickling water feature framing nothing.

Aurienne made no apologies for the gaps in the opulence. In fact, she found them gratifying. She wished that she and Xanthe had pushed for thirty million. No, forty million and the entirety of Rosefell Hall. They could've used the property as an isolation unit after a bit of renovating.

As they walked, a small voice declared, "Cock boil."

Aurienne looked at Mordaunt, who, for his part, grew freshly irritated. "One of those damned critique crickets."

"It followed you from the Downs?"

"Must've hitched a ride. It now lives here. I can't find it to kill it."

"Face like a bollock," said the cricket.

"Fuck off," said Mordaunt.

"Suck a fart out of my arse," instructed the cricket.

"When I find you," said Mordaunt, addressing the room at large, "I am going to make you suffer."

"Perhaps you should deal with your daddy issues first," said the cricket.

Mordaunt, looking grim, led Aurienne onwards.

They came to a sitting room abundant with ormolu, alabaster, and gilt. There was bric-a-brac upon every surface: bronze figures in erotic poses, candlesticks in the shape of storks, jewelled inkwells, fine porcelain dogs, trinket boxes inlaid with precious stones, horses, clocks, globes, marble busts, an enormous golden lobster. The walls were covered in tapestries and a large map of the Tïendoms in finely beaten gold, silver, and copper.

Mordaunt ushered Aurienne into a high-backed chair and sat across from her in another.

Thanks to a fire lurking moodily in the hearth, this was the most well-lit room in the house. The fire burned low and gave off a fragrant, slightly bitter smoke. It lent a Gothic aspect to the scene, flickering against wood panelling and touching Mordaunt's scarred, fine-cut features. He was in only shirtsleeves tonight; they were pushed up to the elbows and showed off particularly vascular forearms. The veins seaming them were a phlebotomist's dream.

A thought, unhallowed and unwelcome, sprang into Aurienne's mind: Mordaunt, dishevelled, princely, bathed by the broody light of the fire, was genuinely attractive.

Discombobulating. Aurienne hadn't found anyone truly attractive since—since *her*.

But it was fine. He had an unfortunate mouth and even more unfortunate morals, and so Aurienne was quite safe. She had better cheekbones, anyway.

She was surprised to find a quantity of old dogs limping about or sleeping in the sitting room. They were a skittish lot; most of them fled as soon as she entered the room. The only one brave enough to remain, an arthritic terrier, did not have a voice. It huffed out aggressive breaths of air that commanded her to leave or perish. Aurienne stared at it. It stared at her. The terrier, satisfied by her courage in the face of its ferocity, returned to its cushion.

On a low table sat a pot of tea and some biscuits, which Mordaunt made a vaguely invitational gesture towards.

"No, thank you," said Aurienne, who remembered Mordaunt's claim about his steward's paramnesiac teas and did not wish to test their potency. "Your deofol said your seith wouldn't come to your tācn."

For the first time since her arrival, Aurienne could make out Mordaunt's face properly. Beneath the scruff of day-old stubble, he looked harrowed.

"Noticed a fluctuation in the middle of a job today," he said. "I was able to finish it, but haven't been able to properly summon my seith since."

He pulled off his glove and raised his tācn to Aurienne. The detestable hellhound's skull flickered a faint red, then faded back to maroon. Mordaunt swore and focused on it again, but his tācn did not respond, and remained as inert as a bloodstain upon his palm.

"Let's have a look," said Aurienne. She put her satchel on the floor and found her feet. "Shirt off, please."

Mordaunt rose and unbuttoned his shirt. "Is this it, then?" he asked in a voice that wanted to be casual, but sounded choked. "Has the rot finally advanced to those—those nodes you pointed out?"

"I don't know," said Aurienne. "We're going to find out."

The terrier sniffed the air and sneezed in objection as Aurienne sprayed her hands with hlutoform.

"Why have you got so many dogs?" she asked.

"I find them, or they find me."

"And why do you keep them?"

"Why not?"

"Everything else in here is rare or beautiful or expensive."

Mordaunt covered the ears of the terrier and told it, "Don't listen to her." He turned to Aurienne. "What's wrong with you? They *are* expensive, anyway; have you any idea what it costs to bring the vet in for eight dogs?"

Aurienne gave up on understanding his logic; it didn't appear that there was any at play. "Right. Turn around. Let's see what's going on."

She rubbed the froth of the hlutoform off her palms and fell into that pre-flow state of calm curiosity, of pleasant problem-solving anticipation. As a Haelan, these moments of discovery were what she lived for—the patient being a Fyren notwithstanding. One could, she supposed, get used to anything.

Mordaunt was anxious. His shield of glibness slipped; his eyes were a clouded, worried grey. The hollows under his cheekbones deepened with the clench of his jaw. The scar across his lips whitened. He half tore his collar as he removed it. He had undone his buttons, but forgotten to take off his braces, which got in the way of removing his shirt. He pushed the straps off his shoulders with jerky hands. He made no eye contact with Aurienne, favouring the unlit chandelier above, as a doomed man might eye the sun one last time, waiting to be hanged.

"I'd be surprised if it was the rot," said Aurienne. "The fact that you can still make your tācn flicker makes me think it's something else."

Mordaunt did not answer. Now shirtless, he continued his gallows stare upwards.

"Right," said Aurienne. "I've had a long day and I didn't conserve my seith. I didn't expect to need any more before bed. I may be slow."

Mordaunt gave her a tense nod.

Aurienne pressed her palm to the spot under his clavicle and activated her tācn. As expected, instead of bursting out of her, as it did in the freshness of the morning, her seith verged on the sluggish. She flowed into Mordaunt.

Most of their previous healing sessions had him facing away from her. This time, she could see his face. His mouth, normally broad with insufferable smiles, was pressed into an unhappy line. Inch by exploratory inch, Aurienne trickled her way through his decaying seith channels.

"Am I done for?" asked Mordaunt.

"Be quiet," said Aurienne.

Mordaunt fell into silence. Aurienne's focus was on her seith, but she could feel him watching her. His breathing was slow and deliberate, but his pulse told the truth and skittered along anxiously under her palm.

In this moment, Mordaunt was devoid of the one thing that gave him power—that made him untouchable—that made him a Fyren.

In this moment, he was mortal.

Aurienne ought to have found his vulnerability enjoyable. She wished she did. She found it merely pathetic.

Seith degeneration could cause excess deposition of extracellular matrix proteins in seith channels. In Mordaunt's left forearm, Aurienne found exactly that: an obstruction where his decayed lines met the healthy. A lovely, juicy textbook seith embolus, impeding the flow to his tācn.

Aurienne withdrew her hand from his chest.

"And?" he asked in a half whisper. He took a twitchy step towards her, then backed off.

Aurienne wasn't cruel. She did not keep him suspended in his agonies. "You'll be all right. A cluster of dead cells has caked up one of your seith channels."

Mordaunt let out a sigh of relief. He clutched at Aurienne's wrists, released them immediately, as though burned, and took quick steps around the room. He swung his arms about, hooked them behind his head, and stared at the ceiling.

These vigours expended, he approached Aurienne again. "Like a clot?"

"Exactly like a clot." Aurienne nodded. "A seith embolus."

"What do we do?" asked Mordaunt.

"*We* don't do anything," said Aurienne. "I clear it."

"Thank the gods for you," said Mordaunt.

"Me in particular, yes. This would normally require an embolectomy—an unpleasant procedure with high risk of permanent damage."

Aurienne waited to be told that she was arrogant. The comment did not come. Instead, Mordaunt observed her with a conflicted expression of unwilling regard, of reluctant appreciation.

"So you can fix it?" he asked. "Now?"

"I could," said Aurienne.

"Could?" repeated Mordaunt.

"You didn't ask me why I'd been delayed today," said Aurienne.

Mordaunt, demonstrating a heretofore unsuspected modicum of intelligence, grew cautious. He was right to; at this moment, Aurienne had Leverage.

"I should've asked," said Mordaunt, with sudden, and insincere, politeness. "Why were you delayed, dear Haelan?"

"In your dealings with the criminal underworld"—Aurienne flung her hand towards an imaginary slag heap—"have you heard of anyone targeting Swanstone?"

"No," said Mordaunt. "Why?"

There was no hesitation in his answer, but that told Aurienne little about whether or not he was lying.

"The Wardens caught four intruders tonight," said Aurienne. "They weren't our usual sorts of trespassers. We get the occasional thief wanting to get into our garden, or addicts breaking into the apothecary's storeroom. But this crew was armed to the teeth—with incendiary devices, if you please—and well funded."

"Any tācn?" asked Mordaunt.

"No."

"Idiots. Bypassing Wardens is near impossible, unless you're me. And civvies, at that? They had a death wish."

"Or they were desperate," said Aurienne. "Or they were being coerced into it. Or they're after something or someone in particular, and it was important enough to risk their lives."

"Interesting," said Mordaunt.

"Will you see what you can find out?" asked Aurienne.

"Are you going to withhold healing this embolus until I agree?" asked Mordaunt.

"Yes," said Aurienne.

The Fyren crossed his arms over his bare chest, which pushed together his pectorals. Aurienne noted in passing that he had more cleavage than she did.

"Well?" prompted Aurienne.

Just as Mordaunt opened his mouth to answer, something banged in a distant part of the house.

There was a cry of "Hallo! Anyone home?"

The voiceless terrier barked. Mordaunt whipped around. Aurienne froze.

"Shit," said Mordaunt.

The next thing she knew, Aurienne had been dragged across the room and stuffed into a wardrobe.

"Stay there," said Mordaunt above her muffled objections. "Don't move."

There was more banging, as of someone running into furniture. Uneven footsteps stomped along the corridor.

The wardrobe's door was ajar. Aurienne could see a sliver of the sitting room. Mordaunt kicked her Haelan satchel under the sofa.

The owner of the uneven footsteps meandered into the room. Judging by his cloak and hood, he, too, was a Fyren. Like Mordaunt, he had a surfeit of weapon holsters strapped to his person, but among knives and swords, his contained a pair of pink safety scissors and a rolling pin.

Mordaunt, still shirtless, strode towards the intruder and hissed, "Leofric. What are you doing here?"

Leofric pulled his hood off to reveal a pale complexion and masses of fluffy red hair springing incongruously upwards.

The ancient dogs surged back into the room and creaked and limped their way around him with wagging tails. Leofric exchanged saliva with the dogs through vigorous kisses (Aurienne shuddered) and flung himself towards Mordaunt for a sloppy hug. Mordaunt countered it with a stiff arm against his shoulder.

"I've got a Concern," declared Leofric.

He went limp and fell into Mordaunt's arms.

"You're smashed off your tits," said Mordaunt.

"Yep," hiccoughed Leofric. He squinted towards the table. "Ooh. Are those choccy biscuits?"

Leofric lurched towards the biscuits, but was unable to muster the coordination to put them in his mouth. Mordaunt crammed a few in for him.

"What do you want?" asked Mordaunt. "What's the Concern?"

Leofric closed his eyes to concentrate upon chewing. Mordaunt glanced downwards, saw that the strap of Aurienne's satchel was still protruding from under the sofa, and nudged it farther in.

"I need to show you something, b-because I trust you," said Leofric.

"What is it?" asked Mordaunt.

Aurienne didn't know what she had expected Leofric to show Mordaunt, but it certainly hadn't involved the removal of his trousers and underthings.

The same went for Mordaunt. "*What* are you doing?"

"H-have you got one ball that hangs lower than the other?" asked Leofric, pointing to the testicle in question.

"Pull your trousers back up, you great oaf."

"Have you, though?"

"I don't know," said Mordaunt. "I've never inspected them for symmetry."

"Show us yours, then," said Leofric, gesturing towards Mordaunt's crotch.

"Fuck off," said Mordaunt.

"W-what should I do?" asked Leofric. "Should I get it looked at?"

"I don't know."

"Slap it, maybe? Pinch it? Might retract it?"

"You need to leave."

Leofric grew philosophical. "D'you know, I don't think my pubes are curly enough. What do you think? Be honest."

Mordaunt was out of view of Aurienne's narrow field of vision, but she heard his exasperated snarl. *"Leave."*

"Why?" asked Leofric, wounded and pouty. "What are you doing that's so important? Why're you half naked, anyway?"

"None of your fucking business."

Leofric looked sly. "'Bout to slap your own balls, I bet."

"No," said Mordaunt.

"'Bout to play with them, then. Let me tell you a thing about that." Leofric pointed a finger in Mordaunt's face, as though he were about to impart some profound advice. Then he said, "Don't get your fingers caught in your pubes."

Mordaunt sounded offended. "How long do you think my pubes are?"

"Dunno. Bet you plait them."

"Fuck off."

"Pube-plait boy."

"I'm not asking you again. Leave."

Leofric grew truculent. "Or what?"

"I'll garrote you with my pube plait."

Leofric tilted his head back and let out a high-pitched giggle.

Mordaunt, losing patience with the proceedings, hitched up Leofric's trousers, grasped him by the shoulders, and steered him towards the door. "Go home."

"Pube plait," whinnied Leofric.

"To the waystone, and I never want to hear about your pubic hair again," said Mordaunt, wrestling him towards the door.

Leofric let out a soul-rending wail about his uneven balls.

There was silence, broken by the occasional thump of Leofric running into furniture, as Mordaunt pushed him out. Finally, there was the slam of a door and the slide and click of several dead bolts.

Mordaunt reentered the room, exasperation wafting off him. He opened the wardrobe, at the bottom of which lay Aurienne, in absolute bits, trying to recover from a fit of silent laughter.

Mordaunt reached a hand down to help her to her feet. The movement was brusque; the grasp was gentler. Aurienne regained her feet, wiped at her eyes, and found her usual seriousness. More or less.

How tragic that she wouldn't be able to share this story with Élodie and Cath.

"That was—" began Aurienne.

"Let's never speak of it again," said Mordaunt. He looked irritated to the extreme. There was a flush of embarrassment across his cheekbones.

"Your friend is—"

"Not a friend," said Mordaunt.

"Who is he?"

"Leofric. He's only got one brain cell, and he uses it to not shit on his own head."

"He seemed nice—"

"He's an imbecile with a perfect instinct for chaos. Impossible to say whether he's the harbinger or the cause. I hate him."

"You know, his pubic hair *was* unusually straight," said Aurienne. "Rigid, like."

"I don't care about Leofric's pubic hair."

"He could take out someone's eye."

Mordaunt shut the wardrobe behind Aurienne with a snap. With an air of immense suffering, he asked, "Must we belabour this subject?"

Aurienne belaboured. "Is his deofol a porcupine?"

"I see we're going for the low-hanging fruit."

"Only one of them was low," said Aurienne. "*Is* it a porcupine?"

"Sea urchin."

Instead of disintegrating into a shriek of laughter, as she wished to, Aurienne said, "A sea urchin. Naturally."

"Naturally."

"Do advise him that testicular asymmetry is normal. However, he ought to see someone if he's in pain, or if he notices any new lumps."

"I will *not* be telling him any of that. Can we carry on with your primitive coercion attempt?"

Aurienne recovered her self-possession in the face of this condescension. Primitive? How dare he?

"It's a *negotiation*," she said. "And I'm keeping the terms basic, given my interlocutor's limited capabilities. I help you with your embolus; you help me find out what those people wanted."

In the face of this—in Aurienne's opinion—eminently fair exchange, Mordaunt let out a dramatic sigh. "If they were as well funded as you, and bold enough to attempt Swanstone, anyone could be behind it. This could take ages. And be exceptionally risky."

"May I remind you that you're an expert at intelligence gathering?" asked Aurienne.

"May I remind *you* that I'm paid handsomely for that particular skill set?"

"Is healing your embolus not handsome enough a payment?"

Mordaunt looked provoked. Aurienne blinked at him with all the innocence in the world.

"You're lucky I need you," said Mordaunt.

"So we have an agreement?"

"Yes, but it's a shit agreement and I'm not happy about it."

"I'm familiar with the feeling," said Aurienne.

Mordaunt narrowed his eyes at her. "Let's get on with it, then."

They resumed their positions in front of the fire.

Aurienne paused before pressing her tacn to Mordaunt's chest. "I should note—simply because I don't trust you—that, as your condition

progresses, you'll have a significant risk of recurrence for more blockages like this one. I hope you'll keep your word, otherwise I won't help
you next time this happens."

"Oh?" said Mordaunt. "It's threats now, is it?"

"You may blame yourself and your noxious influence."

"Congratulate myself, rather," said Mordaunt, like a smug earwig.

Aurienne pressed her tācn to the spot just under Mordaunt's clavicle
and drifted back down his seith lines towards the blockage. She was
fatigued, and her seith flowed slowly, but this particular procedure required finesse over force. She sank into him until she found the blockage again. With an infinitesimally gentle push of her seith, she broke up
the embolus.

The effect was immediate. Mordaunt held out his hand. His hellhound tācn glowed red in all its dead-eyed glory.

"You did it." Mordaunt's smile was back, swift, wide, bright. "Hel's
tits, you made that look easy. I thought I was done for. You're brilliant."

The red glow of his tācn left Aurienne torn between satisfaction at
seeing the thing work as it should and dismay that she had just put an
out-of-order Fyren back in order. He'd had a Murder-Suppression Clot
and she had removed it.

The dismay outweighed the satisfaction. That tācn was an instrument of slaughter. Her spirits plummeted lower than Leofric's ball. She
wasn't certain, suddenly, that she had made the right call. It was one
thing to play along with a deluded moon ritual that would never work;
it was another to actually heal him.

Mordaunt noticed her discomfort. His smile disappeared. "You're
positively dripping with regret."

"I've put a killer back in business."

Mordaunt pulled his gloves on to hide his tācn, as though Aurienne
were a sort of ostrich that would forget which Path he walked if she
couldn't see it.

"I'm grateful that it worked, even if you aren't," said Mordaunt. He offered a low, courteous bow that felt wrong to receive. "Thank you, Haelan Fairhrim."

Aurienne didn't say *You're welcome*, because he wasn't.

The lightest sheen of sweat dampened her brow. She had pushed the limit of her seith a bit tonight, though not enough to trigger her Cost.

Mordaunt buttoned up his shirt—an awkward affair, given the gloves—and flung his cloak on with a jovial swish. The harrowed, pathetic man from earlier became the Fyren again: prepossessing, self-assured, gleeful.

"Fordyce and Shuttleworth were right about you after all," he said. "You *are* a Phenomenon."

"Don't compliment me," said Aurienne.

"Does it make you uncomfortable?"

"Yes."

"Good. I like to see you suffer."

This was accompanied by a wink.

Odious.

"I'll sniff around about your well-funded friends," continued Mordaunt. "Fair warning, though—it could take months to discover anything useful."

He went to a looking glass, of which the room had an abundance, to make some final adjustments to his collar and hair. Aurienne considered the exercise futile; a pustule with good hair is still a pustule.

"I'll walk you back to the waystone," said Mordaunt.

"Not necessary," said Aurienne.

"Yes, necessary," said Mordaunt. "Leofric might still be staggering about out there. I'll go first. You've got enough seith to get to Swanstone?"

A gallant enquiry; Mordaunt had fine manners when he decided to apply them.

"I'll be fine," said Aurienne, who would never drain herself that low on his account.

Mordaunt walked her through the dark kitchens. Like most of the house, they gave off a general impression of disuse, save a section of the worktop where bright copper pots dried under a hanging herb garden.

"Wait here," said Mordaunt. "I'll call you when it's safe."

He disappeared from view in the darkness. Aurienne stood under the crumbling lintel and took in the prospect from this side of the house. The moon remained enshrouded and offered only a veiled suggestion of herself through clouds. Green-black moorland drifted into the horizon under her uncertain light, in ripples of heather and cotton grass, pinned to earth here and there by a stunted tree.

"Come along," came Mordaunt's voice.

Aurienne joined Mordaunt round the corner, on the gravel drive.

The night air was damp with late-spring cold and, after the mouldering house, exquisite to breathe.

They walked in silence until Mordaunt, incapable of peace, broke into chatter.

"I've been thinking about Widdershins and his blackened sun," he said.

"Have you?" asked Aurienne, in a tone suggesting that Mordaunt's inputs thereon were of limited interest.

Mordaunt did not take the hint. He was both clingy and thick, like a tenacious mucus.

"Yes," he said. "For May's Blædnes moon. I'd thought it might be a reference to an eclipse, only there aren't any eclipses, solar or lunar, predicted for months." He gave her a look. "But I see that you already knew that."

"Of course," said Aurienne.

"So what does the blackened sun at land's end mean?" asked Mordaunt. "Clouds? Smoke?"

"It means that Widdershins' entire translation was a fabrication," said Aurienne. "I don't know about the blackened sun, but if we suspend our disbelief—which this entire treatment plan requires anyway—we might find interesting intersections with the data on places at land's end. Peninsulas. Headlands. Capes. There's an obscure annal from For-triu focusing on instances of— Erm, I'm sorry—what's funny?"

"Aren't most instances of anal obscure?"

"*Annal*. Not *anal*. One is a written record. The other has to do with the anus."

"Both can be obscure, then," said Mordaunt.

"Yes."

"Bit darkish in there."

Aurienne gave the Fyren a long look. He certainly giggled a lot about anuses for a thing that had crawled out of one.

"Have you finished?" asked Aurienne.

"Yes."

"I'll send my deofol with instructions when I've worked out where we should meet for May's full moon."

"I hate that little hellrat," said Mordaunt.

"The feeling is mutual. He refers to you as 'the Parasite.'"

The clouds broke as they reached the waystone. Moonlight fell like hoarfrost around them. The gravel drive ribboned into the black moor-lands, a striation of white.

Under the pewter light, everything was distinct, crisp, separate. Shadows mirrored their subjects in livid detail. Light sharpened dark; dark amplified light.

Aurienne pressed her tācn to the waystone.

They did not say good night.

10

GUANO

Osric

Two ladies' maids, seduced; one valet, ditto; one Northumbrian man-at-arms, dead in his bed. Osric was having a good day.

It couldn't last, due to the fact that Fairhrim existed.

She had been of spectacular utility for the embolus, but whatever goodwill Osric had developed towards her was eradicated by the arrival of her deofol.

"Stop interrupting me during jobs," said Osric as Fairhrim's albino genet took shape.

"I can't seem to choose a time when you aren't killing someone," said the hellrat. It twitched its whiskers at the corpse in the bed. "Is he dead enough yet? Are you sure? Perhaps more stabbing?"

"This is hardly an excess," said Osric. "This is industry standard."

"Can you stop fingering him while I'm speaking to you?" asked the deofol.

"First of all, this is my thumb. Secondly, no. He pushed a scroll up his bum. The very scroll that I—unfortunately—was paid to retrieve."

"Grim," said the deofol.

"I know," said Osric. "These gloves were new."

Osric retrieved the scroll and placed it in a pouch. "You'll have to tell your mistress that I can confirm the obscurity of anals."

"What's in the scroll?" asked the deofol, tilting its pointy head. "Other than giardiasis, I mean."

Osric threw his soiled gloves into the fire that flickered in the dead man's hearth. "Plans for Northumbrian fortifications, of interest to Strathclyde."

"What did they pay you?"

"A very small fraction of the fortune I paid for the pleasure of Fairhrim's assistance. What news have you got for me?"

"You're to meet one hour before sunset the day of the Blædnes moon, at Muckle Flugga."

"At what?" asked Osric, unsure if the deofol was clearing its throat.

"Muckle Flugga," repeated the deofol. "In Fortriu. It's the northernmost point of the Tīendoms."

"Romantic appellation."

"There's a lighthouse there. The waystone is at the Woolf. Kindly bathe before you go. You smell like a latrine."

With this concluding remark, the deofol disappeared.

A FEW DAYS LATER, AND VERY MUCH NOT SMELLING LIKE A LATRINE, Osric burst into existence at the Woolf. The pub itself was long abandoned and consisted of a few crumbling walls. The waystone was so worn and low that it served as a passable seat, which Osric placed his buttocks (shapely, muscular) upon.

Before him stretched a lovely vista of rocky shore dissolving into sea, and there, at the end of an outcrop, the lighthouse. Save for a salty breeze and the wheeling of birds overhead, all was still.

Osric wished to take a moment to pause and appreciate the beauty—and so, of course, Fairhrim arrived with the gentleness of a small blizzard.

The waystone spat her into Osric's lap. She rose in a swirl of skirts and things, in uncharacteristic disarray. She was in her stocking feet, her hair was unbound and flopped wetly over her shoulder, and she was only half-dressed.

"What—" began Osric.

"Hold this," said Fairhrim, smacking her satchel into Osric's chest. "And this"—she tossed her cloak over him—"and these," she said, adding her boots to the pile.

With the help of a buttonhook, she worked her way up the long line of buttons of her dress. A round stone with a hole in its centre, usually hidden by her dress's high neckline, hung at her clavicle. The hagstone and its worn leather cord were incongruous amid Fairhrim's other adornments, which were all sharp and silver.

"Shocking," said Osric, due to the fact that she had a throat.

Fairhrim did not deign to reply; his principal function, at that moment, was to prop her up as she pulled on a boot.

"Indecent," said Osric, given that she had an ankle.

Fairhrim's pinchy hand was at his shoulder. "Had to rush. Couldn't miss the tide."

Water from her sopping curls dripped onto Osric's cloak. He smelled soap. "Might I ask why you look like you've just come out of the bath?"

"Because I have," said Fairhrim.

"Why would you have a bath just before we climb up a lighthouse?"

"There was an incident with my last case."

"An incident?"

"Draining an ulcer. It was . . . explosive. Remarkably purulent. Sprayed half a litre of pus into my hair. Do you want to know more?"

"No," said Osric.

"I thought not."

Fairhrim got both boots on. She wrung out her mass of hair and twisted it into its usual Repression Bun, pierced through with a silver curette. She snapped her wrist towards Osric, who duly passed on her cloak and satchel.

After a final straightening of skirts, Fairhrim resumed her usual appearance and composure. She held her chin high, as though she hadn't just landed on Osric like a half-dressed cataclysm.

"Well," she said brightly, "shall we go waste our time again?"

"Oh, do let's," said Osric.

They gave each other false, joyless smiles, and proceeded towards the lighthouse.

"Any changes to your seith since the embolus?" asked Fairhrim.

"None that I've noticed," said Osric.

"Good. And have you discovered anything about those intruders at Swanstone?"

"I'm working on a lead. Have they investigated on your end?"

"Yes, but with limited success. We know they didn't arrive by any of the nearby waystones. The incendiary devices were handmade; our Ingenaut couldn't identify their provenance. And their cadavers revealed nothing." Fairhrim huffed out an impatient breath. "I told Xanthe you're helping us, in exchange for the embolus fix."

"Did you?"

"Yes. She's pleased, and hopes that you will manage to justify your existence by being of some use to the world."

"Optimistic."

"That's what I said."

Fairhrim led him seawards. Underfoot danced a mix of seagrass and wildflowers Osric couldn't name—white, purple, pale yellow.

"Your precious Widdershins told us we must be at land's end, and this is one of the endiest points in the Tïendoms," said Fairhrim. "My dataset for the Blædnes moon favours sunsets at sixty-seven percent of the time—when the stories were good enough to specify a time at all—so that's today's in-between temporal dimension. This place also offers several of those cusps that the data, such as it is, favours—between earth and sky, between tidal shifts, a shoreline. And the lighthouse stands at an ancient crossroads."

"Roman?"

"Norse. A seaway."

"And what of my precious Widdershins' blackened sun?" asked Osric, given that the sun arced bright above them, and was notably not blackened.

"I don't know," said Fairhrim. "You'll have to ask him what he meant. I did check the barometer, and it's supposed to be cloudy today. Perhaps even rainy."

"Oh yes," said Osric, eyeing the violently blue sky. "It's absolutely going to piss down, I can tell."

"This is the North Sea. The weather can't go five minutes without changing."

As they approached the shoreline, the breeze picked up. Osric had expected something bracing and salty, but was instead hit by what could be described only as a reek.

"What is that stench?" he asked as his nostrils filled with acridity.

Fairhrim sniffed and said, "Guano. There's a large gannet colony somewhere round here."

"That's foul," gagged Osric.

Fairhrim was undisturbed by the odour of sun-fermented piss-shit. "After today's purulent drainage, this is downright pleasant."

Serene amid the fetidity, she glided on. "I once had a patient with multiple gastrointestinal fistulas. The ooze that came out of those—*that* was putrid. Necrotising fasciitis is worse, though. You can taste it for days afterwards."

Osric extracted a handkerchief and pressed it to his face.

"Better?" asked Fairhrim.

"Yes," said Osric, in a muffled voice. "Can't smell anything anymore. I think my septum has dissolved."

As they neared the lighthouse, they spotted a few burly figures wandering about at its foot.

Fairhrim stopped. Osric walked into her.

"What?" asked Osric.

"Them," said Fairhrim, pointing at the figures.

Obviously, that's what would have her concerned—a few twits wandering about, and not the immolation of Osric's sinuses.

"This lighthouse is meant to be unmanned," said Fairhrim.

"It looks very manned," said Osric.

"Perhaps they're sightseers," said Fairhrim. "If there are any at the top, I'll ask them prettily to leave so we can carry on with our time wasting unobserved."

"I should do it," said Osric. "I'm prettier than you."

Fairhrim threw her head back, said, "Hah!" as though Osric had made a good joke, and kept walking.

This vexed Osric, because he *was* prettier than her. Wasn't he? Was she prettier than him? Impossible. He surveyed Fairhrim with a new, jealous assessment, but only her back was visible now, and all he could conclude was that she had a good figure.

"This isn't the time for your jokes," said Fairhrim, over her shoulder. "Let's focus on the assignment."

"I *am* the assignment."

Cloak pulled in tight against the wind, Osric followed Fairhrim through a track of crushed grass to the edge of the sea, and they argued about their relative prettiness, and Osric said, "At least admit that I'm handsome," and Fairhrim asked, philosophically, if a disease could be handsome, and vexed him further.

The sightseers at the lighthouse looked remarkably well armed.

"A jolly bunch of holidaymakers," said Osric. "About to have a family picnic, I'll wager. The broadswords are to cut up the roast."

Fairhrim did not share his amusement. "Who are they, and why are they here?"

"I'll go find out," said Osric. "You stay put." Then, because Fairhrim looked as though the instruction displeased her, he added, "I need you alive, and not skewered by Dodgy Gooch and company down there."

"Fine. Try to be diplomatic, won't you?"

"What's that supposed to mean?"

"Don't hurt anyone."

"Oh," said Osric.

This answer was, apparently, insufficient.

"*Promise* not to hurt anyone," said Fairhrim.

Fairhrim's problem was that she had too many principles.

"What about in self-defence?" asked Osric.

"Self-defence," said Fairhrim, in words that Osric immediately planned to make her regret, "is obviously different."

"Right."

"Will you promise not to murder them?"

Osric made a show of considering this, then said, "No."

He strode away. The wind whipped away most of Fairhrim's retort—something about him being horrid. He didn't respond, because he was.

He advanced towards the lighthouse. The tide had receded and left a slippery path of rocks in its wake. Barnacles crunched underfoot as Osric stepped along this provisional bridge.

He was challenged as he approached by a rough "Oi!"

"What?" said Osric.

"What're you doing here?" asked the challenger. With his ill-fitting leather armour and battered sword, there was a whiff of banditry about him.

"Walking," said Osric.

"Well, you can't walk here."

Bandit One was joined by two equally disreputable-looking colleagues, who eyed Osric's kit with interest.

"I like those boots," said Bandit Two.

"I want the cloak," said Bandit Three. "Is that real gold along the edges?"

Osric decided to exercise his limited diplomacy skills, given that he was being observed. "You lot need to clear out for a few hours."

"Lighthouse is ours," said Bandit One, inserting his thumbs into his waistband and broadening his chest. "S'private property."

"Give us your boots," said Bandit Two.

"Is anyone else in there?" asked Osric, jutting his chin towards the lighthouse.

"Twenty men," said Bandit One, at the same time as Two said, "Fifty men."

"No one, then," said Osric. "Good. Off you fuck. Don't make me hurt you."

The men stared at him as they processed his audacity. Osric wasn't the most patient sort and would normally have slit throats at this juncture. However, given that he was under Fairhrim's steely eye, he gave them another chance.

He removed his glove and flashed his tācn at them. "Last warning."

"A Fyren," gasped Bandit One.

"Fuck this," said Bandit Two.

They both fled. That left Bandit Three, the stupidest of the lot. Osric put his glove back on and studied him with mild interest. How to dispose of him while inciting the least amount of pearl clutching from Fairhrim?

"Bet that's a fake mark," said Bandit Three. "Bet it's just a tattoo."

This theory he, apparently, decided to test by throwing a punch at Osric. Osric blocked it; as feeble as the punch was, he considered his nose well shaped, and preferred to keep it that way.

Now that someone else had attempted to draw first blood, Osric's foray into diplomacy came to an end. He delivered a knockout punch, straight into Bandit Three's stupid mouth.

Osric waved Fairhrim over. She picked her way towards the lighthouse as Osric hog-tied the man with his own belt.

"Was that really the only course of action?" asked Fairhrim.

"Yes," said Osric, plucking a tooth out of his glove.

"I thought Fyren were meant to be subtle."

"I'm not wasting my seith on the likes of him."

"How nice to have a choice" was Fairhrim's arid reply.

Osric flicked the tooth at her.

He climbed the spiralling lighthouse stairs. Impressive, how Fairhrim could fix her stare right between his shoulder blades, so hard that he could feel it. Bit stabby, really.

They toiled upwards. They passed through a storeroom scattered with the bandits' belongings. The pungency of the guano receded and gave way to mustiness. The stairs were thick with dust, save for where the bandits' feet had trodden.

Above the storeroom was the old watch room, which had been converted into sleeping quarters.

"Hmm," said Osric.

"What?" said Fairhrim.

"About ten beds in here," said Osric.

He regretted having let Bandits One and Two go now. He should've been proactive and killed them.

"Should we be worried?" asked Fairhrim.

"Worried?" repeated Osric. "Don't be ridiculous. I'm here."

Fairhrim's raised eyebrow informed him that she thought him a bit of a tit.

"If they come up, they're dead," said Osric. "However—I *would* like us to not be interrupted. Help me with this."

With Fairhrim's best attempt at assistance (she flopped her flimsy wrists about and grunted), he shoved and pulled a few crates over the stairwell. They wouldn't stop a determined gang of bandits, but they'd give Osric ample warning that someone was trying to ascend.

The next flight up led to the old lightkeeper's kitchen, scattered with boxes of supplies of dubious freshness.

Finally—and with much huffing and puffing, which both Osric and Fairhrim did their utmost to suppress—they reached the lantern room. It was circular, glass rimmed, and offered a spectacular view of the sea.

The light sat, black and idle, in the centre of the room.

Fairhrim examined the contraption. "I've never seen so many bulbs—have you? A fascinating bit of work by the Ingenauts. I suppose it turns on at sunset. I wonder where the sensors are?"

Lighthouse engineering did not number among Osric's priorities. "Should we be outside, or in?" he asked.

"Out," said Fairhrim.

After a bit of searching, they found a handle on one of the panes of glass, which led to an outdoor platform.

Osric stepped outside, followed, with marked hesitation, by Fairhrim. In response to his eyebrow, she said, "I've no head for heights."

"You live in a tower."

"The tower's got stone walls twelve feet thick. And windows separating me from death."

Osric couldn't further grill her on her contradictions because they were both assailed by the wind. Up here, it was a living thing. It cuffed the back of Fairhrim's head and unravelled her bun. It whisked Osric's cloak up and had a fair go at strangling him. It tumbled and tore around them, and every attempt to correct its chaos—pinning the bun, attaching the cloak, holding down the skirts, saving the cravat—became a game.

Osric gave up first. Cloak and cravat were thrown back into the lantern room.

Fairhrim was more determined, but, after a fruitless fight with her hair, cloak, and skirts, she, too, threw her detachable things indoors. Her hair whipped about in a long, voluminous ponytail, dividing its time equally between lashing her across the eyes and getting into Osric's mouth.

Osric took pleasure in seeing her so discombobulated for the second time today. A bit of chaos among her order might do her some good.

"Less of the guano up here, at least," said Osric. The wind penetrated his open mouth—rude—and came out of his nostrils.

Fairhrim pinned herself to the glass wall, as far from the railing as she could get. Her voice was thready in the wind. "Sunset's in a few minutes."

"Right. And where are your clouds?" asked Osric, because Fairhrim was, obviously, personally responsible for their absence.

"And where is your blackened sun?" asked Fairhrim, as though the fault were his.

A fresh eddy whipped at them as though delivering a smack. Fairhrim's heavy skirts gusted up past her knees. Osric, seeing a flash of white stockings and, above those, a black garter, learned that Fairhrim wore her garters in the new fashion, at the thigh. A nicely shaped thigh—round, with a delicious little indentation where the garter pressed into soft skin.

Which might've been interesting to look at if Osric had a thing for garters, which he didn't, and if he thought Fairhrim remotely attractive, which he also didn't. (So he told himself, with great confidence, suppressing any memory of darkly brilliant eyes and a curl of hair across a damp lip.)

Given that the sight was so uninteresting and that he'd rather be looking at anything but Fairhrim's legs, Osric turned his attention to the sea.

It roiled below them, alive and uneasy. The tide began to rise as the sun began to set. The sky's relentless blue gave way to deep purple.

There was a creak behind them. The enormous set of bulbs in the lantern room turned on and flashed a first beam across the sea. It caught the agitated waves and tipped them, briefly, in gold.

"Look," said Fairhrim. The single syllable was stretched and snapped away by the wind.

Beyond the flashing, gold-glossed waves, a mist was building upon the horizon. At least, Osric thought it was mist. But, unlike mist, it moved with volition. It thickened until it became a cloud bank moving towards them—a cloud bank advancing, impossibly, into the wind.

The cloud approached in stutters, visible only when the flashing beam of the lighthouse hit it.

Osric realised at last that it was a single, frothing mass of birds.

"The gannets," said Osric.

"*Sort sol*," gasped Fairhrim. "It's what they call murmurations in the Danelaw. *Sort sol*—black sun."

With a dizzying din, the colony—thousands, hundreds of thousands, of birds—billowed towards the lighthouse in a single, seething entity.

Osric took a step back, as did Fairhrim. The light flashed again; they saw their own silhouettes flicker against the advancing wall of birds. The beat of wings and hearts without number churned the air until it thrummed. The thrum went through Osric, filled him, reverberated in his bones.

The lighthouse flashed its luminous pulse against the multitude. Osric saw things in it as it swept to and fro above—now a tree line, now cascades, now waves smashing upon rock. Things dim, things shimmering, things Awake.

He felt disoriented and ill. He wanted to touch something solid.

He went for Fairhrim's hand just as she went for his. She clutched at his gloved fingers; his thumb pressed hers.

The maelstrom whirled overhead. They were the only fixed point in the universe; everything else spun around it.

The maelstrom was on them.

It erased the world.

TRANSCENDENCE FLEETING

Aurienne

There was no sea, no sky, no lighthouse. Only air shattered by wings, only the squeeze of Mordaunt's glove against her fingers.

Black-fringed white filled Aurienne's eyes, pleated upon itself, fell, lurched. Light fractured in chinks between wings and through feathers, light from a golden world where an unceasing sun shone.

There was something at work in the celestial clamour—something half-conscious, something not good and yet not evil. Aurienne felt a loosening. The rules became less rigid. Things wouldn't withstand; things wouldn't say no.

She hesitated. Air trembled at her cheek. A window had opened.

Could she do it?

The lighthouse flashed. A hundred thousand bright eyes were on her.

Aurienne, facing Mordaunt, reached for the back of his neck and clasped him in a simple embrace. Her palm found his nape—warm skin notched with scar tissue, and ridged, now, with goose bumps. She felt the breath of wings against her cheek and of Mordaunt against her lips.

A hundred thousand eyes whirled above, below, through, around, within, without.

Aurienne awoke her tācn, and there, at the very rim of the world, in the light of another place, between the winged and the earthbound, between sea and sky, between dark and brightness beaming, she pushed her seith into Mordaunt.

He shuddered. The space between heaven and earth contracted; the sky became something they could touch. Her seith surged; the birds surged; the very air surged. The gannets in their infinities swept upwards, far beyond the lighthouse, far into the violet heavens.

The wind slipped into a murmur, said something too quiet to hear. The window closed.

Aurienne pulled her hand from Mordaunt's neck. They stood and stared at each other, breathless, suspended, astonished.

Mordaunt's collar was crooked; his hair was disastrous. Aurienne felt herself in a similar state, and drained, too—swept up by the moment, she had poured her seith into him in quantities unwise.

Aurienne held her tācn to Mordaunt's clavicle. Low seith or not, she had to know whether it had worked. She cast a live diagnostic.

His eyes were riveted to her. He still clasped her left hand. There was desperation in his intensity; his pulse raced; his lips formed an unvoiced *please*.

The only sound now was the quiet breathing of the sea, as though some great creature had returned to slumber.

Aurienne's diagnostic image glowed feeble white in the intermittent beam of the lighthouse. Her hands began to chap with her Cost; every second of the display was a drain on her already low seith.

Nothing in Mordaunt's seith system had changed.

Aurienne shook her head.

"I really thought," Aurienne began, at the same time as Mordaunt said, "But that felt—"

But no. They had thought and felt wrong.

"Fuck," said Mordaunt.

Aurienne said nothing. Disappointment and relief roiled within her. Disappointment because she had felt so close—so close to an impossibility. Relief that she hadn't managed, because she had always known that this was going to end in failure, and this confirmed that she was right, and—and beyond anything else, a Fyren didn't deserve to be healed. And then the disappointment again, because she had wanted to succeed. And then the relief, because she hadn't.

They were still holding hands.

The emotional roil was joined by the rise of nausea. That live diagnostic had pulled too much from Aurienne's reserves. Black crept into her vision. Her hands stung; her knuckles split; her nails grew bloody.

"Fairhrim?" came Mordaunt's voice.

"I need to sit down," said Aurienne.

She grasped at the glass door.

Mordaunt opened it for her. His hand released hers and moved to her elbow. She pulled away; he kept his hold.

"I don't need you to—" began Aurienne, and then one of her legs buckled.

Mordaunt helped her through the door. He didn't say *Don't be stupid*, but she saw it in the annoyed tightening of his jaw.

Aurienne grasped the doorjamb as she passed it. No tunnel vision, no shakes—she would be fine. She had simply overdone it a bit.

"Seith drain?" asked Mordaunt.

"Yes."

There was a soft intake of breath. He had noticed her hands. "Your Cost?"

"Only the beginning."

"Shit."

Mordaunt propped Aurienne on the ledge that rimmed the inside of the lantern room. He stood in front of her, irresolute, his brows drawn, his mouth an anxious press. The concern on his features was unsettling. His mouth was for snarking, not for looking worried on her account.

"I'm fine," said Aurienne.

Mordaunt's eyes remained on her bloodied hands.

"Ugly, isn't it?" said Aurienne.

"We don't choose our Cost," said Mordaunt. He sat beside her. "If this thing was ever to work, I would've imagined that that was the—the kind of moment."

Aurienne nodded. They had come to the very edge of something today. Something very like what the tales spoke of—a flickering and a fraying of this world and the revelation of another beyond the gossamer. In the thundering rush of wings, it had felt like they were somewhere on that cusp, where the impossible was possible, where the unhealable could heal.

The thrill of Aurienne's early forays into these stories found her again; she almost believed—she wanted to believe. And now she must wait an entire month until the next full moon. (Baffling, to be anticipating her next rendezvous with Mordaunt, but, well—she was rather looking forward to trying again.)

"Are you feeling better?" asked Mordaunt.

"A bit. You can stop looking so concerned. It unsettles me."

"I need you. I need your hands. I'll be as concerned as I like when they look like mincemeat."

"When I've recovered my seith, I'll heal the mess."

"You should rest," said Mordaunt.

Aurienne tilted her head back and leaned, at first, against the glass pane behind her. The glass was uncomfortable and slippery. Exhausted, and past caring what he thought, she slid off it, and rested her cheek upon the soft velvet of Mordaunt's cloaked shoulder.

She closed her eyes and breathed until her breaths matched the cadence of the waves somewhere below them—the long ins, the slow outs. The lighthouse sent its beam out in search of something in the dark. For leagues and leagues over the sea, shadows split, closed up, and were split again.

Aurienne's faintness receded. She opened her eyes.

The lavender sky had given way to black. The Blædnes moon had risen.

Night made a dark looking glass of the windows. Mordaunt was watching her in the reflection. The lighthouse flared and sent his face into sharp relief—the scar across his mouth, the features she wouldn't admit were handsome, the eyes palely reflecting light.

Fyren.

But also—also just a man.

He sat, scarred and imperfect, under a scarred and imperfect moon. Motionless, alert, intent upon her. His breath fanned against her temple, heartbeat-slow, the careful, measured slowness of a man controlling his breathing. The shape of his mouth mattered. His stubble caught her hair.

Just a man. Being so near him in that moment freed the thought from Aurienne. Just a man who, as they stood in the light of another place, had nearly touched his lips to hers. Just a man who had whispered, desperately, "Please."

He leaned into her, or she into him, until their arms touched. Their joined reflection in the window made a soft and pleasing trigonometry. There was a strange intimacy in feeling the heat radiating from him. Aurienne wondered if he thought the same. No answer came, save the mute press of his arm against hers.

It meant nothing. It couldn't mean anything, because of what she was and what he was. These were sweet nothings of an entirely new kind. Meaningless. Futile.

Mordaunt shifted. His signet ring brushed against her; carved stone, blood-warm, caressed her wrist. Her skin received it like a kiss.

Aurienne vacillated between being repulsed and drawn in, between wanting more and wishing to move away, an ebb and a flow as changeful as the waves below, as throbbing and intermittent as the lighthouse strobe. This was the real in-between. Did he, too, feel the push and pull?

The light flared. She glanced up. She caught him unguarded. Instead of mirrorlike silver she found chasmal grey. The intensity in his gaze shocked her even as she found her answer. He looked at her as one who wished to worship, and one who wished to defile.

The next time the light flashed, the mirror was back.

They sat for a long time, leaning against each other, existing in two states at once.

Hate could feel strangely like something else.

AURIENNE DIDN'T USUALLY HAVE TO APPLY HER EMOTION-REGULATION strategies to life outside the wards, but it occurred to her that if she were going to, for example, decide that sleeping on Osric Mordaunt's shoulder was a good idea, she would be wise to. A bit of suppression wouldn't go amiss.

"Sorry," said Aurienne, pulling away from the man in question.

"It's all right," said Mordaunt. His throat sounded dry; he cleared it.

They both found their feet. Mordaunt shook his cloak as though airing it out.

Aurienne ran sore fingers through disorderly curls and pinned them back into place with her silver curette. "The tide's well and truly come in. How long did I sleep?"

"Not sure," said Mordaunt. "An hour, maybe."

"We're stuck here for at least another few hours, then."

"Goody."

Aurienne peered downwards. "With the sea this high, those men won't come back—not unless they've got a boat."

"I wish they would," said Mordaunt. "I'd have some entertainment."

"I suppose you've got to kill people regularly or go wild with boredom."

"Mad with it," said Mordaunt. "Are you hungry?"

"Yes," said Aurienne. "I never leave Swanstone without a few snacks in my satchel, but my departure was so rushed, I haven't anything at all— Erm, where are you going?"

Mordaunt was halfway down the spiral staircase. "The kitchen. You need to eat."

"I'm not going to steal anyone's food," said Aurienne.

Mordaunt's sigh echoed towards her. "They stole the food from someone else. Does that make it better?"

"It compounds the problem."

"No—it cancels itself out. Basic maths."

Aurienne, still feeling a bit lightheaded, decided that she couldn't afford to be picky. She therefore did not further argue about the Fyren's questionable mathematics.

The lantern room's intermittent light faded as she descended the stairs. She discovered the placement of the kitchen worktop by smashing her hip into it.

"I forgot," came Mordaunt's voice. "You're useless in the dark."

Aurienne raised the cold light of her tācn. "How are you seeing anything at all?"

"Trade secrets," said Mordaunt.

"Is it to do with shadow-walking?"

"None of your business." Mordaunt found a gas lamp and lit it. "Stop wasting your seith; you're meant to be recovering it."

"The output for a bit of light from my tācn is absolutely minimal— but, all right. Thank you for the light," said Aurienne. She reserved Mordaunt's trade secrets for future prying.

Mordaunt clattered about the worktop and assembled the bandits' supplies into a heap. He and Aurienne studied them in the lamplight. It was a pile of icebox debris, really—grey potatoes, overripe grapes, things too elusive for identification. The scent of bin juice wafted towards them.

"Lucullan magnificence," said Mordaunt.

"How to choose from among all these delights?" asked Aurienne.

Mordaunt ate a grape. "This feels rather like eating . . . eyes."

"What's this?" asked Aurienne, holding up a bowl of things.

"Earlobes," said Mordaunt.

Aurienne found a plate of scrambled eggs that looked like boogers, which she pushed towards Mordaunt. He traded it for a wrinkled saucisson. Aurienne inspected its mouldy white edge.

"Smegma," said Mordaunt.

"You're disgusting," said Aurienne.

Mordaunt found a carton of something, which he tossed into the centre of the table. It exploded like a full nappy.

"Bechamel?" proposed Aurienne.

"Think it might be a bit off?"

"It's blue."

"Here," said Mordaunt, and he heaved an enormous pumpkin onto the table.

"How am I meant to eat this?"

"Unhinge your jaw."

"It's rotten," said Aurienne, pointing at an ominous crevice in the pumpkin—information which Mordaunt received with stoic dignity by saying, "That smells like a Dreor's arsehole."

"How would you know what that smells like?"

"I'm surmising based upon one encounter."

"You fought a Dreor?"

"Absolutely not. I'm not that mad. I ran away." Mordaunt lifted the lid off a tray of, possibly, pasta. "Thoughts?"

Aurienne inspected it. "Have you ever seen what comes out when someone's taken a tapeworm tablet?"

"Gods," said Mordaunt. "*You're* disgusting."

"I'd kill for just a cup of tea," said Aurienne. She searched the cupboards.

Mordaunt said that he would kill for a cup of tea, too, only literally, unlike her, the coward. Aurienne found a battered pot. Mordaunt found a tin labelled *Tea* containing desiccated remains of things. When consulted, Aurienne opined that it might've been tea, or perhaps floor sweepings; Mordaunt said it was hair from a mermaid's armpit. They boiled it.

Mordaunt gave his mug an aristocratic sniff, as one might when working out the notes of a fine wine. "I'm getting—fish got wanked off into a pot."

They set aside the tea.

AT LENGTH, THE TIDE RECEDED, AND AURIENNE AND MORDAUNT MADE their way down the lighthouse's spiral stair, and back across the bridge.

As they approached the waystone at the remains of the Woolf, they became aware of an imminent problem.

There was a large group of men gathered at the waystone, sitting, standing, milling about. Men who looked rather like bandits who had scampered off to find reinforcements.

Aurienne said that this was Most Inopportune.

Mordaunt made the unoriginal suggestion that he should kill them all.

"No," said Aurienne. "We can find another waystone."

"This is the only waystone out here," said Mordaunt.

"We could negotiate."

"Do they seem willing to negotiate?" asked Mordaunt, rightly, because the men were unsheathing their weapons. There was a gleam in his eye as he studied the assembled men. "I could take them all out from here."

"No," said Aurienne.

"Or I could go in closer and—"

"No."

"What about—"

"No."

"But we really must punish them for that tea," said Mordaunt. "I'll just kill them a little."

"Kill them *a little*? Death isn't divisible."

They were unable to conclude their argument on murder as a fractionable activity because the men fanned out and began an approach. Aurienne recognised two of them from their earlier encounter with Mordaunt. Their reinforcements—four dozen men, perhaps—had given them fresh courage to face the Fyren.

From their chatter, Aurienne understood that they had applied a certain bandity logic to the situation; they had decided that if a lady had hired a Fyren for protection, she must be Worth Something. Some of the men eyed Aurienne, others her satchel. (The latter contained only burn gel, plasters, and a splint, for a total value of thirty thrymsas.)

The bandits had summoned their chief, a large man moving with confidence bolstered by the numbers behind him. He rubbed his hands like a fly that has found a particularly succulent poo.

As for Mordaunt, there was gleeful anticipation in his eye. Aurienne knew that he would have no scruples about murdering all of these men. Scruples did not form a part of his composition.

The bandit chief grinned at Aurienne. He did not have teeth so much as one or two sarsen stones. "A pretty thing like you come to visit us all the way out here? What luck."

Aurienne flung a hand towards him—necessary dramatics, given the Fyren—and said, "Don't come any closer, please. You needn't die today."

"Pretty?" interjected Mordaunt. "Who's prettier, her or me?"

This gave the bandit chief pause. He pressed a meaty finger to his chin and consulted his colleagues.

Aurienne begged them to flee while they could; Mordaunt hushed her and said, "Let them talk." One bandit piped up that she had better eyelashes but he had better cheekbones, and thus mortally insulted them both.

The bandit chief emerged from the conference and said, "About the same."

Aurienne gasped in outrage. Mordaunt, labouring under the delusion that he was prettier, also gasped.

"Well," said Mordaunt, "now you're definitely going to die."

"Don't be a fool," said the bandit chief. "Fyren or not, there's forty of us and only one of you."

Aurienne expected Mordaunt to loose twenty throwing knives and slay the men where they stood. However, he merely bent over to fix the lace of his boot.

The bandit chief took this as a show of submission. "Now," he said, "let's have the lady come over here, nice and slow."

"You're making a mistake," said Aurienne. "He's going to kill you. Let us get to the waystone and he'll leave you alone. I've no money." She rattled her open satchel. "Look: nothing of value."

"You haven't got money here," said the chief, "but you've got money somewhere. It costs millions to hire a Fyren."

"I didn't hire him," said Aurienne.

"Daddy did, then, and he'll pay a pretty sum to get his daughter back."

"No. The Fyren wasn't hired. He's here of his own volition, not for money."

The bandit chief scoffed. "A Fyren? Not here for money?"

"You're right to be cynical," said Aurienne, "but this time, it's true. Please believe me. Let us go."

"The Fyren are good, but they aren't gods, girl. He's only one man."

Mordaunt was still bent over beside Aurienne, fiddling with his boot.

"What," hissed Aurienne, "are you doing?"

"Got to keep things sporting," said Mordaunt. He pulled a bootlace free. "Besides, I don't want to dirty my knives. You stay here and clutch your pearls."

"Clutch my—don't kill them," said Aurienne, stepping in front of him. "They're idiots—utterly lacking in judgement. We must give them a chance."

"You've already given them a chance," said Mordaunt. "Besides, they threatened to kidnap you."

"And? *You* threatened to kidnap me."

"Exactly: only *I* can do that. You can't tell me this lot will be a huge loss to the world."

"You don't get to decide that."

"Death is a normal part of life," said Mordaunt.

"You can't play god and accelerate it," said Aurienne.

"*Tss.* You play god and slow it down; how's that different?"

"Because it's for Good."

"They aren't Good."

One of the bandits, having tired, apparently, of this theoretical exchange, whipped a throwing axe towards Aurienne and Mordaunt. Mordaunt caught it as it spun between them (reflexes, admittedly, impressive), turned to the bandits, and commented at large, "That was a mistake."

He dropped the axe. He moved towards the bandits, armed solely with his bootlace, with such nonchalance that if Aurienne had been a bandit, she would've been offended.

The bootlace dangled. The glove came off. The red tācn glistened like a bloodstain.

There was a shudder among the more intelligent members of the mob at the sight of the hellhound's skull. Then there were rallying shouts about how the lady was worth millions, and this was Only One Man. He couldn't take them all on; obviously—*obviously*—it was all for show, intimidating, like; the tācn probably wasn't even real—what was he going to do, kill them all?

Mordaunt twirled the bootlace as he advanced.

"Arrogant bastard," said the bandit chief.

"Can't argue that," said Mordaunt.

"Run, you idiots," said Aurienne, her hands pressed to her mouth.

"You're going to learn some lessons today," said the bandit chief.

"I think the teaching will be mutual," said Mordaunt.

The bandit chief gestured his myrmidons forward. Their strategy, such as it was, consisted of swarming Mordaunt, who, for his part, turned to Aurienne and, with another of his odious winks, said, "Self-defence."

A strange melee ensued, during which Mordaunt, with an air of roguish enjoyment, strangled men left and right with his bootlace, while they drove their blades towards him and gutted one another instead. He was vastly outnumbered, and yet with his every balletic step, two or three bandits collapsed, and his tācn glowed its diabolical red, and bodies hit the ground, and he had shadow-walked behind his next victim. He was, indeed, very good at what he did. The problem was that what he did was Very Bad.

It was going to be a wholesale single-bootlace massacre until the bandit chief, wielding a spear, hit Mordaunt with a glancing blow over the shoulder. Then Mordaunt grew serious, plucked the spear from the chief's hand, and skewered him and the two men behind him into a grotesque bandit brochette.

All forty died.

Aurienne clutched at her pearls.

OSRIC THE MICROBE

Osric

A few days later, in the depths of a forest, Osric wrapped up a job by dragging corpses into tragic poses next to an upturned carriage. The effect was moving: a terrible accident had befallen the party. There had been a disastrous roll down a hill, resulting in ever so many broken necks. And just like that, the Mercian king had lost one of his chief retainers and Osric had made a fat pile of thrymsas, courtesy of the king of the Danelaw.

Fairhrim had an instinct for catching him post-kill. Her deofol pressed at Osric's tācn with insistence until it was permitted to come through.

The deofol materialised on the highest corner of the upturned carriage. From that vantage, it studied the bloodbath, then leapt to Osric's shoulder.

The genet was only a creature of seith, but Fairhrim's skill was such that it had weight. And, Osric discovered as twenty pins punctured his cloak, tiny seith claws.

"Ouch," said Osric.

"I didn't want to wade through the blood," said the deofol.

"That's barely a puddle," said Osric.

"A puddle? It's so big, it's got its own tide."

"You share your mistress's propensity for dramatic overexaggeration."

"Funny," said the deofol, switching to his other shoulder. "She accuses you of the same."

"What do you want? And retract your damned claws."

The deofol retracted a single claw. "Did you free the horses?"

"Yes."

"Why?"

"They're innocent beasts."

"And you're a champion of the innocents, are you?" asked the deofol.

"What do you want?" repeated Osric.

"Aurienne wishes to enquire about your availability for a meet. Noon, two days from now." With reluctance, and sounding as though it had practised this bit, the deofol added, "She acknowledges your preference for nighttime meetings. However, it'll be her only chance to get away."

"Where?"

"Take a waystone to the Moist Oyster. Follow the signs for the clinic for *Pthirus pubis* infestations."

"The clinic for what?"

"Just follow the signs. She's got something to show you. She asks if you could refrain from committing mass murders on the way, but I see it's already too late."

"I'll be there," said Osric. "I may have an interesting find of my own to share."

The deofol made a retching sound. "We'll have none of that reciprocity malarkey, thank you."

"It's at her request."

"Oh, is it? Well, that's all right, then. She is perfect and can do no wrong. Unlike you."

With a final squeeze at Osric's shoulder, the deofol vanished.

FROM THE WAYSTONE AT THE MOIST OYSTER, OSRIC FOLLOWED THE SIGNS to the clinic. He discovered, incidentally, that *Pthirus pubis* were pubic lice.

There was no queue at the clinic door.

Osric knocked. Fairhrim opened the door.

"You had something to show me?" asked Osric.

"No," said Fairhrim. "I invited you here for the sheer pleasure of your company."

Gods, she could be dry. Osric's lips chapped on the spot.

Fairhrim led him in. She looked severe, as though she were about to quiz him on his multiplication tables.

"Are you going to lecture me about mass murders?" asked Osric.

Fairhrim disconcertingly replied, "No."

"No?"

"You are a Calamity—"

"Thank you."

"—but we've got more important things to discuss."

"More important than me?"

"Have a look at this map," said Fairhrim, as though, indeed, a bit of paper was more important than Osric.

On the clinic's examination table lay a crumpled map of the waystone graticule. A forgettable enough item; everyone had two or three of them hanging about at home or forgotten in pockets, consulted when travelling to an unfamiliar place.

"Waystones," said Osric. "And?"

Fairhrim pointed to the wall over the examination table, on which a regular map was hung, dotted with red pins. "Here are the approximate locations of fifty of the stories—those that contained enough detail for me to map them with something resembling accuracy, anyway. Do you see it now?"

Osric compared a few of the red spots with waystone locations. "Some are near waystones—no surprises there; we've used them—and some aren't. Am I meant to be drawing some sort of conclusion?"

Fairhrim pulled out a dusty projector and slipped the waystone map onto it. The map was thin enough to project a ghost of itself on the wall. After some adjustments, Fairhrim overlaid the image upon the map pinned above the examination table.

Now Osric could see. The red dots from the fairy stories were clustered not around the waystones themselves but rather where the ley lines connecting waystones intersected.

"The crossing of ley lines," said Osric.

"Yes. Cross*roads* have come up in the tales, of course—a classic in-between—but none mentioned the ley lines themselves."

"You're brilliant," said Osric.

Fairhrim gave him an austere look over her silver-sharp shoulder. "Don't compliment me. It was an oversight not to have noticed." She drew her finger across the map. Projected ley lines decorated the back of her hand like new veins. "My first clue was these aggregations at crossroads. Loads of our roads were built parallelling major ley lines. And—coincidentally or not—we have these clusters of data locating stories precisely at those intersections."

"Where's the lighthouse?" asked Osric.

Fairhrim reached towards the map's most northern point. "There." Three ley lines intersected at the island.

"What about points where more ley lines cross?" asked Osric. He pointed at star-shaped bursts where four or five ley lines crisscrossed. "Is that even better?"

"More might be better. Our excursions to the pond and the hot springs—with only a single ley line nearby—were marked failures. I've told you I thought an accumulation of the in-between factors might make the place and time more powerful. However—it won't be that simple. Look at this."

She brushed past Osric to the other side of the map. He found himself distracted by the sensation, by the casualness of it. People didn't simply brush up against Osric Mordaunt. Fairhrim took up a new position a decorous distance away, and Osric focused once again on the map.

She pointed to a spot at the southern tip of the island. Five ley lines intersected there. Osric saw a blurry label for the waystone at the Rummy Thing.

"The South Downs," said Osric.

"At a crossing of five ley lines," said Fairhrim. "*Five*. And we had no success whatsoever."

"Blast it."

"These findings are aggressively inconclusive. And, of course, we can't even call the lighthouse a success. We had a—a *strange* moment, but no result to speak of. This in spite of a full moon, three ley lines, Widdershins' blackened sun, and every in-between dimension of time and place we shoehorned in."

Fairhrim stood pin straight in front of the map. There was something metallic in the glance of her eye and in the hard, dissatisfied line of her mouth. She suppressed a sigh; the merest twitch of her nostrils gave it away.

"Where do we go from here?" asked Osric.

Fairhrim did not answer him. She bent over to make notes.

No one ignored Osric Mordaunt. Osric either charmed or terrorised the trousers off everyone in his vicinity. He was never *ignored*. Who did she think she was?

He glared at Fairhrim's bun in annoyance. At the baby hairs that escaped it at her nape. At her neck, too, because it was in a perfect position for snapping. What a pity she was his Means to an End; she was so very Endable herself.

He stepped behind her to read over her shoulder. Her notes were nearly illegible, but he made out a few fragments: *focus on the crossing of ley lines—in spite of little evidence to support new strategy—pare down locations for June lunation.*

"Right," said Fairhrim, punctuating the final sentence with a full stop.

She straightened. Her bun smacked Osric in the mouth.

"Watch what you're doing," snarled Osric.

Fairhrim passed her hand over her bun to check for damage (gods forbid he'd pulled a hair out of place with his chapped lips). "Watch what *you're* doing. Why were you so close?"

"Watching what *you* were doing," said Osric.

"I don't require supervision from you," said Fairhrim.

She glided off into a back room—the very sweep of her skirts bespoke scorn—and, with much rattling, reappeared with the Franklin diffractor and its knots of wires. "Let's have a look at your progress while we've got the equipment."

Fairhrim pointed to a cabinet and bid Osric to disrobe, and to please, if he would, choose from the adult selection of gowns this time.

Osric was left to study an enigmatic pile of linens. He put a hand in the heap and pulled out baffling bits of fabric: floppy things, long things, things that dangled beyond the three-dimensional, things incomprehensible, bewildering, arcane.

He tied one on like a toga.

The briskness of Fairhrim's knock made him snap to attention, but he recovered his flaneur's slouch in time for her entrance. He leaned against the examination table. His scars cicatrised sexily, his jaw chiselled heroically, his pecs popped manfully—not for Fairhrim, but because that was their usual state. He'd like to see her try to ignore this catalogue of attractions, however.

Fairhrim walked in and did not look at them.

She did observe his attire.

"That," said Fairhrim, "is a table runner."

"I think," said Osric, "it becomes me."

Fairhrim did not opine on this. She said, "Sit."

In a hygienic outburst, she whipped out her hlutoform and sprayed it on her hands—and in Osric's direction, as though he were a handsome microbe that had come too close. Osric sat within the cloud of sanitation. Fairhrim busied herself with her machine.

Osric swept a hand through his hair. She ignored him. He flexed his abs. No reaction. He bit his lip. Disregarded. He made a deep guttural sound when she wiped cold hlutoform against him. She told him to act like a grown man.

She was the Worst.

The toga was shifted to one side; the hlutoform completed its acrid responsibilities; the diffractor's tentacle was pressed to Osric's chest and began its chortling.

"Why are your shoulders scratched up like this?" asked Fairhrim.

"I'm having an affair," said Osric, sexily.

"With a rodent?" asked Fairhrim.

Osric, who was not actually a rat fucker, was compelled to clarify: "It was your bloody deofol who scratched me up."

"Oh," said Fairhrim.

She, notably, made no apology.

Fairhrim attached sticky things on wires to various bits of Osric (not *those* bits, but other, less exciting bits). (Anyway, he hadn't any interest in Fairhrim touching his bits.)

As before, a shiny silhouette, vaguely man shaped, was projected onto the wall by the diffractor. White lines representing healthy seith channels shimmered; black lines vined through them morbidly.

"Don't move," said Fairhrim, as she studied the image.

Osric was disturbed to see bright pinpricks along his seith channels, which certainly hadn't been there before.

"What are those spots?" he asked.

The image on the wall distorted and flickered as he spoke; the diffractor's chuckling grew churlish.

"I said, don't move," said Fairhrim. "Those are my seith markers."

Fairhrim stared at the figure on the wall for an eternity lasting two minutes. She tucked a finger under her chin and said, "Hmm," but Osric did not know if it was a good *hmm* or a bad *hmm*.

She took out a complicated silver instrument, took measurements from the figure on the wall, and noted the results in Osric's chart. The chart was temperamental and twitchy, but grew docile as she began to fill it in. Osric noticed that, under *Patient Name*, she had inserted an alias, which was fine, but that the alias was U. Ganglion, which offended him.

"You may relax," said Fairhrim, as she made her notes. She spoke absently as she wrote. "Your seith system is wonderfully robust, barring the disease. Really makes it a pleasure to study. Much of my work involves civilians, who only use their seith for waystone travel or to send a barely formed deofol. Their channels hardly show up on the diffractor. You've got such well-developed lines. Quite juicy." Fairhrim looked up. "How's the torpraxia? The numbness?"

"Persevering."

"Tell me when you stop feeling this," said Fairhrim.

Osric answered as she ran a cool finger down his arms, and then his thighs and legs, and down his chest and back. Notes were duly taken. No thoughts were had about the nearness of finger to bits; and if the finger was soft, Osric did not notice.

Fairhrim went back to her chart.

"Have you anything good to tell me?" asked Osric.

"No," came the pitiless reply.

"Why not?" asked Osric, in tones that were, admittedly, a bit whingy.

"The rate of the deterioration remains within expected parameters," said Fairhrim.

"So nothing we've done has had any impact?"

"Not a measurable one—not on your seith system, anyway," said Fairhrim, with the implication that there had been diverse nefarious impacts elsewhere.

"We've been wasting our time," said Osric.

"Yes. As I've warned from the beginning."

"Fuck."

"There's not much else I can do at this point."

"Hold me and tell me everything is going to be all right."

Fairhrim's upward glance, begun in scepticism, grew serious, then shifted back to scepticism.

"You almost sounded sincere," said Fairhrim. "Well done."

Osric, who had, obviously, not been sincere, inclined his head towards her like a pleased thespian. "Thank you."

Fairhrim plucked the diffractor's tentacles off Osric and rolled the contraption away. She instructed him to dress and exited the room, and thus deprived herself of further viewings of his superb masculinity, which was her loss.

When Osric had dressed, Fairhrim returned and boxed up her various maps and notes and things scattered about the clinic. ("I'll take these home with me—can't risk someone else seeing," she said, as though the contents were shameful and perverse.)

This exercise completed, she dusted her hands with the air of one moving on to the next item on her list, turned expectantly to Osric, and said, "So."

Osric, having graduated from microbe to bullet point, asked, "What?"

"My deofol told me that you had findings to share with me."

"Oh. That."

"Yes—that. Did you discover something about the intruders at Swanstone?"

"I did."

Fairhrim continued to look at Osric expectantly and, indeed, with far more interest than when he was a microbe. Now he had her attention. Now he wouldn't be ignored.

He would be moderate about it. He wouldn't power trip.

He power tripped immediately.

"I don't know," said Osric. "I'm not certain it's worth sharing."

This had been a coy invitation for a bit of cajoling from Fairhrim.

She did not cajole. She unleashed an imperious command: "Tell me."

"It's very vague. I'd rather tell you when I've got something tangible."

Fairhrim's focus on Osric was intense. Her eyes bored into his. For once, it wasn't Osric who needed something from her, who needed to demand or coerce or beg. It gave him a terrible sort of pleasure to have something that she wanted.

Osric turned away, as if to move towards the door.

Fairhrim took a step sideways to remain in his line of sight. "Tell me."

Yes. He liked it.

"I may have a contact," said Osric.

"For who ordered the intrusion?"

"*Tss*," scoffed Osric. "That'd be too easy. For someone who might know something about who ordered it."

"Who is this contact?"

"You don't need to know. I'm to meet him tonight. I'll tell you if I discover anything worthwhile."

"Can I come?" asked Fairhrim.

"What?"

"Can I come?" repeated Fairhrim. "Tonight? To meet this person?"

"Absolutely not," said Osric.

"Why not?"

"For one, a prissy Haelan popping round to the Bunghole would raise far too many questions."

"The—the Bunghole?" repeated Fairhrim in mild consternation.

"Dodgiest boozer in London. Rough crowd."

Fairhrim digested this information before gathering herself and insisting anew. "I'd be in a better position to talk to them, to get to the bottom of this."

"No. You'll bodge it up."

"I don't trust *you* not to bodge it up," said Fairhrim. "This is important."

"Let me do my job, and you do yours. We'll reconvene when I've got the information and you've helped some invalids, or whatever it is you do with yourself."

"Your job," said Fairhrim, "is murder."

"Espionage is one of my many areas of expertise. Besides, the threat of murder leads to interesting confessions."

"That's your plan?"

"No. My plan is to leave now and advise you of my findings later." Osric considered patting Fairhrim on the head for maximum condescension; however, from the way she was looking at him, he thought she might bite him. "You stay put."

"Find answers without coercion," said Fairhrim.

"No."

"I don't care how you normally do it; *this* time we need reliable information."

"No."

"I've reviewed the literature on the use of torture—"

"Spare me."

"—and the overwhelming scientific consensus is that coercive techniques don't work. It's one of the most ineffective intelligence-gathering tools. You'll get false confessions. People will admit to anything under duress. I need you to get *real* information from this contact. And besides, I don't want further deaths on my conscience—"

"Solution: stop having a conscience."

Fairhrim regarded Osric with queenly hauteur, and Osric, reduced to peasanthood, saw that he had committed lèse-majesté in interrupting her.

"Thank you," she said, "for that incisive recommendation."

"Your alternative is to keep clutching at your pearls."

Fairhrim looked as though, for once, she was wrestling with her temper. She flung up her hand. "I'm leaving."

"Good. Go. Stop waving your stupid swan at me."

"It's an Aer."

"An heir to what?"

"An Aer. *A-E-R*. One of Frīa's companions. Symbol of purity and healing. Those who try to kill one suffer instant death."

"Utter tosh," said Osric.

"Preferable to the singed remains of a dog, anyway" was Fairhrim's retort, accompanied by a vinegary look at Osric's tācn.

She sailed towards the door.

"Go back to your House of Pestilence," called Osric, "though I'm not sure which is the greater Pestilence, you or the House."

"Go back to your derelict country pile and rot there."

They parted with the usual levels of esteem and affection.

THE BUNGHOLE

Osric

Fairhrim occupied an annoying portion of Osric's thoughts. He spent too much time that afternoon continuing their discussion in his head, resulting in an imaginary argument in which he featured prominently with sharp and witty rebuttals. He considered sending his deofol to Fairhrim with a script, so that she knew what he was capable of.

He managed to switch gears as he entered the Bunghole. He needed to be alert and not preoccupied by Fairhrim and her tongue.

Osric was an occasional patron of the Bunghole, one of those grotty little dens of sin, so useful in his line of work, where if no one was actively on fire, it was a quiet night. The pub was small, with a distinct odour and charm. The yellowing tiles lining the wall evoked something between the back room of an abattoir and a men's toilet. The bar was wide enough for perhaps one and a half patrons to stand at. There were pornographic images plastered behind it, in case, Osric supposed, patrons fancied a cheeky wank while waiting for their pints.

Off the bar hung a sign that said *NO CANNIBALISM*.

Osric, his hood up, his cowl raised, and smoked spectacles covering his face, fit right into the crowd; most of the clientele was hooded and sinister. He ordered a pint and retreated to a corner table, from whence he commanded an excellent view of the two dozen turds squeezed into the Bunghole.

He watched the come and go of the local fauna. This was the kind of pub where every regular had a name, which Osric learned as they greeted one another with varying degrees of friendliness: Pissbag Perry, Dandruff, Steve the Builder, Scratch and Sniff, the Artful Todger.

Sharing a table with Osric was the delightful One-Tooth, who wheezed into his whiskers and sipped something that he mysteriously called "long juice," which smelled like pure camphor, before he chased it down with turpentine. Osric suspected that he was a walker of one of the Dusken Paths—because of his gloves—and particularly an Agannor, given the surfeit of purple in his ensemble.

Osric's source had advised him to find a man with a wolf tattoo upon his neck. Osric spotted his mark hunched over a table, chatting with two others who looked as unsavoury as he did. The man was smoking a particularly foul cigar. He leaned back in a stretch that revealed his stomach, upon which he had tattooed *Caution: Choking Hazard*, with an arrow pointing towards his cock.

Charming.

Osric's plan was simple: follow Choking Hazard out, shadow-walk him up a roof, interrogate him about the Swanstone thing, and, if he was of no further use, kill him.

The simplicity of the plan was shattered by the entrance of two women, one in red and one in blue. The red one's dress consisted largely of scarlet fishnet; in a nod to decency, she had covered her nipples in heart-shaped pasties. The blue one was tall, smaller about the bust, but rounder about the hips, wearing boots to the thigh and the shortest of skirts, at the back of which was the lettering: *Make It Bounce.* The women stopped to chat with Madam Miffle, who was ensconced in her wheelchair near the door.

"Ooh." One-Tooth elbowed Osric. "Red girl's Cerys. Isn't she a beauty? Seen a couple of her films at the Sinema." One-Tooth's potent breath exfoliated Osric's face. "Miffle usually has her working at the fancy place up the road. Wonder what she's doing here tonight."

One-Tooth gazed lovingly at the woman in red and updated Osric on her filmography (*Death by a Thousand Sluts* and *Big Tits 4*) and further informed him that her breasts were insured, and also that they had names (from left to right, Thoughts and Prayers).

"Don't recognise the other one," wheezed One-Tooth. "I s'pose she's new. Pretty girl, though."

The new girl stood behind Cerys. She had a gauzy scarf partly covering her hair and lacy gloves over her hands. But yes, thought Osric as she turned towards him and he saw the curve of a cheek and the shape of her mouth, she was a pretty girl. His eye roved up the boots to the edge of the skirt. A pretty girl with the precise kind of thighs of interest to him—until the scarf, the gloves, and the glimpse of her face clicked into place, and he realised who he was looking at.

He clutched at his pint.

"S'matter?" asked One-Tooth.

"That's fucking—that's—never mind," gurgled Osric.

Blessed distraction came. For no discernible reason, the Artful Todger tore off his shirt and challenged Scratch and Sniff to a fight. Dandruff launched himself onto both of them. Choking Hazard and his entourage threw their drinks over the combatants and were dragged into the fray.

Osric joined Cerys, Madam Miffle, and bloody fucking Fairhrim in the corner they'd retreated to.

"Hiya," he said to Fairhrim, by which he meant *I'm going to kill you.*

Cerys wedged herself between Osric and Fairhrim. Thoughts and

Prayers made, frankly, an impressive sort of barricade. "What do you want?"

Osric was about to tell Cerys to fuck off, when he noticed that Madam Miffle might not have had legs but she did have an ancient sabre, which was presently pointed at his groin.

"What museum did you pilfer that from?" asked Osric.

Cerys loomed. The dual threat of suffocation by tit and tetanus of the bollocks made Osric change tacks.

"Your new girl caught my eye," said Osric.

"She isn't having anyone tonight," said Madam Miffle. "She's only learning."

"I just wanted to speak with her. See if we—er—connect."

Madam Miffle and Cerys turned to Fairhrim, who had fixed Osric with a glare of her own. However, she gave them a nod.

"Fine," said Madam Miffle. "Our fee for half an hour of conversation is three hundred thrymsas."

"That's highway fucking robbery," said Osric.

"Pay up or leave," said Madam Miffle, with an ominous sabre rattle.

Osric paid up.

Cerys and her nipple pasties moved aside. "Stay within our sight. And no touching her."

As if Osric would dream of touching the most irritating, meddlesome little Haelan who had ever walked the earth. Other than to murder her, obviously.

Also: Fairhrim had no business having Thighs of Interest.

Osric spat out a proposition to go to the bar. Fairhrim snapped out a tight-necked nod.

They slid along the wall to avoid the brawl and squeezed up to the bar. Their backs were to the room, which was ideal, as their conversation was bound to look anything but friendly.

Osric ordered a Scotch. Fairhrim asked for water.

Gods.

"You didn't tell me you'd moved on to a new career," said Osric.

"A temporary arrangement," said Fairhrim.

"How can you walk in those ridiculous boots?"

"How can you see in those ridiculous spectacles?"

"They're for privacy."

"You look like a bee."

The bartender returned with their drinks, and then, for reasons known best to himself, flung himself headlong into the brawl.

"You shouldn't have spoken to me," said Fairhrim through clenched teeth. "I thought you were meant to be good at subterfuge."

"Your presence has thrown a bit of a wrench in the works, since I now have to make sure you don't get carried off and fucked senseless in the back of a carriage. What a stupid decision to come here. Those women will sell you off to the highest bidder."

"They absolutely will not. I know them. We work together. I asked them to help me come here undercover tonight. Who's our informant?"

"He's *my* informant, found through *my* sources, and *I'll* be talking to him."

"You're here at *my* request, for the safety of *my* Order, and you're doing it in exchange for *my* healing of your little embolus."

Osric sought a rebuttal, but his clever scripts from earlier had evaporated. He wished to stare daggers at Fairhrim, perhaps amplified with a literal dagger, but he didn't want Madam Miffle to trundle over with her castration device. He glared at the pornography behind the bar instead. Fairhrim did the same.

"Why so many vulvas?" asked Fairhrim, with fresh annoyance. "You'd think there'd be more anuses, given the place's name."

"I can't believe I paid three hundred thrymsas to hear you complain about a lack of anuses."

Fairhrim looked grim. They stared at the Wall of Vulvas in silence. The brawl raged on behind them. Someone, bleeding from both eyes, was carried out. A posse entered, snatched up Steve the Builder, and dragged him into a back room. He defended himself with a trowel. The bartender picked up Pissbag Perry and threw him at the dartboard; he did not get a bull's-eye, but he did break Pissbag's neck. Pint glasses arced over the scene like foamy fireworks.

"So, now what?" asked Fairhrim.

"We've reached an impasse," said Osric.

"Since your plan was threats of murder—and, I suppose, actual murder—let me have a go at the informant first, and see what I discover. If he's not cooperative, we can do it your way."

This was, admittedly, a logical proposal. If they did the opposite, Fairhrim wouldn't get much of a go, due to the death and everything. Odds were strong that Osric would be getting his way in the end, too.

"Fine," said Osric.

Fairhrim looked suspicious. Osric did not, apparently, often agree with her.

"Which one is the informant?" she asked.

Osric pointed at Choking Hazard, who was presently pressing Dandruff's face into a heap of broken glass. Choking Hazard moved on to waterboarding Dandruff with a bottle of ale.

Fairhrim observed him as one might observe urinal scum. "I see."

Dandruff fainted. Choking Hazard extinguished his cigar in Dandruff's eye and made his way to the bar. Osric and Fairhrim ceased their conversation as the man approached. He muscled his way between them and slapped his hand on the counter.

"Thirsty work," he declared. "Double whiskey."

Choking Hazard glanced at Fairhrim with mild interest, looked away, and then, with bulging eyes, turned to her again. Osric witnessed the man grow immediately and desperately enamoured with Fairhrim: he went soft eyed, his mouth hung open, and he sighed out a breathy "Wow."

Fairhrim directed a small, shy smile towards Choking Hazard. (She had never managed a small, shy smile towards Osric. Simply a note for the record.)

The barkeep materialised with the whiskey, which he slammed into Choking Hazard's palm before returning to his game of darts.

Choking Hazard, jarred from his stupor, said, "*Phwoar.* You're a sight for sore eyes. Where'd you come from? Haven't seen you round here before."

He attempted to throw back his whiskey and missed most of his mouth because he was staring at Fairhrim, dazed and slack-jawed.

"I'm new," said Fairhrim. She looked demurely downwards and tucked a stray curl of hair behind her ear.

(Since when was Fairhrim *demure*?)

"You're fucking beautiful," said Choking Hazard. "Who do you work for?"

(Was she beautiful? No. Osric was a great connoisseur of beauty. She was not beautiful. All there was to see here was an annoyingly un-afraid gaze and a maddening mouth that alternately spouted nonsense and overly sharp sense at random intervals. She was pretty at best. Just pretty.)

"I've just started working with Madam Miffle," said Fairhrim.

"Where'd she dig you up?" asked Choking Hazard.

"I needed help and she was kind enough to take me in," said Fairhrim.

Cerys, bolstered by Thoughts and Prayers, plunged through the brawl towards them to keep abreast of the situation. Osric jumped when he discovered that Madam Miffle was beside him. He asked her, in a startled whisper, how in Hel's name she had got there, and she answered, "Tunnels."

Fairhrim gestured her two guardians away with a low wave of her hand. Cerys and Madam Miffle backed off, and, incidentally, did not charge Choking Hazard their outrageous fee for conversation with Fairhrim, which was distinctly unjust.

Choking Hazard did not notice any of these subtleties because he was staring at *Make It Bounce* on Fairhrim's arse.

"What are you drinking?" asked Choking Hazard.

"Oh, nothing tonight," said Fairhrim. "It's my first night out. I'm not to drink or take any clients."

"Madam Miffle'll forgive me for getting you a drink. I've given her enough custom over the years." Choking Hazard gestured to the barkeep and ordered Fairhrim a double whiskey, too.

He snatched the drinks in one hand, and Fairhrim's arm in the other, and brought both to his table.

Osric gave them a few minutes, then joined a game of cards at the next table. He noted that Fairhrim was being watched by a great many eyes; every woman in the place found excuses to pass her table and assess her well-being. Cerys was particularly watchful, to the extent that Choking Hazard raised his hands and said, "I'm not fucking doing anything." Cerys patted him on the head and moved along.

Osric did not think of Making It Bounce.

Fairhrim did not appear to like the whiskey, but sipped at it gamely as Choking Hazard described his favourites of Madam Miffle's girls, and what he liked to do with them, and then, in vulgar detail, what he wished to do with Fairhrim.

"You got a dress?" he asked. "A big, poufy dress?"

"Erm—I'd have to have a look—"

"Right. You check. I want you to dress like a princess. You look like you just stepped out of a fucking fairy-tale castle."

(What an idiot. Fairhrim lived in a fortress.)

Choking Hazard shouted towards the bar for a plate of something to eat. The barkeep shouted at him to go fuck himself.

"Speaking of castles," said Fairhrim, shuffling a bit closer to Choking Hazard, "did you hear that someone attacked Swanstone?"

(Subtle, Fairhrim. Very subtle.)

"Where did you hear that?" asked Choking Hazard.

"Some men were discussing it in here earlier," said Fairhrim, with the vaguest of gestures around the pub.

"Which men?"

"Erm—I'm not sure. I think they've left."

Fairhrim wasn't good at playing stupid, but this performance was, apparently, passable enough for Choking Hazard. "No," he said. "I hadn't heard that."

The topic should have come to a natural close at that juncture, of course, but Fairhrim hadn't got what she wanted. She allowed none of her frustration to show on her face; Osric saw it in the twist of a lace glove under the table.

Choking Hazard dragged Fairhrim's chair closer to him, so close that her thigh rode up against his. He stopped her from pulling away with a hand on her knee.

There was a sudden stillness among the ladies in the room. Osric noticed it only because he had, himself, gone still, as he decided where to amputate Choking Hazard's arm because he had touched his Haelan.

A woman passing behind Choking Hazard raised a tray over the back of his head, ready to bludgeon him with it.

Choking Hazard, oblivious to all, said, "You're shy. I like that. We're going to have fun, soon as your minders let you off the lead."

Fairhrim removed Choking Hazard's hand from her person; he grabbed her again. She squirmed off her chair; he snatched her thigh and held her to him.

Osric should have enjoyed her discomfort—he did like to see her suffer. Instead, he found himself seething with a low churn of rage. His blaecblade itched to draw a deep line across Choking Hazard's oily neck.

Fairhrim reached for Choking Hazard's empty glass. "Can I get you another drink, Mr.—erm, I don't even know your name—"

"Scrope," said Choking Hazard.

Fairhrim's fingers around the glass twitched. Osric choked on his drink.

"S-Scrope?" said Fairhrim.

"Yeah. You've heard of me?" asked Scrope, né Choking Hazard, with a grin that was meant to be roguish, probably. (Insufficient teeth. Osric did a much better roguish grin.)

"I think I might've," said Fairhrim. "People say you're in the know about—well, everything. But I must be getting you confused with someone else. You hadn't heard the Swanstone rumour, after all. I'll be right back. It was whiskey, wasn't it?"

Having pricked Scrope with this needle, Fairhrim tottered off to the bar. She asked for another whiskey, then excused herself to the toilet.

Osric rose from his card game. "Flash diarrhoea," he said, and the group asked for no further explanations.

Osric didn't need to ask for directions to the privies; he needed merely to follow the whiff of stale urine. He pushed open the door to the toilet to find Fairhrim undertaking some sort of deep breathing exercise at the sink, and washing her arm where Scrope had touched her.

"What's the next step in your master plan?" he asked.

"I don't know," said Fairhrim. "I'm improvising."

"You might've told me you were going to try to seduce him."

"That wasn't the plan. But, well—if I'm his type—"

"This is appalling to watch."

"To watch? What about me? I'm living it." Fairhrim shuddered. "That man is a vaginal desiccant."

"Get another whiskey down him and try the castle line again. And if it doesn't work, get back to the safety of your friends, and I'll do it my way—just as we should've done from the beginning."

"Fine," said Fairhrim.

"I can't believe I paid three hundred thrymsas to watch you be groped by Scrope."

"Is he *that* Scrope? The ejaculate-in-the-baths Scrope?"

"Ask him. I'm sure he'd be delighted to tell you about his wanking habits."

There was a thump at the door.

Osric and Fairhrim opened the door to find Cerys, Madam Miffle, and two other women waiting outside. They all glared at Osric as though he were the troublemaker here, and not Fairhrim. In their fists were knives, the sabre, and two broken bottles. They were ready to maul him.

"Everything all right?" asked Cerys.

"Everything is fine," said Fairhrim. "Thank you. I've almost got what I need."

Osric lingered in the corridor a bit to give Fairhrim the chance to return to her conversation. The ladies left him behind with suspicious glares over their shoulders.

He rejoined the card game and fielded a few witty enquiries about his bunghole at the Bunghole. Scrope and Fairhrim got to chatting again. One-Tooth won a suspicious number of rounds. Osric found it difficult to focus on his cards, other than how frequently the ace of hearts popped up in his hands.

Scrope was—gods, was he really?—yes, he was asking Fairhrim to feel his muscles.

(Osric never indulged in such ridiculous showing off.)

"You're built like one of the Wardens," said Fairhrim.

"*Pah*," spat Scrope. "Those fucks."

"Don't you like them?"

"Self-righteous cunts. Just like the Haelan, and any of those so-called Bright Path walkers. Think they're better than everyone else."

What a surprise for Osric, to find himself agreeing with Scrope. Fairhrim's impassivity served her well; she did not react to his insult, except for the barest thinning of her smile.

"Bloody good at their jobs, though, those Wardens." Scrope sucked down the dregs of his whiskey.

"Oh?"

Scrope seemed torn between discretion and wishing to impress

Fairhrim. The wishing to impress won out. He leaned close to her and whispered something in her ear.

"Really?" gasped Fairhrim.

Scrope whispered again.

Fairhrim gave him a wide-eyed look. "But who would do such a thing?"

Scrope whispered something else.

Fairhrim looked—well, she looked like she was going for coquettish. "I knew you were *that* Scrope—the one who knows everything."

Scrope pulled Fairhrim in sloppily and muttered something else that Osric didn't catch.

"I've never heard of him," said Fairhrim, pushing her fingers to Scrope's mouth, which was presently attempting to attach itself to her ear. "Is he important?"

"Aye, but not enough to matter to you. You just focus on perfecting your suck jobs, eh?"

Scrope's meal arrived. He spaded it into his mouth. Now that she had the information she needed, Fairhrim's patience wore as thin as her smile. Osric watched her shy-debutante veneer fade. Her jaw found its usual set. Her shoulders dropped and resumed their square. Her bearing grew cold, authoritative, severe.

Scrope, busy at the trough, did not notice these changes. He scratched at his belly. His shirt rode up. Fairhrim caught sight of the *Choking Hazard* tattoo and looked, if it was possible, even grimmer than she had at the Twat Wall. Scrope smacked at his potatoes.

"Must you masticate so loudly?" asked Fairhrim.

"M'what?" was the sparkling response.

Fairhrim made a sound of impatience and rose.

"Where're you going?" asked Scrope in a gurgle of potato.

"Leaving," said Fairhrim.

"Nah. You're not going anywhere. I'm going to have you tonight.

Madam Miffle'll make an exception." Scrope swung a heavy hand to Fairhrim's waist—then it slipped lower, and disappeared under her skirt to grip her arse. "Here, Madam Miffle, you're opening this one's legs up for business tonight, you hear?"

Fairhrim peeled Scrope's hand away. Osric thought of twenty-six ways to kill him using only the potato. Madam Miffle materialised at the table with inexplicable rapidity. Her sabre rested on Scrope's forearm.

"*I* decide, and I said no," said Madam Miffle.

"Come on, Mags. We'll do twice the going rate—how's that?"

"No."

"Three times."

"No."

Scrope, who had obviously considered this an irresistible offer, said, "No? *No?* What's so bloody special about this girl?"

"I'm training her how I see fit," said Madam Miffle.

"You're a dozy fucking cow with no business sense."

"Watch your tongue, or I'll have you blacklisted. You'll have no more girls in the whole of London. You can dig up your dead mum and shag her bones."

Scrope raised his hands. "Fine. *Fine.* There's always tomorrow. Will you be here tomorrow, girl?"

Fairhrim, squeezing past Scrope's chair, her eyes on the exit, made no answer. Scrope groped at her thigh as she passed. It would be one of his last acts on this earth.

Scrope speared the end of a sausage and held it up to her. "Have a little suck of my sausage at least."

"That," said Fairhrim, "looks exactly like a torn-off nipple."

Having delivered this eight-word horror story, she left the pub.

Scrope stared after her; then he, too, made for the door.

He was wrong, by the way. There wasn't always tomorrow. There wouldn't, for instance, be one for him.

CUTLERY, DANGERS OF

Aurienne

Aurienne winced as she stepped out of the pub. Scrope's groping had turned to painful grabs as she had made her escape. A single touch of her tācn could have rendered him unconscious—but it would also have given the game away, and so she had refrained.

It didn't matter. She had got what she came for.

A few steps away from the pub's entrance, Cerys and some of Madam Miffle's girls joined her and returned her satchel. They chatted for a few minutes—how this one's baby was doing; how the other's infection was clearing up; did anyone need contraceptives?—before Aurienne was able to break off towards the pub's waystone. She was desperate for a wash and a change of clothes.

As she walked to the waystone, Aurienne thought she heard the heavy step of a man behind her. Glances over her shoulder revealed nothing, however, and she reached the waystone uninterrupted.

There was a tall shadow waiting for her there; the Fyren had decided to join her.

"Gods," said Mordaunt, pulling his hood down as he stepped out of the penumbra. "The great seduction of the bath-wank bandit. What a show. What did he tell you? What was the name?"

"We can't talk here," said Aurienne. She spotted something shiny in Mordaunt's hand—shiny and suspiciously drippy. "Erm, what's that?"

"Nothing," said Mordaunt, tossing the thing over his shoulder.

The shiny object spun away in the air—a dagger?

No. A fork.

"Why did you have a fork dripping with blood?" asked Aurienne as the thing clattered away.

"I was using it."

Aurienne took a step in the direction of the fork. "For what?"

Mordaunt got in her way. "I thought you were leaving."

"I was, but—"

There was a sort of groan in the direction of the fork. Aurienne sidestepped Mordaunt to pass him, but ran into his chest instead.

"You should leave," said Mordaunt.

Aurienne pushed past him—admittedly not an easy exercise—and strode around the corner. There she found Scrope, studded with at least two dozen stab wounds. Not quite dead, but not quite alive, either.

"What did you do?" gasped Aurienne.

"He fell," said Mordaunt.

"He *fell*?"

"Yes. On the fork."

"He fell on the fork? Twenty times?"

"Yes. Due to . . . fear."

"What was he afraid of?"

"The fork."

Aurienne tore off her glove to heal the dying man. "You're utterly unhinged."

"I'm perfectly hinged," said Mordaunt. "You, on the other hand, have got the survival instincts of a crumpet."

"I beg your pardon?"

"He followed you out here. You can't tell me you think it was to ask you to dinner. He saw you talking to Cerys and the girls. He could've squeezed any one of them for information about you. And I need you alive and well, so—"

"You can't just kill people who inconvenience you," said Aurienne. Scrope's pulse was feeble under her tācn; he was almost gone.

"I can and I do," said Mordaunt.

"People will want to know why he was murdered, and by whom. He'll be missed."

"Missed? A man like this?" Mordaunt nudged Scrope with his boot, as one would a sack of rubbish. "That remains to be seen."

Scrope twitched and died.

"Never mind," said Mordaunt. "The remains are right here. We're seeing them. And look—no one has come running."

"He's a human being."

"Was. A human was."

"Really? Pedantry? Now?"

Mordaunt ushered Aurienne back to the waystone. "Clutch your pearls over here."

"Might we," asked Aurienne, "go anywhere without subtracting from the population?"

"Would you prefer," asked Mordaunt, "that we add to it?"

He dragged Scrope's body into the cesspit behind the Bunghole. There was a splash and a nauseating whiff. He replaced the cesspit lid with a clang and asked, in a chirpy sort of way, "Where to? We need to talk."

Aurienne pressed disbelieving hands to her cheeks. "He's just going to—just going to rot in the cesspit."

"Yes. That's the idea." Mordaunt dusted off his gloves. "This is how one disposes of shit. Shall we go to a clinic?"

"I want a bath. I can still feel his hands on me."

"My house, then."

"What?"

"Well, we're not going to Swanstone for a bath and a confab."

"Have you even got a functioning bath in your great, decrepit manse?"

"No," said Mordaunt, with violent sarcasm. "I bathe in the toilet bowl."

"Fine," said Aurienne. "Your house."

They pushed their tācn to the waystone, were reminded to *mind the gap*, and were pulled into the ley line.

Rosefell Hall was in much the same state as it had been upon Aurienne's previous visit, save for the presence of Mordaunt's steward, whom he introduced to Aurienne thus:

"Ah, Mrs. Parson, there you are. Meet my Means to an End, Haelan Fairhrim. Disregard her attire; she doesn't actually moonlight as a lady of the night. The story is too long and stupid to tell you. Fairhrim—this is my steward, Mrs. Parson."

Mrs. Parson was a stout woman, white skinned and black haired, save the grey streaks running through her bun. She lowered her head. "Haelan Fairhrim, it's an honour."

Aurienne's impression was of a sturdy kind of competence. Mrs. Parson looked so proper in her neat apron that Aurienne wondered whether the poor woman even knew she was working for a Fyren. Perhaps she was normal?

"How do you do, Mrs. Parson?" said Aurienne, inclining her head in return.

Mrs. Parson turned to Mordaunt and, in a tone edging on reproof, said, "I do wish that I'd known we were expecting company."

"Spur-of-the-moment sort of decision," said Mordaunt. "Haelan Fairhrim would like to wash up; she had an unfortunate encounter with a lecherous shitbag."

"What?" gasped Mrs. Parson.

"I took care of him," said Mordaunt. "Couldn't have him harassing our Haelan."

"I hope you made him suffer, sir," said Mrs. Parson.

"I did."

"Is he dead, sir?"

"Yes."

"Send his mother a toe, sir."

"Good idea."

Anyway, reflected Aurienne, it was nice of Mrs. Parson to confirm so early in their acquaintance that she, too, was unhinged.

Mrs. Parson disappeared for a few minutes to sort out the bath and returned with towels wedged under one arm, and two oil lamps. She led Aurienne up the stairs. In the lamplight, Aurienne noticed that Mrs. Parson was missing a few fingers on her left hand. An old injury, based on the maturity of the scars, but a traumatic one. It hadn't been a clean amputation.

The lamps cast shivering shadows over draped-over paintings and fading tapestries. The upstairs of Rosefell was even more desolate than the downstairs had been, and reeked of dry rot. Aurienne, whose mortal enemy was dust, began a rhythmic series of sneezes in time with her steps.

Mrs. Parson was a mix of embarrassed and defensive about the state of the place. "You'll have to forgive the house's condition. It's just me and my husband—he's the groundsman. Mr. Mordaunt doesn't wish to employ anyone else. I can't keep up with all of the rooms. I make sure his chambers are liveable, of course, and I've just given the Magnolia Room a cleaning."

"Have you been with the family long?"

"Oh yes. A few decades. Of course, there's not much of a family to speak of now. Mr. Mordaunt is the last of the line."

They came to the great house's bedrooms, where every door was adorned with a small brass frame. Some still contained, in long-faded ink, the ghostly names of guests from more prosperous times. A path was worn in the plush carpet. Once-fine pieces of furniture sagged along the corridor, topped with tarnished candleholders.

"There was a time when any one of these rooms would have been ready to receive you at a moment's notice," said Mrs. Parson.

"What happened?" asked Aurienne.

"Dissipation."

"Mordaunt's?"

"The younger? Oh, no. He's recovering the fortune. Or was—until you, of course." This Mrs. Parson said matter-of-factly, without the acrimony that laced Mordaunt's remarks on the same topic. "The senior—and his predecessors—were rather less wise."

Mrs. Parson offered no further insights into these unwise ancestors. Aurienne did not pry.

"May I ask . . . ?" Mrs. Parson cast a glance at Aurienne over a round shoulder, hesitated, and fell silent.

"Yes?" prompted Aurienne.

"Is he going to be all right?" asked Mrs. Parson. "Is there a bit of hope?"

"I really can't comment on his prognosis," said Aurienne. "You'll have to ask him."

"He said not much hope. I suppose not much is still a bit."

"I suppose it is" was Aurienne's noncommittal reply.

"He's told me that you've turned to the Old Ways."

"In desperation, yes," said Aurienne. "There's no known cure for his condition."

"It's a great relief that he's, at least, in the best possible hands," said Mrs. Parson. "Though I know—given your tācn, and his tācn—your hands aren't the most willing."

Aurienne produced the most civil answer she could. "Indeed. We seem diametrically opposed on every possible front."

"Perhaps you'll be surprised by points of commonality."

To this, Aurienne could make no civil answer.

Mrs. Parson stopped at a door covered in carvings of tumbling magnolia blossoms. "Here we are. After you, Haelan."

Aurienne stepped into the high-ceilinged suite. There were no lights save Mrs. Parson's lamps. The air was hushed and closed; the sounds of their footsteps were absorbed by the swathes of sheets draped over the furnishings.

The bathroom included the luxury of a hearth. Mrs. Parson had taken the trouble to start a fire. Aurienne sniffed at the smoke—it was the same fragrant smoke she had smelled in the sitting room, with that odd undercurrent of bitterness.

"What wood do you burn here?" asked Aurienne.

"Blackthorn," said Mrs. Parson. "It's all over the estate. We are quite overrun. Half of my husband's waking hours involve cutting it back. But it's not all bad—it makes decent firewood. Burns low and slow."

She turned the tap adorning the large copper tub, muttered something about the boiler, and convinced the tap to produce hot water by striking it with her fist.

Mrs. Parson left Aurienne a lamp. "Mr. Mordaunt's not much one for lights," she said as she placed it next to the bath. "We'd talked of bringing electricity into the house years ago, but, well—with only him here, it'd be of such little use."

Mrs. Parson left. Aurienne stripped out of the clothes she had bought from Madam Miffle's girls and slipped into the bath. She paid particular attention to scrubbing the places that Scrope had touched— the last living memories of a dead man.

Thanks to Mordaunt and his fork, she also had literal blood on her hands tonight, which she washed off guiltily. She and the Fyren had left a pile of dead bandits at the lighthouse, and now another body rotted at the Bunghole. This could not go on.

Aurienne dried. In her satchel was one of her Haelan dresses, a lighter, summer version of her usual habit. She shook it out of its roll, slipped it on, and, feeling much more herself, wandered out of the suite, equipped with the lamp. She took a wrong turn or two among gloomy, forgotten corridors. She discovered more of Mordaunt's collections—a wall of timepieces; a room that housed antique skulls, human and animal. (Aurienne also collected skulls. It offended her to have discovered a point of commonality quite so quickly.)

In her search for the stairs, she came across a locked set of double doors. A book-filled glass display case hinted that this was the library. Aurienne's curiosity was stymied by the lock on the doors; she turned it instead to the contents of the glass case. The glow of her tācn revealed anatomical texts—a set of all seven of Vesalius' *De humani corporis fabrica*.

Aurienne sneezed her way to the staircase under the noble faces of Mordaunt ancestors. She travelled across centuries from time-blackened portraits to modern daguerreotypes as she descended. There were marks of Mordaunt's features in every portrait: a cleft chin here, silver hair there, grey eyes, mouths that hinted at insufferable wide grins. Knightly armour abounded. And now the family's one remaining scion was a Fyren. How far it had fallen. Or was it a regression? Hadn't knightly orders begun their existence being paid for violence?

Mordaunt's critique cricket was still around; a small voice advised Aurienne, as she went, that she smelled like binned mayonnaise.

Aurienne found Mordaunt sprawling in a large armchair in the sitting room. He, too, had washed—presumably he had found a toilet bowl somewhere. He reclined in a Byronic attitude in a half-buttoned white shirt, his damp hair swept artfully to the side, the heels of his boots on the fireguard. The only light came from the hearth. Aurienne quelled the part of her brain that wished her to take note that he was, once again, Being Handsome.

Around Mordaunt were scattered a half dozen of his ancient dogs. This time they did not flee Aurienne's presence; one or two tails fluttered in timid recognition. Only the voiceless terrier emerged from its state of repose. It barked so forcefully at Aurienne that it knocked itself off its feet; then, after their mutual exchange of stares, it retreated to its cushion.

A frail whippet, missing a leg and an eye, was in the armchair with Mordaunt. He ran a gloved hand gently along the dog's bony back. The strange kindness reverberated backwards and clashed violently with what Aurienne knew of Mordaunt; that same hand had just stabbed a man to death with a fork.

Presiding over the sleeping canids like a primal queen was the shadowy form of Mordaunt's deofol. Starlight streamed through a stained-glass window and cast the shape of an elegant greyhound upon her. She lay in the pose of a sphinx. Her unblinking golden eyes met Aurienne's as she entered the room. The wolf offered no greeting. The obsequious tail wags of their last encounter were long gone.

The great wolf turned her attention back to Mordaunt, who said, "You may leave us."

The deofol dropped her muzzle and faded out of view like a Stygian mist.

An aged Great Dane approached Aurienne and shoved its snout into her crotch.

"Sit, Rigor Mortis," called Mordaunt.

"You named the dog Rigor Mortis?" asked Aurienne, as Rigor Mortis ignored the instruction.

"They're named for what was happening when I found them," said Mordaunt. He pointed at dogs as he listed their names. "Arson. Perjury. Forgery. Outraging Public Decency. High Treason. The terrier is Diverse Felonies. The whippet is Crème Brûlée."

"The crème brûlée was a crime?"

"It was the murder weapon."

Mordaunt waved Aurienne towards a sofa. "You'll forgive my state of undress. I decided you weren't important enough for me to wrinkle a fresh neckcloth."

"You'll forgive mine," said Aurienne, extending a foot out from under her skirts. "I didn't fancy putting Cerys' boots back on and I forgot my shoes in my haste to leave."

Mordaunt, his eyes riveted to the hem of her dress, said, "A foot. An *ankle*. Put it away. You'll stir my loins."

Aurienne settled onto the sofa across from Mordaunt and duly tucked away her indecent foot. "Cerys has rubbed off on me."

"That was downright smutty," said Mordaunt. "Perhaps Mrs. Parson can lend you some clogs for the way home."

"Clogs, yes. Just the thing to sneak soundlessly back into my quarters."

Mordaunt's oeillade shifted to Aurienne's face. He observed her with something very like masculine interest, which Aurienne met with a raised eyebrow.

"Are you aware that your throat is exposed?" asked Mordaunt.

"It's only you."

"*Only?* How dare you?"

"I got a bit lost on the way back here," said Aurienne. "I saw your library."

"Which one?"

A question that left Aurienne mildly stunned. "You've got . . . more than one?"

"Haven't you?"

Aurienne ignored this overprivileged, twattish follow-up. "There was a case with copies of *De humani corporis fabrica* just outside the doors."

"Ah. Natural history, then. The other is art history and classical literature."

"Why have you got a copy of *De humani*?"

"I've a small collection of classic anatomical texts."

(Aurienne was vexed anew; another point of commonality.)

"What?" said Mordaunt in response to her frown. "Do you think the Haelan are the only ones who make a study of the human body?"

"I suppose you need to know where to stab."

"Exactly," said Mordaunt. "Also, don't insult me by calling it a copy; it's an original edition. About three hundred years old—"

Mordaunt cut himself off. He had just caught sight of Aurienne's forearm, where Scrope's literal manhandling had left a mark. His eyes, usually heavy lidded with insouciance, real or affected, flew open. His face lost all cynicism. His slouch disappeared. His scar became a vivid white line across his lips.

A second later, it was over. He fell back into his slouch, veiled his eyes, regained his cynicism, and said, "Pity Scrope's already dead. Could've had a bit more fun with him. Are you hungry? I've asked for tea and things. Or will you have something stronger?"

Aurienne healed the marks on her arm. "It's gone half three. Let Mrs. Parson sleep."

"Mrs. Parson can still handle the occasional nighttime adventure," said Mrs. Parson, entering the room with a tray of silverware and porcelain.

"How do you take it?" asked Mordaunt, pouring a cup of tea. "A splash of milk?"

"No, thank you," said Aurienne.

"Sugar?"

"No."

"Nothing fun. I ought to have known."

Aurienne watched Mordaunt pour approximately two cubic feet of milk into his teacup. "Fun? Is that what you call that debauchery?"

"We all have our vices," said Mordaunt, heaping in an equally grotesque amount of sugar.

Mrs. Parson set out a pile of biscuits and a bowl of fruit, and left them to it.

"Pomegranates," remarked Aurienne.

"Yes," said Mordaunt. "They're a metaphor."

Also in the bowl flopped a large, slightly flaccid banana. Aurienne did not ask if the banana, too, was a metaphor.

She left the tea, the pomegranates, and the flanana untouched.

"What happened to Mrs. Parson's hand?" she asked.

"Her hand? Oh, that. An accident with a meat grinder when she was a girl. She does an amusing pantomime about it; you should ask her."

Aurienne did not find such accidents amusing, but she set aside the subject instead of launching into a moral lecture. "We need to talk about tonight."

"We do," said Mordaunt. "It was stupid of you to come out. Kindly preserve your idiotic costume escapades for after you're done healing me. I won't care what happens to you then."

"That's not what we need to talk about," said Aurienne. "But my idiotic escapade got me the information I needed."

"You don't even know if it's good information."

"And I may never know, because you—speaking of idiotic—killed our source. Which is what we actually need to talk about: the trail of cadavers we're leaving in our wake. This isn't how I conduct business."

"It's how I conduct *my* business," said Mordaunt.

"Well, we can't do it your way anymore."

"I'm not telling you to do it my way. I'm telling you to do it right."

"There is nothing right about fork-induced thoracic trauma resulting in death."

A glove was waved Aurienne's way. "You make everything so un-poetic."

"I'm sorry. Would you like me to say it again, in iambic pentameter?"

"Yes."

Aurienne didn't, because she couldn't remember what iambic pentameter was. She regrouped and said, "I'd like us to agree to use violence as an absolute last resort."

"Sounds like a bit of a faff."

"Not murdering people for five minutes is a bit of a faff?"

Mordaunt tilted his head back and sighed at the ceiling. "Violence is a first and best resort. But, very well—I'll let you have your delusions."

"Then we've agreed: no more cadavers," said Aurienne.

"Fewer cadavers," said Mordaunt.

"None."

"Less."

They stared at each other. Aurienne felt the enormity of the gulf between them—morally, ethically, constitutionally. The points of commonality faded to nothing.

"Why does death frighten you so much?" asked Mordaunt.

"Death doesn't frighten me. I am very familiar—*too* familiar—with death. It's you doling it out all willy-nilly that's the problem."

"There's nothing willy or nilly about my approach," said Mordaunt. "I'm a professional; I assess situations and act accordingly."

"*I'm* a professional, and I'm running a course of treatment, not an abattoir."

"An abattoir. That's a good idea."

"A good idea for what?"

"Never mind," said Mordaunt. "Not important."

"Might we therefore turn to what *is* important: the name Scrope gave?"

"Yes," said Mordaunt. "What is it?"

"Bardolph Wellesley."

Mordaunt straightened out of his slouch. "Wellesley? Really?"

"You know him?"

"He's one of the Wessexian queen's retainers. Powerful. Rich. How do you not know of him?"

"I don't keep track of the goings-on among the kings and queens," said Aurienne. "My Order is apolitical."

"As is mine, on paper, but it doesn't mean I wander about absolutely oblivious," said Mordaunt. "All the Orders are under some royal's thumb, somewhere up the line, including yours."

"You're incorrect."

"You're naive."

They stared at each other again.

Mordaunt moved on with a shrug. "The Wessexian queen is the most powerful monarch in the Tiendoms. Bardolph Wellesley, though. That's interesting, if it's true. It mightn't be true—Scrope might've been trying to impress you with the name drop."

"If it *is* true, why would one of the Wessexian queen's men send anyone to Swanstone?" asked Aurienne. "People aren't that stupid. With the exception, of course, of one notable idiot who broke in to see me and pin his hopes on fairy tales."

The Notable Idiot registered the insult with narrowed eyes.

"What have we got that Wellesley couldn't obtain for himself?" mused Aurienne. "Or would want to destroy? Patient records? Prepublication material? Our archives? Our vault?"

"Wellesley is rich," said Mordaunt. "He wouldn't be interested in your vault."

"If Scrope were still alive, we might've interrogated him further on the provenance of his information," said Aurienne.

"If he was still alive, he'd bleed Cerys until she told him who you were and where to find you. And then he'd know too much. And I'd have to kill him anyway."

"Don't be ridiculous. He wouldn't have."

"Which of us is more intimately acquainted with vermin and their ways?"

"You," conceded Aurienne. "You're one of them."

"I *beg* your pardon? Me? A gutter rat like Scrope? Have you seen where I live?"

Aurienne glanced about. Given that there was no gutter immediately within sight, she conceded. "Right. I suppose you're just a rat, then. A plain rat."

"Thank you." Mordaunt, placated, settled back into his armchair.

Aurienne awoke her tācn to summon her deofol. "I've got to inform Xanthe of these developments."

"Developments?" scoffed Mordaunt. "A shit bit of information from a shit source."

"I will remind you that the shit source was your source," said Aurienne, before whispering Cíele's name into her tācn. (A deofol's name was a private thing, and Mordaunt certainly wasn't worthy of knowing hers.)

Her beloved Cíele materialised in her arms and wound his way affectionately up to her shoulder. His fur against her cheek was as soft and intangible as a breath.

When he noticed the Fyren, Cíele said, "Ew."

"You remember Mordaunt, of course," said Aurienne to Cíele.

"As one remembers a particularly distinctive haemorrhoid," said Cíele.

Aurienne did not laugh, though she wished to. "I told you to keep things civil."

"I have kept things civil," said Cíele. "I haven't even drawn blood."

"You have absolutely drawn blood," said Mordaunt.

"He's only a little genet," said Aurienne. "It was an accident."

Mordaunt called Cíele a weasel-faced, pugnacious little squit. Cíele expressed amazement that the haemorrhoid could string together so many words.

"You've got to endure him for the foreseeable future," said Aurienne.

"I know," said Mordaunt and Cíele at the same time.

"She was talking to me," said Cíele.

"She was obviously talking to me," said Mordaunt.

"I was talking to him," said Aurienne, pointing at her deofol.

Mordaunt looked pouty and ate a biscuit.

Aurienne turned to Cíele. "Now, my darling—you must go to Xanthe. Tell her that the Fyren helped me find out who might've sent the intruders to Swanstone: a man called Bardolph Wellesley, who is, apparently, one of the Wessexian queen's men. Mention that the source of the evidence was a drunk lech who is now dead, because the Fyren can't keep his forks to himself—"

"Yes," cut in Mordaunt. "We've established that he's dead. What do you want me to do? Hold a séance?"

"—so ask Xanthe how she'd like to proceed," continued Aurienne. "And don't forget your bows."

"Done," said Cíele.

There was the soft, hardly there pressure of four seith paws against Aurienne's arm; and then, in a puff of white, Cíele was gone.

Aurienne and Mordaunt hardly had time to snarl at each other about Cíele, and whether he deserved to continue to live (Aurienne was strongly in favour; Mordaunt, against), when a push of seith, soft but leathery, tingled at Aurienne's tācn. Xanthe's deofol, Saophal, wanted to come through.

The wrinkled axolotl materialised and took in the room's occupants with slow blinks. "Aurienne: hello. Put on some socks before you catch a chill. Fyren: lukewarmest greetings. No tutu today?"

"Puce wasn't my colour," said Mordaunt.

"Really? I thought it a nice match for your yellow liver." The axolotl's feathery gills fluttered towards Mordaunt. "The evidence on Wellesley's involvement sounds feeble at best."

"It is; it's the slurred words of a sack of shit," said Mordaunt. "He was, admittedly, a well-connected sack of shit."

"It's an avenue for further investigation," said Aurienne. "Which is better than what we had."

Saophal floated towards Mordaunt's face and cocked a beady black eye at him. "Xanthe would like something more concrete."

"Good for Xanthe," said Mordaunt.

"Wellesley's castle will doubtless be a challenge to infiltrate," said Saophal.

"Send the Wardens," said Mordaunt.

"The Wardens aren't at our command—and they don't do infiltrations," said Saophal. "They'd stomp in singing a war song and hang Wellesley from his own ramparts with his limbs torn off. The situation requires a subtle approach. We find ourselves in the interesting position of needing a Fyren."

"What are you paying me?" asked Mordaunt.

"Pay?" repeated Saophal. She turned to Aurienne. "Aurienne, what's the rate of recurrence on emboli for a subject suffering from advanced seith deterioration?"

"Fifty percent chance within the first three months; ninety-five percent within the next six," said Aurienne.

"You're exaggerating," said Mordaunt.

"The data is in publicly available repositories," said Aurienne. "You can conduct your own review if you'd like. Let me know if your conclusion differs."

The axolotl puffed her gills in a satisfied way. "Your pay, therefore, is Aurienne's assistance for your next, inevitable, seith embolus."

"Since when do Haelan bargain with Fyren?" asked Mordaunt.

"You opened the door on that when you first slithered into Aurienne's office," said Saophal. "Don't play coy now. You gather intelligence on Wellesley; we save you from your body's treachery."

"And I'm disposable, should things go wrong," said Mordaunt.

Saophal burbled out a laugh. "Of course. Have a think about our offer. In the meantime, no favours, Aurienne. If he blocks, he blocks. He can go to a chirurgeon for a seith embolectomy if he likes. Those are *great* fun."

Aurienne bowed her head. "Understood."

Saophal spun in a slow circle and fizzled out of existence.

"I won't do it," said Mordaunt, staring at the place where Saophal had floated. "This is shameless coercion. So much for the goodness of the Haelan."

"Xanthe found a point of leverage and she's going to use it to protect her Order," said Aurienne. "Besides—you coerced me in the first place. You deserve nothing but a return in kind."

"I'm just a Point of Leverage, am I?"

"I'm just a Means to an End, aren't I?"

Mordaunt looked sullen in light of this response. But something shifted when his eyes caught Aurienne's—he looked more deeply; he searched her out; he questioned. She met him front on in this interrogation; that was what this was, wasn't it? A purely utilitarian exchange between a Haelan and a Fyren. Nothing lay beyond the transaction. Nothing lay beyond the dichotomy. Did it?

The questions hung unspoken in the indifferent air.

Mordaunt gave her a smile, forced, theatrical. "You're right, Haelan Fairhrim. And so we must remain to one another—Leverage and Means, on this side of eternity."

"We must only endure one another a little longer."

"The dose makes the poison."

"One day it'll be over and we can forget each other."

"You're going to forget me?" asked Mordaunt.

"I hope so," said Aurienne.

"I'm heartbroken."

"You haven't a heart," said Aurienne. "Besides, isn't forgetting you preferable to continuing to hate you?"

"I'd rather you hate me than not think of me at all."

No reply suggested itself in light of this confession, so Aurienne made none. She rearranged her skirts—it was unnecessary; they were irreproachable—and looked into the hearth.

Mordaunt took in a sharp breath, in the way one does when one wishes to make a sudden change in subject. "I suppose you wouldn't even run a diagnostic on me now, to see if an embolus looks to be building up."

"Certainly not," said Aurienne. "You've got to infiltrate Wellesley Keep. You heard Xanthe's deofol; I'm not to grant you favours."

"And you always do as you're told?"

"I'd need an excellent reason to contravene a direct order from Xanthe."

"Me asking nicely isn't an excellent reason?"

"You asking anything nicely is an excellent reason to not do a thing."

"I won't do Wellesley Keep. There's too little benefit to me."

"Too little benefit?" repeated Aurienne. "To have me on hand for your next blockage?"

Mordaunt, seeing from Aurienne's sudden straightening of the spine that he had insulted her, backpedalled: "Well—I mean to say—"

"*Little benefit?* Me? A Haelan who specialises in seith?"

"When you put it like that—obviously, yes, there is a benefit. I meant *monetary* benefits—I'm usually well compensated for assignments of this nature."

Aurienne rose amid the stuttering. With calmness born of searing irritation, she said, "Your compensation is access to me. If that's not good enough, it's not a problem. We'll stick to our original agreement. I'd put a chirurgeon on retainer if I were you. I can recommend a few who've conducted seith embolectomies with minimal butchery. They usually have trouble finding the clot, of course, so they have to make a few incisions and fish about. You're a big, tough Fyren, though—you'll be all right. Your torpraxia is so advanced, you'll hardly feel it. I just hope they don't accidentally sever your seith lines while they're in there. You've got so few left intact."

Mordaunt looked perturbed. "You needn't go. I spoke without thinking."

"You do that as a matter of course," said Aurienne. "I'm off. Thank Mrs. Parson for the tea."

Her satchel over one shoulder and Cerys' boots over the other, Aurienne strode out of the house. The critique cricket called her a gnu as she left.

Little benefit? Years of work, decades of education and practice, to be called *little benefit* by a feckless, blistering ulcer of a man? He could take his next embolus and choke on it.

Mordaunt's decaying house fell behind Aurienne. The night felt large, clear, and still. The air, laden with the smell of heather and clover, soothed her. She took deep, cleansing breaths of it; too much of the evening had been spent in a malodorous pub and, afterwards, in the foundering carcass of Rosefell Hall.

Collaboration with Mordaunt had seemed, briefly, possible. But perhaps it was better not to be entangled in another bargain with him. One ought to keep one's deals with devils to a minimum.

Stars sparkled their eternities above, shrouded by the dapple of a thin cloud. Mist rose from the hollows, redolent with the slow scent of bracken.

Under the curve of the waning moon, an owl drew out a helix.

Aurienne followed the gravel path that led to Rosefell's waystone. Her bare feet hardly made a sound upon the pebbles.

Someone else was even quieter.

"Fairhrim," came Mordaunt's voice.

Aurienne did not turn around. "We haven't anything left to discuss tonight."

"Fairhrim."

"My deofol will find you with instructions for the next full moon."

"Wait."

Fingers in a leather glove caught her hand.

Aurienne turned. The Fyren was behind her, still in his shirtsleeves, bare necked, grave.

He never looked grave.

Aurienne stopped, her hand in his, two steps away from him, as though they were beginning a dance. Even through the glove, his hand was warm.

She waited. A small hushed wind sifted back and forth between them. The moon's all-forgiving, all-encompassing light danced in a scat-

ter upon the mist, stole colours, erased details. The world turned bru-
mous; things grew softer, lost their outlines, became tender and faint.

Nightjars winged between moor and fairy moon. Their shadows
darted and coursed at Aurienne's feet in swift lines; meanings flickered
in and out of existence, visible only if she did not look too close.

Mordaunt stood tense shouldered, wretched, pressing his fingers to
hers. Aurienne felt his struggle with the same clarity as she perceived
the night.

He needed her, and he hated her for it.

"I'll do it," said Mordaunt.

Osric Gets on Fairhrim's Last Nerve

Osric

It had never been part of the plan, this negotiation business, this new round of bargaining, this bit of coercion on black moor turned silver sea. It hadn't been part of the plan to reach with haggard desperation for the only hands that could heal him, to be beholden to a too-bright Haelan, to stand bare souled before her in the shadow of a waystone and, there, bend to her will.

"I'll do it."

Where was his war now? He ought to be back in the skirmish, not in this suspension between war and peace.

It sickened him that he waited for her answer with bated breath, counted time by doomed heartbeats until she said, "All right." He hated the relief he felt, the gratitude, and hated most of all the swell of admiration for her bursting in his chest.

She was the only one who could save him from the chirurgeon's butchery. He had to admire her. She was the only one with the expertise, with the control. He had no choice but to admire her. She was the only one who could even make an attempt to cure his disease. How could he not admire her? He liked rare things. He cherished the exceptional.

Fairhrim softened when he breathed, "Thank you."

Osric stood too long in that silver sea, holding her hand up as though he were about to kiss it. It occurred to him, madly, that he could pull Fairhrim in and crush her to him. It would be so easy. To what end? To what gain? He did not know. The gap must remain. The threshold must not be crossed. That was what they were doomed to: standing upon a threshold. On the verge and only ever on the verge. An almost. He was what he was; she was what she was.

She would never cross over.

Fog-laden air dewed upon Fairhrim's throat, her forehead, her cheek, and netted her with a strange light. She stood between Osric and darkness immeasurable—not only the void of the night sky but the void of death.

Her eyes were wide and gentle. Osric fell into them as one falls into deep waters.

She said, "We can help each other."

He said, "I know."

They slipped a bit over the boundary between enmity and partnership then, into a new place of uncertainty.

She said, "We don't have to like it."

Osric made no answer. He already liked it. He hated that he liked it.

Her hand in his grew restive. He had held it too long. She pulled it from his grasp and was gone.

He hated that he had come to the waystone whole but left it having lost a piece of himself in two star-brilliant eyes.

NONE OF IT MATTERED. OSRIC CONVINCED HIMSELF OF THIS THE NEXT day, when things were less moon touched. It didn't matter that— what?—he had watched Fairhrim wander barefoot and seen a pretty ankle in the moonlight?

What cared he about pretty ankles?

Nothing had ever mattered less.

He must take care not to conflate her with what he needed from her. They were different things. He had a desperate need for her healing, not *her*.

What mattered, really, was that, with this embolus business, Fairhrim had him by the balls. (And why, pray, couldn't it have been someone gentle? Why couldn't it have been someone who'd fondle them while they were at it? Why did it have to be Fairhrim and her iron fist?)

As promised, Fairhrim sent her deofol a few days later, with instructions in preparation for the next full moon. After the usual friendly exchange—Osric threatened to turn the deofol into a toilet brush; the deofol advised him that his chin looked like a testicle—Osric received directions to a clinic in the village of Mortehoe, in Dumnonia.

The signs for the clinic informed him that he was suffering from torn nipples.

Fairhrim thought she was funny.

Osric knocked upon the clinic door, intent on advising Fairhrim that she would soon join the other morte hoes in Mortehoe if she wasn't careful.

He knew that something was wrong when Fairhrim opened the clinic door with a polite "Welcome—do come in" instead of an insult.

On her face was a fixed, triangular smile.

Osric was about to enquire about the mouth trigonometry, but

Fairhrim pointed at her breast. Osric stared at her breast. He saw no cause for concern. Indeed, he had seen it almost bare before and thought it lovely. Fairhrim pointed at her breast more vigorously, until Osric understood that she was indicating something behind her and trying to be discreet about it.

He looked behind her, where a curtain cut the room in half. Two hairy legs protruded from behind the curtain.

Osric raised an eyebrow at Fairhrim. The eyebrow enquired whether he should proceed to kill this person.

Fairhrim did not immediately shake her head no, which was something of a surprise.

Still in that polite voice, she bid Osric to have a seat in the waiting area. With an expression of professionalism frozen on her face, she disappeared behind the curtain to take care of her patient.

"What do you think of my man udders?" came the patient's voice.

Osric knew that voice. There was only one man in the world with that voice.

"Please stop flexing your pectorals" was Fairhrim's reply. "You'll make it worse."

Osric leapt to his feet and swept the curtain aside.

"What in Hel's name are you doing here?" he asked.

Leofric—because of course it was Leofric—looked up. "Osric? What are *you* doing here?"

Leofric was seated in a chair, partially draped in one of the puce gowns. He had a bloody nipple.

"Excuse me," said Fairhrim, snatching the curtain from Osric's hand. "This needs to remain closed."

Leofric was delighted. "It's all right. He's my best friend."

"We aren't friends," said Osric.

"What happened to your nips, Os?" asked Leofric. "Go on—show us. Don't be shy."

"I'll wait my turn," said Osric, and he returned stiffly to his seat, from whence he proceeded to stare down Leofric, and indulge in some fantasising about his death, funeral rites, obituary, etc.

"Right stroke of luck, finding this clinic," said Leofric to Osric over Fairhrim's shoulder. "I was just passing through when I saw the sign. I got too kinky last night."

Fairhrim, even more rigid about the spine than usual, said, "I've got to fetch a few supplies," and disappeared into a back room.

"Nice girl, this Haelan," said Leofric in a whisper. "Bit uptight, though. She could do a Kegel and snap your cock off. But she's warmed up to me. They all do, eventually. Charmed her with my wits and tits. She's a looker."

"Hadn't noticed," said Osric. He was distracted by an unasked for vision of Fairhrim on his cock, doing Kegels.

"D'you think I should ask her about my droopy ball?" asked Leofric.

"This is a clinic for torn nipples."

"How'd you tear yours?"

"Polo."

"Posh cunt," said Leofric. "I'll ask the Haelan if she's hosting a bollocks clinic. Hey—what do you think she'd do if she found out we're Fyren? Should we show her our tācn when we leave? That'd be a laugh, wouldn't it?"

Leofric held up his palm, across which he'd had the Leofricish foresight to place a bandage. As though any Haelan worth her seith wouldn't spot it and demand to see what was underneath.

Fortunately, this particular Haelan knew exactly what Leofric was, and had turned a blind eye to his cunning stratagem.

"Don't do it," said Osric. "She'd report it and cause trouble between our Orders."

"When did you become such a bore bag?" Leofric flopped back in his chair and looked despondent. After a bit of twitching, he rose and wandered towards the worktop, where he found a large test tube, which he held towards Osric. "Pop this in your bum."

Fairhrim returned to instil law and order. Leofric's suggestion did not please her.

"Put that down," said Fairhrim, in tones that would galvanise a mollusc into action.

Leofric jumped and did as he was bid.

"Sit," said Fairhrim.

The single, crisp syllable was delivered with such command that Leofric fell wordlessly back into the chair.

Fairhrim returned the test tube to its rack. Leofric beamed a tentative smile her way. It was not returned. Instead, Fairhrim made him hiss as, with a certain vindictiveness, she applied foam-soaked dressings to his nipple.

"What the fuck is that stuff?" asked Leofric.

"Hlutoform," said Fairhrim.

"It's used all over the Tīendoms," said Osric, knowledgeably.

"Your mum's used all over the Tīendoms," said Leofric.

Osric twirled a knife.

There was the flash of Fairhrim's tācn and a shiver in the air as she pushed her seith into the wounded nipple. Fairhrim's expression was impassive, but Osric knew her enough to read the pinch of her nostrils: how dare yet another idiot Fyren make her waste her seith?

"D'you have any plans to host a clinic on bollocks?" asked Leofric.

Fairhrim, bless her, was a champion of composure. "No. You should go to a physicker." She placed a bandage over Leofric's nipple. "Done. The skin is still new, so mind you don't mess about with clamps again for at least a week. And for Woden's sake, sterilise them before use. This bottle contains a course of antibiotics; take one a day until they've run out."

Leofric took the pills. "Will these give me an erection lasting longer than four hours?"

"No."

"Will you give my nip a little kissie to make sure it's all better?"

Fairhrim's tolerance for nonsense was never high to begin with, but it hit a new low. The ambient air temperature dropped as she stared at Leofric.

Leofric twitched his pec at her in a hopeful sort of way.

"Leave, or I'll undo it all, and remove your other nipple besides," said Fairhrim.

"Ouch," said Leofric.

Fairhrim, in a flurry of efficient gestures, gathered up Leofric's clothes and pushed them into his arms. "Be quick about dressing. I've got another patient to attend to. Goodbye."

Fairhrim strode into the back room again. Osric saw her summon her deofol, who materialised and listened attentively as she went through cabinets and made a list of supplies to replenish the clinic's inventory: "We're low on dextrose gel, indigestion tablets, suture packs, swab sticks . . ."

"That sphygmomanometer looks positively ancient," said the deofol. "Should we ask to have it replaced?"

"Add it to the list, though I doubt they'll approve," said Fairhrim. "And, while we're dreaming, a new trolley—this one's only got one functioning wheel."

The deofol's pointy head turned towards Osric and Leofric. "I see we've gathered all the contraception in one place."

Fairhrim turned her cold gaze towards them, too. "I do like to be organised."

Osric glowered. Leofric was too stupid to be offended. Fairhrim shut the door with a snap.

"I like her," said Leofric as he dressed.

"I don't think it's mutual," said Osric.

"No? I feel like we've got a connection," said Leofric. "Anyway, I don't care what you think—you know nothing about finer feelings."

"And I suppose you're an expert?"

"More than you," said Leofric. "I've never met a Haelan before. She wasn't that bad, honestly, was she? Bit prim, but that's to be expected; they've all got bargepoles up their arses. She didn't judge me in the slightest for the nipple clamps. Shall I wait for you? D'you want me to hold your hand while she diddles your nipple?"

"No."

"All right. I'm off, then. Got a barrister to murder." Leofric turned to the back-room door, cupped his hands around his mouth, and called, "Farewell, sweet Haelan; we could never be."

Fairhrim did not respond.

Leofric left.

Fairhrim emerged from the back room looking as aghast as her features permitted. "Well, that was traumatising."

"Obscene," said her deofol, before disappearing on his errand in a puff of white.

"Good of you not to judge him for the nipple clamps," said Osric.

"With an entire bargepole up my arse, I haven't any room left for judgement," said Fairhrim. "I nearly screamed when I saw him. All I could think about was sea urchins."

She led Osric to the worktop in the back room, upon which lay a messy heap of documents and a half-folded map, looking as though it had been hastily taken down.

"I didn't want Leofric to see," said Fairhrim. With precise, though irritated, gestures, she put her documents back into stacks. "Tore it all down while he was disrobing. Hold this up."

Osric pushed the corners of the map against the wall. Fairhrim ducked under his arms to pin it back up, along with her data tables, a drawing of the Monafyll Stone, and her notes from Widdershins.

As it had last time, her casual nearness surprised him. Those who approached a known Fyren without an iota of fear numbered zero.

Well—now they numbered one. What a pity it had to be Fairhrim.

These musings were interrupted by a sudden, "Ouch—ouch!"

Fairhrim had bumped her bun against him. The silver curette that held her hair in place caught the knife holster at his forearm. Osric attempted to disentangle the mess, but gloved fingers were not adequate for so delicate a task, and all he managed to do was hook more fine hairs around a buckle. Fairhrim gave him two seconds of fumbling before swatting his hand away and doing it herself.

By the time she had got untangled, three hairs had snapped, and fluttered thereafter from Osric's holster like cobwebs, or torn lace, or a secret favour from a Lady.

"Could you stop bobbing about and getting your hair caught everywhere?" asked Osric.

Fairhrim pinned her bun back into place. "Perhaps if you weren't armed to the teeth at all times one could pass you without getting scalped."

And her deofol had called Osric prone to exaggeration.

Fairhrim, her hair in order, turned her attention to the map. "Right. Where was I?"

"You've transposed the ley lines onto this," said Osric.

"Yes—far easier than faffing about with two maps. I've also replaced my pins."

Osric had indeed just noticed that the map was dotted with pink hearts. "Erm . . . are those . . . ?"

"Cerys' nipple pasties, yes," said Fairhrim, wiggling a sheet of nipple pasties. "I like the adhesive; it doesn't damage the map."

Fairhrim had placed the hearts upon areas that they had visited, but also new ones: a place in Somerset, a place in Dyfed, and the empty sea off the coast of the South Downs, where the Hedgewitches had been. ("Those five ley lines," tutted Fairhrim with respect to this last one. "I fancy going back and trying again. But only when we've exhausted our other options.")

"The June lunation takes place in three weeks." Fairhrim tapped at the heart in Somerset. "My proposal for our next attempt is here. I was able to conclusively locate a dozen stories in this specific area, all taking place during the Begbéam moon."

"That's at a crossing of three ley lines," said Osric. "Promising."

"Yes—and at the intersection of two watercourses, which matches your precious Widdershins' translation for June." Fairhrim pointed to her notes, which duly indicated *running waters cross*.

"But, most interesting of all, if we go precisely here"—the tip of Fairhrim's finger stopped at the heart—"we'll add a labyrinth to the mix."

"What's so good about a labyrinth?"

"They're another sort of in-between place. Sacred paths, pilgrim paths—ways to reach a new state of consciousness, ways to approach the Otherworld. Disorienting. Thin." An unimpressed grimace pulled at Fairhrim's lips. "A recurring theme is the importance of trusting the path, even though it seems to be meandering without purpose."

"A bit on the nose for what we're doing at the moment," said Osric.

"Isn't it? I hate it."

"So, we're going to Avalon?"

"Yes. The Færwundor at Glastonbury Tor, to be specific."

"Ah," said Osric, significantly.

"What's wrong?"

"That's a Druid stronghold."

"And?"

"Erm—I might have a history."

Fairhrim's look was full of suspicion. "A history?"

"Might've offed their chief Seer a while ago," said Osric, as innocently as one could when confessing to a murder.

"You *what*? Why?"

"Money," said Osric.

Fairhrim pressed fingers to her temples. "Mordaunt."

(She said his name like it was a swear word and he rather liked it.)

"Bit disappointed he didn't See me coming, to be honest," said Osric.

Fairhrim was as impervious to his wit as she was to his attractions, and remained flinty. "Why," she breathed, "must you complicate everything?"

"Let's try any of these other places," said Osric, gesturing at the hearts on the map. "A place where I won't be subject to the Threefold Death."

"The what?"

"The Druids' Threefold Death. Impalement, stoning, drowning. You haven't heard of it? You need to get out more. Here—what about this place—?" Osric, pointing at the map, noticed that he was talking to himself and turned around. "Where are you?"

"At my wits' end," came Fairhrim's response.

She returned with her satchel, from which she pulled out translations marked with her notes. "Look. Multiple, specific references to the Begbéam moon, all within a half-mile radius of this area."

Osric flipped through the documents. When the stories were good enough to provide them, Fairhrim had identified their time markers, which, indeed, mentioned the Begbéam moon in various forms—the moon at the greening of the dún-heather, the full moon at the month of the strawberry harvest, the sixth full moon, the dogwood bloom-time . . .

"You've bollocksed my idea in a spectacular fashion," said Fairhrim. She turned to the map. Though she stood as straight as ever, there was something disheartened in her stance—in the crossing of her arms, in the downward tilt of her chin.

"Let's do it," said Osric.

Fairhrim threw him a black look. "You're wanted under Druidic law. We can't go traipsing about the Færwundor. I had this all worked out, you know. I was going to ask Xanthe to request a visit of their enclave for a research project. You were to pose as my assistant. But now, the moment they see you—"

"I'm going to introduce you to the concept of being naughty," said Osric.

Fairhrim made a swift gesture of repudiation. "I'm not breaking into the Færwundor. The Druids are allies to the Haelan."

"You're not breaking in," said Osric.

"Good."

"*I* am."

"I'm not trespassing into Druid territory with the man who murdered their chief Seer," said Fairhrim. "We'll be caught."

"You know so very little of my capabilities," sniffed Osric. "If we're caught—which we won't be—they'll go after me. You flash your tācn and tell them I forced you to do my bidding. They won't hurt a Haelan."

She refused.

Osric said that she was Not Pliable.

She agreed.

Fairhrim turned away and began a sort of frustration-driven tidying of the worktop. "Why did you have to throw such a massive bloody wrench in the works? This should've been a simple moonlit stroll. The data on this particular location at this specific moon is the most compelling yet."

"*I'm* being solutions oriented," said Osric. "You should try it."

"Solutions oriented?" repeated Fairhrim. She turned to him, straight and tall. In her hand was a box of scalpel blades. Her gaze flicked from Osric to the blades and back again, and she looked very solutions oriented indeed, assuming that the solution was stuffing scalpel blades down Osric's throat.

He wondered if she mightn't have Valkyrie blood, somewhere up the lines.

She muttered, "Harm to none," through clenched teeth.

"There's another complication, while we're on the subject," said Osric. "Wellesley."

"What about him?"

"Fuckery is what," said Osric.

"Elaborate."

"Things are fraught between the queens of Kent and Wessex. Both sides have been shoring up their fortresses. Wellesley's got five hundred men assembled at Wellesley Keep—it's essentially a garrison."

"I thought you were very good at what you do," said Fairhrim. "Can't you shadow-walk past them?"

"Normally, yes. But I had a little recce and discovered that Wellesley has put up anti-Fyren measures."

"What on earth is an anti-Fyren measure?"

"He's flooded his entire Keep with light," said Osric. "Can't shadow-walk if there aren't any shadows."

"Why? What's he hiding?"

"Don't know. Could be information. Could be paranoia. Could be he's afraid that Kent will hire a Fyren to go after him. The cost of lighting up an entire Keep and its surrounds for weeks on end is exorbitant. He's an idiot for doing it; the message he's sending out is that there is something very worthwhile in there."

"Could it be on purpose?" asked Fairhrim. "Strategic? To draw attention away from something else?"

"If it's a ruse de guerre, it's risky, expensive, and stupid."

"Right. So what are you going to do?"

"Not infiltrate Wellesley Keep, given that I don't wish to be dry fucked in the arse by five hundred spears."

"Be solutions oriented," said Fairhrim.

That was the thing with Fairhrim: you had to choose your words wisely, because she would catch them and fling them back at you, sharper than before. (It occurred to him, by the by, that if a man liked things sharp and pretty, Fairhrim was the sort of woman the man might begin to fancy if he wasn't careful. However: the man mustn't be stupid. That way lay folly.)

"This is no longer a simple infiltration," said Osric. "I can't shadow-walk in."

Fairhrim studied him, then said, with immense significance: "Hmm."

"What?"

"Your hubris has given way to reason; it's refreshing."

"Delighted that my inadequacy pleases you."

"Knowing your limits isn't inadequacy," said Fairhrim. "Xanthe will forbid me from helping you with another embolus, though. Wellesley was your only bargaining chip."

"I've had nothing but the usual fluctuations since the last blockage," said Osric. "I'm convinced that your statistics were nothing but scare tactics—scare-tistics, if you will—"

"I won't."

"—but I am, nevertheless, choosing to put my trust in you."

"Don't. I don't know where it's been."

"Cruel. I was being vulnerable."

Fairhrim held up a warding hand. "You may keep that to yourself, too."

"How can you be so mean to your own patient?"

"You aren't a patient."

"You're caring for me."

"I'm caring for you, not about you."

"Ouch."

Fairhrim, pitiless, continued her interrogation. "How is your torpraxia?"

"Worse. Slammed a jug of lye on my foot and didn't even feel it."

"A jug of lye?"

"I was dissolving a body."

"Dissolving a body." Fairhrim made a tight, pained nod. "Of course." She produced no further comment on the matter, and said instead, "I'll speak to Xanthe."

"Are you Xanthe's pet? Must everything be run by her?"

"It was her call to wrap me up in this debacle, so she gets to share the burden of the decision-making, yes."

"And what are we doing about the full moon?" asked Osric.

"We've got weeks to work it out. I'll find an alternative location. I'm *not* breaking into the Færwundor with the man who murdered their Seer. Why would you do that? The Druids are harmless."

"It was an offer I couldn't refuse."

"Monster."

"The pay funded a large part of your Pox cure, by the by," said Osric.

"It's not a cure; it's an immunisation," said Fairhrim. "And that doesn't make it right. You could've earned the money through any number of pursuits. But I'm wasting my breath." With the air of one Moving On, she asked, "Shall we check on your progress while you're here?"

"Fine."

"You know the routine," said Fairhrim.

"Denude myself, et cetera."

"The things are in that cupboard," said Fairhrim, leaving the room.

This time, Osric made certain to note precisely which cupboard was indicated by Fairhrim. Within it he found not puce gowns but large flannel pantaloons of the same colour. He arranged a pair at a daring angle at his pelvis.

Then he noticed that the pantaloons had a gaping fly and were missing a button, thus leaving the nudest part of the denudation exposed.

He settled on using Fairhrim's ugly fuchsia notebook as a merkin.

Fairhrim, preceded by the rattle of the Franklin diffractor, re-entered the room. At first she noticed only the pantaloons, and asked, "Are you going scalloping?"

Then she saw her notebook and snatched it away.

"My merkin," gasped Osric.

"Close your fly."

"There's no button," said Osric. "Avert your eyes, lest your gaze grow lustful."

Fairhrim, superbly unbothered by the cock dangling before her— *offensively* unbothered, if Osric was honest—produced an overlarge safety pin. "Here. This is a clinic, not a pissoir."

Osric pinned himself shut with great *délicatesse*. "There aren't buttons on any of these pantaloons, so take a note of that in our merkin."

Fairhrim aimed the diffractor at Osric's chest and latched its tentacles upon his person with, it seemed to him, unnecessary force.

Her disinterest in any of the goings-on in his fly crushed Osric to a spiritual pulp. Not that he wanted Fairhrim to look at his cock, necessarily; it was just the principle of the thing. She wasn't charmed by him; she wasn't frightened by him; she wasn't seduced or intrigued by or remotely curious about anything to do with him. Who did she think she was? Her utter lack of interest killed him.

He hated her.

Fairhrim snapped at him to sit up, which Osric did, insofar as pulp can sit up. She faffed about with various silver instruments against the projected figure on the wall, measuring seith channels, intact and rotted, against her bright markers. Once again, she pulled out an irascible, twitching chart (*Pt: U. Ganglion*), which calmed down as she recorded her measurements. And once again, she ran a finger down Osric's appendages (barring the most interesting one) and noted where his numbness began and ceased.

Her brows drawn into a frown, Fairhrim studied the documents before her. She turned off the diffractor, wiped the tentacles with a fresh dose of hlutoform, reattached them, and turned the machine back on. Her silver instruments came in for an encore of their clicking, snapping dance across the projected figure. Fairhrim passed her finger down Osric again, asking if he was quite certain that the numbness stopped just there, and not farther.

"Yes," said Osric. "Why?"

"Mind you," said Fairhrim to herself, "it's hardly been a fortnight since our last measurements."

"What's the matter?"

"And we're still well within normal parameters—though not within *your* normal parameters."

"What parameters? What is it?"

Fairhrim, absorbed in the numbers before her, said nothing. She flew back to the diffractor, tapped at gauges, muttered that it was all in order, *and yet* . . . She returned to her notes, disarrayed, unquiet; her calmness was fragile. She pressed fingertips to her lips. Her eyes ran over and over the columns again and again.

Hope, unchecked, swelled in Osric's breast. "Fairhrim, what is it?"

Once again, Osric measured time by doomed heartbeats until Fairhrim parted her lips. Her gaze, vivid with curiosity, met his. She took a breath. A hundred years passed. He waited, utterly at her mercy. He wished to kneel. He wished to gather her skirts into his fists and prostrate himself at her feet. Please, please, please.

"Your degeneration has, however briefly, slowed," said Fairhrim. "At least, as measured with these instruments. I hesitate to say *stopped*, of course—though, technically, that would be correct. Come here—let me show you."

She divested Osric of the diffractor's sticky tentacles and waved him towards the worktop; he leaned over her shoulder; she ran through the numbers and gave explanations; she smelled of hlutoform and soap; the hope beat wild and thunderous in his chest; she told him to withhold celebrating, as there were many other factors to be accounted for; the numbers and columns swam into one another; she made intelligent observations; he listened and took in strictly none of it, because he was back on the silver sea, enraptured by the woman with the star-bright eyes, the only one who could heal him, the one who was saving his life.

"You and your brains," he breathed. "You and all your pretty edges. You're doing it."

"I've just told you, there could be any number of explanations—"

"But this is good?"

"Yes. It's also medically impossible. But it's good."

Again Osric was breathless and full hearted and swelling with admiration. Fairhrim's bare hand, chapped and dry, lay on the table next to his gloved one.

He brought it to his lips.

Fairhrim was startled, for once, into a gasp.

Osric pressed a gallant kiss into the back of her hand. He should have stopped there, but, like a besotted fool, he kissed smaller, revering ones across her knuckles.

He might have carried on kissing her to her wrist, upon her forearm, past her shoulder, up her neck. He very well could have. He, feeling her cool skin under his warm mouth, quite wanted to. In moments like this, one wished to worship a little.

Her wide, shocked eyes reminded him that her hand wasn't, and would never be, his to kiss.

"Sorry." Osric dropped her hand. "I mustn't sully you with my kisses."

Fairhrim brought her hand up and curled it gently against her collarbone. "A crime of passion. You're forgiven."

"You're doing it. I'm telling you, you're doing it."

On her face, a smile dawned, but did not break.

16

MURDER AT WELLESLEY KEEP

Aurienne

What did having one's hand kissed by a Fyren feel like? Reckless. Heady. Like life being lived. Like an impending disaster.

The moment was a convergence of several strange miracles—the numbers (a thrill), Mordaunt's sudden and wild expression of devotion, and, the greatest miracle of all, sharing in his joy.

Blushes plagued Aurienne whenever she thought of the moment. The way he had swept towards her and seized her hand. The press of his signet ring. The kisses too passionate to be platonic. She told herself it was the excitement of the results. The alternative was appalling.

Aurienne compartmentalised the blushes away (neatly labelled *Inappropriate*) and focused on her morning, which began with a shift in the Pox ward. The little girl from last time was far better—able to see and able to speak; indeed, she was feeling so much better that she had asked Aurienne for an ice lolly. Aurienne, delighted, was quick to dispatch an apprentice to fulfil this important request.

Then it was time for rounds. Aurienne's patients in the Centre for

Seith Research were competing hard for her attention. A fellow Haelan was suffering from a triggered Cost without even using her seith. A kindly old lady from Cardiff was suddenly summoning other people's deofols. The Ingenaut with the seith haemorrhages who had been discharged a few weeks ago was back. She had responded beautifully to Aurienne's micro-occlusion treatment, but had got overexcited about, if Aurienne understood correctly, magnets, and her seith had surged out of control and set a leycraft on fire.

After lunch, Aurienne attended a Haelan robing ceremony. Four new Haelan were earning their wings, including Corinne and Nym. A crowd gathered in Swanstone's largest courtyard, at the foot of a statue of Frīa flanked by two of the Aer in flight. Prendergast, one of the Haelan Order's Heads, was presiding over the ceremony. The new graduates stood with their hands folded before them, listening to his address.

"I feel old," whispered Cath to Aurienne and Élodie. "Look at their baby faces."

"They're no younger than we were when we received our tācn," said Élodie.

"Please," said Cath. "They're legally infants."

"The one on the left is one of yours, Cath, isn't she?" asked Aurienne.

Cath nodded. "She's good. Learned quickly that emergency medicine is the science of making it internal medicine's problem. And the two on the far right are yours?"

"Corinne and Nym. They'll outshine me in a few years."

"Good," said Cath. "You'll need backup; you'll be leading this place by then."

"Never," said Aurienne.

"I can see it," said Cath.

"I can't."

"I know. You've got the imagination of an aubergine."

After Prendergast's address, there were the usual speeches about living the values of *Harm to none*, and always putting the interests of patients before one's own, and professionalism, and compassion—each of which Aurienne received as a lecture addressed specifically to her. When research ethics were discussed, she began to look for exits.

Élodie nudged Aurienne. "Are you all right?"

"You've a hangdog look about you," said Cath.

Aurienne wished very much to burst into an explanation of her flagrant disregard for everything her Order stood for, that she had done the opposite of everything these fine speakers advised, that it was almost worth it because she might have been nearing an incredible breakthrough, but it wasn't worth it because she was working with a Fyren—and, worst of all, the Fyren had kissed her hand, and it gave her blushes instead of shudders of morbid disgust to think about it, and everything was Wrong.

Obviously, she said, "Indigestion."

She was grateful for the ending of the speeches and the concurrent ending of the censure.

Next came the Marking: the Haelan-apparent knelt before the statue of Frīa and her benevolent open arms. They held out their right hands. Prendergast pressed a brand, sizzling with seith, in the shape of the Haelan tācn, to their open palms.

Aurienne, watching the anxious faces of the silver-robed figures, remembered her own time in that position. In spite of Xanthe's assurances to the contrary, she had feared what every apprentice fears—that her years of apprenticeship wouldn't have sufficiently developed her seith system and that the tācn wouldn't take. But it had taken, of course—she had worked too hard, and practised too much, for it not to—and so, too, did the tācn of the four young Haelan kneeling in the courtyard today.

The assembled crowd applauded. The new Haelan held their raw tācn to their hearts, and were robed, for the first time, in the Order's whites. Now their seith would be open to the world, far beyond the small, quotidian uses of civilians. Now they were members of an Order.

They took their oaths for *Harm to none* and swore to be worthy of the privilege of bearing the title of Haelan. Shining silver epaulettes were placed upon their shoulders.

Someone tugged at Aurienne's skirts.

"Beg your pardon," said the apprentice who had done the tugging, bowing low. "You're wanted urgently in Ward Fourteen. Seith transfer. It's Haelan Xanthe."

"Not again," said Aurienne. She waved a rueful goodbye to Cath and Élodie, and followed the apprentice into the fortress.

Haelan sometimes drained their seith empty in succour of particularly challenging patients. Xanthe was notorious for it. Aurienne found her collapsed upon a bed among the sick children in Ward 14, surrounded by a handful of concerned Haelan from Paeds. She lay unconscious and drenched in sweat. She had triggered her Cost—gastroparesis—before fainting; there was a kidney dish on her lap containing the sloshy remains of her lunch.

Lorelei looked up as Aurienne approached. "One of the new arrivals took a turn for the worse this afternoon. He was hanging on by a thread. Xanthe refused to lose him. He's all right. She isn't."

Aurienne was one of the few in her Order who had mastered seith transfers; the procedure required unusual control of seith even among the Haelan. She pressed her tācn to Xanthe's clammy chest and, with great gentleness, infused her own seith into Xanthe's reserves—enough to bring her back to consciousness and bypass another round of her Cost.

Xanthe came to with a muttered "'M fine."

"You mustn't take your system to the brink like this," said Aurienne. "It's hard on you."

"Yes, well, a child will see another day, so it was worth the push." Xanthe sat up with Aurienne's help. She looked sadly at the remains of her lunch in the kidney dish. "Pity about the cheesecake. It was excellent."

"We'll get you another piece," said Lorelei. She called to an apprentice. "You—off to the kitchens. Get her the whole bloody cake."

"More of us need to add seith transfers to our competencies," said one of the other Haelan from Paeds.

"Corinne and Nym have been making progress," said Aurienne. "I think Corinne's got it. Nym's technical competence is excellent; it's her confidence that's low. They both earned their tācn today."

"Oh, bravo," said Lorelei.

"Yes—improvements will follow thick and fast now."

"Have they moved on to cadavers?" asked Xanthe.

"No. Still in the lab. But they will soon."

Colour returned to Xanthe's lips as Aurienne's seith replenished her reserves. Aurienne pulled her tācn away. "Feeling better?"

"Much. Back to your duties, all of you," said Xanthe to the Haelan assembled around her bed. "Those children need you more than I do."

Lorelei and the Haelan from Paeds dispersed. Aurienne took advantage of her tête-à-tête with Xanthe to discuss the Fyren's investigation of Wellesley. She explained Mordaunt's current, unpromising position.

"Let me make sure I've got this straight," said Xanthe, in an exhausted whisper. "The break-in we want the Fyren to do, he can't do, and the break-in we don't want him to do, he can do."

"Correct," said Aurienne. "He can't sneak into Wellesley Keep because of these anti-Fyren measures. But he *is* happy to break into the Færwundor for his next healing, which I strenuously object to."

"Fantastic," croaked Xanthe.

"But please, Haelan Xanthe, let's talk later. You've got to rest."

"*Pish tosh*—let's talk now. I'm not actively vomiting."

"I do hope that next time you'll—"

"Spare me the lecture," cut in Xanthe. "I know the risks. Go fish about in that heap over there; there's something I want to show you."

Aurienne swallowed her gentle, respectful nonlecture, and proceeded towards the indicated heap: Xanthe's satchel and cloak, dropped beside the bed.

"The yellow file," said Xanthe.

Aurienne recognised the loose-leaf file as the register of requests received for Haelan services. She occasionally assisted Xanthe in prioritising the asks, which ranged from requests for Haelan aid in dysentery-infested villages to overwhelmed hospitals. A single Haelan and her seith could change the tide in any of these circumstances—though, given the Pox, all recent requests had been rejected.

Among the letters in the file were the usual suspects; Aurienne recognised the scrawl of the Northumbrian king, the angular script of the king of the Danelaw, the elegant hand of the Kentish queen (always envied by Aurienne, whose writing looked like the abstract blobs of stool culture in a petri dish).

Xanthe extracted a letter from the file. She studied it with her sparse brows knotted into a frown. "Throwing you to the dogs, possibly," she muttered. "But you'd have a wolf with you, so perhaps . . . ?"

Aurienne cast her a look of polite enquiry, but Xanthe didn't see fit to explain herself to anyone at the best of times, and she was particularly deep in thought now.

"I think you've got the coconuts to do it," said Xanthe. "The real question is whether I want to risk you."

"The—the coconuts?"

"The cobblers. The bollocks."

"Ah."

Xanthe carried on an inarticulate dissertation on the relative size of Aurienne's bollocks, their propensity to drag on the pavement, their potential to serve as blimps in times of need.

Snapping out of her reverie, she tapped an age-bent finger upon the file. "We may have the bugger."

"Which bugger?" asked Aurienne, given that there were so many.

"Wellesley," said Xanthe.

"How have we got him?"

"Wellesley requested Haelan assistance for a sick child a few months ago," said Xanthe, passing Aurienne the letter. "Paeds was drowning in Pox cases, obviously, so we declined. I know your source on Wellesley's involvement was questionable, but it's an interesting coincidence."

"Do you think the incursion on Swanstone might've been linked to his child?" asked Aurienne.

"A desperate father, wishing to find a healer for his ailing daughter?"

"Why do you sound cynical?" asked Aurienne, skimming through the letter. "Doesn't he seem sincere?"

"He seems a touch melodramatic. And there were about a hundred courses of action he could've taken before leaping to ingress of Swanstone—if it was him—with incendiary devices, at that. But if we wanted a door into Wellesley Keep, and a neat way to bypass his anti-Fyren measures, that letter is it. I could make the arrangements."

"Right," said Aurienne. "But if Wellesley wants a Haelan for as-yet-unknown nefarious purposes, we'd be handing her over on a silver platter."

"Right," said Xanthe. "But the Haelan could explode his heart with the touch of her tācn, should the situation call for it. And if she was accompanied by a Swanstone guard, as is the usual protocol, who was actually a Fyren assassin, then the two of them could discover something of use, and keep her shielded in the meantime."

"Right," said Aurienne. "And Wellesley wouldn't be stupid enough to harm a Haelan. He'd be incurring the wrath of almost every Order."

"Right," said Xanthe. "And the Wardens would only be a deofol away, should Wellesley be stupid enough."

"Right."

"Right."

Aurienne eyed Xanthe. Xanthe eyed Aurienne.

"Good thing about my blimp-sized bollocks," said Aurienne.

"May they carry you swiftly, and may the winds be fair," said Xanthe.

THUS IT WAS THAT AURIENNE PRESENTED HERSELF AT THE GATEHOUSE of Wellesley Keep with, clanging along behind her, Osric Mordaunt in a full suit of Swanstone armour.

He had reacted to the plan with the expected level of aplomb; that is, immediate hysteria.

His hysteria abated into fuming as they approached the Keep in pouring rain. It was night, but one wouldn't know it looking at Wellesley Keep, which was illuminated by hundreds of humming floodlights.

"Absolute, unmitigated horseshit," muttered Mordaunt between clangs.

"Oh, don't have kittens," said Aurienne.

"I'll have as many kittens as I like. Have you seen all of these lights? Not a shadow to be found. If anything happens, I'm hamstrung."

"It'll be fine once we get inside," said Aurienne.

"Fine? *Fine?* We're putting you in danger—we're walking you right into the Keep of the man we think attacked your Order. If anyone raises a hand against you, they're dead, I want you to know. What arsehole designed this wanky armour? Why am I announcing my movements to every knob end within a mile? My tācn is itchy."

"Stop twitching. Straighten up. You've got to be convincing."

Aurienne and Mordaunt approached the gatehouse in a disgusting rain that came from seventeen directions.

Mordaunt, still seething, did not knock at the door; he smote it with his fist.

With much metallic creaking, he glanced about, squinting through his visor at the bright lights. The Keep glowed as though under the noontime sun.

A peephole slid open from the other side of the door. A suspicious eye protruded in Aurienne's direction. "Who is it?" enquired the eye.

"Haelan Fairhrim and escort," said Aurienne. "Lord Wellesley is expecting me."

The eye grew respectful. "Give us a moment."

The door was drawn open. Aurienne and her soi-disant guard advanced into a sort of vestibule, also bright with lights. Besides the doorman to whom the eye belonged, there was a small complement of guards, as well as an officious-looking round man who introduced himself as Pipplewaithe.

"I'm Lord Wellesley's chamberlain," said Pipplewaithe, doffing his feathered hat and sweeping the ground with it. "At your service, Haelan Fairhrim. And may I say what an honour it is to have one of your Order here."

"Thank you for the kind welcome," said Aurienne.

Pipplewaithe replaced his hat; the ostrich feather sprang to attention. "Before we proceed into the Keep—please forgive me for asking; added security measures out of my control, unfortunately—might I see your tācn?"

Aurienne removed her glove and duly flashed the Haelan tācn at the chamberlain. There was a chorus of *oob*s from the assembled men, to whom the Haelan were, apparently, numinous creatures of legend.

Mordaunt creaked meaningfully beside Aurienne.

"That looks to be in order," said Pipplewaithe. "Or should I say, in Order? Ha! So sorry for the procedural annoyance. One can never be too careful in these unsettled days."

"Are things so unsettled?" asked Aurienne.

"I won't trouble you with the details, but tensions are running high with a neighbour I shan't name." Pipplewaithe's feather turned enquiringly to Mordaunt. "May I ask about your companion?"

Mordaunt clattered into a semblance of a guardish position beside Aurienne, who said, "This is my protector, Phlegmley. He's one of our sergeants at Swanstone. I believe my Order has advised Lord Wellesley of our protocols; I must be accompanied at all times. I'm afraid that he'll have to remain armed and at my side. But you understand—just another procedural annoyance."

"Of course," said Pipplewaithe with another bow. "Welcome, Sergeant."

There was a metallic *chink* as Mordaunt made a nod in his direction.

"Carry out whatever inspections you feel are necessary," said Aurienne with a wave in Mordaunt's direction. "He hasn't a tācn, but I suppose you'd like to check his hands and see for yourself."

Mordaunt removed his right gauntlet.

"Oh, really, it hardly seems necessary," said Pipplewaithe, nevertheless observing Mordaunt's activity closely. "He's here with a proven Haelan. But—procedurally speaking—it would indeed be better."

Mordaunt showed the man his right palm, devoid, of course, of any tācn.

"Excellent," said Pipplewaithe. Then, with rather more trepidation, because Bright Path walkers had their tācn on the right side but Dusken ones had theirs on the left, he waited for Mordaunt to show his left hand.

Mordaunt removed his left gauntlet and presented the man his hand. Pipplewaithe waved for a light, inspected Mordaunt's palm from several angles, and rubbed his fingers across it.

"All clear," said Pipplewaithe. "Thank you, sir. Let us proceed within."

Mordaunt pulled his gauntlet back on. It glided over an immaculate hydgraft, courtesy of Xanthe.

They proceeded through two floodlit courtyards, populated with, it seemed, most of Wellesley Keep's five hundred men.

Pipplewaithe quivered in restrained excitement in Aurienne's direction. Aurienne gave him a smile. He bowed at her again—the feather swept towards her in adoration—and said, "It's a privilege to be able to serve one of the Haelan, however briefly. I've only the highest respect for your Order. Indeed, I am beholden to it, heart and soul."

A snort escaped Mordaunt. Pipplewaithe's feather rose in febrile offence. Mordaunt turned the snort into a faux sneeze.

"Sorry. Allergies," sniffed Mordaunt.

The feather calmed itself. "Ah, indeed? As I was saying, Haelan—beholden. My husband was selected for one of your trials many years ago. Liposarcoma. Extremely poor prognosis. Well, I say *poor*—I mean we were expecting death. But your Order saved him."

"Oh, I am so pleased to hear that," said Aurienne. "Was it under Haelan Linden?"

"The very same. Brilliant healer. Is she still around?"

"Retired a few years ago."

"Well deserved. Right—follow me just through here and we'll have you settling in nicely."

"Settling in?" repeated Aurienne. "Aren't we going to see the patient?"

The feather faltered. "Ah yes, young Gwendolen. Erm—given the lateness of the hour, Lord Wellesley proposed that I show you to your rooms. You can take refreshment, rest, and meet him tomorrow morning so he can discuss his daughter's case with you."

"Shouldn't I see her right away?" asked Aurienne. "Is she so much better?"

"Oh yes, she's much better," said Pipplewaithe. The feather grew evasive. "In no immediate danger whatsoever, to my inexpert eye. One might almost ask why we have disturbed your Order for such a—but, of course, parental worry—nothing like it. Still, to have brought in a Haelan—rather extraordinary—but he does dote on her so."

With these conclusive remarks, Pipplewaithe led Aurienne and Mordaunt into the Keep. The enormity of the task before them began to dawn on Aurienne: what exactly were they looking for, and how were they going to look?

Mordaunt seemed unfazed. In the shadow of his helmet, his eyes jumped from door to door, remembering or counting or doing infiltratey things, while Aurienne kept up the chitchat. The interior of the Keep was, at least, not floodlit.

They went up another flight of stairs. The furnishings grew more luxurious.

"Here we are," said Pipplewaithe, ushering them towards silver-studded double doors. "I hope you'll find everything to your satisfaction. The chambermaids are at your command"—two chambermaids flanking the door curtseyed—"and I'll fetch you tomorrow morning, when Lord Wellesley is ready. He's in the midst of some rather difficult discussions with his commanders. You know how it is."

Aurienne did not know how it was. Pipplewaithe bowed; the feather made its obeisance; both left.

The chambermaids set upon Aurienne in a cloying flurry—could they assist with her hair? With her dress? With unpacking her things?—until she shooed them away, claiming fatigue. They brought in a tray laden with food and stoked the fire high, lest she catch a chill from the damp.

Mordaunt was of much less interest to them. On their way out, they pointed out a bed for him, which consisted of a straw mattress in the antechamber.

"That thing's meant to be a bed?" asked Mordaunt, in the accents of someone with too much privilege and a corresponding absence of grey matter.

The chambermaids were shocked that a guard would query their hospitality. Aurienne elbowed Mordaunt, but hurt herself more than him, due to the armour.

"Er—thank you," grunted Mordaunt. "This will do nicely."

The chambermaids were appeased. They shut the door behind them.

Aurienne stepped into the bedchamber. Mordaunt clanged in too, tearing off his helmet.

As he strode behind her, his helmet under his arm, his breastplate gleaming with the platinum-white wings of a swan, his hair swept messily to one side, he looked, for a moment, noble. Knightly. Valorous. His scars might've been gained in deeds heroic rather than craven.

Then he opened his mouth—"Did you *see* that bed? I thought it was for the dog"—and the mirage faded, and he was the Fyren again.

"What are you looking at?" asked Mordaunt.

"A could-have-been," said Aurienne.

Her gnomic response was of less interest to Mordaunt than the looking glass above the mantel, into which he peered while asking, "Why didn't you let them fuss about your hair?" accusatorially, as though Aurienne had let an occasion slip.

"I'm not here to have my hair fussed over," said Aurienne.

"*I* would've let them, though you're the one in more immediate need."

(A knight in shining armour he wasn't, but a knight in shining passive aggression—yes.)

Mordaunt took a moment to regain that artfully wind-tousled sweep he usually had going.

"And this," he said, pulling the standard-issue Swanstone sword from its sheath. "Rubbish. Horrid balance. No edge to speak of."

"Can you stab someone with it?" asked Aurienne.

"Yes."

"Then it'll do."

Mordaunt, who had been inspecting the length of the blade with one eye closed, cast an intrigued look in her direction. "I thought we were going for fewer cadavers."

"We are," said Aurienne. "However, I would like to not become one myself. Our welcome was odd."

"This entire situation is odd."

"What's your read on it?"

Mordaunt produced a whetstone and sat, with much rattling, upon an ottoman. He began to work on the sword. "Don't think the kid is sick. Don't think the good Lord Wellesley brought in a Haelan for her skills, either—at least, not for the kid."

"Maybe he's got someone else to heal? Himself?"

"Possible. Also, those men out there are ready to march. Don't know if that coincides with your arrival."

"If he thinks he's going to hold me for use as a private field medic, he's in for a nasty shock."

Mordaunt ran the whetstone down the blade in thoughtful strokes. "You'd also be useful if he's got a stubborn captive with some critical intel. Torture, heal; torture, heal."

"That's dark," said Aurienne.

"I'd do it," said Mordaunt. "Doubt he has the brains. Is there a Lady Wellesley? The chamberlain didn't say, did he? What's-his-name—Pumpypipple, or whatever it was; couldn't hear a thing through the helmet—sounded like an angry fart."

"Pipplewaithe."

"Right."

"Lord Wellesley's wife died in childbirth," said Aurienne. "Wellesley mentioned it in his letter to my Order, among other tearjerkers."

"Perhaps his goal is to find a new wife with a useful skill set during a war. Perhaps he's going to seduce you."

"Good luck," said Aurienne.

"I know. Lost cause."

"You're speaking as though from experience."

"I am," said Mordaunt. "I made overtures to you during our first meeting and you were inexorable. Adamantine."

"You? Tried to seduce me? During our first meeting?"

"Well, now you're just offending me," said Mordaunt.

He looked so put out that Aurienne felt the welling of laughter. She tamped it down. "Sorry—which part was meant to be seductive: the part where you broke in, or the part where you wanted to kidnap me, or the part where you bribed my Order to heal you against my will?"

"As I said—lost cause," said Mordaunt, decidedly piqued.

"I've vexed you," said Aurienne.

"Don't hurt yourself rushing to apologise."

"If we haven't aggravated each other to the verge of flying at one another's throats, the day is wasted."

Mordaunt contemplated his sword as well as her words and, at length, conceded: "True."

"How are we going to search the Keep?" asked Aurienne. "The place is enormous."

"That's what you leave up to me," said Mordaunt. "Looking forward to having a look tonight."

"But—how do you know where to begin? We don't even know what we're looking for."

"Human beings are gloriously predictable. Precious lordlings even more so. If there's anything interesting hidden in this Keep, I'll find it."

"What if he's so paranoid that he keeps it on him—whatever *it* is?"

"I'll find it no matter what crevice he's hiding *it* in. I've plunged deep into better men for lesser prizes. And I don't mean that in a sexy way. Although I've also done it in a sexy way. Did your deofol ever deliver my observation about anals?"

"Yes. Pleased you find yourself so amusing. Don't plunge too deeply into Wellesley. If he dies, the repercussions could be outright war."

"And?" asked Mordaunt.

"I'm not here to trigger a war."

"They'll blame Kent."

"But I'll blame me, for whatever hundreds or thousands die," said Aurienne.

Mordaunt looked at her as though she were mildly alien.

"What?" asked Aurienne.

"A conscience must be such a burden," said Mordaunt.

"Managing your lack thereof is the greater strain."

"Might you strain yourself a little further, and pass me that tray?"

Aurienne turned to the elaborate sideboard to her left, upon which rested an equally elaborate tray. "You're going to eat? You trust their food?"

"Absolutely not," said Mordaunt. He picked his way through the tray and began to throw things, with annoying accuracy, into the fireplace. "Let's make it look like you partook."

The bedchamber grew smoky with burnt goose leg, charred leek and cheese pie, and marzipan cakes reduced to ash. The wine they poured into a potted plant.

Mordaunt examined the bottle's label afterwards. "If this was untampered with, what we've just done is criminal."

"Really?" said Aurienne. "That's the criminal part of this endeavour?"

"I'll have to have a look through the man's cellar," said Mordaunt, sniffing the bottle. "Mm—that's champion. Have a nose."

Aurienne had just ascertained that the Bordeaux did indeed smell gorgeous—plush, round, pleasantly spiced—when a shriek echoed through the Keep.

The shriek turned into a high-pitched giggle. There was the sound of footsteps scurrying through the corridor. Mordaunt put his helmet back on and opened the door.

A child streaked past, followed by two huffing nursemaids calling for her to behave herself and get back into bed. From their admonitions, Aurienne gathered that the child—rosy cheeked, bright eyed, glossy curled—was Gwendolen, Lord Wellesley's daughter.

The girl paused long enough to blow a raspberry at Mordaunt, then dashed away again, still giggling. The nursemaids disappeared after her.

Aurienne and Mordaunt regarded each other in silence. He closed the door.

"I've never seen a more vivacious child in my life," said Mordaunt.

"Normally I'd remind you that not all conditions are visible," said Aurienne, "only her father described a litany of symptoms, each more worrisome than the next, and that child didn't look to be bedridden, coughing blood, or continually vomiting."

"There's fuckery underway," said Mordaunt. "Have you got the time? I hadn't the room for a watch in this stupid armour; it hasn't any pockets."

"Should've put it in your codpiece," said Aurienne, consulting her pocket watch.

"My codpiece is already full."

"Of what?"

"My cod."

Aurienne cast a cynical eye towards the codpiece.

"Had to coil it up," said Mordaunt.

"It's half eleven," said Aurienne, among the sound of knocking, as Mordaunt was presently testing the impact resistance of the codpiece.

"Right," said Mordaunt. "Help me out of this armour."

Neither Aurienne nor Mordaunt was versed in plate armour and its foibles; there was much pinching of fingers and muttered swearing as they worked out how to remove it.

The Fyren cloak lay at the bottom of Aurienne's satchel like the unhallowed thing it was. She wished for a pair of tongs with which to extract it, but settled upon forefinger and thumb.

"That's the finest Genoan velvet," said Mordaunt. "You needn't handle it like it's a wet fucking nappy."

Aurienne removed his leather gloves from her satchel in the same manner. Mordaunt snatched them from her. He shook his cloak out and swept it over his shoulders. In a rare flash of brilliance, he hid the Swanstone armour in the dog bed, with a blanket thrown over top, which made it vaguely look as though a man might be sleeping in it.

There was only one thing left to complete Mordaunt's transformation from gallant knight to murderer: the removal of the hydgraft that camouflaged his tācn. He wedged a poker between the room's doors to ensure that they wouldn't be disturbed.

"Excellent," he said as Aurienne took out her instruments. "The itching is unbearable."

"Pruritus. It's normal."

"This entire procedure was unexpectedly disturbing," said Mordaunt.

"I think the Haelan are closer to walking the Dusken Paths than they let on."

Aurienne soaked her hands and his in hlutoform. "Xanthe specialises in regeneration. Don't let it bother you."

"She cut off her own palm," said Mordaunt.

"And healed it back in a minute."

"Why can't she regenerate my seith channels, then?"

"I've already told you—the mechanisms involved in seith-fibre genesis are still under study. In mammals they occur during embryonic development; no one has found a way to replicate it in adults."

"Ow."

"Indeed," said Aurienne, who had pushed experimentally at the edge of the hydgraft. "It seems a shame to remove it; the graft took beautifully."

"Get it off me. It stifles my seith."

"Lovely capillary ingrowth," said Aurienne, tilting Mordaunt's palm into the light. "It's fully vascularised. You're certain you want to remove it? Professionally, it hurts me to undo it—but beyond that, you've a rare chance to start a new life as a man without the brand of a monster."

"I *like* my brand. I *like* being a monster."

"Pity. Sit, then. This won't take a moment."

Mordaunt joined Aurienne on the bed. Aurienne positioned his hand on a pillow. It was altogether less than ideal; she would have had serious words with any apprentice of hers operating in such conditions.

Bit by bit, with a silver curette she removed the graft, as though she were debriding a failed one and removing a flap of necrotic tissue. And bit by bit, the hellhound tācn came into view—the curling horns, the empty eye sockets, the grinning teeth.

She pressed her tācn to the edge of Mordaunt's hand and healed him where the graft had adhered to his palm and the flesh was raw.

Now he was well and truly the Fyren again. Lingering on the inside of Aurienne's eyes, like a sunspot, was that vision of what could have been—of this man in bright armour, proud featured and noble.

But it was a phantasm. She blinked it away.

Mordaunt pushed an experimental flare of seith to his tācn. The hellhound's eyes and mouth glowed their unholy red. "That's better."

Aurienne disagreed, which she expressed by tidying with unnecessary briskness.

Mordaunt pulled his hood over his head and placed his cowl over his face. "I'll be back in a few hours. I'm leaving her with you."

"Her?" asked Aurienne, but Mordaunt answered her question by summoning his deofol.

The smoky form of the great wolf materialised. Normally she had an unsettling tendency of floating her teeth at Aurienne's eye level, but today she hung low. Her golden eyes glowed insolently at Aurienne, then fixed themselves upon the door.

"She'll find me if you need me," said Mordaunt.

"All right."

Now he was a shadow in the darkness of the antechamber. "And Fairhrim—"

"What?"

"Don't look so grim. It's the monster you need tonight, not the man."

Aurienne rolled her eyes so hard, she saw her frontal cortex.

The monster, stiff with vexation, left.

AURIENNE MIGHTN'T HAVE MINDED AMATEUR PHILOSOPHISING ABOUT monsters and men if the monster had been successful. However, he returned at five in the morning, looking pouty and having found nothing of use. His deofol dissipated in a moody smudge of smoke.

"The entire Keep is clean," said Mordaunt, pushing his hood back. "I found things, of course—military plans, billets-doux from mistresses, bits of intel—but nothing that connects Wellesley to Swan-stone."

"Perhaps he wasn't involved after all," said Aurienne.

Mordaunt looked as unconvinced as she felt. "Why have a Haelan in today, then? For a child bursting with health?"

From his cloak he produced letters, scrolls bearing royal seals, maps, and glittering handfuls of jewellery. He proceeded to stuff these into Aurienne's satchel.

"What is all that, and what d'you think you're doing with it?" asked Aurienne.

"Discoveries," said Mordaunt. "Going to sell the military intel to Kent. Hawking the jewels. As for the letters, Wellesley's got seven lovers—one for every day of the week, I suppose—and some of them will be worth blackmailing."

"I beg your pardon? You said you found things—you didn't say you *stole* the things."

"Obviously I stole the things. Didn't kill anyone, by the way, not that you asked. Taking me a bit for granted, I think."

"This isn't what we came here for," said Aurienne as Mordaunt continued to stuff his contraband into her bag. "You can't take those things."

"Of course I can. What are you going to do—call the guards on me?"

Aurienne snatched her satchel from him and inverted it onto the bed. "*I'm* not going to be involved. Do you know how this would look for my Order, if they were to find these things in my bag? Military plans? Really?"

"Well, where am I meant to put them?" asked Mordaunt.

"I don't know. I don't care. Stuff them into your codpiece."

"I also found a kitten."

"You found a kitten."

"Yes."

A hissing, dripping, black ball was placed in Aurienne's hands.

"We can't leave it here," said Mordaunt. "The guards had it half-drowned in a bucket. I can't take it home. Rigor Mortis will eat it. You take it."

The kitten scrambled out of Aurienne's hands and into her satchel, from whence it hissed hatefully at the two of them.

"I also need to do something about these," said Mordaunt, producing two bottles of Scotch from the depths of his cloak. "Wellesley's got a lovely collection and he knows it. The cellar was well guarded. Took me a full quarter of an hour to get in."

Aurienne stared at him. "We are *not* smuggling Wellesley's prized Scotch out of the Keep."

"You really know how to suck the joy out of anything."

"I wouldn't need to if you wouldn't inject unnecessary stressors into already tense situations."

Rustling and chatter began to ring through the corridors as servants made their way to bedchambers to stoke fires and serve breakfasts. Wellesley Keep was waking up.

Aurienne cut her lecture short. "Get back into your armour. We could be summoned to see Wellesley at any moment."

They got Mordaunt back into costume just in time; the chambermaids arrived a few minutes later, bearing a full breakfast tray for Aurienne. For Mordaunt, they brought a single boiled egg.

Mordaunt hadn't replaced his helmet. The chambermaids eyed him as they aired out the room, and Aurienne heard one whisper to the other that if she'd known *that* was under the helmet, she would've offered him the use of her own bed instead of the straw. Mordaunt, however, had eyes only for Aurienne—narrowed ones, accompanied by mutters that she was a Scourge.

As Aurienne finished her breakfast (smeared eggs about and poured tea into the poor potted plant) there was a knock at the door.

"Hello again, Pumpypip—er, Pipplewaithe," said Aurienne.

"Good morning, Haelan Fairhrim, Sergeant." Pipplewaithe swept off his hat. "Lord Wellesley is ready for you. Would you follow me?"

"Of course," said Aurienne. "I caught a glimpse of the patient yesterday, by the way."

"Did you, indeed?"

"By chance—she had escaped her minders. A lively girl. Your inexpert eye was correct. She seems in no immediate danger."

Pipplewaithe's feather shrank in embarrassment. "Did you think so? Well, I'm certain Lord Wellesley will be pleased to hear this assessment. I do offer my personal apologies for your—perhaps unnecessary?—voyage all the way here from the Danelaw. Though I'm sure you will forgive a father's worry. He does like to have the best of the best on hand, as you've no doubt ascertained, but to call in a Haelan for—well, who can truly understand the minds of great men? Ha, ha—shall we?"

Pipplewaithe's feather trembled, Mordaunt's armour clanged, and they were off.

They entered a reception room, overly full of plush seats, where Wellesley's visitors were to mill about before their audiences with the Lord. Aurienne and Mordaunt were the only callers this morning. Pipplewaithe bid them sit, knocked at a great oak door to signal their arrival to those inside, and left.

Aurienne and Mordaunt eyed each other in wary silence.

After some time, the door abutting the antechamber was opened, revealing a high-ceilinged hall. To Aurienne's consternation—and Mordaunt's, no doubt—the anti-Fyren measures were back in full swing within; there were spotlights aimed at every corner of the room, and even the floor was bathed with light. There were no shadows to be seen, much less walked.

Lord Wellesley and his men-at-arms sat around a table scattered with the remains of breakfast. Judging by the decor, Wellesley's chief hobby was the murder of rare megafauna. The taxidermised heads of beasts jutted from the wall—a woolly rhinoceros, a cave hyena, a sabre-tooth, an auroch.

Below this cemetery sat Lord Wellesley himself—bald of crown, red of beard, shrewd of eye. His head, Aurienne noted generously, was shaped like a suppository.

Lord Wellesley exclaimed words of welcome, all while observing Aurienne and her Haelan garb with satisfaction, and turning a calculating eye towards Mordaunt. He seemed pleased with the results of his arithmetic. He gestured Aurienne forwards with a bow.

"Come in, come in, dear Haelan," said Wellesley. "I had lost hope that one of your Order would come."

"We are stretched thin," said Aurienne. "But I'm pleased to be here now. How is your daughter?"

"Much better. May I offer you something? Tea? Have you eaten?"

"I've eaten, thank you," said Aurienne. "I'm pleased she's doing better. You'd listed some worrisome symptoms in your letter."

"It appears to have mostly cleared up. I was too hasty, perhaps, in calling for you. But why don't you sit down? Are you sure you won't take anything?"

He was up to no good. Normally, Aurienne would have castigated him for wasting her time and left in a huff—but she, too, was up to no good.

She sat upon the very edge of a chair. "Shouldn't I have a look at your daughter, since I came all the way here?"

"Of course. It would reassure me to have your expert opinion. But come, rest a moment."

Brief small talk followed, led by Wellesley and responded to in curt, but polite, syllables by Aurienne. The men-at-arms were tense and still.

Mordaunt stood a few feet behind her—the rasp of metal on metal informed her of his shifts in stance—and Aurienne felt comforted. Yes: it was comforting that the Fyren was there.

Which was far and away the most bizarre thought that had ever entered her head.

Wellesley turned the conversation to the Haelan Order, leaned forwards, and seemed to, finally, come to the crux of the matter. "I heard, by the by, that your Order had received an anonymous gift of unusual proportions."

"We did," said Aurienne. She pressed her hands to her heart. "An act of astounding generosity; I can still hardly believe it."

There was a loud sniff from Mordaunt.

"It was rather unconventional, wasn't it?" said Wellesley.

"Most," said Aurienne.

"Have we any idea who this generous donor was?"

This line of enquiry was hilarious, given that the generous donor was right behind Aurienne.

"Not a clue. It was an anonymous donation, as you heard." Aurienne tilted her head, and grew coquettish, and asked, "Was it you?"

Wellesley shuffled closer to Aurienne. He gave her a warm smile, but there was no concordance of sentiment between it and his eyes, which remained cold. "Do you think it could be?"

"Maybe," said Aurienne, returning the smile. "Have I the honour of meeting our incredible benefactor?"

They smiled at each other moronically, until Wellesley's grin disappeared, and he said, "In all seriousness, Haelan—no. It wasn't me. But I'd like to contact the donor, actually, to work out a donation of my own. Perhaps we could make a joint contribution to your Order."

"Oh, that is so kind of you," said Aurienne. "The Heads will be thrilled."

Wellesley came closer. "Surely someone in your Order knows the donor's identity, to assist me in this pursuit?"

Aurienne wished that he would invest in a tongue scraper.

"I'm afraid not a single one of us knows," she said. "The funds were quite literally left in sacks upon our doorstep. No one saw anything—and we have Wardens at Swanstone; if anyone was to have spotted something, it would've been them."

Wellesley's smile was back, pained this time. "Yes, you do have Wardens. One wouldn't expect such a level of protection in a place of healing."

"Unfortunately, not everyone comes to Swanstone with the best of intentions," said Aurienne.

"You'll forgive me for pressing you further—but you're quite certain no one in your Order has any idea who donated these funds?"

"No."

Wellesley's smile was fading. "I need to know who made the donation."

"I can't help you," said Aurienne, in perfect, innocent confusion.

"I'd like you to give me names of people who might know. People I might approach. My enquiries have met with nothing. It's vital that I know the provenance of the funds."

"Why is it vital?"

"The reasons don't concern you," said Wellesley. "Think. You're a Haelan; you know the inner workings of the Order—if you don't know, who might know? One of the Heads, surely?"

"The donation was *anonymous*," repeated Aurienne.

"That's not a good enough answer," said Wellesley.

"I'm not giving you names. You look as though you're about to go and shake them up for information."

"At this stage, yes, that is what I'm going to do," said Wellesley.

"I refuse," said Aurienne.

"So you do have names."

"I don't." Aurienne rose. "I'm leaving. Your behaviour has grown alarming. I thought I was summoned to see to a sick child, not to be subject to an interrogation."

Wellesley eyed Mordaunt, who was now lounging against the wall in a decidedly un-guardish way.

"You'll leave when I say you can," said Wellesley.

His men-at-arms found their feet. Five or six remained next to him; the others moved towards the door.

"I need a few small pieces of information," said Wellesley. "Recommendations. Nudges in the right direction. That's all."

"I won't point you and your men towards anyone in my Order," said Aurienne. "I've already told you: no one knows who gave us that money."

"Think this through carefully, Haelan."

"*You* should think this through carefully," said Aurienne. "You've upset me, but I'm willing to walk away and not mention this ill-conceived interrogation to anybody. I shall consider it a misguided decision by a distressed father. Let me go. I can assure you that the consequences of angering my Order would be dire."

"There are much larger things at stake here than your little Order playing house in that bloody fortress."

"Really? You're on the verge of war. My Order can withdraw every Haelan in Wessex and double those in Kent. Any man of yours who goes down will stay down. Are you sure you want to keep me here?"

Wellesley pressed his hands together until his knuckles went white. "We needn't resort to threats. Give me hints—informally, off the record—that I can pursue, and you can go free. No one needs to be hurt. I just need to know what absolute fool made a donation of twenty million bloody thrymsas to save wretched, Pox-ridden strays."

Aurienne still felt the squeeze at her fingers by one of the wretched, Pox-ridden strays. She mastered her outrage.

"No one knows," she repeated, slowly, so that the words would penetrate the suppository. "I'm leaving. You've wasted my time abominably."

As Aurienne strode towards the door, Wellesley's men-at-arms glanced at him. He made a curt gesture. In a body, they gathered in front of the door, all armed with swords and lances and shields.

There were no shadows for the Fyren to work with. Aurienne made eye contact with him to enquire whether they should be concerned.

Mordaunt lounged against the wall, unperturbed. Which was probably bad news for Wellesley and company.

"Tell your men to stand aside," said Aurienne to Wellesley. "They needn't die today."

It was the second time in so many months that she'd asked a man to stand aside to avoid a massacre. Would this one listen?

No. Wellesley merely looked at her in disbelief. The men guffawed.

"You do realise," said Wellesley, "that you've only got one man here."

"No," said Aurienne, with ruefulness born of sad truth. "I've got a monster."

Now Mordaunt moved. With a clang, one gauntlet hit the floor. With another clang, the other fell. *Clang.* The helmet came off. *Clang.* The pauldrons. *Clang.* The chest plate.

Wellesley's men watched the performance with their brows raised, and with reason, because her guard was armouring down rather than armouring up, as one might imagine a Swanstone sergeant ought to be doing when his Haelan was being threatened.

Finally, Mordaunt stood before them in shirtsleeves and braces, dusting off his palms.

"Hiya," he said. He gave Wellesley's men a coy wave. His tācn was a red glow among the room's white lights.

There were gasps. There was confusion. There was a shrinking back of the assembled men.

"Fyren," someone gasped.

"There are no shadows—he's powerless," said Wellesley, who had himself taken several steps away. "He's got nowhere to hide. Kill the bastard."

Mordaunt flashed a smile uncannily like his deofol's grin.

"Don't," said Aurienne. "You *will* die. Step aside, all of you—just step aside, for Frīa's sake, and let me leave."

"Skewer him," snarled Wellesley, and his men surged forwards.

"Your cheeky little lights didn't get rid of *all* the shadows," said Mordaunt to the approaching men.

And he shadow-walked to the only dark places in the room: their insides.

The first man burst in a wet, bloody slurry as Mordaunt materialised in his chest cavity. The second became a many-legged anomaly as Mordaunt walked through him. The third collapsed into an indistinct pile of organ, bone, and limb. Then the next. Then the next. For added efficiency, Mordaunt held the Swanstone sword at neck height, and decapitated those he wasn't stepping through.

When he had dispatched the men, Mordaunt, dripping with guts and blood, looked down at himself, and said, "Well, this shirt is ruined."

A long piece of intestine slid off his shoulder. A split pancreas dribbled down to the floor with a soft *splish*. He plucked a stray patella off his trousers.

Wellesley, still next to Aurienne, made the mistake—the very grave mistake, the last mistake he would ever make—of laying a hand on Aurienne.

He pulled her against him with a knife at her neck and spat at Mordaunt: "Stay back."

"That," said Mordaunt, "was a bad idea."

But Aurienne, unfond of knives at her throat, did not wait for rescue. She pressed her tācn to the back of Wellesley's hand, sent her seith into him, and pinched his carotid artery shut.

An act which oughtn't have killed him, but, just as everything else today, it derailed spectacularly, and instead of slumping against her into a faint, Wellesley fell backwards and, with a sick crack, smashed his skull open, and scattered his brains on the stone floor.

There was a long silence.

"Shit," said Aurienne.

Mordaunt eyed her with a new interest. "How did you do that?"

"Never mind *how*," said Aurienne. "I've just killed Lord Wellesley."

Mordaunt tutted. "Murderer." He stood over Wellesley's corpse and wiggled a finger over it in a circle. "That was meant to be my job. I was going to enjoy it. But I forgive you."

Aurienne stared at the gory exhibition around them. "What—what's the bloody importance of the name of the donor? Isn't it *good* someone donated? Why the desperate need to know? Why did he want to hurt a Haelan to find out? Why was it worth *this*?"

"Don't know," said Mordaunt. "But we need to get out of here. There's an entire garrison just outside these walls, and when this is discovered—"

"Right," said Aurienne. "Get back into the armour. We were never here."

Aurienne—now, officially, a Murderer—plunged back into the reception room, straightened her dress, sat primly in a chair, and tried to look annoyed, rather than aghast. Mordaunt, his blood-soaked clothes hidden by shining armour and his sword wiped clean on Wellesley's trousers, tumbled in after her, shut the door to the carnage, and stood at attention next to her. A split second later, Pipplewaithe popped his head into the reception room with an enquiring twitch of the feather.

"Hullo!" he said. "Still haven't gone in, eh? They're always behind."

"No, we haven't," said Aurienne. "I'm quite sick of waiting, actually. At this juncture, I'd like to go see the patient, rather than her father."

"I am so sorry, Haelan Fairhrim," said Pipplewaithe. "I shall interrupt them. It's simply unacceptable to keep you like this."

Pipplewaithe knocked, and knocked again, and opened the door, and let out a high-pitched scream.

AURIENNE AND MORDAUNT ACTED THEIR HEARTS OUT AS NEWS OF THE massacre spread through the Keep. They were questioned for hours, but held fast to their story—greatly assisted, credibility-wise, by Pipplewaithe's testimony—that they had been stuck in the reception room, had heard nothing and seen nothing, and had discovered the murders only when Pipplewaithe had opened the door.

The consensus was that a Haelan (*Harm to none*, etc.) and a single Swanstone guard simply could not be responsible for butchery at this scale against ten of Wellesley's best men, fully armed, and that Kent must be to blame.

Lord Wellesley's second-in-command, freshly arrived from some excursion, slammed his fist on several tables, and declared that Wessex must go to war with Kent.

"Oops," said Mordaunt.

Aurienne and Mordaunt were sent back to their rooms between bouts of questioning. No one noticed Mordaunt's half-closed eye under his helmet; when their interrogators had left, he explained to Aurienne that jumping between shadows that weren't connected was far more burdensome on his seith, and hence, he had triggered his Cost.

Their moments alone gave Aurienne ample time to gurgle and churn with guilt. She had not *Harm to none*'d. She had done the opposite. She had killed. She was no better than the Fyren.

She glanced at him. He seemed bored; he had killed ten times the men she had, and on purpose, and he cared not at all. Aurienne, sick with convulsions of guilt, wished she could be as lackadaisical, but no— she was highly daisical.

She sent Cíele to Xanthe with the latest developments and with many apologies, as though apologies were sufficient to atone for starting a war.

Xanthe's axolotl deofol, Saophal, carried her answer to them: "Shit."

"That's what I said. Also, I murdered someone."

"Who?" asked Saophal.

"Wellesley," said Aurienne. "Meant to put him in a faint when he attacked me, but he fell wrong. Cracked open his skull and spilled his brains out. Died instantly."

Saophal looked grave. "He attacked first?"

"Yes."

"Self-defence, then."

"It was." Aurienne held her head in her hands. "I still feel sick."

"Who witnessed it, other than the Fyren?" asked Saophal.

"No one," said Aurienne.

"Then no one will know," said Saophal. "If the Fyren tells anyone, no one will believe him anyway."

"Oi," said Mordaunt from where he lounged on the bed.

"If they don't release you soon, send your deofol," said Saophal. "Xanthe will go directly to the Wessexian queen. There's no proof of your involvement in this mess. They can't hold you long."

The axolotl disappeared. Aurienne the Murderer stewed in more guilt. Mordaunt sauntered towards the table where his pilfered bottles of Scotch still stood.

"Really?" said Aurienne. "You're going to have a drink? Now? Between interrogations? A dead man's stolen Scotch?"

Mordaunt wiggled a bottle at her. "I'm a bon vivant."

"You're a common thief."

"*Common?* How dare you?"

Mordaunt found a goblet, opened one of the bottles, and inhaled.

Aurienne anticipated much waxing eloquent on the Scotch and, wrestling with her own agonies over Wellesley's death, made a swift remark about how it smelled like Malfeasance and Acts of Unwarranted Brutality—but Mordaunt coughed and gagged and cut her off.

"What the hell is this?" he asked of the bottle.

"If it's gone bad, it serves you right," said Aurienne.

Mordaunt tilted the bottle to peer at the liquid therein. "No—it's not Scotch at all."

He passed the bottle under Aurienne's nose. The smell was lightly chemical, acidic, and familiar. It took Aurienne two or three sniffs to place it.

Then, with a gasp, she recognised it: "That's sophoglycolate broth."

"Sack the chef. I've never smelled a worse broth in my life."

Aurienne snatched the cork from Mordaunt's hand and popped it back onto the bottle. "It's a liquid media, a mix of stabilisers and pH buffers. Never mind the details—sophoglycolate broth is used to preserve viruses."

Aurienne plonked the bottle on the table next to its twin.

She and Mordaunt stared at it.

At length, Mordaunt asked, "I was about to drink a virus?"

"I don't know."

"Why's Wellesley got viruses in his cellar?"

"I don't know."

"What virus?"

"I don't know, but I've got a shrewd guess."

"The Pox?"

"The Pox." Aurienne picked up both bottles. "I'm going to have these tested."

"Oh, so *now* we're smuggling bottles out of the Keep," said Mordaunt as Aurienne stuffed them into her satchel. The black kitten was still within; it hissed at her—she had interrupted its nap.

"Were there other bottles?" asked Aurienne.

"There was a whole cellar full," said Mordaunt.

"You said it was unusually well guarded?"

"Yes. Sixteen men."

"None of them saw you?"

"Your question offends."

Aurienne hid the bottles in the depths of her satchel. If her suspicions were right, she no longer felt bad about murdering Wellesley.

They named the kitten Acts of Warranted Brutality.

MR. HUNGWELL

Osric

In the end, Osric had to admit (to himself only, never to Fairhrim) that it had been a grand idea to infiltrate Wellesley Keep. He made out brilliantly. When he went to sell Wellesley's intel to Kent, he took the opportunity to steal Kentish intel, and turned around and sold that to Wessex. Champion.

Now he was having Wellesley's jewels appraised by Sacramore at the Harmacy.

"Quality, quality," said Sacramore, examining them with a loupe. "Lovely finds."

(It was always *finds* with Sacramore. As though Osric came across a ruby worth a hundred thousand thrymsas by pure happenstance. Found it in the soup.)

The useless lug that was Brythe emerged from the corridor leading to Tristane's office.

"Nice baubles, Os," he commented as he passed.

"You can gargle my baubles," said Osric.

"I'll gargle your baubles," said Sacramore to Osric.

"What about mine?" asked Brythe, grasping his balls through his trousers and lifting them in Sacramore's direction.

Sacramore pointed his loupe towards Brythe's crotch. "Show me what's on offer."

"No time for it," said Brythe. "Got places to be. Answers to get. Necks to wring."

"You joining us on the Carnegie job?" asked Osric.

"No. Off to the Danelaw on business."

"What business?" asked Sacramore, his loupe trained on Brythe's face.

"Secret."

"What secret?" asked Osric.

"S'only for top Fyren to know about." Brythe swung the door open. "Got to shower, shit, and shove off. See you povvos later."

Brythe left. The Harmacy's glass door clattered to a close behind him.

"What's he wanking himself over?" asked Osric.

Sacramore stared at the door through his loupe. He turned it towards Tristane's office. "She's accepted, then."

"Accepted what?"

"An ask I didn't think she'd agree to take on. They must have offered a bloody fortune."

"They?"

There was vast disapproval in the squint of Sacramore's eye in the loupe. "Unorthodox. I don't like it. We don't take assignments that are a direct attack on other Orders. It could unbalance things."

"Which Order?"

"I've already said too much," said Sacramore. He turned his attention back to the gems, still disapproving.

It didn't matter. Brythe had mentioned the Danelaw. There was only one Order headquartered in the Danelaw.

OSRIC MATERIALISED AT THE WAYSTONE OF THE PUBLISH OR PERISH A few minutes later. The waystone was tucked against the east side of the pub, offering, in the evening light, progressively deeper shadows of much convenience to a Fyren stalking another Fyren.

Osric summoned Cinder, his deofol, to his side. The she-wolf took partial form in the darkest shadows between the waystone and the pub's stone wall.

"What is it?" asked her glinting teeth.

"Find Fairhrim," said Osric. "Tell her to get somewhere safe. There's a Fyren headed for Swanstone and I don't know why."

The deofol's golden eyes blazed. "Immediately," she said, disappearing even as she spoke.

Osric leaned against the wall and waited. Why had Brythe been sent to Swanstone? And, more importantly, whose necks had he been instructed to wring, and did Fairhrim's number among them?

Had he been hired for a revenge kill for the carnage wrought by Osric and Fairhrim at Wellesley Keep? Impossible. They had been cleared and had left the Keep freely; Kent had borne the brunt of the blame. But if Fairhrim happened to be in the way of Brythe's target? He would kill her without a second thought.

Could Brythe even get past Wardens? Osric had managed his intrusion of Swanstone through every inch of his skill and subtlety. Brythe was a bumbling oaf.

But if he *did* make it past them?

For the next half hour, Osric watched a smattering of travellers pop out of the pub's waystone—Haelan (but not his Haelan), Swanstone staffers, villagers, and even, to Osric's sudden consternation, one of the Wardens—but not Brythe.

No one noticed the Fyren melted into the shadows mere feet away, his blaecblade pressed along his thigh.

Because, yes: after much internal debating, Osric had decided that Brythe was going to die today. Osric was going to interrogate him and kill him. There was no other way to proceed. Brythe was working on something secret that he wouldn't willingly share with Osric. Left alive, he would report Osric's interest to Tristane, and Tristane would ask questions that Osric couldn't answer, and so Brythe must die. Answer Osric, and then die.

Cinder returned to Osric's side. Her ears were back and flat; her voice was low. "The Haelan wouldn't let me through."

"Again?" snarled Osric, because this wasn't the first time Fairhrim had rejected his deofol.

"I've been trying every few minutes. She might be in the company of others."

"Go back. Push until she lets you. Hurt her if you must."

Cinder vanished with an irritated growl.

Osric had just found his comfortable, one-legged lean against the wall—his favourite stakeout position—when a cloaked figure shimmered into existence at the waystone.

Brythe, materialising in a homely little village in the Danelaw, did not have his guard up. Osric took two strides forwards. His blaecblade found that favourite juncture between neck and shoulder and stabbed deliciously downwards.

A moment later, he was stabbing thin air; Brythe had shadow-walked. Osric's blade dripped red in the evening light. He held his tācn towards the shadow of an awning ahead—the place where he would've jumped to had he been stabbed—and moved there, and found Brythe bent over, holding his hand to his neck, gasping. Osric had, perhaps, been a little too enthusiastic. The wound was fatal. They would have a few minutes for a brief interview and Brythe would be dead.

Brythe, still unaware that he was dealing with a Fyren, reached his tācn ahead of him and shadow-walked towards a dark garden.

Osric materialised behind him and, wishing him to stop running so that they could chitchat, severed both of his hamstrings.

Brythe shadow-dragged himself to an old stone wall abutting the courtyard of a massive glassworks. A desperate flurry of knives flew towards Osric—most of Brythe's arsenal, by the look of it—but Brythe's right hand hung useless, and so he used his left, and hit Osric with only a few glancing blows. Brythe clutched his maul where he lay, but it was a worthless threat without the momentum that made it deadly.

Osric sank his blaecblade into Brythe's left arm, between his radius and ulna.

The maul fell.

"Osric?" gasped Brythe, finally catching a glimpse of him. "Wh-what—why?"

Osric sat on his haunches and pressed a friendly hand to the uncontrolled haemorrhage at Brythe's neck. "Who gave Tristane the Swanstone job?"

"F-fuck you," said Brythe.

"Who were you sent to kill?"

Brythe's words came with difficulty. "Fuck. You."

Osric removed his blaecblade from Brythe's arm with a tug. He pressed it into Brythe's tācn instead.

Brythe screamed.

"Who were you sent to kill?" asked Osric. His knifepoint pried into the eyehole of Brythe's tācn.

"Never going to—you're a traitor. Hel will curse you for this—"

"I'm Hel's favourite." Osric slipped the blade between two metacarpals in Brythe's palm. "Answer me."

The blood loss was hitting; Brythe was beginning to fade. Osric turned the blade. The delicate metacarpals in Brythe's hand separated. He sprang back to screaming life as his tācn was destroyed.

"I will make your last moments a misery," said Osric. "Who were you sent to kill?"

Brythe's jaw was set. The death grimace was creeping upon him. He would rather spite Osric and die without giving him what he wanted.

Again Osric's blade turned. Again Brythe screamed.

The sound attracted attention in the quiet village. People stood upon their stoops, asking one another what was happening.

Osric moved his blaecblade to Brythe's neck. "Tell me."

Brythe, full of spite, slumped forwards with the last of his strength. Osric's blade, honed to the sharpest edge, severed tissue, artery, and vein. Brythe slouched against Osric's arm, partially decapitated.

No last words, then.

It was time to go. The flames of the glassworks' enormous forge provided a convenient place to dispose of the body.

Osric retreated to the safety of the sod roof of the Publish or Perish as villagers stepped out to investigate the source of the screams.

The coolness of Fairhrim's seith was at his tācn. Her deofol was asking to come through.

"Finally," spat Osric as the white genet took shape.

"What do you want?" hissed Fairhrim's deofol, its ears so far back that they disappeared and made its head a flat triangle. "She's busy; can't your deofol take a bloody hint?"

"A Fyren was headed for Swanstone," said Osric.

"What?"

Osric held up his wet blaecblade. "Threat extinguished. You'll find him roasting in the glassworks forge."

The deofol's self-possession left it. The fur along its back stood on end. "Why was he going to Swanstone?"

"He killed himself before I could finish enquiring," said Osric.

"Do you know you're bleeding?" asked the deofol.

"A few scratches," said Osric, looking down to take stock.

"That's a substantial sort of scratch," said the deofol.

Brythe's blaecblade was sticking out of Osric's side. So advanced was his torpraxia that he hadn't even noticed; there was no pain, only a dull ache that grew more acute now that he was aware of the injury.

"Fuck," said Osric.

He did not need the deofol's advice to know that this was Not Good, but the deofol nevertheless said, "That's Not Good."

"*No.* Really?"

"You need a Haelan," said the deofol.

"I do happen to know one," said Osric. He strode across the roof, in the direction of Swanstone's high-turreted silhouette.

Fairhrim's deofol scampered in front of him. "No—wait—Aurienne isn't at Swanstone."

"She's not at—what? Where is she?"

"The opera," said the deofol. "That's why she couldn't let your deofol through—bit awkward to have a great bloody wolf materialise in the middle of the third act—"

"The opera? *The opera?* That's where she is, and I've just got myself gutted for her?"

The deofol's whiskers twitched in consternation. It was doing some quick thinking. "Take the waystone to the Higgledy-Piggledy in London. Go to number three, just across the way. It's her parents' house. She'll be on her way there shortly, if she isn't already. I shall try to warn her that you're coming, but she's surrounded by people. Your timing is appalling, as usual. Don't pull out the knife, whatever you do—hide the wound. To the waystone, *go.*"

The deofol disappeared.

The little village of Swanstone-on-Sea was lit with torches as its inhabitants searched for the source of the screams. Someone discovered the puddle of Brythe's blood under the awning.

Osric descended from the pub's roof to the waystone and pressed his tācn to it. Down into the ley line towards London he went. He whirled back into himself upon shining cobblestones. This London was different to the London in which Osric normally conducted his business—it was a London of wide, leafy streets illuminated by electric globes instead of gas lamps, and bordered by elegant, if narrow, homes. No soot, no fumes, no reek of boiled fish and cheap spirits. Osric moved towards number three, catching glimpses of soft-lit drawing rooms as he passed.

His preference would have been to shadow-walk the house until he found Fairhrim, but, given the rather urgent state of affairs, he went directly to the front door.

Osric climbed the dozen white marble stairs, an exercise that ought to have been excruciating, given his injury, only the torpraxia-induced numbness made the knife feel like an unfriendly poke more than anything else. He drew his cloak around himself to cover the worst of his state, including the hilt protruding from his side. He made sure that his crisp collar was visible, and pulled on his gloves to hide his tācn.

A serving girl opened the door. Osric had a general impression of glittering bustle behind her—many voices, trays being conveyed to and fro by harried servants.

"Yes?" prompted the girl.

"Who is it, Tartiflette?" asked a voice, unknown and yet, with its intonations of authority and impatience, familiar. "Did we leave someone behind?"

"I'm a friend of Fair—erm, of Aurienne's," said Osric to the serving girl.

A woman popped over the serving girl's shoulder and observed Osric coolly. "Oh? Aurienne didn't mention that she had invited anyone."

The woman was unmistakably Fairhrim's mother. She had the same brown skin and masses of hair (though white at the temples)—and, more intimidatingly, the same darkly flashing, intelligent eyes.

She turned towards the well-dressed crowd behind her. "Aurienne! Your guest is here. Kindly make introductions." She turned back to Osric. "Do come in and forgive the chaos—we've just got home. You must join us for a drink."

Osric entered the foyer. Tartiflette, who had fallen in love with him immediately—because who didn't?—blushingly offered to take his cloak. Osric made a polite refusal, claiming to have caught a chill. He did feel chilled—it probably had to do with the half litre of blood he had left at the waystone.

Fairhrim's mother tutted. "Cold? On such a fine evening? Turn up the furnaces, Tartiflette."

A figure emerged from the crowd behind Fairhrim's mother. Fairhrim's voice, resplendent with annoyance, preceded her. "Mum, did you say a guest of mine had—"

"Yes, your Friend," said Fairhrim's mother.

Fairhrim came into view. She froze when she saw Osric.

He froze when he saw her, too. This was Fairhrim off duty, nigh unrecognisable in a flowing mauve gown, elbow-length white gloves, and hair off the side of her neck in a soft wave. She was stunning—a disturbing development, and one that Osric set aside to cope with at a later moment.

Fairhrim's surprise at the sight of Osric was such that it was clear her deofol hadn't been able to get her somewhere private to explain. Her impassivity was challenged—her fingers gripped at the stem of a glass of wine; her jaw clenched. In the press of her lips Osric saw her fury: that he had harassed her all evening with his deofol, that he had the gall not only to come to her but to enter her parents' home—that he dared to call himself her *friend*.

Osric would have to get her alone as soon as possible to explain.

Also to help with the small matter of the knife.

Fairhrim's mother, whose attention was mercifully on a tray of champagne being whisked by, did not see their mutual gawping. "You might've mentioned, Aurienne. You are so forgetful sometimes—just like your father—but no matter; the more, the merrier."

Fairhrim, who had, in Osric's experience, a mind like a steel trap, said, "I'm sorry. I forgot to mention."

An older man joined them, tall, white skinned, slightly stooped about the shoulders. "What am I accused of this time?"

"Forgetfulness, among your many sins," said Fairhrim's mother. "Aurienne invited her newest Friend for drinks and neglected to tell me—an inherited trait."

Fairhrim looked as though she wished to strangle Osric with his own collar. "Yes. This is my—Friend," she said, having never sounded so constipated around a word.

"Osric Hungwell," said Osric, offering his hand to Fairhrim's parents.

Fairhrim took his alias in her stride, though twitchily. "May I introduce my mother, Radia, and my father, Rosbert?"

"Pleasure," said Osric, shaking hands with both.

The father's handshake was firm; the mother's was pinchy. Radia's eyes ran down his ensemble, which, though dusty (and bloodstained, if she approached enough to observe it), was obviously quality, and seemed to satisfy her. Fairhrim's father regarded Osric with mild curiosity, as though his daughter had brought in a stray dog and he wished to make friends with it.

They had a definite whiff of the nouveau riche: the earrings in the mother's ears, the cane in the father's hand, the house—no, they were not old money. Osric continued to feel superior to Fairhrim, and all was well in the world, except for the knife in his guts, and the fact that she might, after all, be prettier than him.

He wanted a quick word with her to inform her that he was actively in the process of dying, but they were swept into the crowd and deposited in a reception room. Fairhrim recovered her composure from her initial shock and was glassy and restrained as Osric was introduced to various other Fairhrims whom he did not care about.

"Might I have a word—" began Osric, but Aunt Plectrude drew him into conversation about the state of the roads. Had he heard of the tragic accident that had befallen those Mercians? (He had, actually.)

"If we could step out a moment—" tried Fairhrim, but she was asked for an update on the Pox, and made some curt, generally optimistic pronouncements, only many of the poor surviving children were not quite right; the Pox inflamed the brain—there was a general consensus that this was a pity.

Osric nodded, then said again, "Perhaps we could, just for a minute—"

A drink was pushed into his hand by Fairhrim's father. Scotch. Very good Scotch. Osric drank the Scotch. Would it pour out of his perforated intestine? He felt this would be difficult to explain. He was made to try bits of food. Some of it was unusual—salads with no salad but, rather, tomatoes, cucumbers, and onion; beans marinated in something called *chermoula*. All exceptionally good; he could not appreciate it fully, however, because he was dying.

"You're pale," said Fairhrim. "Your hands are shaking. What's the matter?"

"He said he was cold," said Radia. "Poor thing. Tartiflette! The furnaces."

"I've turned them up, madam," said Tartiflette. "Shall I go higher? What setting?"

Radia, wild-eyed and imperious, said, "Inferno."

The world grew distant. Osric didn't wish to overreact, but he thought this might be getting urgent. "I—"

"So, tell us, Mr. Hungwell," came Rosbert's friendly enquiry, "how did you and Aurienne meet?"

Osric cleared his throat in a pained sort of way. He had very little blood in his brain to fabricate an answer, given that much of it was presently soaking through his shirt and waistcoat. "Well—erm—that's an interesting story—"

Fairhrim, bless her, immediately took over the tale. "He's a consultant. We hired him a few months ago. He's an expert in—"

"Knife," blurted Osric.

"Y-yes," said Fairhrim. "He's reviewing our surgical-instrument inventory at Swanstone."

Osric made a mild recovery and said, "Metallurgy is one of my areas of speciality."

"He's produced some truly remarkable dissecting and dressing sets. Artery forceps to die for. And the episiotomy scissors, frankly gorgeous—they keep their edge like nothing else—"

"Metallurgy!" said Radia. She removed her glove and showed her right palm to Osric. The tācn there consisted of golden gears. "I'm an Ingenaut. Am I in the company of a fellow member of the Order?"

So Fairhrim's mother was a brain, too. Good to know, but also, at the moment, he didn't care.

"Er—sorry to disappoint, but no," said Osric.

"Oh, well, never mind," said Radia, replacing her glove with obvious disappointment. "What are your thoughts on the ecgium alloy that's making such waves?"

"Some interesting applications," said Osric, "but it's got nothing on blaec, of course."

Radia blinked at him. "Well, blaec isn't exactly widely available, is it?"

"Right. No."

"What's blaec?" asked Rosbert.

"A wonder metal," said Radia, "whose secrets are kept by that awful, obscure little Order—what's-their-name, the murdery sorts—"

"The Fyren," bit out Fairhrim.

Dimly, through the black fuzz encroaching on his vision, Osric was aware that he was an idiot for talking about blaec. Fairhrim reaffirmed this by bayonetting him with her eyes. He should definitely not open his cloak to show Fairhrim's mum the blaecblade jutting from his side, then; his brain, gurgling through what remained of his blood, was certain of this, at least.

Osric tucked a hand into his cloak. Things felt rather wet and sticky even through his glove, and not in a sexy way. He realised that he couldn't remove his hand, lest everyone see the blood.

"Fair—er—Aurienne, might I steal you away for a moment?" he asked, feeble voiced.

"Yes," said Fairhrim.

"Are you quite all right, Mr. Hungwell?" asked Rosbert.

"Of course. Just need to talk business for a moment—scalpel order—wouldn't want to bore the party."

"Excuse us," said Fairhrim. "We'll be back in a minute."

Osric followed Fairhrim to the foyer, mercifully devoid of people.

When Fairhrim had ascertained that they were alone, she let Osric see the full brunt of her wrath in the form of flared nostrils. "*What* is going on? You'd better have a good explanation for coming to my parents' home and inviting yourself in—"

"Fairhrim."

"What?"

"I'm bleeding out."

"You're—what?"

Osric pulled his dripping glove out of his cloak. "But I hate to interrupt—quite a lovely party, if it wasn't for you perforating me with your eyes every few seconds. Going to leave me bloodier than the knife—"

"The knife?" repeated Fairhrim. "Show me."

Osric fumbled with the clasp of his cloak. His hands shook; his fine motor skills were shot. In light of his futile attempts with the clasp, Fairhrim made an impatient click of the tongue and reached for it herself. She tugged at it with brisk movements, threw it open, gasped, and flung it closed again.

"Mother, would you give us a bit of privacy?" she called over Osric's shoulder. Osric was pleased that he wasn't the only one in the world towards whom she could direct that precise, Fairhrimish ring of Supreme Irritation.

"I was just coming to see if everything was all right, but I see that it is," said Radia, shimmering into existence next to her daughter. "Might we refrain from getting handsy just before we serve the sweets?"

There was something martyred in Fairhrim's expression—that her own mother would suggest such antics with a known Murdery Sort . . .

"Mum, please," said Fairhrim, holding Osric's cloak shut, as Osric stuffed his blood-soaked glove into a pocket. "He's unwell. I'd like to examine him in private."

Radia grew serious. "Oh? Shall we have him lie down? Take him upstairs—oh, but the guest rooms are all taken—"

Aunt Plectrude hobbled out into the foyer. "Where is Aurienne's young man? I was just going to tell him about my collection of taxidermised bits."

"No one wants to hear about your bits," said Radia.

"I want to hear about Aunt Plectrude's bits," said Osric.

The delirium of blood loss was upon him. Everything seemed funny. Also, he was about to faint.

"Let's get him to my room," said Fairhrim. "Stairs. The lift is too far." She was looking at Osric with something very much like worry. Her glove was off. Her tācn glowed with readied seith. She snatched his hand.

A serving boy scuttled past with some kind of steamed pudding.

"Oh," said Radia, "let's send up something sweet with him—bring that here, Arthur. Have a look, Mr. Hungwell. May we tempt you into something naughty?"

Osric wished to say something witty about how the woman holding his hand and dragging him to her bedchamber was the only thing tempting him into Something Naughty. Gods, he was cold. Everyone had their collars open and glistened with a sheen of sweat, and he was frozen. Was this how he was going to die? Hand in hand with Fairhrim on her mother's polished floor?

"Not now," said Fairhrim. "He needs rest. Come on, Mor—er, Osric."

It was lovely to be fussed over, Osric thought. Tartiflette was sent to set a warming pan in Fairhrim's bed. The serving boy held up the pudding for Osric's inspection. Fairhrim's hand squeezed his. He took a step towards her. She was a dreamlike blur in his fading vision. In spite of all her finery, she smelled like herself, like hlutoform and soap. Her eyes were dark with concern, only she hated him, so they weren't, but it was lovely to pretend.

So very lovely.

He fainted face-first into the pudding.

OSRIC FADED IN AND OUT OF AWARENESS. SOMETHING NEW HAPPENED every time he opened his eyes—he was carried into a bedchamber by Fairhrim's relatives—Fairhrim chased everybody out—blackness—sharp pain at his side, followed by coolness—a gentle hand in his hair—blackness again.

Osric came to in a soft-lit room. It was Fairhrim's hands he saw first in his blurred, queasy return to consciousness. She washed them in a basin beside the bed. She scrubbed carefully along fingers, across palms, around nails, up and around wrists. She had overused her seith and triggered her Cost—her knuckles were red and cracked; her fingertips had blistered open; long wounds ran up her wrists. Between his gutting and her hands, this had been a real orgy of self-sacrifice.

Osric watched the glitter of water and the slow, frothy drip of bloody soap, backlit by a yellow lamp. The swan on Fairhrim's palm tilted towards him; its blank, triangular eye observed him between sweeps of white towel. Then came a spray of hlutoform. Fairhrim didn't flinch as she applied it directly to her wounds.

The soft glow came from diagnostic images floating above him.

"Dress—ruined," pointed out Osric.

"Don't talk," said Fairhrim.

"Have I got custard in my hair?"

"You're an idiot," said Fairhrim. Her voice was tight and clipped; she was withholding a high-pressure torrent of further opinions.

"Answer me about the custard."

Fairhrim's withheld torrent found a crack. "Do you know how lucky you are that your bowels weren't perforated? I'm still not certain whether or not I need to involve Cath—"

"Who's Cath?"

"A trauma specialist."

"Short for Catheter, I suppose."

"No. Stop talking." The crack widened; Fairhrim's torrent gushed forth. "What were you thinking? What was the operative theory here, Mr. I'm-Nigh-Untouchable? Well, you certainly got touched. And then what? You thought you'd just . . . hold the blood in? Keep your guts braced through sheer force of will? Flirt with Aunt Plectrude with a knife thrust into you? Find death in a pudding?"

Osric raised a feeble finger. "It seems unfair to tell me to stop talking and then ask questions."

"The questions are rhetorical. Honestly, what's in your head? Close your eyes. Can you manage that? I'll happily sedate you if you can't."

Fairhrim's palm was at his side. The torpraxia didn't affect his ability to feel her seith; it swept into him in cool, controlled pushes. Unlike his seith degeneration, Osric had, this time, presented Fairhrim with a problem that was enormous but solvable—and she solved. He had known that she was brilliant, but he truly understood now what that brilliance meant. Her seith surged into him in a curative wash, impossibly knitting him closed from the inside out.

He was going to be all right, thought Osric as he sank back into unconsciousness and Fairhrim's seith flowed through him.

Blood on her cheek and sharpness on her tongue, she was going to save him.

AURIENNE THE CRIMINAL

Aurienne

After two hours of work, Aurienne, lightheaded from seith depletion, her hands a mess of livid wounds, her neck aching, her favourite dress a blood-splattered disaster, sat back, satisfied; Mordaunt was stable.

Cíele had told her what he'd seen and thus converted her frightened anger into confused gratitude.

Her deofol hovered above Mordaunt's face. His tail swept about restlessly. "I haven't got to get Cath?"

"He'll be fine," said Aurienne. "By some miracle, the blade avoided his intestines."

Mordaunt had been lucky—and therefore she'd been lucky. The complications of a bowel perforation would've been far beyond her scope of practice; if he'd presented with a perforated viscus, she wouldn't have had a choice but to call in Cath.

Cíele ceased his hovering and perched his near-imperceptible weight upon Aurienne's shoulder. "Thank Frīa. Would've been rather difficult to explain to Cath why you've got a wounded Fyren in your childhood bedroom."

"I'm not entirely sure I can explain to myself why I've got a wounded Fyren in my childhood bedroom," said Aurienne.

"Everything happened so fast. He said something about a Fyren headed for Swanstone. He thought you were there. And, given that he didn't know what the other Fyren wanted, he killed him. The Fyren—our Fyren, I mean—didn't even realise he'd been stabbed."

Aurienne contemplated the man, drifting somewhere between unconsciousness and true sleep, lying on her bed. His face was ashen, his hair—she had rinsed off the custard—soaked with new sweat. His left hand, in a blood-crusted glove, lay on his chest. Aurienne had left the glove on, lest any visitors spot his tācn.

"This is mad," said Aurienne.

"I know," said Cíele.

"*He's* mad. He killed one of his own Order."

"And roasted the corpse," added Cíele.

"I find him far more disturbing when he's quiet."

"D'you think it matters to him? Having murdered one of his own?" asked Cíele. "Do you think it's normal for Fyren to kill each other?"

"I don't know how far this strays beyond whatever their code is—if they've even got one."

Cíele fixed Mordaunt with a searching look. Aurienne did the same.

The deofol voiced the question Aurienne hadn't dared ask: "Should we have let him die?"

The answer came more readily than the question had. "I couldn't have."

"I saw," said Cíele. "You saved him before you even knew what he'd done."

"Seeing him so hurt was—it was—"

Aurienne stopped trying to describe it, because words were insufficient. No utterance could capture the fear she'd felt when she had pulled off his blood-soaked cloak and understood how close he was to Hel's final embrace. The touch of his fevered hands had no grammar; there was no orthography to the pain of her heart squeeze.

At the edges of all this emotion lapped, as always, little waves of reason. She owed him healing only for the seith rot; he was a Fyren; hundreds had died because of him, and now, because of her, he would go on to kill hundreds more. Had she done Right? Had she done Good?

Cíele's red eyes were on Aurienne. He sat with all four paws gathered below him, unusually still.

"He's more important to me than I would wish him to be," said Aurienne.

"For what it's worth, I think you're more important to him than he'd like you to be, too."

"*Important* is all right," said Aurienne. "*Important* is—justifiable. We're valuable to one another."

"But nothing beyond?"

"Nothing beyond," said Aurienne. "Beyond would be impossible. He is what he is."

"He is what he is," repeated Cíele, with a grave nod.

Aurienne wished that she were satisfied by this conclusion, by this retreat into the safety of definitions, of classifications and structure. Mordaunt was a Fyren. Just a Fyren. But was he *just*? When a man kills one of his own Order for you, nearly gets himself eviscerated for you, shows up half-dead at your door because of you, and collapses into your arms—is he *just*?

When Cíele had first explained what he had seen, Aurienne had felt things she hadn't a name for—or, more honestly, that she didn't want to name. She did not wish to admire the Fyren, to hold him in regard, or to glow with gratitude at the thought of him. And yet, what massacre might the other Fyren have wrought at Swanstone? How many people had Mordaunt saved?

She knew that Mordaunt had sound, perfectly solipsistic reasons to do what he had done, of course. He was protecting his Means to an End. He hadn't done it for her so much as for himself. And yet, he had done an act of Good.

A sigh fluttered Cíele's whiskers. "I'd better go. I'm draining your seith. Your hands already look like you stuck them into a bin of scalpels and waved them about."

"Right. I think I'd still like to consult Cath on management and rehab."

"Is that wise?" asked Cíele. "Won't she ask questions?"

"She will. I'll tell her I can't answer them at the moment. She's the specialist; I've got to make sure I've done everything right. He deserves that much. Will you go to her, and ask if I can see her tomorrow? I think she's in the operating theatre in the morning. I can pop by the pub at lunch."

"Very well," said Cíele. He spun in a solemn circle and disappeared.

When he was gone, Aurienne allowed herself to fix Mordaunt's hair. A living Mordaunt would never permit his hair to be in this state; the mess made him look like he must be dead.

It was the excuse she made for herself, anyway, as she ran her fingertips through silver-white strands.

There was no excuse for brushing a gentle hand along his cheek.

AURIENNE HELD HER CONCERNED FAMILY AT BAY BY TELLING THEM that Mr. Hungwell was out of harm's way, and if they could give her a bit of time alone with him, he would be back on his feet within another day, thank you (this accompanied by a firmly closed door).

What Aurienne really wanted, after this massive seith exertion, was a hot meal, a steaming bath, a massage, and (while she was at it) an orgasm or two, to relax herself into sleep. Instead, she ate cold leftovers in the kitchens and dozed upon an uncomfortable sofa. She regenerated enough seith to fix up the absolute state of her hands and took the way-stone early the next morning to the Publish or Perish.

She left Tartiflette with instructions to stand guard outside Mordaunt's room: no visitors. The man needed rest.

Before meeting up with Cath at the pub, Aurienne stopped at Swanstone for supplies. It was a Saturday, and mercifully quiet in the Centre for Seith Research. Aurienne nevertheless summoned Cíele to stand watch as she slipped into the supply room.

Cíele floated at the door, his tail sweeping back and forth in displeasure. "We're stealing. I hope we don't go to prison. I don't think I'd do well in prison."

"We won't go to prison for a few cannulae and clamps," said Aurienne as she stuffed her satchel with those, along with IV tubing, pain-killing infusions, antibiotics, and packets of powdered bhreue. "My parents' first aid kit is, unfortunately, not quite up to par for our needs."

Also to note: she was now a thief as well as a murderer. Mordaunt really was rubbing off on her.

"What about an infusion stand?" asked Cíele.

"Can't exactly stuff one into my bag," said Aurienne. "I'll work something out at the house—a coatrack or something."

When she had crammed her pilfered stock into her satchel, Aurienne realised that because she kept impeccable inventory at the Centre, she would also have to modify the books to spare herself and other Haelan interrogations from Quincey when the numbers didn't add up.

A bit sweaty about the armpits, Aurienne added forgery to her list of crimes.

A sound made her and Cíele jump. It was only Acts of Warranted Brutality, the black kitten that Mordaunt had found at Wellesley Keep. The kitten hated everyone, including Aurienne, except when she was hungry. She crept out from between shelves and mewled her distinctive meow—less of a meow than an *eep eep*—at Aurienne. Aurienne had nothing to offer and told her to go to the kitchens. Acts of Warranted Brutality turned away in disgust.

"Someone's coming," whispered Cíele.

Quincey's footsteps shuffled along the corridor, preceded by cheerful humming.

Cíele darted out of the supply room to hold him off long enough for Aurienne to close her satchel. She heard Cíele greet Quincey with unusual friendliness (Cíele was, as a rule, not friendly with anyone who wasn't Aurienne). When she joined the two of them in the corridor, Cíele was feigning a profound interest in Quincey's marmalade toast.

"Haelan Fairhrim," said Quincey when Aurienne rounded the corner. "Is something the matter?"

A fair question, given that it was rare for Aurienne to ever be mucking about in the supply room.

Aurienne, unused to being in the wrong, and struggling to recover her self-possession, spoke in a voice approximately four octaves higher than usual: "No, nothing."

"Can I help you find something?"

"No, no—I was merely inspecting."

"An inspection?" asked Quincey. He nearly dropped his toast. "But—but we just conducted an audit. Have you found anything out of order? Anything I can correct?"

"I think the manufacturer recommends that those impregnated gauze pads be kept out of light. I'd move them to one of the drawers."

Quincey took the misplaced gauze pads personally. He wilted over his marmalade. "Right—of course—thank you."

"Otherwise, it's perfect. Well done, you. Enjoy your toast. I'd best crack on; I'm meeting Cath. Goodbye."

Quincey received the compliment with a blush. Aurienne, her satchel bursting with contraband, strode away with exceptional briskness.

A group of villagers was hanging about outside the Publish or

Perish. They greeted Aurienne with respectful bows. She heard their conversation pick up again after her passage; there had been a Mysterious Incident in the village the night before—loads of screaming and blood, no bodies found, but a peculiar smell of burnt pork had lingered all night.

Aurienne wouldn't know anything about that.

Neither did Cath, who was sitting in a back corner of the pub, putting away a curry, and blessedly out of earshot of the villagers. She sat with Felicette, the Ingenaut-in-residence who maintained and developed Swanstone's seith-powered equipment, and occasionally introduced less popular advancements, such as the sentient charts.

The chimes at the door of the Publish or Perish consisted of a dozen stirring rods all tied together. Aurienne's presence was announced by their metallic clang. She returned waves from the Paeds matron, Breage, and a few nurses and fellow Haelan. She received bows from apprentices swallowing lunchtime pints and pies, and nods from a few village grannies setting the world to rights over their cups of tea.

The walls and ceiling of the Publish or Perish were plastered with scientific papers produced by Swanstone—accepted papers, rejected papers, papers scribbled all over with notes, first drafts, final editions. Aurienne's works were there, too, pasted in during celebratory rounds or dejected rejection pints. A few cheeky scholars had even glued in full books, the pages of which fluttered amid the pong of fried fish and onions, and added their own esoteric whiff to the place. The walls of the Publish or Perish were thus always interesting to stare at; even in their most drunken stupors, patrons always Learned Something.

At the counter, Aurienne flagged down old Grette, the publican. Instead of her usual small ale, Aurienne asked for an entire bottle of Rathcroghan's Fortified Wine, calculated to please Cath.

"You're going to get absolutely wankered," said Grette, who fancied herself an oracle as well as a publican.

"I thought you'd be proud of me," said Aurienne. "You take the piss out of my usual."

"If I took the piss out of your usual, it wouldn't have any flavour at all," said Grette.

She handed over the bottle; Aurienne pondered how much urine she had ingested in her lifetime.

"Here," said Grette, softening the blow by handing Aurienne a plate of bread-and-butter pudding. "Last piece—have it before it goes stale. On the house."

"You're sure you don't want it yourself?"

"Milk gives me wet shits."

Grette placed the pudding on a tray, upon which she arranged some deformed glassware in lieu of cups. Her husband was the Haelan Order's glassmaker; pieces that were flawed or otherwise didn't reach the quality standards set by Swanstone's laboratories were put to use in the pub.

Aurienne took her tray and bottle, and approached Cath with her bribe.

Cath kept her head shaved because of her Cost, which caused hair loss. On days when she had triggered it, she hadn't any eyebrows, either, and painted them on in various colours. Today, they were an iridescent shade of mauve.

Felicette was observing something under a large, illuminated magnifying glass.

"Felicette has made friends with a fly," said Cath, drily, to Aurienne.

"Our conceptualisation of sight is pathetically simplistic," said Felicette. "They can teach us so much."

The fly flew off; Felicette followed it with her magnifying glass held high.

"What's this for?" asked Cath when Aurienne placed the bottle of Rathcroghan's Fortified before her.

"Buying."

"What?"

"Your silence."

Cath's brow shimmered an interrogative purple. "Continue."

Aurienne sat. She served Cath and herself in a crippled beaker and a wonky flask, respectively. Cath took a generous swig of her wine. Aurienne was more careful; Rathcroghan's Fortified consisted of wine, brandy, caffeine, and the potential to reduce Aurienne to a talking pile of vomit.

"I need your advice on wound management," said Aurienne. "But it's top secret, and I will deny that we had this conversation."

Cath's eyes, edged with impeccably sharp purple wing tips, narrowed at Aurienne. "What sort of wound?"

"Penetrating abdominal trauma," said Aurienne.

"Ooh," said Cath. "My favourite."

"The individual was impaled by something long and metallic."

"If they were stabbed, you can just say so," said Cath.

"I can't," said Aurienne. "You'd have to report it."

"*You* ought to be reporting it," said Cath.

"Yes, which is why I will deny having had this conversation," said Aurienne.

She explained what she had done so far, accompanying the explanation with a diagram on a napkin to demonstrate the curve of organs and the knife's near penetration thereof.

She thought the diagram masterful and clear, but Cath asked, "Why have you drawn a tit wank?" and offended her.

"It's not a tit wank."

"That's a cheeky cock."

"That's the kni—er, the implement."

Cath set aside the tit wank. "You're positive that there was no perforation of the intestinal tract?"

"None."

"You've closed him up?"

"Yes."

"He's hemodynamically stable?"

"Yes."

"No signs of peritonitis?"

"No. It's early, but no."

"Antibiotics, analgesics, and observation, then," said Cath. "But if you notice any signs of clinical deterioration, you're to shut down your illicit personal hospital immediately. I'll send my deofol to check in on you."

"No, no," said Aurienne. "Don't send your deofol."

"How else d'you want me to reach you? Cork up a message in a bottle and fling it into the sea?"

"I'll send mine if I need you."

Cath, looking suspiciously at Aurienne over the edge of her beaker, drank. Aurienne watched the liquid descend from two hundred fifty millilitres to ninety millilitres.

"How did this patient come into your care?" asked Cath.

"He's not a patient," said Aurienne. "And I can't tell you."

Again came the shimmer of a brow. "Not a patient? But you're caring for him?"

"Yes."

"What's so special about this nonpatient?"

"Nothing."

"He's special enough to make you break the rules." Cath rapped her fingertips against her defective beaker. "Do you *care* care for him?"

Aurienne, suddenly rigid, replied: "Absolutely not."

"Where is he?"

"At my parents' house."

Cath's eyebrows became acrobatic. "Was your mother the one who stabbed him?"

"No."

"You're sure? She'd have it in her."

"You must stop asking questions."

"You'd be all in a lather if I did this to you," said Cath.

"Foaming at the mouth," agreed Aurienne.

Cath took another pull at her beaker, whose contents had now descended to forty millilitres, with no noticeable impact on her cognitive functions. Aurienne was impressed; the fumes alone were making her lightheaded.

Cath leaned back and said meditatively: "If Aurienne Bloody Fairhrim is breaking the rules, there has to be a good reason. I won't ask any more questions."

"Thank you," said Aurienne.

"You're not welcome. Your lack of trust offends me."

"I'm sorry."

"Shall I be quite honest?"

Aurienne, who would actually prefer Cath not be honest at all, nodded.

"Your secrecy reminds me of the situation with the Hedgewitch," said Cath.

"Too honest," said Aurienne.

"Sorry," said Cath.

Aurienne watched broken bits of star anise float about asymmetrically in her flask. She had a sip. It tasted like despair. The perturbing thing—the miserable thing—was that Cath wasn't wrong. There were certain parallels. This was how it had begun with Amagris. Furtive attractions. Illicit rendezvous with someone from another Order, outside the scope of her duties as a Haelan. Was she headed towards the old error by new paths?

No. She was older and wiser now. Besides, she had loved Amagris. She could not love Mordaunt.

"I would betake myself to the scaffold before letting that happen again," said Aurienne.

Cath, serious now, reached across the table and squeezed her forearm. Aurienne stared at the wall and learned about intracerebral haemorrhages.

The cluster of stirring rods at the pub's door jingled, heralding the entrance of Élodie. She floated towards Aurienne and Cath, nymphlike, with her Haelan whites drifting behind her in ways Aurienne's never did.

Constitutionally incapable of walking anywhere without picking flowers, Élodie approached with a roadside bouquet of alliums, which she examined while muttering about their resemblance to spike glycoproteins.

Aurienne, who had been wilting over her wine as pathetically as Quincey over his marmalade, sat up and said, "New dress. Lovely."

"I put it on just to fascinate you," said Élodie.

"It's working."

Élodie spun. Aurienne kissed fingertips her way. Cath said, "Stop flirting with my fiancée."

"Mightn't I join your marriage?" asked Aurienne.

Élodie drifted into her chair. "I thought you'd sworn off love?"

"Right. I did."

Élodie slipped an allium behind Aurienne's ear. "Stupid idea, but I suppose even you must have those on occasion."

Cath's glance towards Aurienne suggested, for example, secretly healing a Mysterious Stabbed Man.

Aurienne, who had come for a consult, and not repeated deep cuts to her psyche, said, "I've got to go."

"Aren't you meant to be in London?" asked Élodie. "Or were you called in for the novitiate assessment?"

"I'm meant to be in London, and I'm going back there now. I'm not on this assessment rotation."

"You'll miss all the adorable baby deofols. Last time there was a fawn. But wait—sit. You mustn't leave just yet. You've got to celebrate with me."

Aurienne sat. Élodie waved Grette down for an additional glass, which came in the form of a U-shaped absorption tube.

Aurienne poured wine into the tube. "What are we celebrating?"

"We've got a vaccine candidate," said Élodie.

"What?" gasped Aurienne.

"Incredible," said Cath.

They each planted a kiss upon Élodie's dimpled cheeks. The flask, the wonky beaker, and the absorption tube came together in a cheerful clatter, with cries of "Bravo!" and "Cheers!"

"Official announcements to follow," said Élodie. "But I wanted to give you *la primeur de la nouvelle*—the what's-it-called—the scoop."

"The nightmare is drawing to a close," said Aurienne.

Cath topped up their glasses and, having run out of room in hers, drained the bottle into her mouth.

Élodie caught sight of Aurienne's diagram. "Who's been drawing penises?"

"Aurienne was explaining her plans for the evening," said Cath.

"*Félicitations,*" said Élodie. "Is he as well-endowed in good humour as he is in girth?"

"It's not a penis," said Aurienne, snatching the napkin from Élodie.

She left Élodie perplexed and Cath cackling into her beaker.

BACK AT MORDAUNT'S BEDSIDE, AURIENNE OFF-LOADED HER PILFERED goods onto his (her) bedside table. She descended to the kitchen to fetch boiling water for a few doses of bhreue. Mordaunt was awake when she returned—still not quite himself; his eyes were unfocused and his greeting was uncharacteristically affectionate ("You're back. I missed you").

Aurienne stirred powdered bhreue into a mug. "I'm pleased you're awake. You're to drink this."

"You brought me a flower," said Mordaunt, holding up Élodie's allium.

There were tears in his eyes. Aurienne did not correct him, given that he might actually cry. She, however, was fighting down the bubbling of hysterical laughter.

"You may keep the flower if you finish this," said Aurienne.

She helped Mordaunt higher onto the pillows and tilted the mug towards him. Mordaunt—unusually docile—drank.

After three or four sips, he grimaced, and said, "I've got to tell you, darling, this is awful."

"It's bhreue—it's very nutritious. It'll help you recover. Don't call me darling."

Aurienne put together an impromptu IV stand by removing the shade from a tall lamp.

Mordaunt gave Aurienne what she interpreted as an eyebrow wiggle. "I found your note."

"My note?"

"Well, your diagram." Mordaunt fished about on the table upon which Aurienne had dumped her ill-gotten gains. He held up the napkin. "Is this . . . what you want to do?"

"It's what I did," said Aurienne. "I was explaining the procedure to Cath."

"The procedure?"

"Yes."

"You've already done it?"

"Yes."

"With me? Last night?"

"Yes."

Mordaunt looked pouty. "You might have waited until I was conscious, so I could enjoy it, too."

Aurienne stopped untangling tubing, because it dawned on her that she was, once again, being haunted by the tit wank. "It's not a tit wank."

"It's a tit wank," said Mordaunt.

"That's not a penis," said Aurienne. "It's a blaecblade. And those are semilunar folds, not tits."

Mordaunt, argumentative even in delirium, said, "The tits have got nipples."

"Those are omental appendices, not nipples."

Mordaunt's eyes were closed. His voice had gone soft; he was fading into sleep. "I'd do it if you wanted to—"

"I don't want to."

"—but I'd really rather be suffocated by your thighs."

He fell asleep. Aurienne bustled about with the homemade infusion stand.

Hundreds, thousands, of idiotic things had been said to her by half-conscious patients over the years.

This marked the first time she felt the warmth of a blush on her cheeks.

THAT NIGHT, WHEN MORDAUNT HAD FALLEN ASLEEP, AURIENNE DREW herself the bath she had desired all day. She sank into the hot water for a well-deserved soak. Amid the fragrance of lavender sachets and soapy steam, her stresses melted away—mostly. Two knots in her upper back would remain until she died, probably. She ought to name them Mordaunt One and Two.

Mordaunt was doing much better, however. That was the principal thing. And she had got advice from Cath on his care without having disclosed too much about who, exactly, she was healing. A bloody Fyren. There was a Fyren presently asleep in her childhood bed. Mad. Her mother would kill her.

It was—Frīa forgive her for this thought—in many ways a great pity he was a Fyren. He had a quick wit—intermittently charming, more oft mocking, but well matched to hers. He was considerably competent and wasn't deficient physically (quite the contrary, unfortunately). He was well educated, though with a questionable specialisation. Mannered, though occasionally caddish. And he trod the fine line between expertise and arrogance. Aurienne supposed people could say the same about her.

She sighed and sank deeper into the tub. He was what he was.

She was tired. She was stiff.

She wanted an orgasm.

Moreover, she deserved one.

She closed her eyes. Her hand travelled from the edge of the bathtub to her breast, brushed at a wet nipple, and slipped between her legs. The ceiling faded away and was replaced, a bit unusually for her, with the idea of a man between her legs. She paid him little heed other than the novelty of it. He was nondescript; his face was a blur; all that mattered was his capable tongue moving back and forth in a rhythm matching her fingers. She leaned her head back and pressed her palm against herself in small circles. The gentle climb towards orgasm began. Her breathing came heavier; her breasts rose and fell in little movements, an inch above and an inch below the waterline, pleasantly stimulating her nipples with the switch between hot and cold. She was getting close. Behind her closed eyelids she put her hand in the man's hair and guided him upwards a bit, a little to the left, please, and harder. Her fingers matched her command. Her heartbeat accelerated. She was beginning to crest.

That was when she noticed the man's hands clasping her thighs. He wore black leather gloves. And his hair—

"No," gasped Aurienne, but it was too late. She was over the edge.

She came, unwilling, pulsing with horror and pleasure and horror and pleasure, knowing exactly who she had come to.

She lay in silence, breathing hard, staring at the ceiling, slick and swollen with the memory of him.

When she had towelled off, and got over the shock, Aurienne told herself, with supreme conviction, that it meant nothing. It had been scratching an itch. Mordaunt and his stupid comment from earlier happened to be on her mind; that was all.

She would never think about it again.

She was very good at compartmentalising.

SHARING YOUR TRAGIC BACKSTORY WITH YOUR HOT ENEMY

Osric

When Osric next awoke, Fairhrim was beside him. She had returned to her usual whites, but in the form of a soft, high-waisted dress. Her hair was in a loose, curling knot at the base of her neck. Her edges were still there, however—her posture was perfect; her shoulders were square beneath gauzy fabric.

Fairhrim saw that he was awake. With a surprising lack of edge, she said, "Someone once told me it's rude to stare."

"Not sure I've got the strength to turn my head," said Osric. It was mostly true. "Are we alone?"

"Yes."

"What time is it?" asked Osric, his voice a weak rasp.

"Half past two, two days after. How are you?"

"In grand fettle," said Osric.

"How's your pain?"

"Feel like I got filleted."

"You'll have a new scar for your collection."

"What's all this I'm tied up with?" asked Osric, lifting a hand from which tubing emerged. "Why am I so tubey? Why am I entubed?"

"Plasma volume expanders. Intravenous antibiotics. I'll take you off them soon."

"Lucky your parents had all this handy."

"They didn't," said Fairhrim. "I stole it from Swanstone."

"You stole?"

"Don't be smug."

"*You're* the common thief."

Fairhrim gave him the sort of look that could skewer a man fifty paces out.

Osric ceased his teasing, given that he already suffered from one grievous injury.

He lifted his weak, entubed hand. "How long will I be this useless?"

"I'll give you recommendations to shorten your convalescence," said Fairhrim. "Abide by them and you may be ambulatory again within two or three days."

"Two or three days? I haven't got *days*."

"Oh, yes, you have. Here." Fairhrim handed Osric pills and a glass of water.

"What are these?" asked Osric.

"A dose of reality."

"You aren't funny."

"They're for the pain. Also, a stool softener."

"Brilliant," said Osric. "I love the idea of you worrying about the softness of my stool."

"I'm not worried about it; you're on stool softeners."

Osric swallowed the pills along with his dignity. Just what he wanted: Fairhrim's solicitude over hard poos. He felt about where the blaecblade had impaled him. "Am I all closed up?"

"Yes."

"Are my guts where they should be?"

"Yes."

"Thank you," blurted Osric.

He didn't like that. The blurting. He preferred his words, like his murders, nice and premeditated.

Fairhrim folded her hands together. Then she moved them to her thighs. Then she brought them together again. She, who always decidedly knew how she felt and did not hesitate to express it, seemed to not know how to feel or how to express it.

Finally, she sat herself at the foot of the bed and said, "I'm the one who owes you thanks. My deofol told me what he saw. So—so thank *you*."

She looked as uncomfortable as he had felt with thanks—only his had been expelled, like thanks-vomit, whereas hers had needed to be pushed, like thanks-constipation. He ought to propose a stool softener to her, for her mouth.

Anyway, Osric was gratified. "All in a day's work."

"You're mad," said Fairhrim. "You killed one of your own Order."

"Fairhrim?"

"Yes?"

"Sometimes violence really is the answer."

Fairhrim didn't disagree with him. Perhaps she was being nice because he was still convalescing. She did have a weakness for invalids.

"Though, to be technical about it, he landed the finishing blow himself," added Osric.

"Will you explain what happened, from the beginning?" asked Fairhrim.

She sat straight backed and attentive as Osric explained, starting with the gargling of the baubles, and ending with Brythe's spiteful suicide.

Fairhrim stared at him for a long time, expressionless save for a new, peculiar gravity in her eyes.

"I will never reject your deofol again," said Fairhrim. "And I'm sorry I did."

Osric felt that he had won something—but what it was, he wasn't sure.

Fairhrim looked at her hands, rather than at Osric, and said, "You almost died."

"Am I detecting concern?" asked Osric, delighted.

"You're in my care. And you put yourself at great risk."

"I hadn't a choice. There was a chance that he might kill you—and if you die, I die. Couldn't let that happen."

"I understand."

"I've still got a use for you."

"Of course."

"It was pure self-interest."

Fairhrim appeared to consider smiling. "There is no occasion in which I would imagine you acting out of anything other than pure self-interest."

Satisfied that they had mutually established that they didn't care about each other beyond professional necessity (her) and personal agenda (him), Osric said, "Can't believe you were faffing off at the opera. Had no idea you weren't at Swanstone. Could've spared myself the disembowelment."

"There's one less Fyren in the world," said Fairhrim, looking pleased at the prospect.

"He was instructed to wring necks at Swanstone until he found an answer, only I don't know what the question was."

Fairhrim shifted on the bed. Osric felt her weight against his shin. Her seriousness returned. "Our Orders have their differences, but we never directly attack one another. We simply don't. You know the Peace Accords. It would destabilise things."

"I know."

"Do you think this has to do with the other infiltration attempt?"

"If it does, it means Wellesley was just a pawn. Whoever it is has moved on to another level if they're hiring Fyren. They must be bloody flush. I don't see how else they would've convinced Tristane to take it on."

"Tristane?" asked Fairhrim.

"My warchief," said Osric. "Also the most lethal Fyren in existence. Might be Hel herself, walking among us."

"How long have we got before Brythe's death is discovered?"

"I didn't leave a body. They'll never know if he simply fucked off. Tristane will start asking questions when he doesn't report back. We've probably got a week or so before she realises something's wrong."

"What will she do?" asked Fairhrim.

"Rage. Send someone else. Go herself. I don't know."

"I've got to warn Xanthe," said Fairhrim. "We'll take additional protective measures."

"Be careful with your measures," said Osric. "It'll be suspicious if Swanstone is suddenly swarming with Wardens and lit up like it's Yule. Tristane can't suspect there was a leak."

Fairhrim made a sound of agreement. She rose and fetched a sort of wrist brace. "Let's get this on you."

"What's it for?" asked Osric.

"To hide your tācn for now," said Fairhrim, slipping the brace over his left hand. "We'll say you injured your wrist when you fainted. It covers your palm."

"Ah."

"We'll have to get you new gloves. Yours are rather on the crusty side."

"I'll send my deofol to Mrs. Parson for clothes."

"I've tucked your things under there," said Fairhrim, pointing to a floorboard. "Including Brythe's and your blaecblades. My mother mustn't know how close she is to real blaec."

"Floorboard. Classic."

"Gloriously predictable, as you once said. What's the meaning behind the gold threads?"

"Which?"

"The ones that wrap around the hilts of the blaecblades. I noticed yours and Brythe's had different amounts."

"Oh, those. They're a marker of, erm—rank."

"I thought they might be." Fairhrim nodded. "Thought it could denote years of service, like Haelan wings, only you can't have over eight hundred years of service, so what are they counting?"

Osric took too long to fabricate an answer. Fairhrim stared at him, then said, "Gods. It's kills, isn't it?"

"Ask me no questions and I shall tell you no lies."

Fairhrim gave no answer but a resigned sigh. She cocked a hip against a sofa and shoved it over the floorboard. "Rest while you can. There'll be a stream of curious relatives itching to see you. I'll do my best to stem the flow."

"Why are there so many relatives here?"

"The party."

"What party?"

"My parents' fortieth anniversary party is in a few days. They decided to make a Thing of it." Fairhrim looked as though she had opinions on parties and Things. "Now, if you want to get better quickly, you need to rest. I'll leave you."

"I'm sorry about your dress."

"It doesn't matter."

"At least it wasn't one of your usual perfect white ones."

"Haelan whites are made of an impermeable polymer. They don't stain."

"Oh."

"Sleep," said Fairhrim.

She strode towards the door.

"Fairhrim?" called Osric.

"What?"

"What's an episiotomy scissor?"

320

"It's used in childbirth."

"A scissor? In childbirth? What for?"

"Cutting the perineum, between the vagina and anus."

Having delivered this newest eight-word horror story, Fairhrim quit the room, taking whatever was left of Osric's innocence with her.

IT WAS GOOD FUN BEING FAIRHRIM'S AILING FRIEND. IT OBLIGED HER TO be kind to him whenever there were others present, which was a nice change, and one he took advantage of (it was unnatural, pleasurably novel). It also provided endless scope to annoy her, while forcing her to keep the most cutting of her remarks to herself.

She disbursed them liberally upon him whenever they were alone, however. That night, feeling considerably better, Osric asked for a Scotch, of the same bottle, preferably, as the one he had been served from the night of the opera. Fairhrim told him that if he was feeling well enough for a Scotch, he could go fetch it himself instead of lying there twitching his mandibles at her like some sort of larva.

Her childhood bedroom held a single bed, the sofa, and the spirit of young Fairhrim. On the walls were botanical plates and framed pages torn from medical texts—illustrations of humans and animals in various states of dissection. ("Yes," said Fairhrim, when she saw Osric observing them, "I disappointed my mother early by being more interested in the biological sciences than the harder stuff. Too whimsical, she said.")

There was a balcony at the far end of the room, giving onto the back garden. The favourite activity of Osric's guests was to come in and throw the curtains open with gasps about the salubriousness of the sun; he stumbled up after they were gone to draw them closed again.

For the benefit of Osric's visitors, Fairhrim made up a complicated Syndrome that explained his collapse and long recovery. No one questioned her—she was a Haelan, after all—but Radia remarked with a sniff that they invented a new Syndrome every day. To explain his constant wearing of gloves to hide a rather telling tācn, Fairhrim declared that he had eczema.

Osric got to know Fairhrim's parents through their visits to his suite. Radia was a more outgoing version of Fairhrim—intelligent, wry, gleefully critical. She had come to the Tīendoms from the Rif region of Tamazgha as a teenager and earned her tācn—as well as a slight Dublin accent—from the Ingenaut Order a few years thereafter. Osric learned that she was the one responsible for the *riche* in *nouveau riche*; she had made her family's fortune by inventing some sort of tube.

"A compression fitting," specified Radia, when Osric called it a tube. "Really, Aurienne, are we certain he hasn't suffered brain damage from his Syndrome?"

Fairhrim's response was a mere tightening of the mouth.

Anyway, the compression fitting was, apparently, now a part of the irrigation booms used by every farmer in the Tīendoms, and so the tube had made the family.

"Poor creature," said Radia, standing at the foot of Osric's bed. "And what about his eczema? Haven't your lot at Swanstone worked out anything better than a salve and gloves?"

"Treatment takes time," said Fairhrim. "Short of transplanting a new set of hands on him, there's nothing to be done but wait."

"That's the problem with human beings," said Radia. "Insufficient spare parts. I've noticed a bit of a limp when he walks, too. Have you looked into it?"

Was this what they were doing? Cataloguing what was wrong with him, and why Fairhrim hadn't fixed it?

"It's part of his flare-up," said Fairhrim. "He'll get better."

"And mightn't we do something about those scars?" asked Radia, pointing a dissatisfied finger towards Osric's face. "Poor man could've been handsome if he didn't have the blueprint for Carn Euny on his face."

"Mum, kindly stop troubleshooting my guest," said Fairhrim, steering her mother out of the room.

Fairhrim's father was a professor of botany. He was a chatty, bookish sort of man, and the master of a large greenhouse that took over most of the back garden. When he discovered that Osric was possessed of moderate intelligence and was too infirm to run away, he adopted him as a personal companion for his afternoon teas, and spent many hours at his bedside discussing algal mats.

From these conversations, Osric discovered that he was one of a series of occasional Friends whom Fairhrim's parents had met over the years, and that it was expected that he would not be the last. These Friends inevitably made catastrophic errors, such as breathing too loudly, or blinking moistly, or existing, and Fairhrim swept them out of her life as swiftly as she had let them in.

"You're different to Aurienne's usual type, though," said Rosbert. "Bit less tweed on you."

"Oh?"

"Sugar?"

"Four lumps."

"Madman." Rosbert delivered the sugar. "I know you won't trifle with her affections, if she is serious—there's a decency about you."

Osric wished to assure him that between himself and Fairhrim there was no affection to be trifled with whatsoever, but he choked on his tea, because *decency*.

"Don't be modest," said Rosbert. "She's told us all about you. You've apparently saved her from a hostage situation. And you donate to paediatric disease research. And you rescue dogs."

All of which was simultaneously true and strikingly inaccurate.

From her parents Osric saw where Fairhrim got her brains, but her sharpness was entirely her own invention. These were soft people. There was a purity in their hospitality and an innocence in their concern for

Osric that felt foreign. There were no knives here—no plots, no back-stabbing, no need to look over one's shoulder.

On the second day of his convalescence, Osric took Fairhrim's hint about ending his career as a mandible-twitching larva to heart, and began to make forays on his feet. His first was remarkable; he declared to Fairhrim that he was, in fact, ready to leave, then strode to the first available door, swung it open, and walked into the toilet.

"That's the toilet," said Fairhrim, unnecessarily.

The world spun and Osric almost cracked his head open on the toilet bowl, and so he lay back down and decided to try again later.

Exploring the house was an adventure. The mark of the Ingenaut was everywhere. Radia had equipped her home with all of her Order's luxuries and combined them with the artistry of her homeland. Elaborately carved doors swung open as Osric approached. A lift that was a magnificent, soundless marvel of engineering carried him from floor to floor, all gleaming brass levers and bright buttons, decorated with seas and stars. Globes of light etched with geometric patterns recessed into the ceiling when they weren't needed, and descended when required. The corridors used by the servants were camouflaged with mirrors and paintings. Illuminated curio cabinets lined walls. Radia had an extensive collection of timepieces, beautifully polished, one or two of which caught Osric's eye, but she also had an impressive alarm system, so Osric decided to let only his eye be caught, and not his hand.

Fairhrim could have lived a soft life here. She was generally a logical sort, but this was inexplicable: why did she toil and sacrifice at Swanstone and live in a spider-filled attic? Altruism? The toilets here had contraptions that washed one's entire undercarriage. A French import. There was simply no way Swanstone had those. That was what altruism got you: spiders in your arsehole.

At night, Fairhrim slept on the sofa, wrapped in a spare blanket, and dressed in oversized flannel pyjamas that looked as though she'd borrowed them from her father. Osric liked to think that he had recovered from his blood-loss-induced delirium and ceased to find her stunning.

However.

However.

One night—when he was still, he would later tell himself, in the delirium of his recovery—there was one moment—he blamed it on the drugs in his system—one moment—he wasn't himself yet—when he succumbed to a low, terrible weakness.

It was four in the morning. He woke up hard. The dream had involved a woman—possibly Fairhrim, but he preferred to tell himself that he didn't remember.

In normal circumstances, he would have rubbed out a quick wank and gone back to bed, only he was in Fairhrim's room, and Fairhrim was asleep right there.

He did not, in his defence, touch himself.

Not immediately, anyway.

He thought of unsexy things. He thought of disgusting things. He thought of episiotomy scissors. Gangrene. Torn nipples. Mathematics.

His erection remained, achingly hard. His balls felt heavy. He was so aroused that the merest twitch of his hips upwards against the resistance of the sheets made his cock jump. Small blessing: his torpraxia had not advanced to his cock; it could still feel perfectly. Was it a blessing? Perhaps not in this specific moment.

He knew what he wanted to do. He didn't know if he was filthy enough to do it.

Fairhrim was right there. It would be wrong. It would be profane.

He was filthy enough to do it.

He watched her through half-lidded eyes, telling himself, at first, that it was to make sure that she wouldn't wake up while he relieved himself. That was all he was doing: relieving himself. It had nothing to do with her.

He observed her hand, dangling from the sofa as she slept, her tācn half-visible. He—to his shame—imagined that hand running along his cock as he slipped his own hand under the sheets and stroked himself. He watched her breathe. He tightened and relaxed his grip upon himself in keeping with the rise and fall of her chest. He thought of the chapped roughness of her palm along the underside of his erection. Thought of her fingers swirling around his head as he mirrored the movement under the sheets. Thought of her lips next, kissing their way upwards, and then opening—

Gods. He was disgusting. He was abhorrent. She had just saved his life, and slept exhausted next to him, and this was how he repaid her?

He continued his imaginings. Her lips—that tongue that she wielded so masterfully against him in their verbal spars—ran up his shaft. His cock jumped under the sheets; pre-come dribbled onto a knuckle. He was ashamed. His cock throbbed. He imagined her breath feathering across his wet tip. His hips bucked. This was obscene. He should stop.

He tried to stop. Saw the outline of her hip in the dark. Stroked himself again. Slipped into a new phantasm. His mouth on her hip, kissing and biting its way to the delicious inside of a thigh, then dragging wet kisses upwards. Pulling away her underthings. Delving into her, tasting her, intoxicating himself on her arousal, smearing it all over his mouth and chin. The press of thighs on either side of his head. Fairhrim sighed in her sleep. He imagined that her lips parted thus because of his tongue. Trembled. Gave himself a final stroke. His free hand gripped sheets, grasped at something—anything—on the bedside table to catch his come. He found a bit of napkin. Held back a gasp. White light bloomed behind his eyelids.

His orgasm came in bursts of guilt and pleasure. He rode it out in silence as he spilled himself into the napkin. When the pleasure-guilt pulses twitched out their last in his fist, he stared at the ceiling. Recovered his breathing. Found that his face was burning.

He wiped the evidence of his shame off his cock and noticed that the napkin was *that* napkin. He hoped that Fairhrim wouldn't have need of her diagram anymore.

Gods.

Her father had called him decent.

Gods.

It was all right. It would be fine. No one had witnessed his solitary indecency. No harm could come of it.

The only problem was that there now lived, in his head, visions of Fairhrim that should never have been there, and that he knew he wanted to see again.

FOUR DAYS AFTER OSRIC'S ILL-FATED ARRIVAL UPON RADIA AND ROS-bert's doorstep, it was the night of the party. The back garden was turned into a green and gold arbour lit up with free-floating lamps. Fairhrim friends and relatives showed up en masse and ate, and drank, and danced. Over it all lay the scent of greenhouse blooms and the glamour of a perfect June evening.

Osric watched the goings-on from the shadows of the balcony. Fairhrim's parents had invited him to attend, but she had flashed him a look that said *Don't you dare*, and Osric had declined. They sent Tarti-flette up with bites of food from the party, as well as a pity bottle of Scotch. Fairhrim had flashed Osric a second look, and warned him that he could have two drinks, and not more. It was a miracle that he hadn't gone blind from all these flashes of hers. She was a bloody heliograph.

It was a tranquil way to pass an evening, anyway: eyeballing the jewels on the hands of various aunts, watching Fairhrim, counting how many drinks Uncle Pilheard downed, watching Fairhrim, assessing the string quartet, watching Fairhrim . . .

Why was he watching Fairhrim? Oh, many reasons. Because it was interesting to see her outside the usual context of dusty clinics. Because she danced unexpectedly well. Because there was nothing better to do. Because he actually had brain damage from the Syndrome.

If it wasn't for the fact that it was Fairhrim whom he was observing so attentively, he could almost think he fancied her. What a joke that would be. What a celestial irony.

It was clear, from Fairhrim's spinning about the garden in the arms of others, and kissing cheeks, and laughing, that she was well liked, even well loved.

Fairhrim bestowed swift smiles on all who asked her to dance (point of interest: she never bestowed swift smiles on Osric) and left behind her a trail of discarded adorers as she moved from one to the next. They were all underbred youngbloods with nothing to recommend them; Osric was far more handsome. And richer.

Poor Tartiflette kept coming upstairs with offerings for Osric. This time she joined him on the balcony with oblong brown things on a plate, like some sort of poo sommelier.

"Thank you," said Osric.

The brown things were chocolates. Tartiflette gurgled in an agony of lovestruck shyness and left again.

Osric watched Fairhrim release the chinless wonder she was dancing with and move on to another. This one was tall. Admittedly good-looking. Love-light in his eyes. Presently dancing with Fairhrim for a third time. Osric was taken over by a savage jealousy.

It was the Season of Betrayal.

No. One couldn't get possessive over a thing that wasn't one's to begin with—and that one had no desire to possess anyway. That would be ridiculous. Osric went back to watching the aunts to decide if anything was worth stealing, due to a sudden, unrelated-to-Fairhrim, urge to join the party. A solid gold torc caught his eye, as did a jewelled lorgnette.

He stress-ate chocolate.

Where had Fairhrim got to?

There she was—at the door of the bedroom, rapping her distinct knock.

Osric had known, of course, having watched her below, that she was wearing a lovely champagne gown, and had gathered her dark hair in a crown braid with orchids tucked into it, but it didn't lessen the shock when she came in looking not at all like the Haelan and looking, instead, fresh, sylphidine, and very much beautiful.

Not beautiful. Just pretty.

Just pretty.

Osric did not want Fairhrim to be beautiful. He was susceptible to beauty. He was an Appreciator of beautiful things. He wanted to acquire them. He wanted them to be his. Now, as Fairhrim neared, he fought a momentary panic that his beauty-loving heart would want Fairhrim in any way, that her loveliness tonight would trigger some latent kleptomaniac urge.

He hated Fairhrim. Ergo, she was not beautiful. This was the only solution; the cognitive dissonance would be unbearable otherwise.

He conceded a vast prettiness that took her to the very edge of beauty. Besides, this was temporary. Soon the night would be over, and Fairhrim would return to the choke of her high-necked dress and her usual froideur, and be the Haelan again. This was a moment as ephemeral as the orchids in her hair.

Also—*also*—he wouldn't be attracted to her because she wasn't attracted to him. One-sided attraction was a power differential he used to his advantage, and he did not wish to be on the receiving end of any such thing from Fairhrim.

There was a totter in Fairhrim's step. She was loose limbed from a few drinks. The flush of the dance was on her cheeks. (Most certainly the dance, and not the influence of the Tall Good-Looking Other Man.)

She joined Osric at the railing and, with unlooked-for familiarity, put a hand on his arm to hold herself up as she took off her shoes.

It struck him; it threw him off-kilter; it made him daring; it made him stupid.

He found himself torn between saying things ugly and beautiful, between lies and truth.

"You look—you look—" he began.

"Not objectionable?" came the breezy suggestion.

"Yes."

"I saw you lurking up here," said Fairhrim, her voice still warm with whatever she had been smiling about with the Tall Other Man. "Pleased you've been able to stand for so long. How are you feeling?"

"Lonely."

"Lonely? You? You hate everyone."

"Do I?"

"Don't you?"

"You're right—I do."

Fairhrim adjusted long gloves that went past her elbows. "I suppose we look like we're having too much fun. You can come down if you wish, only promise you won't exert yourself—and keep the bloody tācn covered."

Osric, however, had no reason to go down, now that Fairhrim was up here. "Who was your overly handsome partner?"

"Which?" Fairhrim looked over the balcony. "Oh—Aedan?"

"Is it?"

"Sweet Aedan," said Fairhrim. She propped her elbows upon the railing. "My mother's still not forgiven me for not marrying him; he's caring, and wealthy, and an Ingenaut."

Osric made some calculations and concluded that he hit a solid one out of three on Fairhrim's mum's marking scheme for desirable husbands. Not that he had any wish to be a desirable husband; it was simply good to know where one stood.

Tartiflette's timorous knock rang and she brought in a single trembling flute of champagne. Osric, still working on his Scotch, declined. Fairhrim took the flute with a pitying look at Tartiflette as she left.

"If only she knew what you are," said Fairhrim.

"Wouldn't matter," said Osric. "I'm irresistible."

Fairhrim, with offensive tranquillity, said, "Load of rot."

She watched Sweet Aedan below with a gaze that was remote. At least when she looked at Osric, there was a spark of something there—vast irritation, usually, but still, something. This detachment would kill him.

"Sweet Aedan looks as though he still carries a flame for you," said Osric.

"I've told him I have a new Friend—a Friend at this very party. And yet . . ."

"I suppose this is but a small sample of your prospects," said Osric with a gesture to the adorers.

"There are no prospects," said Fairhrim. "I loved once. It was a mistake. It will never happen again."

"I'm intrigued."

"I won't tell you what orifice to stuff your intrigue into," said Fairhrim. "Stop prying, or I shall pry at you in return."

"I haven't anything to hide," said Osric.

"No? No tales of past heartbreaks?"

"No heart to break," said Osric. "I'm safe."

Fairhrim sipped at her drink. She touched her neck, tense jawed. "Wise of you."

"What happened between you and Perfect Aedan?" asked Osric. Before Fairhrim could snarl at him for his continued curiosity, he made a sweeping invitational gesture towards himself. "And yes—you may pry at me in return. You may even go first."

"May I? So kind."

"Ask me whatever you'd like."

"Anything?"

"Anything."

Fairhrim pondered her question, one finger running up and down the stem of her champagne flute. Osric prepared to discuss the details of his most lurid affairs in such a way as to spotlight his prowess as a lover.

Then Fairhrim asked: "Why did you kill your father?"

Which was not at all where Osric had wanted this to go.

"I had hoped," said Osric, "that we could confine the conversation to our lovers."

"You said *anything*," pointed out Fairhrim, as though Osric weren't suddenly and acutely aware of his strategic misstep. "But we needn't see this through. We can withdraw our pryings by mutual agreement."

"My father was a bastard," said Osric.

"In which sense of the term?" enquired Fairhrim.

"Metaphorical. I, however, am a bastard in the literal sense."

Fairhrim was strong; he offered her an overture to indicate that she thought he fit both definitions quite neatly, but she made no comment.

"My father, of the great Mordaunt line, refused to marry my mother when she fell pregnant. Said I wasn't his. Her family—minor nobility, Wessexian—disowned her. We lived in absolute poverty while father had thirty rooms at Rosefell in which he got drunk every night. His lowliest under-housemaid ate more in a day than we did in a week. The housekeeper snuck food to us on her off days."

"Mrs. Parson?" asked Fairhrim.

"Yes. My mother brought me to my father every few years to ask him to recognise me as his son—he never did, even as I grew into his spitting image—and to get a few thrymsas out of him. He gave us beatings along with the thrymsas. The very last time he tried to beat us, I had begun to apprentice with Tristane. He didn't know. Neither did my mother, for that matter. I hadn't yet earned my blaecblade or my tācn, but I had learned to handle a knife. He had just thrown my mother into a wall. He went for my throat; I went for his. Mother never woke up. Father died by my hand. I was fourteen years old."

Fairhrim studied Osric for a long time in silence. "I suppose I didn't expect it to be a happy story."

"Does the tragedy of it all absolve me of my sins?"

"An explanation isn't an excuse."

Classic Fairhrim rationalism. "It *is* a happy story, anyway," continued Osric. "I'm happy now."

"Your poor mother."

"Avenged and not forgotten."

"This explains why some of your scars are so old," said Fairhrim. "Old enough to precede your career, I mean."

"He did have a knack for decorating us both," said Osric.

"How did you end up with Rosefell Hall if you were a bastard?"

"Terrorised father's legal man into forging documents legitimising my birth. Killed him later to be safe. Hired tutors and masters to learn how to be a nobleman's son—whatever my mother hadn't been able to teach me. Father had pissed away most of the family fortune; I've been rebuilding it ever since. Until you. Now I'm basically destitute."

Fairhrim was not as pity struck as he would have hoped. She served him a look tinctured with criticism rather than sympathy. "You're far from destitute."

"I'm far from as rich as I was, too."

"Sell your collections."

"Unmerciful creature," said Osric.

"I'll buy the *De humani* off you."

"You couldn't afford it," said Osric.

"Try me."

"Another time. It's your turn now. You must tell me what happened between you and Sweet Aedan."

"Between me and Sweet Aedan," repeated Fairhrim, with a look towards the man in question, who danced below. "Nothing happened. That was, perhaps, the problem. There was no quarrel; there was no explosion. Aedan is too perfect. He has no faults to love him by."

"You require faults in your lovers?"

"One or two, judiciously chosen."

"Hah," said Osric, who had many to choose from. Not that he wished to be her lover; it was simply a fact.

An enquiring eyebrow curved Osric's way over a bare shoulder.

"Never mind," said Osric. "A joke that was funnier in my head."

"I think they're all funnier in your head, but thank you for showing restraint." Fairhrim was still looking at Too-Perfect Aedan. "It doesn't matter. We're still friends. At least, I'm friends with him."

"One of your many Friends, I'm given to understand."

A measure of Fairhrim's usual rigidity returned to her neck. "And who would've told you that?"

"The last source I shared with you wound up dead, so I shan't disclose," said Osric. "I suppose you haven't quite found the balance of desirable faults."

"Not that it's any of your business, but—yes, the correct ratio is difficult to achieve. And, of course, they must find my faults palatable." To Osric's annoyance, she preempted him and added, "I've got a few."

"Name them," said Osric.

"Low tolerance for Fyren continuing to pry about my personal life," said Fairhrim.

"I'll constrain my prying to your professional affairs."

Fairhrim shifted into a sweeping contrapposto. "Constrain it, full stop."

"No."

"Yes."

"No."

Annoyance accumulated on Fairhrim like a patina—the pinched nostrils, the tightened jaw, the majestic drawing upwards as she prepared to unleash some trenchant remark.

Then she saw his smirk.

"You're winding me up," said Fairhrim.

334

"You really are delicious."

Fairhrim never troubled to flirt with him, but her dark look, the amused press of her lips, and the brush of her elbow against his all had much the same effect on Osric; all mingled with the drink, was more potent than the drink, warmed his blood, threatened to heat his face. He thought forbidden thoughts about her lips again, what they had done in his imaginings, what he would like to do to them.

She was a thing between desire and impossibility.

Was he becoming one of those pathetic men who found a woman more desirable in direct proportion to how unattainable she was?

She held up her glass and said, "Well done."

Thank you, and I would like to die suffocated by your thighs did not seem an appropriate response at this time.

Osric said, "I serve at your pleasure," and held up his glass to hers.

She pressed her flute of champagne to his Scotch with a smile hidden in the corner of her mouth.

No, there was nothing worth stealing at the party below. But up here? It occurred to him that he would like to steal a dance.

THE SECRET CALLIGRAPHIES
OF RAIN

Aurienne

It was difficult, thought Aurienne as she leaned next to Mordaunt on the balcony, to hold him in her habitual disdain. Could one admire someone for acts of goodness, however self-interested, while simultaneously holding them in contempt? Aurienne found it impossible to maintain both perspectives concomitantly. Ultimately, he was a Fyren. And yet, and yet, and yet.

The man dying in her bed and his hot grasps at her hands were a memory. But what a memory. It should've been the best thing in the world to see him suffer, but it had been the worst thing in the world to see him suffer—so where did her peace lie? Certainly not here, not in the murk of this rapprochement, where he almost gave his life to protect her and she, with her own excuses, brought him back from the brink of death.

Aurienne, who revelled in accurate categorisation, hated that she no longer knew what to do with Mordaunt. He was an extraordinary combination of monster and man, of villainous and meritorious, base and noble—and, on occasion, he did good. It changed the anatomical diagram of Mordaunt in her mind. Her labels no longer made sense. The bottles he had found with the suspected Pox virus were undergoing testing at Swanstone; if they came back positive, it would be yet another point in his favour, yet another source of unwished-for gratitude, yet another challenge to her neat categories.

Aurienne cast a glance towards Mordaunt, who was nearly himself again. She had noted, as she joined him on the balcony, the cross of braces between muscular shoulders, and the shirt, of a markedly good cut, raffishly open at the neck. Everything about him was, once more, posed and intentional, from his casual recline against the rail to the scruffy beginnings of a beard along his jaw to the smoothness of *I serve at your pleasure* to the shirtsleeves pushed up to his elbows. So careless. So deliberate.

The brush of his arm against hers gave her a thrill. It was clandestine; it was wrong; it was the pretty foretaste of a kiss. Her heart skipped a beat.

"You know, it's a good thing I listened to your advice," said Mordaunt.

Aurienne, startled from her musings, intelligently replied, "Hmm?"

"Two drinks in and I'm positively mortalled." Mordaunt swirled the remains of his Scotch. "Perfect Aedan is looking for you, by the way."

Aurienne followed Mordaunt's line of sight to the crowd below the balcony, where Aedan was indeed casting about with a glass in each hand.

"Poor bastard," said Mordaunt. "That suit looks exactly like someone vomited on it." He turned to Aurienne and added, inconsequentially, "We should dance."

A draughty silence ensued.

"Why?" asked Aurienne.

"To convince him that you've moved on."

"With an episiotomy-scissor peddler?"

"With faults and everything."

"I'm not sure that's necessary."

"Look at him. Poor lovelorn pup." Mordaunt's pitying words did not match the stare he shot over the rail. "Although Perfect Aedan *has* got faults."

"Which?" asked Aurienne.

"Have you seen his ears?"

"What's wrong with them?"

"They're massive."

"They aren't."

"Look at those things, scooping up the very air. Could he leave some decibels for the rest of us?"

Why was the only man who could make her laugh tonight a Fyren? Mordaunt could be a fine conversation partner if one set aside what he was. It was like setting aside gravity—doable, but only for brief moments.

Anyway, Aurienne didn't wish to speak about Aedan. Desiring to move on from the cloying subject, she made some inapposite remarks about the weather. (The subject was cloying; Aedan was cloying—the more she was clung to, the more she desired escape.)

Mordaunt, with a notable lack of interest in the weather, said, "I'm your Friend du jour; surely that warrants a dance. People would think it strange otherwise."

"As laudable as your commitment to the charade is"—Aurienne held up the shoes dangling from her fingertips—"I'm done for the night. Couldn't do another minute in these."

"Dance without them," said Mordaunt.

"Don't be ridiculous."

"No one can see your indecent ankles from down there. It's only me."

"*Only* you?"

"Only. My near-death experience has left me humble and lamblike."

Strains of music floated up to them as the first bars of the next song began. Mordaunt held out his hand to Aurienne. Aedan, looking every inch the lovelorn pup, chose that moment to look up, and spot her on the balcony.

If he saw her refuse Mordaunt's hand, it would send a signal to him, and Aurienne didn't wish to send signals to Aedan. Well—unless the signal was that she had moved on with another. In which case—

Aurienne tossed her shoes to the side and took Mordaunt's hand. "Very well. I will dance as nature intended."

"Barefoot, tipsy, and with flowers in your hair."

"You paint a lovely picture."

"You are a lovely picture."

"I thought I was an uptight little fusspot?"

Aurienne was rewarded by one of Mordaunt's brilliant smiles. "Do you know," he said, "sometimes I don't mind being wrong?"

They came together, hands guarded from touch by gloves of leather and silk. Aurienne had lost the added height of her heels; she stood at eye level with Mordaunt's mouth.

They danced slowly, because he couldn't go very fast, and because the song was a low, romantic ballad. It meant nothing—it was a stupid little dance that was part of a stupid little charade—but her pulse was all aflutter. Aurienne took refuge in the clinical. She quizzed Mordaunt on any lingering symptoms: dizziness, confusion, palpitations, tachypnoea, and, finally, oliguria—"And when's the last time you urinated?"

Mordaunt, who looked increasingly discontented as her evaluation progressed, said, "Really?"

"What?"

"We're dancing and you're interrogating me about urine?"

"It's important," said Aurienne.

"You really can wring the romance out of anything," said Mordaunt.

"What romance?" asked Aurienne. "This is a sham."

"Well, *I* was enjoying the sham—and the garden, and the lights, and the music; it all pleases my sense of Aesthetics."

Aurienne dismissed the Aesthetics with a flick of her fingers. "Answer me about the urine."

"Yes, I had a piss," said Mordaunt, with slight, alcohol-induced slurring. "Since we're ruining everything with vulgar reality."

"Quantity?"

"Well, I didn't *measure* it."

"Normal?"

"Yes. Gods."

"Excellent. You're well enough to leave tomorrow. We can draw the charade to a close. You may go back to enjoying the Aesthetics."

Mordaunt resumed this activity by observing the glittering crowd below. "Your family likes their jewels."

"They do," said Aurienne. "Have you seen anything you like?"

"Some."

"Have you stolen anything from the house yet?"

"You still don't trust me?"

"No," said Aurienne. "I know you've thought about it."

"It is a fascinating house. So automated. Mine must seem rather—"

"Primitive," suggested Aurienne.

"Traditional," said Mordaunt. "Your mother is quite the horologist."

"Her favourite holiday location is La Chaux-de-Fonds, if that gives you an idea."

Mordaunt's eyebrows rose at this mention of the cradle of Swiss watchmaking. "I'm even more tempted now. Her alarm system has, admittedly, given me pause."

"I was right: you're a common thief."

"Not common. *Not* common."

"Have you no pleasure in life but to acquire things that aren't yours?" asked Aurienne.

Mordaunt gave her a look veiled by heavy eyelids and drink. "I have other pleasures," he said, and did not elaborate further.

"I ought to go warn my aunts to count their diamonds."

Mordaunt's fingers tightened at her waist. "But then you won't be here to supervise me. Anyway, you can't leave yet—the song hasn't ended. It'll look like we had a falling-out."

"We exist in a perpetual state of falling out."

"Others needn't know the sordid truth," said Mordaunt. Aurienne matched him in a slow spin. "These few days have been a pleasant interlude, false as they were."

"For you, perhaps," said Aurienne. "I'll be subject to questions about you until I tell my parents it's over."

"What excuse will you give for my ignominious loss of your favour?"

"A selection of sordid truths," said Aurienne. "I shall tell them you were too smug, too arrogant, too convinced that you were right all the time, and that these things suffocated all your other attractions. To the bin with you."

"All of those things are equally applicable to you," said Mordaunt.

He was right, so Aurienne said, with vast matter-of-factness: "Nonsense."

"What other attractions?" asked Mordaunt.

"I can't think of any, but, for the sake of your dignity, I'll pretend they exist."

The scar over Mordaunt's mouth twitched. "I fish for compliments, and instead of taking the bait, you slap into the stratosphere."

Aurienne squeezed at their joined hands. "I know what's under here; it casts a pall over any possible attractions."

"What if my tācn were something else?" asked Mordaunt. "What would the attractions be then?"

The question was posed with sarcastic, boozy interest—only Aurienne caught real curiosity in Mordaunt's downward glance. A moment later, it was gone. There again was the quirk in the lips; there was the mordacity.

"That tācn has tainted everything I know of you," said Aurienne. "I couldn't answer the question."

"Not even as a thought exercise?"

"A thought exercise? Of this scope? Mid-dance?"

"Try."

"Arm veins," said Aurienne.

"Arm veins?" repeated Mordaunt.

"I'd love to pop a large bore into this one," said Aurienne, running a finger over the juiciest one.

"I am absolutely wasted on you."

Mordaunt had used her soap today; Aurienne could smell it on him. He was very near. Had they begun the dance this close together? And if they hadn't, which of them had closed the gap? It might have been her. She hoped it had been him. She looked at the hollow at the base of his throat. It was the lighthouse all over again, the pull of the wanting to be near, the natural repulsion, the back-and-forth.

It began to rain.

There were gasps from the garden below and a faltering in the music as the quartet backed itself under a canopy. The music picked up again, as did the chatter, all dampened by the soft percussion of a gentle June-time shower. It scattered itself upon Aurienne and Mordaunt in glittering handfuls, lit by the green and gold lights below.

"It's raining," said Aurienne.

"I know," said Mordaunt.

"Shouldn't we go in?"

"Why must you be sensible?"

"One of us ought to be."

But they weren't sensible. They were tipsy. They danced in the rain.

Besides, they were indoors, sort of—as well as outside: a bit of both, all at once. Aurienne's bare feet danced from the balcony's cold stone to the bedroom's warm floorboards and back again. The wet splashed indoors; the lamplight glowed outdoors; the rain washed the distinctions away. Water dripped against Mordaunt's neck, and Aurienne's bodice, and his temples, and her lips, and wrote things there in calligraphies long forgotten.

Their shadows also spoke things in their twine and untwine against balcony railing and white curtains, cast now by the lamps in the bedroom, and now by the light of the half-moon. The space between her and Mordaunt was a sparkling, rain-studded thing; they pulled it apart and tightened it with every spin, over and under, farther and nearer; they wove and unwove, and wove and unwove.

What was between them? An ebb and a flow, curiosity and guilt, today's fatal daydream and tomorrow's scars.

Delighted laughter echoed below as partygoers noticed Aurienne and Mordaunt's rain-drenched dance. There was applause—a celebration of a thing that was not, and could never be.

Aurienne sought Mordaunt's gaze to see how much longer he wished to keep up the pretence of the dance, but his eyes were on their joined hands. Their star-crossed tācn pressed against each other's. Their Orders were in their veins, as inescapable as their own blood.

He held his arm overhead; she spun out and spun back in; pale skirts clung to black trousers.

What was between them? Once it had been a theatre of war; now it was a no-man's-land. They had grown entangled in each other through reciprocities. Healing and killing, killing and healing.

The music swelled. Mordaunt radiated warmth; Aurienne could feel it through the front of her dress where it brushed his chest, through her glove where he clasped her hand. He was loose and relaxed; his head hung low, the scruff at his jaw brushed her cheek. The hand that had been decorously perched at her waist slid into the small of her back. Through the fine fabric of her dress, she felt the press of his signet ring.

Their faces were near each other's. Mordaunt looked at her mouth like he thought of kissing it.

He was a very good actor.

To their audience below, a kiss would be utterly unremarkable—normal—expected, even. Aedan had found a recipient for his drink, but he was still looking at Aurienne.

"Let's put the poor bastard out of his misery," said Mordaunt, his voice more warmth than word against Aurienne's mouth.

A lie—that's what was between them now.

Their cheeks touched. Their noses brushed. His eyes flashed ardent, wanting.

"I don't kiss patients," said Aurienne against his lips.

"I thought I wasn't a patient," said Mordaunt.

"Right. You're just a Point of Leverage."

"You must make use of me."

And, because Aedan was watching—and only because Aedan was watching—Aurienne rose to her tiptoes and ran silk-clad fingers through Mordaunt's hair.

He didn't hesitate, didn't give her time to change her mind. He pulled her in close, put a hand around the back of her neck, tilted her head upwards.

Then came the tender apocalypse of his lips on hers.

She felt Mordaunt's scar against her mouth, felt the tightening of his hand at her neck, savoured Scotch and chocolate and lies from his lips. Her body didn't know what her brain knew; her heart beat wild in her chest; breathing became an act of discipline, irregular ins and outs and ins and outs between the press of rain-wet lips.

While it lasted, the kiss was eternal.

And it was too much and too little, and it was unhallowed, and it was sacrosanct.

There was warmth at the side of her neck. Mordaunt mapped the course of raindrops against her throat with his mouth. He released a long, shuddering breath against her skin. He held her against him rather possessively for a kiss that meant nothing.

The audience sighed about a thing that did not exist.

Aurienne stilled. The music carried on; the violins made a rapturous chorus with the dripping melody of the rain. She released her hold on Mordaunt's shoulder, but his lingered at her waist. He kept her hand clasped in his. His nearness, the kiss, her rushing blood, all heightened her perception, and, as at the lighthouse, she saw warring in his eyes: vulnerability, yearning, desperate unhappiness.

He retreated into irony. Grey hardened into silver. He said, "Didn't think you would."

As for Aurienne, she regretted the kiss immediately—because it blurred already-blurred lines, because of what he was and what she was, because it felt good.

She blinked rain-misted eyes. She liked her precious categories. She liked things sharp and delineated. She liked contrasts. Clarity. Knowing where she stood.

She did not care about the secret calligraphies of rain.

She said, "I'd better go."

He said, "If you must."

Aurienne turned away. She dropped his hand and its profane tācn.

He released hers slowly. Leather slid against silk, palm slid against palm, fingertip slid against wet fingertip, and whatever had been woven between them stretched and tore and severed with a snap.

SOMETHING BECOMING

Osric

When Osric had asked Fairhrim to dance, she had, at first, done nothing but stare at him. A very dark time in his life had followed, taking on the proportions of approximately ten years of agony and suspense, until her shrugged "Very well."

That was where it should have ended. Osric had never intended to steal a kiss, and certainly never intended to linger along her neck. It was meant to be only a dance. But she had looked up at him, and he had discovered how her wet hair caught pentagrams of stars, and watched raindrops trickle down her throat and make a necklace of moon glitter there, and the kleptomaniac urge had risen, and he, weak-willed fool that he was, had yielded to it.

When he had asked her to put the poor bastard out of his misery, he hadn't been referring to Perfect Aedan. He had been talking about himself.

He had played the smitten fool a little too well. Well enough to believe it.

Afterwards, Fairhrim had fled from him, and left him with an unfinished dance and a fear.

He wished he could unknow what she had tasted like. What it had felt like to hold her quivering stillness in his arms as he made his way down her neck.

Once again they had met upon a threshold, once again they had reached an Almost, and once again she had fled.

She would never cross over. And he was burdened now, with the memory of a swiftly beating heart, exhilaration and pleasure, and the weight of regret.

He wished he could unkiss her.

A FEW DAYS AFTER OSRIC'S STAY WITH FAIRHRIM, TRISTANE'S ILL-tempered polecat deofol summoned him to the Fyren HQ.

Thanks to Fairhrim's attentions, he was by then able to walk normally, and not as though he had been stabbed in the gut by a fellow Fyren who was, incidentally, missing under mysterious circumstances.

The Fyren headquarters had moved to an abandoned abattoir. Osric had scouted the place out after one of Fairhrim's more piquant remarks. It was perfect; there were exsanguination and blood-storage facilities on-site, and no one in the neighbourhood investigated if things got smelly. Fairhrim would no doubt be thrilled to know her input had had such an impact on Osric's Order.

Upon the abattoir's rusted gates lingered the cheerful slogan *We kill so you don't have to!*

Below it was carved a rough rendition of the Order's hellhound fangs.

Sacramore was in the abattoir's dingy reception area, sorting through a diverse pile of contraband.

"Good luck, darling," he said as Osric walked in. "The butcher is in a mood."

Osric pondered Why That Could Be.

He followed a cracked-tile corridor to the killing floor, where Tristane stood, accompanied by Lady Windermere. Around them were enormous meat hooks, upon which recent victims of Tristane's interrogations were hung upside down. A few of them were still alive. One wheezed aerosolised blood.

There was a sign on the wall indicating the days since the last injury: fourteen. Osric felt that it needed updating.

Tristane gestured him closer. She wore an enormous rubbery apron and yellow boots.

"Lovely outfit," said Osric. "Crime-scene chic."

"Thank you," said Tristane. "It has pockets."

"What are you doing with these fine gentlemen?"

"A bit of forensic accounting," said Tristane. "Have you had any word from Brythe recently?"

Lady Windermere, who had been standing beside Tristane in silence, let out a staccato breath, and wiped away a tear.

Osric, with perfect innocent concern, said, "Brythe? Saw him last week at the Harmacy."

"That's the last time anyone saw him," said Tristane.

"He's missing." Lady Windermere turned sunken eyes to Osric. "My deofol can't get through—can't even find a trace of his seith."

"Neither can mine," said Tristane. "Which means he unlinked us—"

"Brythe would *never* unlink me," said Lady Windermere in a fierce hiss.

"—or he's dead," finished Tristane.

"Dead? Brythe?" Osric scoffed. "Impossible."

Lady Windermere wrapped her arms around herself. Her thin form swayed. "Then where is he?"

"The alternatives are limited and unsatisfying," said Tristane. "Few could kill Brythe. Perhaps *des circonstances insolites*—a freak accident of some kind."

"I refuse to believe that," said Lady Windermere. "But you're right—few could kill him. If he's dead, that will narrow down my list." She gave both Tristane and Osric a look, and he knew that the two of them had just made it onto her list.

"Cast your suspicious gaze elsewhere," said Tristane, pressing a warning fingertip to the hilt of her blaecblade. "Your lover may be dead, but I remind you that I've also lost one of my Fyren. And Osric a friend and colleague."

Osric, who had been personally responsible for converting the dear friend and colleague into ash, nodded gravely.

Lady Windermere lowered her gaze to the floor.

One of the wheezing, upside-down men—a redheaded, skinny fellow—created a timely diversion by burbling for mercy. Tristane poked about through some crates, muttering about gags. She found a harmonica in her apron pocket, which she jammed into the man's mouth.

"There," she said, patting him on his upside-down chin. "You may do something useful with your breathing. Give us a bit of ambience."

The harmonica's discordant whistles filled the room.

"Kind of you," said Osric. "This is cosy."

"I know," said Tristane. "I'm a real softie when it comes down to it. That's my trouble."

Amid the harmonica's sepulchral melody, Osric asked, "Will you launch a search for Brythe?"

"Windermere will be leading it," said Tristane. "Beaufort and Sacramore will help her."

"If I hear anything through my contacts, I'll let you both know immediately," said Osric.

"Thank you," said Lady Windermere.

She left. The harmonica turned melancholy.

"You said you last saw Brythe at the Harmacy?" asked Tristane when Lady Windermere was gone.

"Yes—Sacramore was there, too."

Tristane sighed. "He was heading out on a job that day. I think he's dead. He can't be on the run. He had the payout of a lifetime coming his way."

"What job was it?" asked Osric.

"One that it was imperative he not fail," said Tristane.

"You're sure you don't want me to look for him?"

"No," said Tristane. "That's not the priority. The priority is completing the job."

"Shall I take care of it? I do like a payout."

Tristane listened to the sad harmonica. Her triangle of hair swayed mournfully. "It wasn't a job I would normally agree that we would take on. It involves another Order."

"Oh?"

"I made an exceptional decision on an exceptional basis."

"What exceptional basis?"

"Money."

"Well, obviously."

Tristane's hard eyes surveilled Osric. "Aren't you going to query me about the advisability of attacking another Order?"

"Did Brythe?"

"No, but Brythe considers nothing beyond the money. It's why I asked him in the first place. You're just as rapacious, I know—but you've got a Particle of intelligence and political acumen."

"An entire Particle?" said Osric. "You flatter me. Can the job be done without evidence of Fyren involvement?"

"That was, of course, the idea," said Tristane. "Otherwise I'd be pulled up to the Stánrocc to explain myself to the Heads of every other Order, and probably sentenced to death."

"What Order was the target?"

"That's not for you to know," said Tristane. "Sacramore was against my taking it on. Bit of a traditionalist. *However*, if no one knew our Order was responsible, his reservations would be moot."

"Who's the client?"

"Someone worth breaking a few rules for." Tristane meandered through the hanging men as one would through a peaceful Zen garden, with her hands behind her back. "Some *sombre idiot* donated a substantial wodge—twenty million—to an Order when all other funding avenues had been strategically blocked by the client."

This was a bit awkward for Osric, given that the *sombre idiot* was, you know, him.

"And now Brythe has disappeared," continued Tristane. "He can't have been caught—if they'd caught a Fyren, I'd have been dragged before the Stánrocc already to explain why I've broken two hundred years of Peace Accords."

Osric gestured to their bloodied audience. "Haven't this lot heard a little too much?"

"I suppose," said Tristane. She paused. A knob on the wall caught her attention. "What do you think this does?"

"A mystery knob," said Osric. "Pull it."

"I have tugged a few mystery knobs in my lifetime," said Tristane.

Tristane pulled the mystery knob. It severed the man next to her clean down the middle.

"Ah," said Tristane, observing the result. "Very good. I wouldn't go to a pie shop round here for a little while if I were you."

"Thank you for the tip."

"You're dismissed," said Tristane. "Come to me if you hear anything about Brythe. I will pass the information to Lady Windermere. You saw today that she's . . . quite emotional about this."

"Understood. And the job?"

"Leave the job to me." Tristane walked pensively away from Osric, her boots squelching in fresh offal. *"On n'est jamais si bien servi que par soi-même."*

Which, Osric understood from his rudimentary French, meant that she was going to do it—whatever *it* was—herself.

Which meant that Tristane was going to pick up where Brythe had left off, and go to Swanstone.

Which meant that Osric needed to see Fairhrim immediately.

A few other Fyren were milling about the reception area when Osric exited the killing floor. Sacramore asked him whether he'd join them at the Dog's Bollocks for drinks. Osric, panicky, produced some sort of strangled gurgle from his larynx—he hoped it sounded like a viable excuse—and strode off.

Safely away from the abattoir, Osric summoned Cinder, his deofol, with instructions to find Fairhrim sharpish, and tell her they had to meet. Fairhrim had told Osric that she would never reject his deofol again—and yet, a few minutes later, Cinder returned, her ears pinned back, to report that she hadn't got through.

"She's either ignoring me or sound asleep," said Cinder, her voice husky with displeasure.

"Sound asleep? At half two in the morning? Ridiculous," said Osric.

"What do you want to do?" asked Cinder.

"You're going to keep trying and I'm going to make my way to Swanstone. Come back to me if you get through."

Cinder nodded and faded from existence in a smudge of smoke.

Osric took a waystone to the Publish or Perish, from whence he sped to Swanstone. The frozen waterways bordering the fortress during his February visit had melted into proper ponds and moats, populated now by flocks of drowsy swans. They were, like Fairhrim, pretty, foul tempered, and best appreciated from a distance. They detected something of him as he shadow-walked past and hissed in his direction.

The white fortress's battlements loomed overhead. Osric slipped into shadow, awaiting the touch of the returning Cinder against his tācn. None came. Osric stared at the ramparts above him, glowing here and there with warding. Very well: he would be visiting Fairhrim in person once again.

Slowly, carefully, using his utmost finesse to dodge the Wardens' trapping wards, he made his way to the roof of the highest tower of Swanstone.

"I CAN'T BELIEVE FAIRHRIM DOESN'T TRUST ME," SAID OSRIC TO HIMSELF as he broke into her bedroom.

The window was large and round. Its lock gave him no trouble. He swung it open. However, there was a significant, Warden-driven upgrade to the security, if one actually wished to go inside: there was a ward around the entirety of the window frame, glowing midnight blue. This was not a ward that could be dodged or danced around. Osric would no longer be able to enter Swanstone undetected.

The good news was, neither could Tristane.

He peered inside. Fairhrim's quarters were larger than he'd expected, encompassing the full circumference of the tower, with a high, vaulted ceiling. The decor consisted of angular furnishings looking singularly inhospitable, on which lay many books, and when not books, plants under glass cloches, and when not plants, meticulously labelled skulls. Into one of the cloches gazed a pubey sort of cat, black and scruffy. Osric recognised it as the kitten he had found at Wellesley Keep and consecrated to Fairhrim's care. The ungrateful creature hissed at him.

Fairhrim lay in a bed against the far wall. She was in a deep sleep— the senseless, boneless sleep of one recovering from seith exhaustion. Her arm hung off the side of the bed. Osric was pleased to discover that the sight of her hand did not, this time, turn him to lewdness. It was bloody with evidence of her Cost. Her tācn shimmered with a glowing pulse now and again as Cinder tried to get through.

His deofol's efforts came to fruition. Fairhrim sighed herself awake, cracked an eye open to stare at her tācn, and pointed it at the floor.

Cinder took shape. Fairhrim's cat, seeing the shadow of the great wolf, fled.

In a sleep-cracked voice, Fairhrim muttered, "What?" to Cinder.

"Good evening," said Cinder.

"Hiya," said Osric, given that he was there, too.

Fairhrim's bleary stare turned to Osric's silhouette at the window.

"I wish to awaken from this bad dream," declared Fairhrim. Then, having processed the reality of the situation, she sat up with a jerk. "Don't touch the window. There are wards—"

"I saw."

"You're mad to have come here." Fairhrim kicked off her sheets. "Has something happened? Are you all right?"

"I'm fine," said Osric. "But I've made a worrying discovery."

He dismissed Cinder, who dissolved into smoke.

Osric cursed inwardly, because Fairhrim, bereft of all her party accoutrements, her eyes black rimmed with fatigue, her hands crusted over with scabs, was, unfortunately, still beautiful. When she wasn't sharing a room with him at her parents' house, she slept in a thin, satiny nightdress, which clung to her in interesting ways. Given that her sleeping attire was of no consequence to him, he directed a powerful curiosity towards his knee while she put on a dressing gown. Her hair was pulled into a sleep-frizzed plait that unravelled down her back.

As she approached Osric, wide-eyed in the dark, she looked unusually vulnerable. Something about it made him want to be gentle.

"Did they add wards to every point of entry?" asked Osric, gesturing with distaste at the blue glow tucked into the frame.

"Yes. The Wardens brought in Tenet."

"Who?"

"One of their ward specialists."

"Aren't they all ward specialists?"

"Yes, but she's an expert among experts. She's been added to their detachment here. She mapped out all of our seith signatures—every Haelan, every member of our personnel, every guard, every patient. Any person crossing any threshold who isn't from Swanstone will trigger alarms—and probably lose a limb. It cost a bloody fortune, but you said we had to be discreet in our enhancements."

"The one time you follow my advice, it inconveniences me," sighed Osric, settling into a seated position on the roof.

Fairhrim pushed aside a few plants and, after a moment's hesitation—and decidedly not looking down—she clambered onto the window's broad ledge, so that she and Osric were separated only by the space of the open window.

"Nice flowers," said Osric.

Fairhrim repositioned one of the glass cloches. "Orchids. I'm fond of them; their blooms last a very long time."

"Ah," said Osric. (Desperate feeling: he had thought they were ephemeral.)

"Tell me what's going on," said Fairhrim.

"Complications."

Osric described what he'd learned from Tristane—the questions raised by Brythe's disappearance, the outrageous payout involved in the hit, the mysterious client who had deliberately blocked the Haelan Order's funding.

Fairhrim absorbed Osric's every word, her fingers pressed to her lips. She studied him in silence when he had finished his accounting. "It terrifies me that you're terrified of Tristane."

"As it should," said Osric.

"Why are you so frightened of her?"

"She's French."

"Be serious."

"Everything I can do, she can do better, faster, bloodier. Her shadow-walking is a thing of legend. She can move from one shadow to the next over real distances, not only a few dozen feet, like me—and *I'm* considered outstanding. Her blaecblade might as well be her hand. She's taken over three thousand souls—in this lifetime, anyway. I told you some of us call her Hel herself. The goddess of the dead, walking among us."

"What do we do?" asked Fairhrim. "How do we prepare?"

"These new wards are a good starting point. You want to deter her—make her think twice about entering Swanstone. She won't risk being caught by Wardens. Add wards everywhere, not just at points of entry to the fortress proper. The bridge connecting Swanstone to the mainland. Any waterways below the fortress. Hatches. Dumbwaiters. Holes in roofs. Sewers. Everywhere there's a shadow. She's formidable, but you're forewarned. That's an advantage her victims don't usually get."

They talked. And something extraordinary happened, because, for once, their talk wasn't arguments; it wasn't negotiations; it wasn't provocations; it wasn't wheeling and dealing—it was the terra incognita of collaboration. It was coming up with a plan, together.

Night deepened and cooled, but the fortress's sun-filled stones released the rays that had baked them all afternoon, and kept Osric and Fairhrim warm. And it was lovely to sit there, leaning against his side of the window while Fairhrim rested against hers, mind pressed against mind, untangling. There was pleasure in it. He thought that she, too, was enjoying it; her words were appreciative rather than cutting; her looks, encouraging; her nods, satisfied.

Fairhrim recollected something with a jolt. "Gods—it's been so hectic, I haven't had a chance to send you my deofol with the news."

"What news?"

"I just received the test results for the substance in the bottles from Wellesley Keep."

"And?"

"It was the Pox."

"We knew it."

"We were right. Appallingly, we were right."

"I almost *drank* it."

"It wouldn't have affected you. It only infects the young." Fairhrim's face was drawn. "I think they're using the bottles to store the virus. The cellar would be the right temperature. Not sure how they're producing it, or spreading it. But do you know how horrific this is? Do you know how many brain-dead children we're struggling to bring back, quarantined in our wards here? Hundreds. And that's just at Swanstone. There are survivors everywhere, just—surviving, if someone is giving them care. They may never live again, not really."

"Wellesley had entire crates of those bottles in his cellar."

Fairhrim sat up with a sudden combativeness. "Every bottle will soon be useless. Élodie is rolling out an immunisation programme. Our lead virologist," she added, in the face of Osric's blank look. "It explains so much about the virulence of the Pox outbreak to know that it was deliberately being unleashed. But it also raises a thousand more questions, such as, you know—*why* anyone would do such a thing. Why would Wellesley trigger an outbreak of an obscure disease that had all but disappeared? To what end? To what possible benefit? And if what Tristane told you is true, it means Wellesley was working for someone else. Someone even more powerful, who blocked all the funding avenues for researchers seeking to stop the spread of the Pox—and who is now furious that my Order sidestepped those blockages. Someone who has now paid millions upon millions to have Tristane herself involved. Do you know how mad that is? Incomprehensible. Absurd. What's worth this much money?"

"The only thing ever worth this much money—this many expenditures, this many resources—is war," said Osric.

"What war? Whose war? Wessex and Kent?"

"I know your Order is apolitical, but you need to step outside of your ivory tower occasionally," said Osric. "Take your pick of any two of the Tiendoms sharing a land border. Actually, sharing a border is optional. Throw two darts at a map."

"What war is fought by brain-dead children?" asked Fairhrim.

"I don't know," said Osric.

"I couldn't think of worse soldiers," said Fairhrim. "Of what possible utility . . . ? They've no souls left, the poor things—they're just shells whose biological functions are continuing to—"

Fairhrim cut herself off.

A slow horror dawned on her face. "Mordaunt?"

"What?"

"How—how are Dreor made?"

There was a long silence.

Osric said, "Fuck."

Fairhrim pressed her damaged hands to cheeks gone pale.

It was a night of breath-held, uncanny stillness. The moon, waxing, drew a white path over the flat black sea. There wasn't the slightest shiver of a breeze. Only their talk disturbed the silence, strange whispers passing to and fro, bridging two loyalties; the soft, portentous whispers of something becoming.

"I owe you—we owe you—so many thanks," said Fairhrim. "The only reason Élodie could work on her inoculation project was because of you. We only discovered the Pox bottles because of you. You killed one of your own for the protection of my Order—"

"For you" was Osric's swift correction.

"—and you've just helped me work out, possibly, the why behind this awful plague."

She regarded Osric with a gaze full of wonder.

(Such witchery, such witchery in a pair of bright eyes.)

"Why are you helping me?" asked Fairhrim.

"Someone is going to die at Swanstone, and I can't have it be you," said Osric.

Fairhrim, who could pass the ward at the window unhindered, pressed her fingers to his arm, which sent, as always, a rush through him. There was a time when she had flinched away from touching him at all. "Thank you—truly."

Then, more exhilarating still, she asked, "Are you free Friday next?"

"Why?"

"It's the full moon. And we're going to break into the Færwundor."

Osric stared at her in shock. She had been categorical in her refusal. "You—you're going to do it?"

"You won't let us get caught," said Fairhrim. After a beat, she added, "I trust you."

The words landed heavily on Osric's chest, ran deep, heightened the exhilaration.

"We've managed to slow your degeneration," continued Fairhrim. "Let's see if we can reverse it. After what you've done, it's the least I can do."

The sparkle in her eyes might have been the stars; it might have been a secret smile.

Osric felt the weight of some doomed and inexpressible truth.

They tarried long at that window, not quite in, and not quite out. They succumbed to the slow enchantment of a June night. White moths, pale and brilliant in the dark, spun by in shivering constellations, flowed into one another, collapsed in and out of one another, and, whirling upwards, became part of the sky. In the east, clouds gleamed with to-morrow in them.

They talked until the stars went out.

Fairhrim, silver framed in the window, became a focal point: a notan study of light and dark. Unimportant things became important. Her lashes painting their own shadows against her cheeks. Moonlight subliming her hair. Her hand beside Osric's on the windowsill, so close their fingers brushed.

Her touch was an aching, fragile beauty. It was a hinge that swung him into something else. An awareness. An understanding that came in a bursting, ecstatic, agonised thrill.

He and she sat in the moonlight as lover and beloved.

He hadn't paid attention. He had been stupid—gods, so stupid. He no longer owned his heart.

The thief was unconscious of her crime. She asked, "Is something the matter?"

And, for once in Osric's life, the lie didn't come easily. It was too enormous. He shook his head and held the truth between his teeth.

The realisation was a breaking point. He saw before him the beautiful impossibility of it all, league upon league of impossibility stretching between them. It was ruthless folly; it was the sorrow of a thing ending before it could begin; it was a new circle of torment; it was a delicious wound. What joy seamed by misery. What pleasure fraught with pain.

It hadn't been love at first sight, but at last sight—gods, at last sight—

Far above, the moon hung like a promise.

The Orders

In the Tīendoms, eight Orders emerged over centuries out of guilds and other consortia grouping together like-minded specialists working to master seith. The Heads of the Orders meet once a year at the Stánrocc. The Orders operate under the Peace Accords, which include provisions banning cruel training techniques and an agreement to avoid direct hostile actions against another Order.

On paper, the Orders are apolitical, and owe allegiance to no particular Tīendom. In practice, Orders maintain strategic ties with certain governments for mutual benefit.

Members of Orders are said to walk the Bright, the Dusken, or the Dim Paths. Walkers of the Bright Paths have their tācn on their right palms; the Dusken Paths have theirs on their left. Hedgewitches, who walk the Dim Path, choose on which side to place their tācn, in alignment with their practice.

THE BRIGHT PATHS

HAELAN

Harm to none

From OE *hælan*, "cure, heal, revive." Order of healer-scholars. Differentiated from physickers and chirurgeons in their use of seith in healing and research, which has permitted significant advancements in their practice. Headquartered in the Danelaw. Tācn: white Aer (mythological swan).

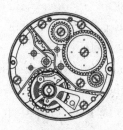

INGENAUT

Mind over matter

From ME *ingeny*, "gadget, apparatus," + Ancient Greek *naútēs*, "sailor." Order of engineer-scholars. Like with the Haelan, the integration of seith into their practice has allowed the accelerated development of engines and devices beyond the work of the engineers of the day. Headquartered in Īrland. Tācn: golden gears.

LEYFARER

Hail the traveller

From Old French *lier*, "to bind," + OE *faran*, "to journey." Occasionally also *Leynaut*. Order specialising in the management and navigation of ley lines and ley-line travel through waystones or using leycraft. Headquartered in Fortriu. Tācn: bronze compass.

WARDEN

Will over want

From OE *weard*, "keeper, guardian, protector." Order of paladins hired at great expense throughout the Tīendoms for their specialisation in defence and protective warding. Headquartered in Dumnonia. Tācn: blue auroch's head.

THE DUSKEN PATHS

AGANNOR
Mind over flesh

From OE *āgan*, "to own." An Order whose members possess others against their will and, depending on the practitioner's skill, without their knowledge. Headquartered in Wessex. Tācn: purple eye.

DREOR
Death devours all

From OE *drēor*, "gore, blood." Obscure, near-extinct Order of death-knights. Headquartered in Mercia. Tācn: black death's-head.

FYREN

Fear not the dark

From OE *firen*, "wicked, crime, sin." Order of assassins trained in shadow-walking. Notoriously costly to hire and notoriously lethal. Headquarters location shifts throughout the Tīendoms. Tācn: red hellhound skull.

THE DIM PATH

HEDGEWITCH

As above, so below

From OE *hægtes*, "witch, sorceress." Once persecuted almost to extinction, the Hedgewitches remain a secretive Order. Headquartered in Kent. Tācn: three green hares.

PRONUNCIATION GUIDE

Agannor: *AH-gan-or*

Aurienne Fairhrim: *OR-ee-en FEHR-rim*

Cíele: *TCHEE-el*

Deofol: *DAY-o-fol*

Dreor: *DREE-or*

Fyren: *FY-ren*

Haelan: *HAY-lan*

Ingenaut: *ING-eh-not*

Leyfarer: *LAY-fair-er*

Osric Mordaunt: *OZ-rik MORE-dint*

Seith: *Sayth*

Tācn: *TAH-kin*

Tīendoms: *TEE-en-doms*

Xanthe: *ZAN-thee*

Acknowledgements

These are the giants in whose shadow this book germinated: W. B. Yeats, whose collection of fairy lore and folktales in *The Celtic Twilight* inspired both plot and world, and Jerome K. Jerome and P. G. Wodehouse, whose heights of drollery and wit I am fated to admire and never attain. I must also mention three scholars whose works have been stacked upon my desk for the past few years: Robert Macfarlane and his fabulous books on language and landscape, Ronald Hutton and his extraordinary explorations of magic and paganism, and Hana Videen and her fresh approaches to Old English (I hope she never reads this book, however, due to my various butcheries thereof).

This story wouldn't have reached book form without my brilliant agent, Thao Le, with whom it has been such a privilege to collaborate. Thao found the perfect home for this book at Berkley and Orbit UK, with two spectacular editors, Cindy Hwang and Nadia Saward. Their acumen, dedication, humour, and patience were critical in shaping the book into what it is now. For this Ace edition, special thanks to editorial assistant Elizabeth Vinson and production editor Daniel Walsh for their professional expertise, and to Eileen Chetti, Jamie Thaman, and Lisa Lester Kelly for their lynx-eyed attention to the text. On the publicity side, all gratitude to Kristin Cipolla and Yazmine Hassan, and on the marketing side, Jessica Mangicaro and Kim-Salina I for working

ACKNOWLEDGEMENTS

their magic. Thank you also to map artist Rebecka Champion for the gorgeous rendition of the Tïendoms and to the lovely Katie Anderson for the cover design. Finally, I am so thrilled and honoured to be able to thank cover artist Nikita Jobson for sharing her glorious talents and bringing Osric and Aurienne to such vivid life.

Deep gratitude to fandom in general, for providing me with two decades of writing practice, and to the Dramione girlies in particular, whose enthusiasm for my work put me on this new, unexpected path.

Finally, and forever, love to my family.